The Perilous Cemetery
(L'atre Périlleux)

The Perilous Cemetery
(L'atre Périlleux)

Edited and Translated by
Nancy B. Black

Routledge
Taylor & Francis Group

First published in 1994 by Garland Publishing, Inc.

This edition first published in 2018 by Routledge
2 Park Square, Milton Park, Abingdon, Oxon, OX14 4RN
and by Routledge
52 Vanderbilt Avenue, New York, NY 10017, USA

Routledge is an imprint of the Taylor & Francis Group, an informa business

Publisher's Note
The publisher has gone to great lengths to ensure the quality of this reprint but
points out that some imperfections in the original copies may be apparent.

Disclaimer
The publisher has made every effort to trace copyright holders and welcomes
correspondence from those they have been unable to contact.
A Library of Congress record exists under ISBN:

ISBN 13: 978-0-367-18681-4 (hbk)
ISBN 13: 978-0-367-18682-1 (pbk)
ISBN 13: 978-0-429-19758-1 (ebk)

GARLAND LIBRARY OF MEDIEVAL LITERATURE
VOL. 104, SERIES A

THE PERILOUS
CEMETERY
(L'ATRE PÉRILLEUX)

The Garland Library
of Medieval Literature

General Editors
James J. Wilhelm, Rutgers University
Lowry Nelson, Jr., Yale University

Literary Advisors
Ingeborg Glier, Yale University
Frede Jensen, University of Colorado
Sidney M. Johnson, Indiana University
William W. Kibler, University of Texas
Norris J. Lacy, Washington University
Fred C. Robinson, Yale University
Aldo Scaglione, New York University

Art Advisor
Elizabeth Parker McLachlan, Rutgers University

Music Advisor
Hendrik van der Werf, Eastman School of Music

Paris, Bibliothèque Nationale, fonds français 1433, folio Av
(Photo: Bibliothèque Nationale.)

THE PERILOUS CEMETERY
(L'ATRE PÉRILLEUX)

edited and translated by
Nancy B. Black

GARLAND PUBLISHING, Inc.
New York & London / 1994

Library of Congress Cataloging-in-Publication Data

Atre périlleux. English & French (Old French)
  The perilous cemetery (L'atre périlleux) / edited
and translated by Nancy B. Black.
      p.   cm — (Garland library of medieval liter-
ature ; vol. 104A)
  Parallel texts in English and Old French, with criti-
cal matter in English.
  Includes bibliographical references and index.
  ISBN 0–8153–1897–9
  1. Gawain (Legendary character)—Romances. 2.
Romances—Translations into English. 3. Arthurian
romances.   I. Black, Nancy B. II. Title. III. Series:
Garland library of medieval literature ; v. 104A.
PQ1425.A605E5 1994
841'.1—dc20   94–18392
                                                      CIP

Printed on acid-free, 250-year-life paper
Manufactured in the United States of America

To
Frank Stuart
and
Mabel Allebach
BreMiller

Paris, Bibliothèque Nationale, fonds français 1433, folio B
(Photo: Biliothèque Nationale.)

Preface of the General Editors

The Garland Library of Medieval Literature was established to make available to the general reader modern translations of texts in editions that conform to the highest academic standards. All of the translations are originals, and were created especially for this series. The translations usually attempt to render the foreign works in a natural idiom that remains faithful to the originals, although in certain cases we have published more poetic versions.

The Library is divided into two sections: Series A, texts and translations; and Series B, translations alone. Those volumes containing texts have been prepared after consultation of the major previous editions and manuscripts. The aim in the edition has been to offer a reliable text with a minimum of editorial intervention. Significant variants accompany the original, and important problems are discussed in the Textual Notes. Volumes without texts contain translations based on the most scholarly texts available, which have been updated in terms of recent scholarship.

Most volumes contain Introductions with the following features: (1) a biography of the author or a discussion of the problem of authorship, with any pertinent historical or legendary information; (2) an objective discussion of the literary style of the original, emphasizing any individual features; (3) a consideration of sources for the work and its influence; and (4) a statement of the editorial policy for each edition and translation. There is also a Select Bibliography, which emphasizes recent criticism on the works. Critical writings are often accompanied by brief descriptions of their importance. Selective glossaries, indices, and footnotes are included where appropriate.

The Library covers a broad range of linguistic areas, including all of the major European languages. All of the important literary forms and genres are considered, sometimes in anthologies or selections.

The General Editors hope that these volumes will bring the general reader a closer awareness of a richly diversified area that has for too long been closed to everyone except those with precise academic training, an area that is well worth study and reflection.

James J. Wilhelm
Rutgers University

Lowry Nelson, Jr.
Yale University

CONTENTS

Introduction ix

Acknowledgments xxxi

Select Bibliography xxxiii

L'Atre Périlleux 1

List of Emendations 341

Textual Notes 353

Index of Proper Nouns 381

Appendix 387

Paris, Bibliothèque Nationale, fonds français 1433, folio 55
(Photo: Bibliothèque Nationale.)

INTRODUCTION

Authorship

L'Atre Périlleux (The Perilous Cemetery) belongs to a new category of literature that became popular in France from approximately 1190 to 1300. This genre, Arthurian verse romance, was inspired by Chrétien de Troyes's narratives, from which individual lines and sometimes whole episodes are borrowed. The later romances are characterized by the invention of new motifs, artful linking of episodes, word play, reinterpretation of character, and, occasionally, mockery of romance conventions. Some of the later stories continue the adventures of Perceval left unfinished by Chrétien. Others introduce new protagonists into the Arthurian landscape: Gliglois, Meraugis, Durmart, Yder, Jaufré, Fergus, Mériaduc, Hunbaut, Floriant, Claris, Laris, and Escanor. This particular romance, *L'Atre Périlleux*, is unusual among the verse romances in making Gawain the central figure.

Although we know the names of the authors of many verse romances, such knowledge does not necessarily make the date of composition, historical identification of the author, or the circumstances surrounding composition any easier to ascertain than when the romance has, like *L'Atre Périlleux*, no named author. The few clues we have about the anonymous author can be deduced from study of the linguistic features of the three extant manuscripts and from analysis of the style and content of the narrative.

In his 1905 study of the rhyming words in *L'Atre Périlleux*, Theodor Wassmuth was the first to suggest that the author came from eastern Normandy, or more precisely, from the western portion of the French department of Eure. Brian Woledge, in his extensive study of the language of the three extant manuscripts of the work, which he completed in 1930 in preparation for his critical edition, rightly objected to Wassmuth's overly circumscribed location of the author in a particular region of one department, a conclusion that was based on faulty dialect maps (*Etudes* 53–54). Woledge identified eight features of the author's language which suggest that he came from the western region of the *langue d'oïl*, a conclusion that Woledge repeated in the introduction to his critical edition: "Pour le pays de l'auteur, plusieurs traits semblent prouver qu'il était de l'Ouest, sans qu'on puisse préciser davantage" (As to the native land of the author, numerous characteristics indicate that he came from the West, without being able to specify the region more precisely; *L'Atre* viii).

Study of the phonology and morphology of the author's language indicates a date of composition earlier than the date of the three extant manuscripts, the earliest of which was written in the late thirteenth century (see p. xxiv below). The author is familiar with Arthurian themes and romance conventions and makes frequent reference to the works of Chrétien de Troyes. These features suggest that the earliest possible date of composition is the first quarter of the thirteenth century.

It has been proposed that the latest date of composition might be established by a passage borrowed from *L'Atre Périlleux* and used in a later romance, *Claris et Laris* (Paris 127–8). Because the latter work refers to the capture of Antioch in 1268, that date would constitute a *terminus ad quem* for the earlier romance (Woledge, *Etudes* 62). However, the "borrowed" passage referred to is not a quotation or verbal echo of *L'Atre Périlleux*. Rather, the passage relates an adventure in which Claris fights the devil who has been keeping a maiden prisoner in a castle (ll. 8673–8870). The similarities between this episode and Gawain's battle with the devil in the Perilous Cemetery, fought in order to free a maiden kept imprisoned in a coffin, are too vague to establish a direct link between the two works for purposes of dating.

In the absence of a precise date or any reference to historical events in the work itself, scholars of the French verse romances have found that the best procedure for dating is not to establish a *terminus a quo* and *terminus ad quem* but to group the work with similar romances. As Keith Busby writes, "the notion of generations of romances...may prove more useful than attempts to date individual texts" ("Diverging Traditions" 93). Accordingly, *L'Atre Périlleux* may be placed in the period 1230–1250 along with *Fergus, Le Chevalier aux deux épées*, and *Hunbaut* (Schmolke-Hasselmann, "Der französische Artusroman" 419). The conclusion reached by this method of dating is not dramatically different from Woledge's conclusion that the work was written around the mid-thirteenth century (*Etudes* 63).

The style and content of the text itself provide clues that result in contradictory impressions of the author. Certain romance conventions, such as abrupt transitions from one episode to the next, frequent references to food, and the praise of Arthur's generosity in paying jongleurs and musicians at the conclusion of the work, suggest that the author might have been a professional storyteller. On the other hand, the presence of religious themes—fragmentation of the body, resurrection of a dead man, and a miraculous cure of blindness—may imply a clerical role for the author. Alternatively, we might read these episodes as ironic commentary on the proliferation of saints and relics in France and England in the early thirteenth century. From the following, we can probably ascertain that the author was literate: many verbal echoes of the works of Chrétien de Troyes; several references to a written source for his story; explicit reference to *The Song of Roland* in the climactic battle of twenty knights against ten.

There are a few hints about the circumstances that might have occasioned the poem's composition. At the opening of his romance, the author states that a woman has ordered him to tell a story of an adventure that happened to "the good knight":

> Ma dame me conmande et prie
> Que une aventure li die
> Qu'il avint au bon chevalier,
> Et je nel puis mie laiscier
> Quant ele le m'a conmandé,
> Des qu'il li plaist et vient a gré. (ll. 1–6)

The author is probably imitating the opening of Chrétien de Troyes's *Lancelot* (Walters 22), a work probably written for a female patron, Marie de Champagne.[1] It is impossible to know who the patroness was or what the occasion for the commission of *L'Atre Périlleux* might have been. However, because the romance ends with the performance of multiple marriages[2] and because, by the end of the narrative, Gawain has become a kind of marriage broker,[3] it is tempting to think that the poem was composed to celebrate a marriage.[4]

On the basis of female patronage, we might expect the author of *L'Atre Périlleux* to be particularly attuned to the female members of his audience, but he also makes anti-feminist remarks at two places in his narrative. In one episode a knight discovers his *amie* in the presence of Gawain, who has removed his armor to rescue a sparrow hawk; the knight falsely accuses his *amie* of being a whore, concluding that "A woman is quick to find words/ To escape from a tight place" (ll. 2690–91). The narrator adds his own comment:

> Por mon conte que je n'aloing,
> Ne veul lor barate descrire.
> Assés m'en avés oï dire
> En autres lius, si m'en tairai. (ll. 2692–95)

Woledge claims that this passage indicates that the poet is the author of other works maligning women (*Etudes* 41), a conclusion unwarranted by the passage. The author merely says he has made anti-feminist remarks in other places or on other occasions.

The second passage containing anti-feminist remarks occurs just before Gawain goes to help Cadrés fight off twenty knights. The sparrow-hawk woman, who has been accompanying Gawain in his adventures, develops a sudden hunger and thirst, and demands that Gawain go to a nearby castle for food and drink. This deflection from the chivalric path prompts Gawain to cite a proverb, "The ass crumbles under too heavy a load" (l. 4004), and the author to comment:

> Salemons dist en un sien livre
> Que cil n'est pas del tot delivre
> Ki conpaignie a fenme prent.... (ll. 4009–11)

In the thirteen-line passage that follows, the author warns that "he is no longer free/ Who holds company with a woman" (ll. 4010–11).

At first glance, these passages may seem to contradict the celebration of marriage in the poem and the idea of female patronage. However, similar contradictory points of view are found elsewhere in romance literature, including Chrétien de Troyes's *Le Chevalier au*

Lion (Yvain) and *Perceval.*[5] It would appear that male teasing of women is not an uncommon feature of works written for mixed-gender audiences, even in works where female patronage is certain.

Artistic Achievement

Although *L'Atre Périlleux* appears in three important medieval codices and a good critical edition of the work has been available since 1936, it is only recently that the romance has begun to receive sustained critical attention from scholars. A call for reappraisal of the late Arthurian verse romances by Schmolke-Hasselmann (1980 and 1983) and Busby (1988) initiated modern interest in the romance. A French translation of the work appeared in 1989, and there have been several articles on the program of illustrations contained in one of the manuscripts (B.N.fr. 1433), which also contains Chrétien de Troyes's *Yvain.*[6] The Garland edition, with the first English translation, should stimulate further scholarly interest. As a verse romance, written during a period when most Arthurian stories were being written in prose, and as one of the few romances in which Gawain is the protagonist, the work deserves to be better known.

Although Gawain appears in many romances, he usually performs a secondary role, acting as a foil for the exploits of the hero, with whom he is often unfavorably compared.[7] In *L'Atre Périlleux*, as in the fourteenth-century English romance *Sir Gawain and the Green Knight*, Gawain is presented in a mainly positive, but hardly unambiguous light. In the opening lines of the romance, even before his name is mentioned, we learn that the story is to be about the *bon chevalier.*[8] In this romance, Gawain's reputation precedes him: he is the paragon of virtue, the most courteous, and the bravest; as the king's nephew and therefore in line for the throne, he ranks as the highest noble in the court; he is the upholder of honor and justice; and, of course, he is a ladies' man.

Although Gawain's reputation is high at the start of the romance, his performance hardly justifies it. He fails to prevent the abduction of a maiden from Arthur's court and delays chasing the offending knight. Rebuked by Arthur and finally shamed into leaving the court, Gawain finds that, in the world outside, he no longer exists.

Incognito, he encounters three maidens and a wounded, blinded knight who tell him a grisly story of Gawain's death in battle and the subsequent dismemberment of his body. This erasure of Gawain provides one of the inciting moments of the romance, and the protagonist, now referred to as *celui qui a perdu son nom* ("he who has lost his name"), begins a quest for the recovery of his identity as well as for revenge on the offending knight.

Lori Walters has argued that the author of *L'Atre Périlleux* made a conscious attempt to rehabilitate the reputation of Gawain (7–8). That reputation had experienced a steady decline in the previous century: criticism of Gawain, evident as early as Chrétien's romances, is most obvious in the prose Grail romances written under the influence of Christian clerical tradition, such as the *Quest of the Holy Grail* or the *Prose Tristan* (Bogdanow 160–61). In *L'Atre Périlleux*, Gawain succeeds in his quests, despite his inauspicious beginning: by purging the Perilous Cemetery of its devil; by taking vengeance on the proud knight, Escanor, who abducted the maiden from Arthur's court; by rescuing a number of damsels in distress; by helping at least five knights reconcile themselves with their loved ones; and by avenging the death of his double. In fact, Gawain facilitates the miraculous resurrection of his double and a cure of the blinded youth who had come to his double's defense. The final fruit of Gawain's labors is the celebration of multiple marriages in the final scene of the romance.

L'Atre Périlleux, then, represents not only one of the few narratives in which Gawain is the central figure but also one of the few in which his accomplishments are treated positively. The development of his character in the course of his adventures differs, however, from that of his prototypes, Erec, Yvain, Lancelot, and Perceval. Unlike the earlier Arthurian protagonists, Gawain is not motivated by love for a woman, nor does he develop in his understanding of love or marriage. Rather, he is motivated by loyalty toward his uncle, King Arthur: the fulfillment of his responsibilities as Arthur's right-hand man is his primary goal, and Gawain develops within the context of these responsibilities. By removing the false self, he becomes the knight he should be, the true self—the one who insures that the laws of courtesy and chivalric behavior are upheld. The wholeness achieved at the end of the romance is not simply Gawain's bodily wholeness but also the legal and social wholeness of the realm he represents, in which law and order finally prevail, in which tyrannical and discourteous knights have been brought into line.

One scholar has attributed the lack of development of Gawain in the earlier romances to the fact that he "undergoes no real crisis whence he emerges a wiser and better knight" (Busby, *Gauvain* 387). By contrast, real crises are encountered by Gawain in *L'Atre Périlleux*. A first crisis occurs when he delays pursuing Escanor in order to free the abducted lady, a crisis that is resolved early in the narrative (by line 2492). A second, more important crisis occurs when he hears the report of his own death and the fragmentation of his supposed body. It is this latter event which provides the structural frame for all succeeding episodes and which is ultimately resolved by the resurrection of his double's body toward the end of the narrative.

From the point of view of medieval law, the fragmented body suggests the customary punishment for a treasonous crime (Barron 36–7). The author may thereby imply that, by failing to protect the abducted maiden, Gawain has committed treason. Or perhaps the fact that a knight can enter Arthur's court and freely abduct the king's personal cup bearer implies the inadequacy of centralized judicial control in Arthur's court (Bloch 11). Read against contemporary hagiographic texts (Bynam 268–84), the fragmentation of Gawain's double suggests that Gawain is, perhaps ironically, being portrayed as a saint, the saint of courtesy, parts of whose body are carried to different parts of the country and even venerated (for Tristan has had a reliquary constructed for the false Gawain's arm—ll. 5176–86).

For the reader, much of the delight of this story lies in narrative play on this conventional paragon of chivalric virtue. Gawain is persistently, but gently, mocked for his failings. A first example appears in the opening scene: a young woman arrives at Arthur's court and asks to become his cup bearer; Gawain is assigned as her protector and, on the following day, just as everyone is seated at the table and she is assuming her role as cup bearer, an arrogant knight, Escanor, arrives and kidnaps her. Gawain—the supposed paragon of courtesy—doesn't move, for he thinks that it would be impolite to get up from the table in the middle of a meal right there in front of the King. Not until rebuked first by Kay and then by Arthur himself does he make his move.

Further mockery of Gawain's polite behavior occurs later in the narrative during his attempt to rescue a damsel in distress. The woman's lover has left her alone in the forest with orders to guard his favorite sparrow hawk. The bird has flown up into an oak tree and refuses to come down. Hearing the maiden's lament, Gawain arrives in full suit of armor, tries to call the bird back, but fails in this endeavor. He has to take off his armor and climb into the tree to recapture the sparrow hawk. While he is in this compromising position, the woman's lover returns and, concluding that Gawain is a rival lover, takes Gawain's beloved horse, Gringalet, and leaves Gawain stranded with the woman.

Although there is much that is comic about this romance, the darker theme of death is also explored. The theme is addressed in the story of the dismemberment of Gawain's double, already mentioned above, and, more importantly, in the adventure that gives the romance its title, "The Perilous Cemetery." While the dark side never dominates the romance, it does lend depth to a story that is otherwise characterized by a sense of the playful and celebratory.

In the "Perilous Cemetery" adventure, Gawain is required to fight the devil himself. In repayment for having cured a young woman of madness, the devil keeps her entombed in a grave by day and requires her by night to fulfill his sexual desires. By freeing the woman from the devil's lustful clutches, Gawain establishes himself as the guardian of sexual morality; he also legitimizes his pursuit of Escanor, the arrogant knight who abducted the maiden from Arthur's court in the first scene of the romance. An ironic reversal of the devil's abuse of his whore by night occurs, for Gawain sees to it that for two nights Escanor is unable to sleep with the woman he has abducted.

Nearly as interesting as the depiction of the hero is the narrative structure of the poem. *Entrelacement*, or interlacing of narrative episodes, is carried out with great intricacy in this romance. One adventure is constantly interrupted by another, so that Gawain's affairs become very complicated indeed. Interruption of one adventure by another, or "deflection from the right path," is, in fact, characteristic of Gawain (Busby, *Gauvain* 389). In some romances, such as *The Quest of the Holy Grail*, this results in an aimless series of adventures, rather than a quest in the proper sense of the word. In *L'Atre*

Périlleux Gawain's early adventures may appear aimless; however, at a certain point in the narrative (l. 3930) the unfinished adventures begin to be resolved. The turning point is, in fact, what appears to be the most senseless of interruptions, the demand of the sparrow-hawk woman that her three-day hunger and thirst be assuaged. Surprisingly, each new adventure thereafter represents a resolution of an earlier adventure that had been interrupted and left unresolved. By the final scene, all adventures have been knit together in a *bel conjointure*.

Beneath the seemingly senseless interruptions, then, is a hidden rationale, a mysterious force that brings about, almost miraculously, a resolution to all the adventures begun by Gawain. The use of this narrative device leads to a type of suspense—not quite what a modern-day reader of a mystery story would experience in awaiting the announcement of "who done it"—but something nonetheless similar, what we might call the "expectation of surprise." The reader cannot help but wonder how the narrator will work out this story so that all narrative threads are resolved happily in the end.

The narrative structure of the romance—with all its interruptions and resolutions—can be depicted schematically as follows:

$$\{A^1+B^1+A^2\}+\{C^1+D^1+E\}+\{F^1+C^2+D^2+C^3+F^2\}+\{B^2+A^3\}$$

A^1 Initial conflict at Arthur's court: Gawain pursues Escanor, abductor of Arthur's cup bearer.

B^1 New conflict: Gawain, incognito, encounters three weeping maidens and a blinded knight who tell him Gawain has been killed and dismembered by three knights; Gawain decides to delay pursuit of the knights.

A^2 Initial conflict resolved: after pursuing Escanor for three days and two nights, Gawain finally fights and kills him.

C^1 New conflict: leaving his party near Carlisle, Gawain rides off to inquire why a maiden nearby is weeping; the adventure with the sparrow hawk and loss of Gringalet follow.

D^1 New demand: Ragidel of Angarde appears and supplies Gawain with a horse in return for a future boon; Ragidel takes the sparrow hawk as pledge.

E New conflict: Espinogre appears and tells a long story about his hard-to-get lover, whom he is about to leave for another woman; Gawain fights with him to enforce his fidelity to his first *amie*. This episode is resolved without interruption.

F[1] New conflict: Espinogre, the sparrow-hawk maiden, and Gawain encounter Cadrés, who is on his way to a dangerous battle to rescue his *amie* from a rival accompanied by twenty knights. Espinogre and Cadrés leave together for the battle, but Gawain is deflected from the path.

C[2] New demand: from a nearby castle, Gawain must get the sparrow-hawk woman food and drink, which he must discourteously seize from its reluctant owner, a woman whose seven brothers are out hunting.

D[2] Old demand resolved: Ragidel of Angarde suddenly reappears and demands his boon, that Gawain should agree to abduct and bring to him his *amie*, the woman with the seven brothers.

C[3] Old conflict resolved: the cries of the abducted maiden cause the eldest of her brothers, Codrovain, to come to the rescue; he turns out to be the original owner of the sparrow hawk and the abductor of Gringalet; Gawain fights him, gets his horse back, and—in return for his life—makes him promise to give his sister to Ragidel in marriage and reconcile himself with his *amie*. The other six brothers agree with this arrangement and offer to fight with Cadrés.

F[2] Old conflict resolved: while Codrovain accompanies the women back to the castle, Gawain, Ragidel, and the six brothers join Espinogre and Cadrés in their battle with twenty knights; Codrovain later joins the battle, and the *amie* of Cadrés is liberated.

B[2] Old conflict resolved: Espinogre and Gawain seek the three weeping maidens, but meet instead Tristan Who Never Smiles, who tells them where to find the two outrageous knights. Espinogre and Gawain defeat the two knights, named Gomeret and the Proud Magician. The reformed Magician restores the fragmented knight to life and gives sight to the blinded young man, whose name is Martin.

A[3] Final resolution of conflicts: all return to Arthur's court where several marriages are celebrated.

One consequence of this complex interlacing of episodes is that Gawain constantly gains followers, leading to a type of narrative *amplificatio*; thus, in the climactic battle to free Cadrés's *amie* (which has echoes of *The Song of Roland*), Gawain and nine other knights successfully battle twenty opponents at a narrow pass. In the course of his adventures, Gawain encounters so many damsels in distress that he nearly always has one or two women riding with him at any one point in the narrative, a feature that carries particular irony with a hero named Gawain.

Further insight into the structure of the romance may be gained by comparison with another lost version, of which we have only an eighteenth-century summary. The "Fabliau ou Conte de l'Atre périlleux, c'est-à-dire du Manoir périlleux" was published in July 1777 as part of the *Bibliothèque universelle des romans*. It is not known what manuscript formed the basis of this prose summary of *L'Atre Périlleux*, but it is clear that the original differed sharply from the narrative found in the Garland edition.

In the opening episode of the prose summary (compare A[1] above), there are important differences in details. Gawain is not asked to defend the maiden until the day after her arrival. When she is abducted, everyone in court rushes to follow, but Arthur directs only Gawain to pursue the knight; despite this order, Kay rushes out ahead. Gawain does not hesitate to leave in this version. There is no breaking of Kay's arm, and Kay himself is at fault for seeking to take the adventure from Gawain.

A more significant difference revealed by the summary is the absence of the intermediary encounter with the three weeping women, the fragmented body, and the blinded young man (B[1]); thus the whole motif of Gawain's lost name is omitted. Accompanied by the squire from the castle and the lady from the cemetery, Gawain battles, defeats, and kills Escanor during the second day of his pursuit. Before Gawain can return to court with his companions, he hears a maiden weeping in the forest. The episode with the sparrow hawk in the oak tree and the loss of Gringalet follows (C[1]). The next day Espinogre arrives (E), and this episode is followed directly by the appearance of Cadrés (F), omitting the appearance of Ragidel (D[1]). In this abbreviated version, Cadrés is prevented from marrying his *amie* only by the father, whom Gawain fights and defeats. Gawain has thus brought two couples together (Espinogre and Cadrés with their *amies*) in a more direct manner than in the Garland version of *L'Atre Périlleux*.[9]

Whether this shorter version of *L'Atre Périlleux* represents an earlier stage in the composition of the romance or a later abridgment we cannot know. Certainly the succession of events is much more straightforward, easier to comprehend and remember. It is tempting to speculate that the author of the longer version knew and built upon the shorter one. If such is the case, we can see the adapter/author of the Garland text darkening the theme by introducing the false death of Gawain, focusing events on the reestablishment of Gawain's reputation, and interlacing the episodes so as to build toward the climactic battle.

In one of the three extant manuscripts of *L'Atre Périlleux*, we have evidence of another *remaniement*, or reworking of the text. In Bibliothèque Nationale fonds français 1433 (see discussion of "Manuscripts" below), the adapter added a 666-line interpolation, which is reprinted in this edition in the Appendix. In B.N.fr. 1433, this addition is placed between episodes D^1 and E, that is after the first appearance of Ragidel and before Espinogre appears to tell his story about his hard-to-get *amie*. The new episode tells the story of another arrogant knight, Brun Without Pity, who treats a woman abusively. For four days out of each week, this knight, who is King of the Red City, keeps a beautiful young woman naked and immersed up to her waist in a cold spring. Fifty-four knights have challenged him and been defeated by the king; after defeat their bodies are dismembered, and their heads and gleaming helmets are placed on stakes. Gawain, after a long and difficult fight with the king, defeats Brun, takes him prisoner, and sends him off to report to Arthur's court. By adding this adventure, the adapter, in B.N.fr. 1433, has not only lengthened the romance, he has also skillfully highlighted several themes introduced in earlier episodes: knightly arrogance, the abuse of women, and fragmentation of the body.

It should be evident from the preceding discussion that *L'Atre Périlleux* is a considerably more interesting romance than earlier scholars supposed. The comment of Alexander Haggerty Krappe in 1932 that, aside from the episode of the Perilous Cemetery, "tout le reste du conte n'est que lieux communs, combat banal et quelques radotages pieux" (all the rest of the narrative consists merely of commonplaces, conventional battles, and pious nonsense; 261) would not be advanced today. Bringing new approaches to the romance, current scholars are enhancing our appreciation of it: by placing it within the context of contemporary verse romances; by analysis within its social and historical contexts; by study of *entrelacement* and other rhetorical devices; and by studying the relationship of illustrations to text.

In the early fourteenth century, at least one reader, the compiler of B.N.fr. 1433, thought that *L'Atre Périlleux* was to be valued as much as Chrétien de Troyes's *Yvain*, for the two romances were placed side-by-side in one codex, conceived of as a unit, written in one hand, and illustrated by one artist, who produced four illuminations for *L'Atre Périlleux* and nine for *Yvain*. It is unlikely that any modern scholar would make the claim that the literary value of this romance equals that of Chrétien's *Yvain*; nonetheless, the romance deserves more appreciation than it has previously received from readers and critics.

Sources and Influences

The influence of the romances of Chrétien de Troyes on the author of *L'Atre Périlleux* is extensive.[10] The opening formula, in which the author responds to the request of his lady to tell a story about the *bon chevalier*, echoes the opening of Chrétien's *Lancelot* (Walters 22, n.18). Further, the initial narrative pattern found in *Lancelot*—Arthurian knights gathered for a feast, interruption by a challenging knight, and an unsuccessful attempt by Kay to meet the challenge—is repeated, although with changes in many details, in *L'Atre Périlleux*. The lady with the sparrow hawk reminds us of *Erec et Enide*. The oft-repeated episode of Gawain's incognito battle with another Arthurian knight first appears in *Yvain*. There is an explicit reference (ll. 5124–35) to Perceval's defeat of the Red Knight in *Le Conte du Graal*.

Both John Reinhard and Brian Woledge tentatively suggested that *Amadas et Ydoine* might provide a source for Gawain's battle with the devil in the cemetery in *L'Atre Périlleux*. However, the earlier romance, dated 1190–1220 by Reinhard, displays important differences from the scene in *L'Atre Périlleux*: Ydoine only appears to have died and is entombed in the cemetery where a fairy knight comes to claim her, while in *L'Atre Périlleux* the maiden is under the spell of the devil, who keeps her entombed by day and sexually enslaved by night. The parallel passages Reinhard cites are unconvincing;[11] similar words and phrases might be found in any number of romance battles.

A better parallel to the story of Gawain in *L'Atre Périlleux* occurs in *Mériadeuc*, also known as *Le Chevalier aux deux épées*. Stoyan Atanassov has shown that in both romances there is a split between the reputation (*renon*) of Gawain and his identity (*non*). In both romances Gawain must confront a knight whose lover will only consent to love him if he defeats Gawain in battle. In *Mériadeuc*, when Gawain is severely wounded in the battle, news of his death circulates throughout the land. His future adventures are attempts to disprove the report of his own death. In *L'Atre Périlleux*, a knight reported to be Gawain is killed and his body chopped up into six pieces by two knights whose loved ones insist upon the defeat of Gawain before granting them their love. Gawain must find and battle the two knights before recovering his name. Despite the similarities between the two romances, it is impossible to determine the direct influence of one upon the other.[12]

The prose romance *Perlesvaus* contains several episodes set in a cemetery. The most important of these occurs when Perlesvaus's sister enters a cemetery specifically called L'Aitre Perilleus (Branch VIII, l. 5034). Although the narrative action is quite different from what Gawain encounters in *L'Atre Périlleux*, there are distinct verbal echoes here and in the other episodes. The editors of *Perlesvaus* found the parallel passages convincing enough to suggest that the author of the prose romance "divided a single episode and distributed its traits among several, and that *L'Atre périlleux* was a source for P at these points" (Nitze and Jenkins, II 309).

Stock motifs and formulas found in other Arthurian romances also occur frequently in *L'Atre Périlleux*, and they may be best summarized by means of the following list:

A woman appears at court requesting help—*Lanzelet*; *Diu Crône*; *Hunbaut*; *Durmart le Galois*; *Amadas et Ydoine*; *Quest of the Holy Grail*; *La Mule sans frein*.
An adventure in a cemetery—*Amadas et Ydoine*; *Perlesvaus*; *Rigomer*; *First Continuation of Perceval*.
The woman who loves Gawain without ever having seen him—*Le Bel Inconnu*; *Mériadeuc*; *Hunbaut*; *Vengeance Raguidel*;

First Continuation of Perceval.

The incognito battle with another Arthurian knight—*Hunbaut* (with Gaheris); *Prose Lancelot* (with Lancelot); *Méraugis de Portlesguez* (with Méraugis); *First Continuation of Perceval* (Gawain with his son); *Mériadeuc* (with Mériadeuc).

Woman with sparrow hawk—Malory's *Morte d'Arthur; Durmart le Galois.*

The knife broken in anger—*Prose Lancelot*; *First Continuation of Perceval*; Wolfram's *Parzival.*

The wedding at the close of the romance—*Durmart le Galois*; *Fergus*; *Claris et Laris.*

In addition to the above motifs, the 666-line interpolation found only in one manuscript of *L'Atre Périlleux* (see Appendix), contains episodes found elsewhere in Arthurian romances. The King of the Red City, who keeps his naked lover sitting in water four days a week, has parallels in *Dame à la Lycorne, Roman de la Violette, Claris et Laris,* and *Valentine und Namelos.* The motif of the heads on stakes, which the tyrannical king collects, derives ultimately from *Erec et Enide,* but is also found in *La Mule sans frein, Vengeance Raguidel,* and *Durmart le Galois.*

Names of non-Arthurian knights who appear in *L'Atre Périlleux* also make an appearance in other Arthurian narratives: *Durmart* has a character named Cardroain (Codrovain); *Méraugis de Portlesguez* has a minor character named Espinogre; and *Hunbaut* has a character named Espinogre involved in an episode reminiscent of his role in *L'Atre Périlleux.* The character Ragidel may be taken from *Vengeance Raguidel,* believed to have been written in the first quarter of the thirteenth century, or the influence may be the reverse. Lais Hardis, with whom Gawain fights in the final battle of the romance, is mentioned as an Arthurian knight in Chrétien de Troyes's *Erec et Enide,* and he makes appearances in the *First Continuation of Perceval, Claris et Laris,* and *Escanor.* The last-mentioned romance, written by Girard d'Amiens (ca. 1280), appears to have borrowed the name of its hero, Escanor, from *L'Atre Périlleux.*

Although it is easy to find parallel episodes in other Arthurian romances, there is no single source for *L'Atre Périlleux,* nor is there definitive evidence that the author of any later romance knew or imitated *L'Atre Périlleux.* Scholarship of the last fifty years has failed to alter Woledge's conclusion regarding the author's use of sources: "Son roman est une combinaison nouvelle de traits et d'incidents déjà racontés par ses prédécesseurs, à laquelle il a ajouté quelque chose...de lui" (His romance is a new combination of deeds and events already narrated by his predecessors, to which he has added something...of his own; *Etudes* 81).

Editorial Policy for This Text and Translation

The Manuscripts

L'Atre Périlleux exists in three manuscripts, to which Woledge, in his critical edition, assigned the following sigla:

N¹—Paris, Bibliothèque Nationale, fonds français 2168, late 13th century.
N²—Paris, Bibliothèque Nationale, fonds français 1433, early 14th century.
A—Chantilly, Musée Condé, MS 472, late 13th century.

A fourth manuscript, now lost, was recorded as present in the library of Charles V (Delisle, *Recherches,* II 190). Woledge assigned the siglum X to this lost manuscript (*Etudes* 18–19).

A modern French version (assigned siglum S by Woledge) of *L'Atre Périlleux* was published in the *Bibliothèque universelle des romans* (July 1777) under the title "Fabliau ou Conte de l'Atre périlleux, c'est-à-dire du Manoir périlleux." Because the narrative differs markedly from that found in the three extant manuscripts, it may indicate that yet another manuscript once existed.[13]

The earliest, most reliable extant manuscript is B.N.fr. 2168 (Anc. 7989; Baluze 572), the base manuscript for this edition.[14] The codex contains a number of disparate works in 241 folios, plus 24*bis* and 117*bis*, of which folios 46 and 97 are blank. The codex contains the following works: *L'Atre Périlleux* (folios 1–45, including 24*bis*); *Li Vilains de Farbu* (folio 45); *Li Lais de Eudemarec* (incomplete at the start; folio 47); *Li Lais de Gugemer* (folios 48–54); *Li Lai de Lanval* (folios 54–58);

De Narciso li lais (folios 58–65); *L'Aventure de Graalent* (folios 65–70); *Aucassin et Nicolete* (folios 70–80); *Li Favliaus d'Infer* (folios 80–84); *Li Faveliaus de quaresme et de carnage* (folios 84–88); *Du Secretain, ou li fablax du moine* (folios 88–91); *Li Fabliau de la veuve* (incomplete at end; folios 91–94); Gautier de Metz's *L'Image du Monde* (incomplete at start; folios 95–156); *La Vie de Charlemagne* (incomplete at end; folios 156–158); *Fables* of Marie de France (folios 159–186); *La devision des quinze singnes* (folios 186–188); *Li Drois bestiaires de la devine escripture* (folios 188–209); *Du Bouchier d'Abevile* (folios 209–213); *Du Tort contre le tort* (folios 213–214); *Lucidaires en romans* (folios 215–239); *De le Vielle truande, ou, De la Viellete* (folios 239–240); *Li Fabliaus de Dagombert* (folios 240–241).

The work of two scribes is evident in B.N. fr. 2168: the first in lines 1–5740; the second in lines 5741 to the end. The work is written on vellum in two columns of 37 lines each. Red ink is used for capitals to mark the start of new stanzas and for the incipit and explicit.

B.N.fr. 1433, which contains the 666-line interpolation (see p. xx above), is a later copy of N[1], or a manuscript related to it and now lost.[15] The codex consists of 120 folios (numbered in a later hand), plus two illustrated folios Av and Br at start. The last two numbered folios are blank. The text is written in two columns of 31 lines each. Decorations include the two full-page, multi-compartment illustrations at the start; eleven additional panel illustrations interspersed in the text; two historiated initials, one at the start of each romance; and 112 illuminated initials. The codex contains two romances: *L'Atre Périlleux* (folios 1–60) and Chrétien de Troyes's *Yvain* (folios 61–118). B.N.fr. 1433 is a moderately luxurious copy, written on vellum by one scribe. As has been argued convincingly by Lori Walters, the codex was conceived, artistically and thematically, as a unified whole.

Chantilly 472 contains 260 folios, plus 153*bis* (a small scrap leaf), 203*bis*, 217*bis*, and 231*bis* (folio 56 is missing).[16] The following works are contained in the codex, which consists mainly of Arthurian romances: *Rigomer* (folios 1–55); *L'Atre Périlleux* (folios 57–77); *Erec et Enide* (folios 78–99); *Fergus* (folios 100–122); *Hunbaut* (folios 122–133); *Le Bel Inconnu* (folios 134–153); *La Vengeance Raguidel* (folios 154–173); *Yvain* (folios 174–195); *Lancelot* (folios 196–213); *Perlesvaus* (folios 214–243); four branches of the *Roman de Renart* (folios 244–260).

Although as many as six scribes may have worked on the codex as a whole (Micha 39), one scribe was responsible for *L'Atre Périlleux*. On folio 122, the scribe identifies himself as Colins li Fruitiers. The texts are written on vellum in three columns of 50–52 lines for poetry and two columns for prose. The titles of each work are given in alternating red and blue capitals.

The text of *L'Atre Périlleux* in Chantilly 472 is shorter than in the other two manuscripts, and it contains many substantive variants from N^1 and N^2, including a 58-line passage not found in the other texts. It thus represents, according to Woledge, a separate manuscript group.

Woledge's study of the morphology and phonology of the four scribes demonstrates that, unlike the author, all come from the North of France (*L'Atre* ix). The presence of Picardisms is particularly strong in the work of the main scribe of N^1 and the scribe of N^2. The second scribe of N^1 demonstrates the influence of Francian on Picard dialect; the scribe of A has characteristics of Walloon and Eastern dialects (*Etudes* 65–79).

Previous Editions

Two previous editions of *L'Atre Périlleux* have been published: an unreliable text, attributed to Schirmer (1868); and the critical edition of Brian Woledge for the Classiques français du moyen âge series (1936). In addition, Wolfram von Zingerle published the two interpolations in a 1910 article in *Zeitschrift für französische Sprache*.

The Present Edition

Both previous complete editions of *L'Atre Périlleux* were based on N^1, which I have also chosen as copytext for the present edition. I have been conservative in making emendations, preferring to retain differences in orthography between its two scribes, variants in spelling within the work of each scribe, and even inconsistencies in syllabification of lines. A number of typographical errors found in Woledge have been corrected and are indicated in the Textual Notes at the end of this volume. I have followed Woledge in printing the

58-line interpolation in A as a major substantive emendation of N[1], since the text would otherwise make little sense without it.

Like Woledge, I have also placed the 666-line interpolation found in N[2] in an appendix to the Garland text. The episode is referred to at line 6614 in N[1], and thus an argument could be made for inserting it after line 3002 in any critical edition, as does Ollier in her modern French translation of the romance. The decision to print the interpolation in the Appendix reflects my desire to have the Garland edition follow copytext as closely as possible.

The anonymous author of *L'Atre Périlleux* provides a title in the closing verses of the romance:

> Si sacent tuit bas et haut
> Car li Aitres Perilleus faut
> Des que Gavains a tant erré
> Qu'il est a cort a sauveté,
> Si fine ichi nostre romans. (ll. 6669–73)

The earlier, main scribe of the base manuscript, B.N.fr. 2168, spells the title variously as "li atres perellox," "latre perellox," "latre perillox," "latre perelox," or "latres perilleus"; a rubric at the start has "cest de latre perillous." The explicit, in the hand of the second scribe, reads "Explicit——/ de latre perelleus." This edition retains the modern French title assigned by Woledge, as well as his line numberings.

Indentations in the Garland text and translation indicate the presence of a large capital in N[1]. Folio numbers are bracketed and printed in italics in the right-hand margin of the edition. Line numbers are printed in the left-hand margins of both text and translation.

Diplomatic transcriptions of all three manuscripts were typed onto computer diskettes from photocopies and then checked against the manuscripts themselves. The Garland text was established after a line-by-line comparison of the three manuscripts and Woledge's edition.

I have followed current practice in the editing of Old French texts by making the following changes in accidentals without comment: resolving all abbreviations, including those for numbers; distinguishing *u* from *v* and *i* from *j*; dividing words that are run together; providing punctuation and capitalization, including use of quotation marks for direct speech; using the apostrophe to represent an elided vowel. I have followed the recommendations of Foulet and Speer on use of diacritical marks.

A list of all changes made from copytext, other than the accidentals indicated above, may be found in the List of Emendations following the Garland text and translation (pp. 341–52). From this list it is possible for the reader to reconstruct the copytext. Square brackets are used only to indicate emendations based upon writing in a modern hand at one repaired portion of copytext (see Textual Notes, ll. 1225–37).

I have translated the Old French octosyllabic couplets into prose, aiming for a lively, flowing English narrative style. When faced with dangling relative clauses or awkward parataxis, I have taken the liberty of reordering the lines or substituting a more idiomatic English syntax. I have supplied proper names when necessary to correct the frequently vague pronoun references. Although the Old French verbs frequently shift from past to present tense to convey a sense of immediacy, I have not attempted to reproduce this trait in English.

NOTES

[1] For Busby the reference to *bon chevalier* also recalls an earlier, very brief Gawain story, *Le Chevalier à l'épée* ("Diverging Traditions" 102).

[2] The text is ambiguous about how many marriages are celebrated at the end of the romance. Gawain asks King Arthur to hand over two *amies* to two knights, presumably the two sisters to Gomeret and the Proud Magician (ll. 6604–05), who have pursued them throughout the romance. A few lines later, he asks Arthur to marry Espinogre, Cadrés, and Ragidel to their loved ones (ll. 6608–11). However, a triple marriage is depicted in the illustration on f. 60 of B.N.fr. 1433.

[3] Busby was the first to use the term "marriage broker" to refer to Gawain's role in *L'Atre Périlleux* ("Diverging Traditions" 105).

⁴ The bishop who, according to the text, performed the marriages, Reniés of Chester, does not, so far as I have been able to determine, correspond to any actual bishop of Chester in the first half of the thirteenth century. Volume 1 of Conrad Eubel's *Hierarchia Catholica Medii Aevi* lists bishops for the period 1198–1431. The reader is told to see Cenventren for information about bishops of Cestren, but then no list under that heading appears. There is no listing for Reniés (or the Latin Rainaldus) under the bishops of Chicester, which might presumably have been confused with Chester (187). Chester was the seat of a bishop briefly from 1075–1102, and thereafter it was an archdeaconry attached to the see of Lichfield. According to P. Heath the "brief elevation of Chester in the eleventh century was tenaciously commemorated long after the bishops had ceased to style themselves by that title" (244). The name is probably fictional and meant to refer to the historical past. Chester was, with Carlisle, an important location in Arthur's kingdom; it is probably the City of the Legion mentioned by Nennius as the site of the ninth of Arthur's twelve battles (Ashe 40–41).

⁵ See *Yvain* (Roques 1644–45) and *Perceval* (Roach 5855–60). Ollier also notes the frequency of anti-feminist remarks in romances and mentions an example in *Le Chevalier à l'épée* (*La Légende* 673, n. 1).

⁶ See articles listed in the bibliography by Walters, Hindman, and Black.

⁷ The unfavorable comparison of Gawain with other Arthurian knights begins as early as Chrétien's *Yvain*, *Lancelot*, and *Perceval*. Busby notes that, in *L'Atre Périlleux*, Gawain becomes "for the first time in Old French literature the hero of a romance" ("Diverging Traditions" 103). He is the hero of one German romance, *Diu Crône* by Heinrich von dem Türlin, and the hero of numerous Middle English romances.

⁸ Gawain is also referred to as the *bon chevalier* in *Le Chevalier à l'épée*. See Busby, "'Li Buens Chevaliers'."

⁹ The two couples proceed with Gawain and the sparrow-hawk woman back to Arthur's court. Before their arrival, they meet the jealous knight who took Gawain's horse (C² in the Garland edition). Gawain defeats him and reconciles him with his *amie*. Gawain thus returns to Arthur's court with three couples. The two women whom Gawain had rescued at the start of the romance (the maiden abducted by Escanor and the lady imprisoned by the devil in the cemetery) are also paired up with two knights of the Round Table. The

romance ends with the celebration of the marriage of five couples.

[10] Verbal echoes are noted in the Textual Notes.

[11] See Reinhard 32–33, for cited passages; Micha also concludes that "differences in treatment...exclude the derivation of one version from the other" (368).

[12] As mentioned above, pp. x–xi, *Mériadeuc* is placed by Schmolke-Hasselmann in the same "generation" of verse romances as *L'Atre Périlleux*, 1230–1250. Keith Busby in *The Arthurian Encyclopedia* says "second quarter of the thirteenth century" (382); Alexandre Micha in *Dictionnaire des lettres françaises* says first third of the thirteenth century (1007).

[13] Not having found any trace of this manuscript among Sainte-Palaye's collection in the Bibliothèque de l'Arsenal, Woledge conjectured that the title may refer to a copy of N[1] made for his use (*Etudes* 19–20).

[14] Descriptions of this manuscript may be found in Woledge (*Etudes* 13–15) and Bourdillon (11).

[15] For descriptions of this manuscript, see Micha (*La Tradition* 44) and Woledge (*Etudes* 15–16).

[16] Fuller descriptions of this manuscript may be found in Winter (xi–xiv), Frescoln (2–5), Micha (*La Tradition* 38–39), and Woledge (*Etudes* 16–18).

ACKNOWLEDGMENTS

Thanks are due to many institutions and their staff, as well as to colleagues, friends, and family members. First, to the Bibliothèque Nationale in Paris and the Musée Condé in Chantilly for providing microfilm copies of the three manuscripts and for permitting me to study the manuscripts in person. The librarians of the Brooklyn College Library, in particular William Parise and William Gargan, provided prompt service for many interlibrary loan and purchase requests. Research was supported in part by a grant from The City University of New York PSC-CUNY Research Award Program.

In 1991, during a National Endowment for the Humanities summer institute held at Stanford University on "The Grail and the Rose," I first began to talk to colleagues about my translation project. Encouragement came from Brigitte Cazelles, Kevin Brownlee, Paula Giuliano, Gale Sigal, Beverly J. Evans, Duane W. Kight, and Gerald E. Seaman. Gerry Seaman helped with a number of specific translation problems, and since then Beverly Evans has continued to make herself available to answer questions, enlisting occasionally the aid of Victoria Guerin.

Special thanks are due to Mary Pagurelias, who gave generously of her time in helping to transcribe many lines of Old French from microfilm and who read and commented on early drafts of the introduction and translation. Judith S. Neaman offered constant encouragement, provided advice on several of the textual notes, and commented on a draft of the introduction. Michael L. Black introduced me long ago to the intricacies of editing texts; as a reader for this project, he saved me from many stylistic blunders. Camera-ready copy was produced by Jessica W. Black, and Wade N. Black was my computer consultant.

I am particularly indebted to the editorial staff of Garland Publishing for their helpfulness, to Joyce Coleman for proofreading the Introduction, and to James J. Wilhelm for his careful reading of the entire text and translation.

Paris, Bibliothèque Nationale, fonds français 1433, folio 60
(Photo: Bibliothèque Nationale.)

SELECT BIBLIOGRAPHY

I. Editions and Translations of *L'Atre Périlleux*

"Fabliau ou Conte de l'Atre périlleux, c'est-à-dire du Manoir périlleux." *Bibliothèque universelle des romans* (July 1777): 70–86. Summary of a version of *L'Atre Périlleux* which is now lost.

Ollier, Marie-Louise. "*L'Atre périlleux* (Le Cimetière du Grand Péril): D'une aventure de Gauvain, le Bon Chevalier." *La Légende Arthurienne: Le Graal et la table ronde*. Paris: Robert Laffont, 1989. 605–708. Translation into Modern French prose, based on Woledge's edition, with consultation of other manuscripts.

[Schirmer]. "Der gefahrvolle Kirchhof." *Archiv für das Studium der neueren Sprachen und Literaturen* 42 (1868). 135–212.

Woledge, Brian. *L'Atre périlleux: roman de la table ronde*. Classiques français du moyen âge, 76. Paris: Champion, 1936.

Zingerle, Wolfram von. "Zum altfranzösischen Artusroman 'Li Atres perillox'." *Zeitschrift für französische Sprache* 36 (1910). 274–93. Edition of 666-line interpolation in N^2 and 58 lines of A.

II. Bibliographies and Other Reference Works

BBSIA: *Bulletin bibliographique de la Société Internationale Arthurienne*.

Bossuat, Robert. *Manuel bibliographique de la littérature française du moyen âge*. Melun: Librairie d'Argences, 1951.

Bossuat, Robert, Louis Pichard, and Guy Raynaud de Lage. *Dictionnaire des lettres françaises: le moyen âge*. Paris: Fayard, 1964.

Brault, Gerald J. *Early Blazon: Heraldic Terminology in the Twelfth and Thirteenth Centuries.* Oxford: Clarendon Press, 1972.

Broughton, Bradford B. *Dictionary of Medieval Knighthood and Chivalry: Concepts and Terms.* New York; Westport, CT; and London: Greenwood Press, 1986.

———. *Dictionary of Medieval Knighthood and Chivalry: People, Places, and Events.* New York; Westport, CT; and London: Greenwood Press, 1988.

Brown, Michelle P. *A Guide to Western Historical Scripts from Antiquity to 1600.* Toronto and Buffalo: U of Toronto Press, 1990.

Chantilly: Le Cabinet des livres. 3 vols. Paris: Plon, 1900.

Delisle, Leopold. *Le Cabinet des manuscrits de la Bibliothèque impériale.* 3 vols. Paris: Imprimerie impériale, 1868–81.

———. *Recherches sur la librairie de Charles V.* 2 vols. Paris: Champion, 1907.

Dictionnaire historique de la langue française. Paris: Dictionnaires Le Robert, 1992.

Encomia, Bibliographical Bulletin of the International Courtly Literature Society. Published annually since 1976.

Euble, Conrad. *Hierarchia Catholica Medii Aevi.* 3 vols. Regensburg: Regensburg Monastery, 1910–14.

Flutre, Louis-Fernand. *Table des noms propres avec toutes leurs variantes figurant dans les romans du moyen âge écrits en français ou en provençal et actuellement publiés ou analysés.* Poitiers: Centre d'études supérieures de civilisation médiévale, 1962.

Foerster, Wendelin. *Wörterbuch zu Kristian von Troyes' sämtlichen Werken.* 2nd ed. Halle: Niemeyer, 1960.

Foulet, Alfred Lucien and Mary Blakely Speer. *On Editing Old*

French Texts. Lawrence: Regents Press of Kansas, 1979.

Godefroy, Frédéric. *Dictionnaire de l'ancienne langue française et de tous ses dialectes du IXe au XVe siècle.* 10 vols. Paris: 1880–1902; rpt. Paris: Librairie des Sciences et des Arts, 1938.

Greimas, A. J. *Dictionnaire de l'ancien français jusqu'au milieu du XIVe siècle.* Paris: Larousse, 1968.

Kibler, William W. *An Introduction to Old French.* New York: Modern Language Association, 1984.

Lacy, Norris J., ed. *The Arthurian Encyclopedia.* New York: Peter Bedrich Books, 1986.

Marcuse, Sibyl. *Musical Instruments: A Comprehensive Dictionary.* New York: Doubleday, 1964.

Morawski, Joseph. *Proverbes français antérieurs au XVe siècle.* Classiques français du moyen âge, 47. Paris: Champion, 1925.

The New Grove Dictionary of Musical Instruments. Ed. Stanley Sadie. 3 vols. New York: Macmillan, 1984.

Omont, H. *Catalogue général des manuscrits français de la Bibliothèque Nationale.* Paris: Leroux, 1900.

Pickford, Cedric E. and Rex Last. *The Arthurian Bibliography.* 2 vols. Cambridge: Brewer, 1981–83.

Reiss, Edmund et al. *Arthurian Legend and Literature: An Annotated Bibliography. Vol. 1: The Middle Ages.* Garland Reference Library of the Humanities, 415. New York and London: Garland, 1984.

Sachs, Curt. *Real-Lexikon der Musikinstrumente.* 1913. New York: Dover, 1964.

Schulze-Busacker, Elizabeth. *Proverbes et expressions proverbiales dans la littérature narrative du moyen âge français, recueil et analyse.* Paris: Champion, 1985.

Tobler, Adolf and E. Lommatzsch. *Altfranzösisches Wörterbuch.* Berlin: Weidmannsche Buchhandlung; Wiesbaden: Franz Steiner, 1925—.

Vielliard, Françoise and Jacques Montrin, ed. *Manuel Bibliographique de la littérature française du moyen âge de Robert Bossuat.* 3rd supplement (1960–1980). Paris: Editions du centre national de la recherche scientifique, 1986.

West, G. D. *An Index of Proper Names in French Arthurian Prose Romances.* U of Toronto Romance Series, 35. Toronto: U of Toronto P, 1978.

———. *An Index of Proper Names in French Arthurian Verse Romances.* U of Toronto Romance Series, 15. Toronto: U of Toronto P, 1969.

III. Critical Studies

Adams, Alison. "La Conception de l'unité dans le roman médiéval en vers." *Studia Neophilologica* 50 (1978): 101–12. Discussion of narrative techniques employed to achieve unity in *Durmart le Galois, Le Bel Inconnu,* and *Méraugis de Portlesguez.*

Alton, Johann, ed. *Li Romans de Claris et Laris.* Tübingen: Bibliothek des litterarischen Vereins in Stuttgart, 1884.

Ashe, Geoffrey, ed. *The Quest for Arthur's Britain.* St. Albans: Paladin, 1971.

Atanassov, Stoyan. "Gauvain: malheur du nom propre et bonheur du récit." *Le Récit amoureux* (Colloque de Cerisy, juillet 1982), PUF, Champ Vallon, 1984. 11–21. Study of the rupture between *renon* (reputation) and *non* (name) in *Le Chevalier aux deux épées* and *L'Atre Périlleux.*

Barron, W. R. J. *Trawthe and Treason: The Sin of Gawain*

Reconsidered. Manchester: University Press, 1980. Thematic analysis of *Sir Gawain and the Green Knight.*

Baumgartner, Emmanuele. "A propos du *Mantel Mautaillé.*" *Romania* 96 (1975): 315–32.

Black, Nancy B. "The Language of the Illustrations of Chrétien de Troyes's *Le Chevalier au Lion (Yvain).*" *Studies in Iconography* 15 (1993). Forthcoming.

Bloch, R. Howard. *Etymologies and Genealogies: A Literary Anthropology of the French Middle Ages.* Chicago and London: U of Chicago P, 1983. See especially Chapter 5 on "The Economics of Romance."

——. *Medieval French Literature and Law.* Berkeley: U of California P, 1977. Explores the relationships between legal and romance discourse.

Bogdanow, Fanni. "The Character of Gauvain in the Thirteenth-Century Prose Romances." *Medium Aevum* 27 (1958): 154–61. A succinct summary of changes in depictions of Gauvain according to genre and authorial intent.

Bourdillon, F. W. ed. CEST DAUCASI(N) (ET) DE NICOLETE. Facsimile Edition. Oxford: Clarendon, 1896.

Boutet, Dominique. "Carrefours idéologiques de la royauté arthurienne." *Cahiers de civilisation médiévale* 28 (1985): 3–17. Four romance episodes illustrate the deterioration of the Arthurian ideal of universal order.

Busby, Keith. "'Li Buens Chevaliers' or 'uns buens chevaliers'? Perlesvaus et Gauvain dans le *Perlesvaus.*" *Revue Romane* 19 (1984): 85–97. Examines the romance's positive depiction of Gawain and use of two epithets.

——. "Diverging Traditions of Gauvain in Some of the Later Old French Verse Romances." *The Legacy of Chrétien de Troyes.* Vol. 2. Ed. Norris J. Lacy, Douglas Kelly, and Keith Busby.

Amsterdam: Rodopi, 1988. 93–109. The positive depiction of Gawain in *Hunbaut, Chevalier aux deux epées, L'Atre Périlleux,* and *Les Merveilles de Rigomer.*

———. *Gauvain in Old French Literature.* Amsterdam: Rodopi, 1980. Survey of depiction of Gawain in romances written 1155–1225.

———. "Gauvain in the Prose Tristan." *Tristania* 2 (1977): 12–28. This romance represents the nadir of Gawain's reputation.

Bynum, Caroline Walker. *Fragmentation and Redemption: Essays on Gender and the Human Body in Medieval Religion.* New York: Zone Books, 1992.

Cadot, Anne-Marie. "Le motif de l'*Aitre périlleux*: la christianisation du surnaturel dans quelques romans du XIIIe siècle." *Marche Romane* 30 (1980). 27–36. Comparative analysis of the Perilous Cemetery episode in *Amadas et Ydoine, L'Atre Périlleux,* and *Perlesvaus.*

Chênerie, Marie-Luce. *Le Chevalier errant dans les romans Arthuriens en vers des XIIe et XIIIe siècles.* Publications romanes et françaises, 172. Geneva: Droz, 1986. Exhaustive study of motifs associated with Arthurian knights.

Colliot, Régine. "Un Visage de la 'Demoiselle Arthurienne' du treizième siècle d'après les neuf Rencontres de Gauvain dans l'*Atre Périlleux,* comparées à celles de Laurin, dan le *Roman de Laurin, fils de Marques.*" *BBSIA* 31 (1979): 265–66.

Dickson, Arthur. *Valentine and Orson: A Study in Late Medieval Romance.* New York: Columbia, 1929.

Dingemans-Zuurdeeg, Alice. "Les Thèmes unifiants de *L'Atre Périlleux.*" *BBSIA* 31 (1979): 317.

Dufournet, Jean, ed. *Aucassin et Nicolette.* Paris: Garnier-Flammarion, 1973.

Foerster, Wendelin, ed. *Le Chevalier aux deux épées.* Halle: Niemeyer, 1877.

———. *Cligés von Christian von Troyes.* 1884. Amsterdam: Rodopi, 1965.

Foulet, Lucien. "De *icest* à *cest* et l'origine de l'article." *Romania* 46 (1920): 570–77.

Frappier, Jean. "Le Personnage de Gauvain dans la *Première Continuation de Perceval (Conte du Graal)*." *Romance Philology* 11 (1957–58): 331–44. Reshaping of Gawain's image in the First Continuation.

Freeman, Michelle. "*Fergus*: Parody and the Arthurian Tradition." *French Forum* 8 (1983): 197–215.

Freymond, E. "Ueber den reichen Reim bei altfranzösischen Dichtern bis zum Anfang des XIV Jahrhunderts." *Zeitschrift für romanische Philologie* 6 (1882): 1–36, 177–215.

Gildea, Joseph, ed. *Durmart le Galois: roman arthurien du treizième siècle.* 2 vols. Villanova, PA: Villanova Press, 1965–66.

Gimpel, Jean. *The Medieval Machine: The Industrial Revolution of the Middle Ages.* New York: Penguin, 1977.

Grivot, Denis and George Zarnecki. *Gislebertus: Sculptor of Autun.* New York: Orion Press, 1961.

Guillaume le Clerc. *The Romance of Fergus.* Ed. Wilson L. Frescoln. Philadelphia: Allen, 1983.

Hanning, Robert. *The Individual in Twelfth-Century Romance.* New Haven and London: Yale UP, 1977.

Heath, P. "The Medieval Archdeaconry and Tudor Bishopric of Chester." *Journal of Ecclesiastical History* 20.2 (1969): 243–52.

Hindman, Sandra. "King Arthur, His Knights, and the French

Aristocracy in Picardy." *Contexts: Style and Values in Medieval Art and Literature*. Ed. Daniel Poirion and Nancy Freeman Regalado. Yale French Studies, Special Issue. New Haven: Yale UP, 1991. 114–33.

Holden, Anthony John. "Ancien français *tresoïr*, 'entendre bien,' 'entendre mal,' ou autre chose?" *Romania* 97 (1976): 107–17. Discussion of *tresoïe* in l. 4301 of *L'Atre Périlleux*.

————, ed. *Richars li Biaus: roman du XIIIe siècle*. Classiques français du moyen âge, 106. Paris: Champion, 1983.

Johnston, R. C. and D. D. R. Owen, eds. *Two Old French Gauvain Romances: "Le Chevalier à l'épée" and "La Mule sans frein."* New York: Barnes & Noble, 1972.

Kelly, Douglas. *The Art of Medieval French Romance*. Madison, WI: U of Wisconsin P, 1992. Analysis of statements about romance artistry found in medieval works.

Kibler, William W., ed. and trans. *Chrétien de Troyes: Lancelot or, The Knight of the Cart (Le Chevalier de la Charrete)*. Garland Library of Medieval Literature, Series A, 1. New York and London: Garland, 1981.

Klose, Martin. *Der Roman von Claris und Laris in seinen Beziehungen zur altfranzösischen Artusepik des XII. und XIII. Jahrhunderts*. Halle: Niemeyer, 1916. See pp. 249–52 for influence of *L'Atre Périlleux*.

Knight, Stephen. *Arthurian Literature and Society*. New York: St. Martin's Press, 1983. Commentary on class conflict in Arthurian romances.

Köhler, Erich. *Ideal und Wirklichkeit in der höfischen Epik: Studien zur Form der frühen Artus- und Graldichtung*. 2nd rev. ed. Tübingen: Niemeyer, 1970. Analysis of relationships between romance ideals and political realities.

————. "Le rôle de la 'coutume' dans les romans de Chrétien de

Troyes." *Romania* 81 (1960): 386–97. Structural importance of customs in Chrétien's romances.

Krappe, Alexander Haggerty. "Sur un épisode de l'*Atre Périlleux*." *Romania* 58 (1932): 260–64. Explains incongruities in Perilous Cemetery scene by positing Indian folktale origins.

Larmat, Jean. "Le personnage de Gauvain dans quelques romans arthuriens du XIIe et du XIIIe siècle." Vol. 2 of *Etudes de langue et de littérature française offertes à André Lanly*. Nancy: Publications de l'université de Nancy, 1980. 2 vols. 185–202. Brief survey of the disintegration of Gawain's reputation from Wace to the *Prose Tristan*.

McGillivray, Murray. *Memorization in the Transmission of the Middle English Romances*. New York and London: Garland, 1990. Analysis of manuscript variants of four English romances for evidence of memorial transfer.

Micha, Alexandre. *La Tradition manuscrite des romans de Chrétien de Troyes*. Geneva: Droz, 1966. See pp. 38–9 for description of Chantilly 472 and p. 44 for description of B.N.fr. 1433.

———. "Miscellaneous French Romances in Verse." *Arthurian Literature in the Middle Ages*. Ed. Roger Sherman Loomis. Oxford: Clarendon Press, 1959. 358–99.

Michelant, Heinrich, ed. *Der Roman von Escanor von Gerard von Amiens*. Bibliothek des litterarischen Vereins in Stuttgart, 178. Tübingen: 1886.

Nitze, William A. and T. Atkinson Jenkins, eds. *Le Haut Livre du Graal Perlesvaus*. 2 vols. 1932–37. New York: Phaeton, 1972.

Offord, Malcolm. "Reflexions sur la construction du français médiéval démonstratif et phrase relative avec adverbe locatif." *Romania* 97 (1976): 195–217.

Ollier, Marie-Louise. "The Author in the Text: The Prologues of Chrétien de Troyes." *Yale French Studies* 51 (1974): 26–41.

Prologues establish a new literary space for self-conscious establishment of a written text.

Owen, D. D. R. "Burlesque Tradition and *Sir Gawain and the Green Knight.*" *Forum for Modern Language Studies* 4 (1968): 125–45.

Paris, Gaston. "Romans en vers du cycle de la Table ronde." *Histoire littéraire de la France*, vol. 30. Paris: 1888. First published notice of the existence of three manuscripts of *L'Atre Périlleux*.

Pauphilet, Albert, ed. *La Queste del Saint Graal: roman du XIIIe siècle.* Classiques français du moyen âge, 33. Paris: Champion, 1984.

Perceval. The Story of the Grail. Trans. Nigel Bryant. Brewer: Cambridge, 1982.

Picot, Emile. "Le Duc d'Aumale et la Bibliothèque de Chantilly." *Bulletin du Bibliophile et du Bibliothécaire* (1897): 305–48. An account of Henry of Orleans's efforts (1830–89) to preserve the Chantilly collection.

Reinhard, John R., ed. *Amadas et Ydoine: Roman du XIIIe siècle.* Classiques français du moyen âge, 51. Paris: Champion, 1926.

———. *The Old French Romance of Amadas et Ydoine: An Historical Study.* Durham, NC: Duke UP, 1927.

Roach, William, ed. *The Continuations of the Old French "Perceval" of Chrétien de Troyes.* 5 vols. Philadelphia: University of Pennsylvania Press/American Philosophical Society, 1949–83.

———. *Le Roman de Perceval ou Le Conte du Graal.* Geneva: Droz, 1959.

Roques, Mario, ed. *Aucassin et Nicolete: Chantefable du XIIIe siècle.* Classiques français du moyen âge, 41. Paris: Champion, 1925.

———. *Le Chevalier au Lion (Yvain).* Classiques français du moyen âge, 89. Paris: Champion, 1980.

————. *Erec et Enide.* Classiques français du moyen âge, 80. Paris: Champion, 1981.

Rychner, Jean, ed. *Les Lais de Marie de France.* Classiques français du moyen âge, 93. Paris: Champion, 1983.

Schmolke-Hasselmann, Beate. *Der arthurische Versroman von Chrestien bis Froissart: zur Geschichte einer Gattung.* Beihefte zur Zeitschrift für romanisiche Philologie, 177. Tübingen: Niemeyer, 1980. See especially Chapter 4 on Gawain and pp. 100–15 on the false death motif in *Le Chevalier aux deux épées* and *L'Atre Périlleux.*

————. "Der französische Artusroman in Verse nach Chrétien de Troyes." *Deutsche Vierteljahrsschrift für Literaturwissenschaft und Geistesgeschichte* 57 (1983): 415–30. Definition of the verse romance genre after Chrétien.

Stones, Alison et al., eds. *The Manuscripts of Chrétien de Troyes.* Amsterdam: Rodopi. Forthcoming.

Suchier, Hermann, ed. *Aucassin et Nicolette: Texte critique accompagné de paradigmes et d'un lexique.* 5th ed. Paderborn: F. Schoeningh, 1903.

Walters, Lori. "The Creation of a 'Super Romance': Paris, Bibliothèque Nationale, fonds français, MS 1433." *The Arthurian Yearbook I.* Ed. Keith Busby. New York and London: Garland, 1991. 3–25.

Wassmuth, Theodor. "Untersuchung der Reime des altfranzösischen Artusromans 'Li Atres perillox'." Diss. Bonn, 1905.

Weston, Jessie L. *The Legend of Sir Gawain: Studies upon Its Original Scope and Significance.* London: D. Nutt, 1897.

Winters, Margaret, ed. *The Romance of Hunbaut: An Arthurian Poem of the Thirteenth Century.* Leiden: E. J. Brill, 1984.

Woledge, Brian. *L'Atre Périlleux: Etudes sur les manuscrits, la langue*

et l'importance littéraire du poème, avec un spécimen du texte.
Paris: Droz, 1930. Reviews: Gifford, *Speculum* 6 (1931): 494–95;
Jeanroy, *Romania* 56 (1930): 296–97; Bossuat, *Revue critique
d'histoire et de littérature* 97 (1930): 350–52; A. M., *Studi
Medievali* 4 (1931): 396–97.

————. "Bons vavasseurs et mauvais sénéchaux." *Mélanges Rita
Lejeune.* Vol. 2. Gembloux: J. Duculot, 1969. 2 vol. 1263–77.
Analysis of etymologies and literary uses of the two terms,
vavassseur and *sénechau.*

Wolfthal, Diane. "'A Hue and a Cry': Medieval Rape Imagery and Its
Transformation." *The Art Bulletin* 75.1 (1993): 39–64.

Wolfzettel, Friedrich. "Arthurian Adventure or Quixotic 'Struggle
for Life'? A Reading of Some Gauvain Romances in the First
Half of the Thirteenth Century." *An Arthurian Tapestry: Essays
in Memory of Lewis Thorpe.* Ed. Kenneth Varty. Glasgow:
French Department of the University of Glasgow, 1981. 260–74.
Discussion of sparrow-hawk woman's demands for food in
L'Atre Périlleux, l. 3930 ff., and Gawain's encounter with the
bourgeois host, l. 1669 ff.

Wulff, F. A., ed. "Le Conte du *Mantel*: Texte français des dernières
années du XIIe siècle, édité d'aprés tous les mss." *Romania* 14
(1885): 343–80.

The Perilous
Cemetery
(L'Atre Périlleux)

C'EST DE L'ATRE PERILLOUS

1   Ma dame me conmande et prie   [1ra]

1   Ma dame me conmande et prie   [1ra]

Que une aventure li die

Qu'il avint au bon chevalier,

4   Et je nel puis mie laiscier

Quant ele le m'a conmandé,

Des qu'il li plaist et vient a gré.

Or oïés com il li avint.

8   A une Pentecouste tint

Li rois Artus feste moult grant,

Ne remest chevalier errant

De la mer des que en Cornuaille,

12   Ne damoisele qui rien vaille,

Qui a cele cort ne venist.

Et li rois grant honor lor fist,

Car moult lor dona rices dons.

16   Quant venu furent les barons

Et asanlé le samedi,

Aprés le none avint, issi

Que li rois s'aloit deduisant,

20   Qu'il ont veü venir errant

Toute seule une damoisele

Qui moult ert acesmee et bele.

Moult estoit de grant aparel:

24   D'un moult rice samit vermel

Fu sa robe fresce et novele;

De son lorain et de sa sele

Et de son autre acesmement

28   Deviser or plus longement

Ne me veul je mie entremetre,

Car grant paine i convenroit metre

Au dire, tant est acesmee.

32   Ensi est en la sale entree

Que onques son frain ne retint

Desi que devant le roi vint.

        "Rois," fait soi, "cil sire vous saut,

THIS IS ABOUT THE PERILOUS CEMETERY
   My lady orders and requests me
  To tell her an adventure
  That happened to the *bon chevalier.*
4 I cannot fail to do
  What she has ordered
  If it will delight and please her.
  Now listen to how the story goes.
8 One day at Pentecost,
  King Arthur held a great festival.
  There was no knight errant
  In all of Cornwall,
12 There was no maiden of any worth,
  Who did not come to his court.
  And the king honored them magnificently
  By giving them many expensive gifts.
16 All the barons had arrived
  And assembled together on Saturday.
  After the hour of nones, it happened,
  As the king turned to courtly pleasures,
20 That they saw, riding up on horseback,
  All alone, a young woman,
  Who was very beautiful and well-dressed.
  What magnificent clothing!
24 Made of luxurious, bright-red silk,
  Her dress was in the latest style.
  Of her harness and saddle
  And the other equipment on her horse—
28 I don't want to attempt
  To describe it in more detail.
  Only with great effort could I
  Put it into words, so ornate was it.
32 Thus she entered the great hall,
  And she didn't pull back on the bit
  Until she came up right before the king.
    "King," she said, "may the Lord protect you,

36   Cil qui gouverne bas et haut
     Le ciel et la mer et la terre.
     De mon païs vous vienc requerre   [1rb]
     Que vous me creantés un don.
40   Ja ne vous querrai mesproison
     Ne outrage ne vilonnie. "
     Li rois bonement li otrie
     Que volentiers le don ara.
44   "Dites," fait il, "que ce sera
     Et vous l'averés sans mentir,
     Por tant que jel puisce aramir."
          "Sire," fait ele, "vostre merci.
48   Or oiiés donc que je vous pri.
     Je veul demain boutelliere estre
     De vostre coupe la plus mestre
     Et servir a vostre mengier.
52   Et si veul que un chevalier
     De çaiens, tout le plus prisiés,
     Cil qui li mix est enteciés,
     Me gart et desfende et honort
56   Tant conme j'ere a vostre cort,
     Que jou ni aie vilonnie;
     Car jou n'i oseroie mie
     Demorer sans moult bone garde."
60   Li rois moult bonement l'esgarde:
          "Bele," fait li rois, "li servise
     Ferés a la vostre devise;
     Mais je ne sai mie jugier
64   Trestout le mellor chevalier
     De çaiens ne de ma maisnie.
     Tant estes prox et ensegnie,
     Espoir dit l'avés por aucun,
68   Et si vous plaist, només ent un,
     Li quex vous volés que ce soit.
     Je li quemant des orendroit
     Que il bien vous gart et desfende
72   Et que a vous servir entende
     Tant com çaiens estre vaurois."
     "Sire," fait ele, "n'est pas drois
     Que j'en doinse a un tout le pris,   [1va]

36	He who reigns over high and low,
	Over heaven and earth and sea.
	I travel from my country to ask you
	To grant me a boon.
40	Be assured I will not ask for anything evil,
	Nothing excessive or villainous."
	The king graciously promised her
	That he would freely grant this wish.
44	"Tell me," he said, "what it is
	And, on my word, you shall have it,
	So long as I am able to arrange it."
	"Sir," she said, "many thanks.
48	Now listen to what it is I ask of you.
	Tomorrow I want to become
	Your personal cup bearer
	And to serve at your table.
52	Let one knight in this hall—
	He who is most prized,
	He who is most qualified—
	Let him guard me and defend my honor
56	As long as I am at your court,
	So that I will not suffer any villainy.
	For I would not dare to stay
	Without very good security."
60	The king regarded her with much good will.
	"Beautiful one," he said,
	"Perform this service, however you want.
	But I don't know how to judge
64	Who is the best knight of all
	Those in the room or in my company.
	You are so wise and learned.
	Perhaps you have someone in mind?
68	If you please, name him.
	You may have whomever you want.
	I will immediately order him
	To guard and defend you.
72	He will be at your service
	As long as you want to be with us."
	"Sir," she said, "it is not right
	That I should give the prize to any one knight.

76 Ains en ai sor vous le fais mis,
 Qui le don m'en avés doné.
 Je cremiroie avoir mal gré,
 Se par moi seule l'eslisoie."
80 "Ja Dix," fait li rois, "ne me voie
 Quant j'en sai le mellor eslire,
 Mais je vous veul proiier et dire
 Que vous m'otroiiés une riens,
84 Se vous veés que ce soit biens:
 Sans ellire, vous veul baillier
 En la garde a un chevalier
 Bel et prox et courtois et sage;
88 Et s'il ne fust de mon lignage,
 J'en deïsce une grant parole."
 La pucele qui n'ert pas fole
 Li dist: "Sire, només le moi,
92 S'il vous plaist, ains que je l'otroi."
   "Bele," fait li rois, "c'est Gavain
 En cui garde serés demain,
 Et tant com onques vous plaira."
96 "Sire," fait ele, "quant je vinc ça,
 Me fu forment Gavain loé,
 Et g'i remain par vostre gré,
 Car ne vous demant se lui non."
100 Ensi li est greé le don,
 Com la cose vous ai contee,
 Et Gavains l'a tantost menee
 A moult grant joie a son ostel;
104 Et saciés que il li fist tel
 C'on n'i seüst rien que reprendre,
 Car moult durement fist entendre
 A li servir une pucele
108 Et sa seror qui moult ert bele,
 Qui li porterent conpaignie.
 Moult menerent joieuse vie
 Cele nuit dusqu'a l'endemain.
112 A grant joie leva Gavain   [1vb]
 Et les puceles toutes trois.
 Puis ala o itel harnois
 Au moustier oïr le servise,

76   I would never take over this role from you,
Who have agreed to my request.
It would not be gracious
For me to be the one to choose."

80   "May God," said the king, "not take offense,
If I dare to choose the best.
But I ask and pray you
To grant me one thing,

84   If you judge it appropriate.
Without exactly choosing, I want
To entrust you to the care of a knight
Who is handsome, brave, courteous, and wise.

88   If he were not related to me,
I would praise him at great length."
The maiden, who was no fool, said,
"Sir, tell me his name, if you please,

92   Before I consent to it."
       "Fair one, " said the king, "it is Gawain.
You will be under his protection tomorrow
And for as long as you please."

96   "Sir," she said, "when I came here,
Everyone praised Gawain highly,
So I will stay with him as you advise.
I ask for no one but him."

100   Thus the maiden was granted her wish.
Everything happened as I have told you.
Gawain immediately led her
With great rejoicing to his apartment.

104   Be assured that he arranged everything there
So that there would be no reason for reproach.
He entrusted her to the care
Of a young woman

108   And his very beautiful sister,
Who became her companions.
They had a joyous time together
That night and straight through until morning.

112   In a good mood, Gawain
And the three young women arose.
Armed with these companions, Gawain
Went to church to hear the morning service.

116   Car li rois ert ja a l'eglise,
        Et la roïne et ses puceles,
        Quant Gavains o les damoiseles
        I est de son ostel alés.
120   Quant li services fu finés,
        Si s'en revindrent tout ensanble.
        A la pucele, ce me sanble,
        Si com el li fu creantee
124   Fu la maistre coupe livree,
        Car les tables erent ja misses.
        A tant conmença li services,
        Moult grans et moult biax et moult rices,
128   Car li rois Artus n'ert pas nices,
        Que voloit qu'il fust moult pleniers.
        Mais ne m'est ore nus mestiers
        De dire qu'il fist ne coument,
132   Fors tant conme ci en apent.
           De la coupe sert la mescine.
        Les le roi seoit le roïne,
        Et li rois de Wales aprés;
136   Gavains et Tors, li fix Arés,
        Et Erec sist de l'autre part,
        Et Carados Briesbras li quart;
        Aprés sont tout li autre assis.
140   Maint chevalier i ot de pris
        Et mainte cointe damoisele;
        Maint hanap et mainte escüele
        Ot devant ax d'or et d'argent.
144   N'orent pas mengié longement,
        Car il n'orent c'un mes eü,
        Quant un chevalier ont veü
        Venir par mi le porte errant,
148   Et saciés, s'il ne fust si grant,
        Sous ciel n'eüst plus bel de lui,   [2ra]
        Mais trop estoit grans a anui;
        Moult par ert bel et bien armés.
152   Ensi est en la sale entrés,
        Fors sa lance que il laisça,
        Que dehors la sale apoia.
           Tant fu orgellox le vassal

116   The king was already there,
        Along with the queen and her women,
        By the time Gawain and the three women
        Had left their rooms.
120   When the service was finished,
        They all returned together.
        Just as had been promised,
        The royal cup was delivered
124   To the young woman,
        For the tables had all been set up.
        At this the meal began—
        Everything was grand! So beautiful and elegant!
128   For King Arthur was no fool.
        He wanted everything full of splendor.
        But it is not necessary right now
        For me to tell you all about what happened,
132   Just what is necessary for my story.
            The young woman served from the cup.
        Next to the king sat the queen
        And the King of Wales next to her.
136   Gawain and Tor, the son of Arés,
        And Erec sat on the other side;
        Carados Briesbras made the fourth.
        After them all the others were seated.
140   Many a worthy knight was there
        And many an elegant lady.
        Many trenchers and bowls of gold
        And silver were placed before them.
144   They hadn't been eating for long—
        They were still on the first course—
        When they spied a knight riding
        Right up through the door. Be assured
148   That, if he hadn't been so large,
        He would have been the most handsome
        On earth, but he was just too big.
        Well-armed from head to foot,
152   He entered into the hall,
        Leaving only his lance outside
        Resting against a wall.
            So proud was the knight that he

156 Qu'ainques ne retint son ceval
     Tant que il vint devant le roi,
     Et se vint par itel desroi
     Que son frain hurta a le table;
160 Onques uscier ne connestable
     Nel contredist de nule cose.
     Quant esgardés les ot grant pose
     Sauf çou que mot ne lor sona,
164 Vers la pucele se torna
     Si l'a par les espaules prise,
     Puis si l'a devant lui asise
     Desor le col de son destrier.
168 "Rois," fait il, "celer ne te quier,
     Ceste damoisele est m'amie,
     Si l'ai en mainte cort sivie
     Puis que l'oi enprise a amer.
172 Onques mais ne la peuc trover
     En cort u jou l'osasce prendre;
     Mais je senc la toie a si tendre
     Et de bons chevaliers si vuie,
176 Je di por ce qu'i lor anuie,
     Et que de li la saisine ai,
     Que ja par ex ne la perdrai,
     Ains l'en porterai sans dangier.
180 Ja par le cors d'un chevalier
     De cex qui çaiens sont assis
     N'en ert vers moi son escu pris.
          Sire rois," fait il, "je m'en vois
184 Le haut voie vers ce bois,   [2rb]
     Qui me menra en mon païs.
     Savés por quoi je vous devis
     Par u je m'en doi repairier?
188 S'il avoit çaiens chevalier
     Qui par savoir u par folie
     Rien nule que je ci vous die
     Vuelle desdire par bataille,
192 Ne die pas que jou m'en aille
     Par une autre voie fuiant.
     Oiant tox ensanle me vant
     Que par icele m'en irai,

156   Did not restrain his horse until
       He came right up in front of the king.
       He approached in such a reckless way
       That the bridle bumped the table.
160   No guard, no official, was there
       To prevent such a thing.
       After he had looked around at them,
       Without saying a word,
164   He turned toward the young woman,
       Grabbed her by the shoulders,
       And sat her up before him
       On the neck of his war horse.
168   "King," he said, "I'll not hide what I seek.
       This young woman is my *amie*.
       I have followed her to many a court
       Since I undertook to love her.
172   I was never able to find her
       In a court where I dared to seize her.
       But I sense that your court is so weak—
       So lacking in good knights—
176   (I say this because they are upset
       At my kidnapping of the young woman)
       That I have nothing to fear from them
       And can carry her off without danger.
180   Not one knight of all the knights
       Who are seated here in this court
       Will take up his arms against me.
          "King Arthur," he said, "I will take
184   The highway that goes toward the woods,
       The one that leads into my country.
       Do you know why I tell you
       The route I am about to take?
188   So that, if there were here in this hall
       A knight who, cleverly or foolishly,
       Wanted to contradict through battle
       Anything that I have said to you,
192   He cannot say that I
       Scuttled off by another road.
       Let it be publicly stated
       That I am taking this road

196   Ne ja del petit pas n'istrai
      Desi la qu'i m'avesperra.
      Je weul que cil qui me suirra
      M'ait a aise, s'il ne se faint,
200   Ains que je viegne au bos, ataint."
            A cest mot a sa voie enprise;
      Por sa lance vient, si l'a prise,
      Car il nel vaut mie laisier;
204   Le petit pas de son destrier
      En est isçus hors de la porte;
      Ensi faitierement en porte
      La damoisele en son païs.
208   Gavains fu dolans et pensis,
      Qui les le roi sist au mengier.
      Ne se set pas bien consellier
      Li quex li ert plus honerable
212   U salir par desor la table
      Por parsuïr le chevalier
      U a seoir tant au mengier
      Que le service soit fini.
216   Longement a ensi pensi,
      C'onques ne but ne ne menga;
      Au deerain se porpensa
      Que le soufrir li ert plus bel.
220   Tant sent son ceval a isnel
      Que tost l'ara aconseü.
      Et Qex, qui tout çou a veü,   [2va]
      A ses conpaignons apelés:
224   "Segnor," fait il, "or entendés
      A servir ceste cort a droit,
      Car il m'estuet sivre orendroit
      Cel chevalier qui tel sorfait
228   A, voiant tox ces barons, fait,
      Qui par orguel et par derroi
      A saisie devant le roi
      La damoisele a son mengier.
232   Onques n'i ot nul chevalier
      Qui desdeïst de nule rien.
      Une cose saciés vous bien:
      Onques mais a roi ce n'avint,

196 And will not stray from it one bit
     Until night begins to fall.
     I want anyone who follows me
     To catch up easily, if he doesn't delay,
200 Before I reach the woods."
          With these words he set out,
     But first he went to pick up his lance:
     He would never leave it there.
204 Letting his horse go at a walk,
     He rode out through the gate.
     And so he carried off the maiden
     And headed for his own country.
208 Gawain was sorrowful and thoughtful,
     Sitting at his place beside the king.
     He didn't know how to decide
     Which was more honorable—
212 To jump up from the table
     And follow the knight
     Or to sit at the table
     Until the meal was finished.
216 He was rapt in thought a long time,
     Without even drinking or eating.
     At long last he decided
     That to wait was the better course.
220 He knew that his horse was so fast
     That he would soon overtake him.
     Kay, who had observed everything,
     Called to his companions:
224 "Milords," he said, "continue
     To serve at this court as is custom;
     But right now I must go after
     This knight who acted so outrageously
228 Here in front of all the barons,
     Proudly and foolishly seizing
     The maiden right here in front of the king
     While he was sitting down to eat.
232 There was not a single knight here
     Who said a word against it.
     You can be sure of one thing:
     Never before has this happened to the king.

236   Des puis que primes feste tint,
       Nule si grant desconvenue
       Quant ce faili ne se remue
       En qui garde li rois le mist.
240   Cent dehais ait qui primes dist
       Qu'en lui eüst bon chevalier."
       A tant se vait aparellier
       A son ostel moult ricement.
244   Quant armés fu delivrement,
       Sor le bon ceval est montés,
       Puis est u grant cemin entrés
       Par u li chevaliers s'en va.
248   Devant lui a terre esgarda,
       Si en a coisi les esclos.
       A tant se met es grans galos
       Por ataindre le erranment.
252   N'ot pas cevaucié longement
       Quant un tertre le vit monter.
       Il conmença a escrier:
       "Estés, estés, sire vassal!
256   La damoisele et le ceval
       En menrai jou ensanle o moi,
       Et vostre cors rendrai le roi
       A faire del tout sa justise.
260   Mar i fu la pucele prise   [2vb]
       Devant lui si estoutement.
       Se mort u pris ne vous en rent,
       Je ne me pris une prounele."
264   Cil descendi la damoisele,
       Si guenci ariere son frain,
       Puis si a dit: "Est ce Gavain
       Qui ci me suit si derreés?"
268   "Nenil," fait il, "ançois sui Kés,
       Li senescax le roi Artur."
       "Ore," fait cil, "a mal eür,
       Que vous ne demandoie mie:
272   De la vostre chevalerie
       N'est pas grans le los en ma terre."
       Lors va li uns l'autre requerre,
       K'onques n'i ot autre tençon.

236 Not since holding the first festival
Has he been so terribly mortified,
While this coward, in whom the king entrusted
The care of the maiden, failed to budge.

240 A hundred curses on him who
Would call him *bon chevalier*."
Thereupon Kay went to his room
To put on his splendid armor.

244 In no time he was well-armed
And mounted on his good horse,
So that he was soon on the highway
That the knight had set out on.

248 He looked at the ground before him
And noticed some footprints there;
So he set out at a great gallop
To catch up quickly with the knight.

252 He had not been riding long
When he saw him mounting a hill.
He began to call out:
"Halt, Sir Knight, halt!

256 I am going to take you,
Your horse, and the maiden
Back with me to the king so that
He can carry out justice.

260 Woe to you for having taken this maiden
So ingloriously before his very eyes.
If I don't turn you over dead or captured,
I'm not worth beans!"

264 At this the knight had the maiden dismount;
He pulled back on his bridle,
And asked, "Is this Gawain
Who chases after me?"

268 "Nay!" he said, "it is Kay,
The seneschal of King Arthur."
"Now," said the other, "that's bad luck.
I certainly didn't ask for you:

272 About your chivalric virtues
We don't hear much praise in my country."
Then they started to attack one another,
Without any further debate.

276   Kex le feri tout a bandon
     Desox la boucle de l'escu,
     Qu'el trové li a et fendu,
     Mais li haubers le garanti,
280   Onques maille n'en desmenti.
     Kex l'enpaint bien sa lance frousce.
     Cil feri lui par tel angousce
     Que l'abat lui et son ceval.
284   Kex caï el pendant d'un val,
     Qui moult fu quaisciés et bleciés;
     Ses destres bras li fu brisiés
     Par entre l'espaule et le coute.
288   Li cevax saut sus, si s'aroute
     Tout le cemin par u il vint.
     Et cil a Keu nul plait ne tint,
     Ains le laisça iluec gisant;
292   A la pucele vint errant,
     Si la remonte devant lui.
     "Bele," fait il, "si com je cui,
     Dans Kex ne vous en maine pas."
296   Lors s'en vait vers le bos le pas,
     Demenant grant joie a s'amie.   [3ra]
     Au roi et a sa conpaignie
     Me covient des or reperier,
300   Qui encor seoit au mengier
     De l'aventure moult pensis.
     Voiant tox a un coutel pris,
     Si l'a ficié par mi un pain,
304   Puis i apoia si sa main
     Que le coutel froisça en dox.
     Des chevaliers ne fu uns sox
     Qui ost enquerre et demander
308   Seul l'ocoison de son penser,
     Et li rois s'est aperseü
     Et set de voir qu'il ont veü
     Coment li coutiax fu froisciés.
312   "Segnor," fait il, "moult sui iriés
     De ceste mesentance d'ui.
     Sin ai encor grengnor anui
     Por la mesproison de Gavain,

276   Kay struck him with full force,
On the boss of his shield,
So that he split and pierced it.
But the knight's chain mail saved him:
280   Not a piece sprang out of it.
Kay threw his lance, but it broke.
Then the knight struck him so hard
That he and his horse fell down.
284   Kay dropped down on a little incline,
For he was badly wounded.
His right arm was broken between
His shoulder and his elbow.
288   His horse got up and ran off
Down the road he had just come up.
That knight didn't do anything to help,
But just left him lying there.
292   Instead, he went over to the maiden
And put her back up on his horse.
"My pretty one," he said, "I don't think
That Sir Kay will be riding off with you."
296   Then he went off on the path through the woods,
Very happy to be with his *amie* again.
Now I need to return to the story
Of the king and his company.
300   The king was still sitting at the table,
Deep in thought about this adventure.
In front of everyone, he picked up a knife
And plunged it into the middle of a loaf of bread.
304   He leaned on his hand with so much force
That the knife broke in two.
There was not one knight there
Who dared to inquire or ask
308   What he was thinking about.
The king became aware of them
And realized that they had seen
How the knife was broken.
312   "Lords," he said, "I am very angered
By today's unfortunate event.
I am even more troubled
By Gawain's failure to act.

316   Je cuidoie estre bien certain
        Que n'eüsce ja enconbrier
        Par le cors d'un seul chevalier
        Dont Gavains ne me desfendist;
320   Et s'a un autre avenist
        Qui la pucele en garde eüst,
        Par mauvaistié que en lui fust,
        Que il ne l'osast pas desfendre,
324   Si deüst bien Gavains enprendre
        A desfendre la por m'onor.
        Moult me poise qu'a si bon jor
        M'en est tel anui avenu."
328   Dont li dist Iders li fix Nu:
            "Sire," fait il, "ne vous cremés,
        Li senescax i est alés,
        Qui bien vengera ceste honte."
332   Et li rois dist: "Ce est nul conte;
        Or croist et double men anui.
        Tant a grant prouece en celui   [3rb]
        Et tant est fors et sorquidiés
336   Que ja par Keu n'ert damagiés.
        Moult i puet voir vaselage;
        Onques sais en tout mon eage
        Plus outragex de lui me vi."
340   Et Gavains dist: "Sire, merci!
        Vous avés dit vostre plaiscir;
        Mais je ne veul pas tresailir
        Par en son le table au mengié.
344   J'en cremisce avoir reprovier
        Se je l'eüsce tresailie.
        Tant estes de grant segnorie
        Et tant vous a Dix fait haut home
348   Que, se l'enpereor de Rome
        Vous venoit çaiens manecier,
        Por quoi seïsciés au mengier,
        Ne mais que pis ne vous feïst,
352   Que ja por cose qu'il deïst
        Ne s'en devroit nus desrengier;
        Quant il vendroit aprés mengier,
        Si alast cil qui vous plairoit,

316   I believed I could depend on,
        If I was ever challenged—
        Especially by one lone knight—
        Gawain to defend me.

320   If it had fallen to another
        To have the maiden in his care,
        He might not have dared, on account of
        Cowardice, to defend her.

324   But Gawain should have undertaken
        To defend her, for the sake of my honor.
        It depresses me that on a feast day
        Such misfortune has occurred."

328   Then Yder, the son of Nuc, responded:
        "Sir," he said, "have no fear.
        Your seneschal has gone
        To take revenge for this dishonor."

332   And the king said, "That's of no account.
        It only doubles my worry.
        There is such prowess in that knight,
        He is so strong and arrogant,

336   That Kay will do him little harm
        No matter how much prowess he might have.
        Never before in all my life
        Have I seen anyone more outrageous."

340   Now Gawain spoke up: "Sir, have mercy.
        You have made your wishes clear.
        But I didn't want to jump up
        From the table right in the middle of a course.

344   I feared I would be blamed
        If I had gone off like that.
        You are of such high nobility—
        God has made you such a great man—

348   That if the Emperor of Rome
        Came inside here to menace you
        While you were seated down to eat—
        So long as he didn't do you harm,

352   Except for things he might say—
        No one should break ranks.
        Only after the meal has ended
        Then the one who would please you,

356   A cui la cose en aferroit,
Vengier vostre anui et le suen.
Je sent mon ceval a si buen
Que je l'arai moult tost ataint.
360   Ne cuidiés pas que il en maint
La damoisele sans calonge.
Ja puis Dix honor ne me donge
Quant onques par il le laisçai.
364   Et se de riens mespris en ai,
Je sui tox pres de l'adrecier."
A tant est levés du mangier,
Si a ses armes demandees,
368   Doi vallet li ont aportees;
Il s'est moult vistement armés,
Puis est u bon ceval montés
Q'onques estrier n'i a requis;   [3va]
372   Et quant il a son escu pris,
Et on li ot baillié sa lance,
De l'errer se haste et avance.
       Gavains erre vers la forest.
376   A grant mervelle li desplest
Quant il nel voit ne long ne pres.
A tant es poignant a eslés
Le destrier Keu le senescal;
380   Gavains connut bien le ceval,
Sel saisi au destroit d'un mont.
Auques ot escorcié le front,
Si que tox jors venoit sainnant;
384   L'arçon de la sele devant
Ot tout quassé et esmiié,
S'ot le frain rout et depecié,
Si qu'il n'i ot fors la cevece.
388   "Dix," dist Gavains, "si grant prouece
Ot cil qui si vous abati."
De çou fu auques amati,
Qu'il crient qu'il ne soit mors u pris;
392   "A! Dix," dist il, "tant ai mespris,
Tant il m'est wi mesavenu,
Quant par moi a li rois perdu
Le chevalier qu'il amoit tant.

356	He whom this affair concerned,
	Would revenge your insult and his.
	I know my horse is so good that
	I will soon overtake the knight.
360	Don't think that he will hold onto
	The maiden without a challenge.
	May God never grant me honor
	If I let this happen to her.
364	And if I have made any mistake
	I am quite ready to make up for it."
	Then he got up from the table
	And called for his armor.
368	Two squires carried it to him.
	He was armed very quickly;
	Then he mounted his horse
	Without even using his stirrups.
372	And when he had taken his shield
	And had been handed his lance,
	He hastened to go on his way.
	Gawain rode toward the forest.
376	He was quite displeased
	To see nothing far and wide.
	Suddenly, he saw galloping toward him
	The war horse of Kay the seneschal.
380	Gawain knew the horse well
	And grabbed him at a narrow pass.
	Someone had battered his forehead
	So that he was bleeding profusely.
384	The saddlebow was broken
	And crumbling into pieces,
	And the bridle was also split and broken
	So that only the halter remained.
388	"My God," said Gawain, "whoever struck you
	Must have had great courage."
	At this he became depressed, for he feared
	That Kay might be dead or captured.
392	"Ah, God," he said, "what a crime!
	What misfortune has come to me,
	If, on my account, the king has lost
	The knight he loves so much!

396 Il m'ert tox jours mais mis devant
En tox lius u j'ere trouvé,
Si m'ert laidement reprové.
Je ne di pas que ce soit tors:
400 Il est par ma defaute mors,
Qui la pucele en garde avoie."
Lors garde lions en mi la voie
A ce grant duel que il demainne;
404 Voit Keu lever a quel que painne
De la u cil l'avoit laiscié.
Il a le ceval eslaiscié,
Si est venus poignant a lui.
408 "Sire," fait il, "de vostre anui   [3vb]
Sui moult dolans et abosmés,
Car je dout que vous me retés
Qu'il vous soit par moi avenu."
412 "Malvais," Kex li a respondu,
"Il m'est or avenus par vous.
Moult estes fiers et orgellox
Dedans la canbre le roïne;
416 N'est mie povre ne frarine
Cele a cui vous degniés parler.
Qui alec vous orroit vanter
De hardement ne de prouece
420 Ne diroit pas que par perece,
Par mauvaistié ne par soufraite
Qui soit en vous, fust au roi faite
Par le cors d'un seul chevalier
424 Tel vilenie a son mengier.
Moult vous ai wi veü restif."
"Sire," fait Gavains, "pas n'estrif
Que je n'en aie moult mespris;
428 Mais j'ai ci vostre ceval pris,
Si i montés, se il vous plest,
Et jou irai vers la forest
Por parsivrre le chevalier,
432 Qu'il m'estuet en oire vengier
Le grant anui que il m'a fait.
Et Kex li dist, "Cent dehais ait
Qui ja de vos mains le prendra,

396   It will be constantly thrown up to me
In every place where I am to be found,
And I will be sorely reproached.
I don't say they will be wrong.

400   It is my fault that he is dead,
For the maiden was under my protection."
While succumbing to this great anguish,
He looked far ahead on the road.

404   He saw Kay getting up with great difficulty
From the place where the knight had left him.
Gawain loosened the reins
And galloped up to him.

408   "Sir," he said, "on account of this trouble
I am dismayed and embarrassed,
For I fear that you will blame me
For what has happened to you."

412   "Great misfortune," Kay replied,
"Has indeed happened because of you.
How very brave and proud you are
In the chamber of the queen!

416   Those to whom you deign to speak
Are never poor or feeble!
Who, hearing you bragged about there
For your bravery and prowess,

420   Would dare speak of the laziness,
Dirty tricks, or lack of manners
In you that made the king suffer,
At the hands of only one knight,

424   Such humiliation in the midst of dining?
I saw how you jumped up today!"
"Sir," said Gawain, "I don't deny
That I have made a big mistake.

428   But, see here, I have caught your horse.
Mount it, if you will.
And I will go off toward the woods
In pursuit of that knight

432   So that I may speedily take revenge
For the anguish he has caused me."
And Kay replied, "A hundred curses
On him who would take it from your hands

436   Ne qui ja tant vous prisera
      Qu'il vous doie nul gueredon."
      Gavains n'ot soing de sa tençon,
      Sel loia les lui a un saus;
440   Puis vait vers le forest les saus
      Et les grans galos enforciés.
      Mesire Kex s'est esforciés
      Tant que il vint a son ceval,
444   Puis l'acosta devers le val;
      A quel que painne i est montés,   [4ra]
      Si est en son païs alés
      A tout sa grant malaventure.
448   Et Gavains suit grant aleüre
      Le chevalier qui oirre a plain
      Et quant il ot passé le plain
      Et fu en la forest entrés.
452   Quant aprés lui fu aroutés,
      Soventre lui u bos entra;
      Une grant piece issi erra,
      Qu'onques nel vit ne pres ne loing.
456   A tant oï a grant besoing
      De trois damoiseles le cri,
      Qui dissoient: "A! Dix, merci!
      Ices caitives que feront,
460   Quant toute la joie du mont
      Est wi cest jor tornee en ire?
      Bien peuent les puceles dire
      Que tout lor secors perdu ont."
464   Por le grant duel que eles font
      A Gavains son cemin laiscié
      Et vint a eles eslaiscié.
      El cief les trova d'une lande;
468   Doucement enquiert et demande,
      Quant il lor ot son salut fait,
      Por qu'eles sont en tel dehait,
      Ne por qu'eles font si grant duel.
472   "Lasse," fait l'une, "mien wel
      Fussiens nous toutes trois ocises.
      C'est dolors que nous sommes vives,
      Quant nous avon tel perte faite

436   Or value you to such an extent
That he would be obligated to you!"
Gawain could offer no excuse.
So he left the horse by a willow tree.

440   Then he turned toward the woods, letting
His horse gallop at a great speed.
Sir Kay forced himself to move
So that he got himself near his horse.

444   Then he got it lined up by a hill.
With great difficulty, he mounted it
And returned to his own land,
Defeated by this great misadventure.

448   And at top speed Gawain followed
The knight, who was travelling fast,
For he had already crossed the plain
And entered into the forest.

452   After Gawain had pursued him a while,
He too entered into the forest.
He went some distance without
Seeing anything far and wide.

456   Just then he heard the cries
Of three young women in great anguish
Who said: "Ah, God, have mercy!
What are we poor wretches to do?

460   All worldly joy has vanished
From our lives today and turned to sorrow.
Well can we women speak of it,
We who have lost all our solace."

464   Hearing this great lamentation,
Gawain turned from his path
And rode at top speed toward the women,
Whom he found at the edge of a heath.

468   After he greeted them,
He gently made inquiries and asked
Why they were in such a sad state
And why they displayed such grief.

472   "Alas," said the one, "better that
All three of us were dead!
The worst is that we live.
We have suffered such a loss

476   Qui ja mais ne sera retraite,
       Ne par bouce d'ome contee."
       A tant ciet a terra pasmee,
       Se ist reconmenciés li dex.
480   Il a regardé deriere ex,
       Si vit gesir un damoisel
       Moult grant et moult gent et moult bel,   [4rb]
       Qui moult estoit bien atornés,
484   Mais il avoit les ex crevés
       Ileuques tout nouvelement,
       Qu'encor en ot le vis sanglent.
           Moult par en fu Gavains iriés:
488   Tant ert biax et bien atiriés
       Que bien paroit de haute gent,
       Si quidoit bien a escïent
       Que tout ce duel fust por lui fait.
492   "Bele," fait il, "icest forfait
       De cest vallet que je ci voi,
       Coment fu il fais ne por quoi?
       Grant talent ai que je le sace."
496   L'autre respont: "Ja Diu ne place
       Que je vive mais longement,
       Quant l'onor et l'afaitement,
       La largece et la segnorie
500   Et le flor de chevalerie,
       Ai ci veü morir ensanble."
       A cest mot li cuers li trestranble,
       Si que toute descouloree
504   Kaï dalés l'autre pasmee.
           Gavains mist le terce a raison:
       "Bele," fait il, "par gueredon
       Vous requier et pri par servise
508   Qui soit fais a vostre devise
       Que me dites, se vous poés,
       Dont ce duel vient que vous avés."
       La damoisele a respondu:
512   "Sire, por çou que j'ai veü
       Que vous avés si bel parlé,
       Vous ert de cief en cief conté
       Et la dolor et l'ocoison.

476   As can never be recovered,
Nor even spoken of by human voice."
At this she fainted
And the other two renewed their cries.

480   Gawain looked behind them
And saw a young man lying on the ground.
He was shapely, noble, and handsome,
And was very elegantly dressed,

484   But his eyes had been punctured.
He must have been recently wounded,
For the blood was still flowing.
    Gawain was quite angry at this sight:

488   The young man was so handsome and well-dressed
That he appeared to be of high rank.
And certainly Gawain realized
That all the sorrow was on his account.

492   "Fair one," he said, "the crime
Against this squire whom I see here—
How and why did it happen?
I would very much like to know this."

496   The second young woman replied:
"May God grant that I not live long,
Now that I have seen the embodiment
Of all honor and good manners,

500   Generosity and lordliness—
The flower of chivalry—die."
With these words, her heart beat fast,
She turned totally pale,

504   And then fainted next to the other one.
    Gawain tried reasoning with the third one:
"Fair one," he said, "as a favor,
I pray you, in return for my service

508   Doing whatever you might require,
That you tell me, if you can,
The source of your anguish."
The young woman replied:

512   "Because I have observed
That you speak so politely,
You will be told from start to finish
Both about the sorrow and its cause.

516   Sire, le duel que nous menon
       N'est pas si grant que nous devroit,
       Car se trestout le mont savoit
       Le grant damage et le dolor   [4va]
520   Qui est avenu wi cest jor,
       Si en feroit il autretant.
       Car li damages es si grant,
       Onques si grans ne fu veüs,
524   Quant il sera partout seüs.
            "Mendre est li diex que li damages,
       Car cil qui tant ert prox et sages
       Et qui du mont avoit le pris
528   Est en ceste forest ocis
       Orendroit ici devant nous.
       Bien poés savoir a estox
       Qui cil est de cui je vous di."
532   "Bele," fait il, "quant je nel vi,
       Je n'en puis estre bien certains."
       "Sire," fait ele, "c'est Gavains,
       Li niés le rice rois Artu,
536   Le bon chevalier esleü,
       Qui tant ert proisiés et amés.
       Wi erroit trestous desarmés
       Par ceste forest en deduit,
540   Sans conpaignie et sans conduit;
       Il n'avoit arme o lui portee,
       Fors lance et escu et espee,
       Et si erroit sans conpaignie.
544   Trois chevalier que Dix maudie,
       Qui de viés l'avoient haï,
       L'orent desque ci parsivi.
       Quant il fu isçus de ce val,
548   Li uns lait corre le ceval
       Et vint poignant desi a lui;
       Enbuscié se furent li dui,
       Et li tiers a lui se mesla.
552   Tant longement l'estors dura
       Que Gavains en vint el desus;
       Li doi nel peurent soufrir plus
       Que cil avoit el bos laiscié,

516   Sir, the grief that we display
    Is not as great as it should be.
    If all the world knew about
    The great injury and suffering
520   That has occurred today,
    They would grieve the same way.
    For the loss is so great—
    A greater one has never been seen—
524   When it will be known by all.
        "Our sorrow hardly measures the loss,
    For he who is so brave and wise,
    Who is the best knight in the world,
528   Has been killed here in this forest
    Just now, right before our eyes.
    Certainly you are able to guess
    About whom I am speaking."
532   "Fair one," he said, "since I saw nothing
    I can't be completely certain."
    "Sir," she said, "it is Gawain,
    The nephew of rich King Arthur,
536   Known as the *bon chevalier*,
    Who is so esteemed and loved.
    Today he wandered totally unarmed
    Into this forest for pleasure,
540   Without companions or armed knights.
    He carried no arms with him
    Except for lance, shield, and sword.
    He went about quite alone.
544   Three knights—may God curse them!—
    Who had hated him all their lives,
    Followed him up to this place.
    As he passed out of the valley,
548   One of them let his horse run
    And came up to challenge Gawain.
    The other two lay in ambush,
    And the third fought with him.
552   The battle raged for a long time,
    And eventually Gawain got the upper hand.
    The other two, who had been left in the forest,
    Couldn't stand to look on for long.

556 Ains i vinrent tout eslaiscié   [4vb]
     Por aidier a lor conpaignon.
     Gavain misent en tel randon
     Qu'il ne se peut desfendre d'ex,
560 Qu'il erent trois et il ert sex
     Et s'estoit cascuns bien armés.
     Cil vaslés qui vous la veés,
     Qui de grant hardement ert plain,
564 I poinst por aidier a Gavain;
     Son pooir fist de lui aidier,
     Mais ne li peut avoir mestier,
     Car cil erent et grant et fort;
568 A ex valut peu sen esfort,
     Car il estoit tous desarmés.
     Au vallet ont les ex crevés,
     Et Gavain ont tout detrencié.
572 Sire, le duel et la pitié
     Que nous avons et la grant ire,
     Loiaument le vous poons dire,
     N'est pas por cestui seulement;
576 Ains avons le grant mautalent
     Del bon chevalier qui est mors."
     Lors conmenca uns dex si fors
     Que nus nel vous porroit retraire:
580 "Lasse," font eles, "que porrons faire?
          "Ahi! Mors! Tant par es avere!
     Nous n'avions fors cestui frere,
     Et si avons cestui perdu.
584 A! Mors delente, que fais tu,
     Quant orendroit ne nous ocis?
     C'est ta costume de toudis
     Qu'a celui qui ta venue aime,
588 Et a son besoig te reclainme,
     Ne veus secorre ne aidier.
     Tu as mort le bon chevalier,
     Dont tox li mons sera en paine.
592 Ahi! Mor, tant par es vilaine,
     Qui les bons prens tout a eslais   [5ra]
     Et laisces vivre les mauvais:
     En toi n'a raison ne mesure.

556   They came at top speed
         To aid their companion.
         They took Gawain with such force
         That he could not defend himself,
560   For they were three and he was one,
         And they were each of them well-armed.
         This squire whom you see here,
         Who was very brave,
564   Came forth to assist Gawain.
         He did all he could to aid him,
         But he himself needed help,
         For his opponents were big and strong.
568   His effort against them was of little value,
         For he was completely unarmed.
         They pierced the eyes of the squire,
         And they cut Gawain up into pieces.
572   Sir, the sorrow and pity
         That we have, as well as our great anger,
         We can honestly tell you,
         Are not only for this one.
576   We have the great distress now
         For the *bon chevalier* who is dead."
         At this they began to cry so hard
         That no one could describe it.
580   "Alas," they cried, "what are we to do?
           "Ah, Death, you are so greedy!
         We had no friend other than him
         And now we have lost him.
584   O sorrowful Death, what now
         If not to kill us immediately?
         It is always your custom
         That the very one who desires you
588   And claims you in his own need,
         To him you fail to offer aid.
         But you killed the *bon chevalier*,
         For which the whole world is in pain.
592   Alas! Death, you are such a villain,
         Who rushes to take the good men
         And lets the evil ones live.
         You know neither reason nor moderation.

596   De ces trois lasses n'as tu cure
        Qui lor vie ont en grant despit?"
        Et mesire Gavains a dit:
            "Beles, ne vous desconfortés.
600   Por trop grant nient vous cremés,
        Car je vieg de la cort tot droit,
        Si i vi seoir orendroit
        Au mengier monsegnor Gavain,
604   Et saciés que jel vi tout sain
        A la cort quant je m'en parti."
        Et li vallés li respondi:
        "Biax sire, ains est mors a estrox."
608   "Amis," fait il, "que savés vous?
        Coment en estes vous certain?"
        "Je fui," fait il, "vallés Gavain
        Antan a un tornoiement,
612   Et si sai tout certainement
        Que c'est il qui est decaupés."
        "Amis," dist il, "car me moustrés:
        Je conisterai bien le cors."
616   "Sire," fait il, "cil sont ja fors
        De la forest qui l'ont ocis.
        Quant il en orent le cief pris,
        Trestox les membres li cauperent;
620   Laidement le desfigurerent,
        Qu'il n'i remest ne pié ne poing.
        Il sont ja bien trois liues loing
        O le cors qu'il en ont porté
624   En lor païs a sauveté.
        Il ne doutent wi mais nului."
        Se Gavains ot ire et anui
        Del vallet qui si ert destroit
628   Et des puceles que il voit
        Por lui si grant dol demener,
        Il ne fait mie a demander.   [5rb]
            Por le vallet est tox dervés,
632   Car hom qui a les ex crevés
        Vit tox jors puis a grant anui;
        Et set de voir que c'est por lui
        Que on li a cest mal tout fait;

596 Have you no care for these three
Who have no regard for life?"
And Sir Gawain then said:
"Fair ones, don't be discomforted.
600 You torment yourselves for nothing.
For I come straight from the court
Where just now I saw Sir Gawain
Sitting at the table.
604 Be assured that I saw him in good health
There in the court when I left."
And the squire replied:
"Dear sir, he is definitely dead."
608 "My friend," Gawain asked, "what do you know?
How can you be sure of this?"
"I was in Gawain's service
At a tournament a year ago,
612 And thus I know for certain
That it is he who was killed."
"Friend," Gawain said, "please show me,
For I will easily recognize the body."
616 "Sir," he said, "those who killed him
Are now outside of the forest.
After they had cut off his head,
They cut off all his limbs.
620 They so disfigured the body
That neither foot nor finger was left.
They are three leagues away by now.
They carried off the body
624 To their country to preserve it there.
They need have fear of no one."
Gawain was angered and troubled
About the squire who was so badly injured
628 And the three maidens that he saw
Display such sorrow on his account.
He couldn't ask anything more.
He was most angry about the squire,
632 For he whose eyes are destroyed
Lives ever after in great anguish.
And Gawain realized it was for his sake
That all this evil had happened.

636   Et del chevalier qui s'en vait,
        Qui en porte la damoisele,
        Par quoi ses dex li renouvele,
        Si qu'il ne set que il fera,
640   La quele aventure il suirra,
        La premiere u la daraine.
        Vis li est que la premeraine
        Doit il premierement furnir,
644   Et si il s'en puet revenir
        Sans peril et sans enconbrier,
        Si doit a cesti reperier,
        Et vengier le s'il onques puet.
648   "Amis," fait il, "errer m'estuet.
        A Diu soiiés vous conmandé;
        Et saciés bien de verité
        Que, se g'i fusce ançois venu,
652   Ains en fust percié mon escu
        Et mon hauberc rout et fausé
        Et jou par mi le cors navré
        Que on vous eüst fait cest anui.
656   Ne ja ne sarés qui je sui
        Devant la que je revenrai,
        Ne ja mais jor ne finerai
        Puis que je serai reperiés,
660   Ains ere mors u vous vengiés."
            Les puceles a Diu conmande;
        Poignant s'en va par mi la lande
        Tant qu'en sen droit cemin entra.
664   Une grant piece ensi erra
        Tant que la forest ot passee;
        De l'autre part de la valee
        Voit loing le chevalier errer.   [5va]
668   Il conmença a avesprer,
        Et Gavains point tant son ceval
        Qu'i fu de l'autre part d'un val.
            Lors vit devant lui un castel,
672   Tout clos de piere et de quarrel,
        Dont li murs ot cent piés de haut:
        Li castiax ne redoute asaut,
        Tant estoit ricement fremé.

636   And as for the knight who was riding away,
Carrying off the young woman—
At this thought his anger was renewed!
But he didn't know what to do—
640   Which adventure should he follow?
The first or the second?
He realized that he ought to complete
The first one before the other,
644   And then, if able to get away
Without losing his life or being harmed,
Then he ought to return
To try to avenge the second.
648   "Friend," he said, "I must be on my way.
May God protect you!
Believe me when I say
That if I had arrived earlier today,
652   It would have been my shield that was pierced
And my coat of mail that was broken
And my own body wounded
Before anyone had caused you this grief.
656   You will not know who I am
Until I return.
I will not rest
Until I have righted this wrong
660   And am either dead or avenged."
       He commended the maidens to God.
Quickly he rode off across the plain
Until he came to the right road.
664   He went quite a distance
Until he had passed through the forest.
At the other side of the valley
He saw the knight riding far ahead.
668   It was nearly nightfall,
And Gawain pressed his horse so hard
That he was soon on the other side of the valley.
       Suddenly he saw before him a castle,
672   Well-fortified with stone and spire,
With walls a hundred feet high.
The castle need not fear an assault,
No matter how powerful.

676   Il vit bien qu'il ert avespré,
       Tant qu'il ne porroit sans mescief
       De sa bataille traire a cief,
       Porpensa soi qu'il souferra
680   Et que demain se conbatra
       Au cevalier qu'il parsivoit;
       Car a escient set et voit
       Qu'el castel se herbegera,
684   Et il meïsmes i gerra
       Por atendre iluec sa bataille.
       Ansi quide faire sans faille,
       Mais moult li avint autrement,
688   Car li chevaliers erranment
       Dedens le premier baile entra,
       Et li solax lors esconsa,
       Si furent les portes fermees.
692   Il a les rues trespasees
       Tant qu'il vint amont u castel.
       Devant le tor en un prael
       Seoit li sire aveuc sa gent.
696   Il le salue belement;
       Aprés li a l'ostel requis,
       Et il li dist: "Biax dous amis,
       Vous l'arés," fait il, "volentiers."
700   Lors sailli sus uns chevaliers
       Qui descendi la damoisele.
       Li sire ses vallés apele
       Por le chevalier desarmer;
704   Aprés li a fait aporter   [5vb]
       Un bliaut et un mantel gris.
       Quant il l'ot delés lui assis,
       Si li enquier moult bonement
708   Son estre et son contenement,
       Dont il vient ne quel part il va,
       Et li chevaliers li conta,
       Qu'onques ne l'en degna mentir.
712   A Gavain m'estuet revertir
       Qui encor oirre par la plaigne,
       Ne li caut mais que il ataigne
       A estre de jor herbegié.

676	He saw clearly that it was starting to get dark
	So that he could not, without distress,
	Bring the battle to an end.
	He thought that he should be patient
680	And fight the battle tomorrow
	With the knight he was chasing.
	For he was certain that he could
	Be lodged within the castle
684	And that he would be able to rest
	There while awaiting his battle.
	He thought surely he could do so,
	But things happened very differently.
688	For the knight very quickly
	Entered within the first wall,
	And just as the sun went down,
	They closed the gates.
692	The knight crossed over the roads
	Until he had ridden up to the castle.
	Before the door within a courtyard
	He found the lord seated with his people.
696	He greeted him courteously
	And then asked for lodging.
	And the lord said: "Dear sweet friend,
	You will have it," he said, "gladly."
700	Then a knight got up and helped
	The young woman down off the horse.
	The lord called over his squires
	To disarm the knight.
704	Afterwards he had them bring
	A long tunic and grey coat.
	When he had seated him at his side,
	He inquired very courteously
708	Who he was and why he was travelling,
	Where he came from and where he was going.
	And the knight told him
	Without lying about anything.
712	Now it is necessary to return to Gawain,
	Who was riding at great speed across the plain.
	He cared for nothing except
	Finding lodging for that day.

716 Il a son ceval eslaiscié,
Si vint poignant droit a le porte.
Por le vile qu'il voit si fort,
A moult le castel regardé.
720 Il a le portier apelé
Si durement qu'il l'entendi,
Et li portiers li respondi:
"Biax amis, por noient criés,
724 Car li solax est esconsés;
N'i ara wi mais porte ouverte,
Ne le matin por nule perte,
Devant çou que sera grant jor.
728 Car li sire de ceste honor,
Et li clerc et li chevalier,
Serjant, borgois, et escuiier,
Ont tout conmunement juré,
732 Que ja por home qui soit né
N'ert li guicés destorelliés,
Puis que li solax ert couciés,
Ains sera levés el demain."
736 "Amis," ce li a dit Gavain,
"Travelliés sui, si est moult tart;
Car me di donques de quel part
Je porrai wi mais ostel querre."
740 "Sire," fait il, "en ceste terre,   [6ra]
De grans dis liues environ,
N'a il ne borde ne maison.
Je ne vous sai consel douner:
744 Toute nuit porriés errer
Par mi bruieres et par bois."
"Amis," fait Gavains, "je m'en vois.
A Diu soiiés vous conmandé."
748 N'ot pas le trait d'un arc alé
Quant il coisi un capele
Dalés le cemin haute et bele,
Dont l'atre estoit enclos de mur.
752 Ileuc quida estre aseür
Gavains et la nuit herbegier,
Mais s'onques li fu nul mestier
D'estre prox, or l'en ert gregnor;

716 He let his horse run at full speed
So that he came galloping up to the gate.
Seeing the town so well-fortified,
He looked a long time at the castle.
720 He called to the gate-keeper
Loud enough for him to hear,
And the gate-keeper replied:
"Dear sir, you shout for nought,
724 For the sun has gone down.
No door will be opened
For any reason until morning,
Not until broad daylight.
728 For the lord of this manor himself,
Clerks and knights,
Sergeants, merchants and squires,
All are judged alike!
732 For no one on earth
Will the door be opened
After the sun has gone down.
It will not be raised until morning."
736 "Friend," Gawain said to him, "I am
Completely worn out, and it is very late.
Please tell me then where else
I will be able to find shelter."
740 "Sir," he replied, "in this country
There is neither hut nor house
Within an area of ten leagues.
I don't have any advice to give:
744 You could wander the whole night
Through heath and wood."
"Friend," said Gawain, "I am going.
I commend you to God's care."
748 He had not gone a bow's length
When he saw a chapel,
Tall and beautiful, at the side of the road.
Its cemetery was enclosed by a wall.
752 Gawain thought this would surely be
A secure place to rest the night,
But if he ever before had the need
To be brave, he would need it more here.

756   Onques mais de si grant paour
       Jor de sa vie n'escapa.
       Desi a la capela va,
       Si est en l'atre descendu;
760   Sa lance osta et son escu,
       Si l'apoia a la capele.
       Del bon destrier osta la sele,
       Sel forbi bien et conrea;
764   De l'erbe paistre li laisça,
       Puis est assis sor un tonbel.
       A tant oï un damoisel
       Venir le trot sor son roncin
768   Devers le bos tot le cemin.
           Il est du cimentire isçu,
       Si li demande: "Que es tu
       Qui si tart trespasses par ci?"
772   Et li vallés jeta un cri,
       Puis dist: "Dame Sainte Marie,
       Tenés moi en sens et en vie.
       Gloriex Dix, tenés mon cors
776   Que je n'isce de mon sens fors
       Et que diables ne m'afot."
       Gavains de ce grant mervelle ot: [6rb]
       "Amis," fait il, "ne vous cremés.
780   Li vrais Dix que vous reclamés
       Deffende moi et vous de mal."
       Ci guenci vers lui le ceval
       Quant il l'oï de Diu parler;
784   Tantost li ala demander
       Qui il ert et de quel païs.
       Et il li dist: "Biax dox amis,
       Je sui Gavains, li niés le roi.
788   Por quoi eüstes vous de moi
       Paor quan je vous aparla?"
       "Sire," fait il, "jel vous dirai:
           "Sire," fait il, "ne savés vous
792   Que c'est li Atres Perellox
       U vous avés vostre ostel pris?
       Cascune nuit, je vous plevis,
       Ne tenés pas mon dit a fable,

756   Not without great fear would he
Escape with his life this day.
He rode up to the chapel
And dismounted in the cemetery.

760   He took off his shield and lance
And rested them against the chapel.
He unsaddled his war horse
And looked after him well;

764   He let him eat the grass,
And then sat himself down on a tombstone.
At this he heard, from the sound
Of hoofbeats, a young man coming

768   Along the road by way of the woods.
     He came out of the cemetery
And asked: "Who are you
Who crosses over this land so late?"

772   And the squire, startled, cried out,
Then said, "Mary, Mother of God,
Keep me alive and sane.
Glorious God, protect my body

776   So that I don't lose my mind.
Don't let the devil get hold of me."
Gawain was quite surprised at this.
"Friend," he said, "don't be afraid.

780   The true God that you call upon
Protects us both from harm."
The squire turned his horse toward him
When he heard him speak of God.

784   Immediately he asked
Who he was and from what country.
And Gawain said to him: "Dear friend,
I am Gawain, the nephew of the king.

788   Why did you have such fear of me
When I spoke to you just now?"
"Sir," he said, "I will tell you.
     "Sir," he said, "don't you know

792   That this is the Perilous Cemetery
Where you have taken refuge?
Each night, I assure you—
Don't take this for a fairy tale—

796   S'i vient herbegier le diable,
      U dex u trois, je ne sai quans.
      Bien a passé plus de cent ans
      Qu'il n'i herbega chevalier,
800   Ne nul home de nul mestier,
      K'on ne trovast au matin mort.
      Arivés estes a mal port,
      S'autre ostel de cest ne querés.
804   Mais se vous croire me volés,
      Je vous herbegerai moult bien,
      Car ce castel la sus fu mien,
      Si le dounai un chevalier,
808   Et ma suer a tout a mollier.
      Encor se dormoient trestuit
      Jewi quant j'alai en deduit
      Por berser en ceste forest:
812   C'est uns deduis qui moult me plest.
      Eneslespas un cerf feri;
      Trestoute jor l'a parsivi
      Tant que l'ataint un men levrier;   [6va]
816   Au desfaire et a l'escorcier
      Me sui longement demouré,
      Vers le ci u je l'ai torsé;
      Sin arons ja endroit moult tost
820   Assés en esçau et en rost.
         "Sire," fait il, "por Diu vous pri
      Que vous ne demourés pas ci,
      Se vous avés vostre cors cier;
824   Mais venés laiens herbegier
      U vous arés moult bon ostel."
      Et Gavains dist: "Or n'oï tel:
      Je vinc ore a le porte errant,
828   Si me respondi un serjant
      Que je crioie por noient,
      Et m'afica moult durement
      Une rien dont moult me mervel:
832   Puis que coucié est le solel
      Sont tox jors les portes barees,
      Ne ja ne seront desfremees
      Devant la qu'il ert grant matin."

796   The devil comes to rest here,
        Or two or three—I don't know how many.
        Not for a good one hundred years
        Has a knight taken refuge here,
800   Nor a man of any other occupation,
        And not been found dead the next morning.
        This will turn out badly,
        If you don't find some other place to rest.
804   However, if you want to trust me,
        I will provide you much better lodging.
        For the castle up there is mine.
        I gave it to a knight
808   And my sister when they married.
        They were all still sleeping,
        When I went out for fun
        To hunt in this forest.
812   This is a pleasure I delight in.
        Immediately I spotted a deer
        And followed it all day long
        Until finally one of my hounds caught it.
816   I was delayed a long time
        Cutting it up and skinning it.
        You can see it tied up here.
        We will soon have enough of it
820   Boiled or roasted.
        "Sir," he said, "for God's sake,
        I pray you, do not stay here,
        If you value your life;
824   Rather come spend the night with me
        Where you will have very good lodging."
        And Gawain said, "Now I heard differently:
        Just now I went to the gate
828   And a sergeant responded—
        To whom I shouted in vain—
        And insisted quite firmly about
        Something that surprised me very much.
832   As soon as the sun has gone down
        The doors are barricaded
        And won't be opened again
        Until full daylight."

836   "Par foi," fait il, "ce est li fin;
        De çou vous dist il verité.
        Mais nous venrons ja au fossé,
        Ens jeterai ma venison,
840   Et nous meïsmes i sauron,
        Puis irons vers les murs amont.
        Mi vallet qui la dedens sont,
        Qui or ne sont pas aseür,
844   Aront tost trait en son le mur
        La venison et vous et moi."
        "Amis," dist Gavains, "quel conroi
        Seroit il de nos cevax pris?"
848   "Sire," fait il, "par cest païs
        Les lairons paistre toute nuit.
        Le mien en est moult tres bien duit:
        Ja del mur ne s'eslongera."
852   "Li miens," fait Gavains, "que fera,   [6vb]
        Qui ne counoist pas le païs?
        S'or le m'avoient leu ocis,
        U aucune beste sauvage,
856   Il me seroit tout mon eage,
        Qu'il ne poroit estre celé,
        En ma contree reprové
        Que je l'aroie seul laiscié
860   Conme couart par mauvaistié,
        Si l'aroient estranglé lex.
        Certes ja ni remanra sex,
        Ains prendrai o lui bien et mal."
864   "Si vous," fait il, "por un ceval
        Vous i laisciés de gré morir,
        Por fol vous en porrés tenir.
        Cevax recouverrés assés,
868   Mais se vous croire me volés
        Vous en venrés ensanle o moi
        A ce castel u aler doi."
            Gavains li dist: "Ce est l'estrox;
872   Je n'irai pas ensanble vox
        Quant mes cevax n'i enterroit.
        Mais je vous pri, s'estre pooit,
        Que vous me creantés un don,

836 "In faith," the squire said, "this is quite true.
He spoke honestly about this.
But we will go by way of the moat.
I'll throw over the venison,
840 And we ourselves will jump over there,
And then we'll climb up the wall.
My retainers, who are inside there,
Who are now somewhat uneasy,
844 Will quickly have pulled over the wall
You, me, and the venison."
"Friend," said Gawain, "what care
Will be taken for our horses?"
848 "Sir," he said, "in this country
We let them graze through the night.
Mine is quite used to it.
He won't wander far from the wall."
852 "But mine," said Gawain, "how will he make out?
He doesn't know this countryside.
If wolves—or some other
Savage beast—kill him,
856 I would be, for my whole life,
(Because it couldn't be hidden)
Rebuked in my country
For having left him alone,
860 Like a coward out of wickedness,
So that they could kill him.
I will never leave him here alone.
Whether for good or evil—I will stay with him."
864 "If you," the squire replied, "let yourself
Die on account of a horse,
You could be taken for a fool.
You will easily get another horse.
868 But if you want to trust me,
You can come along
To the castle where I must now go."
Gawain said to him, "It is decided.
872 I will not go with you
If my horse cannot enter too.
But I ask you, if it is possible,
To grant me a boon,

876   Dont vous arés bon gueredon
       Se je puis escaper de ci."
       Et cil li dist: "Jel vous otri,
       Sor la loiauté que jou ai,
880   Que, se je puis, jel vous donra."
       "Amis," dist il, "or enten donc:
       Un chevalier qui trop est lonc
       (Se ce ne fust, si fust trop bel)
884   S'est herbegié en ce castel;
       Si en porte une damoisele,
       Grande et gente et cortoise et bele,
       Si le prist wi par son derroi
888   En ma garde a le cort le roi.
       Moult par en ai esté mari;   [7ra]
       Trestoute jor l'ai porsivi,
       Onques ataindre ne le poi.
892   Ainc de rien si grant corox n'oi
       Com s'il la gardoit anuit mais.
       Por m'amor en prendés tel fais,
       S'il onques puet estre a nul fuer,
896   K'anuit mais le gart vostre suer,
       Si m'arés moult servi a gré.
       S'il en faisoit sa volonté,
       Je n'aroie ja mais honor;
900   Et demain quant il sera jor,
       Si en soit tout en pais saisi.
       Se faire le poés issi,
       Ne m'en caut puis quel part il aille,
904   Que lors venrai a ma bataille."
            Cil li respont: "Il ert bien fait."
       Les grandismes galos en vait,
       Que plus demourer n'i osa.
908   Au fossé vint, si apela
       Ses vallés, qui as murs estoient,
       Et qui moult grant paour avoient
       Qu'il ne fust mort u afolé.
912   Sa venison jete u fossé,
       Et il meismes i sali;
       Son caceor el camp guerpi,
       Quant le harnois en ot osté;

876 For which you will have good reward
   If I escape from here."
   And the squire replied, "I will grant it,
   Out of loyalty to you;
880 If I am able to, I will fulfill it."
   "Friend," he said, "now listen to this:
   A knight who is excessively tall
   (If this were not so, he would be very handsome)
884 Has taken refuge in this castle.
   He has with him a young woman,
   Who is tall and beautiful, noble and courteous.
   Today he foolishly took her
888 From the king's court while under my guard.
   I have been most grieved by this.
   All day long I have followed him—
   I never could catch up with him.
892 I have never had such great anger at anything
   As at the thought that he would keep her tonight.
   For love of me, take on this deed.
   If, one way or another, you are able to,
896 Have your sister guard her tonight.
   You would provide me a great service,
   For if he would have his way with her,
   I would be completely dishonored.
900 And tomorrow, when it is daylight,
   Let him peacefully regain possession of her.
   If you can do things this way,
   It won't matter which way he leaves;
904 I will finally have my battle with him."
    The squire replied, "It's as good as done."
   He went at top speed,
   For he didn't dare stay any longer.
908 He came to the moat and called
   To his retainers, who were on the wall
   And who had very great fear
   That he was dead or wounded.
912 He threw his venison over the moat,
   And then he himself jumped over.
   He abandoned his good horse on the plain,
   After he had taken off the harness.

916   Tout en aveuc lui porté
       Le harnois et la venison.
       Ainc n'i ot autre arestison:
       Vistement l'ont sor le mur trait.
920   Au segnor la novele en vait
       Que li vallés estoit venus.
       Il est contre lui acourus
       Hors du castel par une rue,
924   Liés et joians de sa venue;
       La dame meïsme i acort,
       Et toute la gent de la cort: [7rb]
       N'i remest ni wiscier ne gaite.
928   Onques tel joie ne fu faite
       Por le cors d'un seul damoisel
       Com on fist de lui u castel,
       Qu'a escient savoient tuit
932   Qu'il estoit alés en deduit
       En la forest por arcoiier,
       Si cremoient qu'au repairier,
       Por çou que tant ot demouré,
936   L'eüst le diable afolé
       Qui gardoit l'Atre Perellox.
       Si en furent moult peürox,
       Qu'il n'en i ot nul si hardi
940   N'en fust trestout acouardi.
             Lors s'en sont en la sale entré,
       Et le vaslés a regardé
       Le chevalier qui se seoit
944   Et la pucele que il voit,
       Dont Gavains li fist la proiiere.
       Auques le counut a la ciere
       A le maniere et au sanblant
948   Del chevalier qui si ert grant.
       Lors mist a raison le segnor:
       "Sire," dist il, "si grant dolor
       N'avint onques, ce saciés vous,
952   La hors en l'Atre Perellox,
       Ne si grant mais n'i avenra,
       Com en ceste nuit i ara.
       Bien doit tout le monde plorer,

916   He carried with him only
The harness and the venison.
There was no other delay.
In no time they had pulled him over the wall.

920   The news travelled to the lord
That the squire had arrived.
He ran ahead to greet him
On a road outside the castle,

924   Happily celebrating his arrival.
The lady of the castle herself
And all the nobles of the court also rushed there.
Neither gatekeeper nor watchman stayed behind.

928   Never had there been such joy
On account of a single young man
As there was here in this castle for him.
For they all knew perfectly well

932   That he had gone for pleasure
Into the forest to hunt with bow and arrow.
They feared that he, in returning—
Because he had been so delayed—

936   Had been wounded by the devil
Who guarded the Perilous Cemetery.
And they were full of fear,
So much so that there wasn't one so brave

940   That he wasn't frightened by it.
       Then they entered into the grand hall,
And the young man looked at
The knight seated there,

944   As well as the young woman
For whom Gawain had asked a favor.
Anyone could recognize him from his face,
From his manner, and from the appearance

948   Of this knight who was so large.
Then he began to reason with his lord:
"Sir," he said, "there has never been
Such great suffering, this you should know,

952   Outside in the Perilous Cemetery,
Nor will there be in the future,
As is going to occur tonight.
Right it is that everyone should cry

956 Car el monde n'avoit son per
   De largece et de cortoisie,
   Et por sa grant cevalerie
   N'estoit il nient plus orgellox.
960 Maudis soit l'Atre Perellox
   Quant il onques s'i herbega.
   Quant li rois Artus le sara,
   Tout en destruira cest païs;   [7va]
964 Car li bons rois poesteïs
   Nous demandera tout par doit
   Son neveu qu'il pert orendroit.
   Il le pert, c'est moult grans damages;
968 A Dix, com grant duel ses lignages
   En aront quant il le saront!
   Et trestoute le gent del mont
   Qu'il connoiscent nes d'oïr dire
972 Aront de sa mort duel et ire,
   Car moult ert proisiés et amés.
   Sire," fait il, "or escoutés
   Par quel sorfait et par quel tort,
976 Et l'ocoison dont il est mort.
    "Cel chevalier que je la voi
   Vint orains a la cort le roi,
   Quant il seoit a son mangier;
980 Cele pucele i vint des ier
   Presenter au roi son servise.
   A la cort remest en tel guise
   Que de la coupe serviroit
984 Et que Gavains le garderoit
   D'enconbrier de honte et d'anui.
   Orains le saisi devant lui
   Cis chevaliers par son orguel.
988 Par mi la forest de Carduel
   L'a Gavains toute jor sivi;
   En l'Atre Perellox le vi,
   U j'ai grant piece o lui esté,
992 Si m'a de cief en cief conté
   Com il l'a sivi toute jor.
   Je li priai par grant douçor
   Qu'il venist caiens herbegier,

956 Because the world contains no equal
In generosity or courtesy,
And yet, for all his chivalric virtue,
He is not full of pride.
960 Damn the cursed Perilous Cemetery
For ever having lodged Gawain!
When King Arthur hears of this,
He will destroy this land.
964 For this good, powerful king
Will rightfully call us to account
For his nephew, whom he is about to lose right now.
To lose him is a great injury.
968 Ah God! what lamentation in his family
When they learn of it!
And all the people in the world
Who have only heard of him
972 Will be sad and angry at his death,
For he is highly valued and loved.
Sir," he continued, "now listen
To what outrage and offense
976 Are the cause of his death.
    "This knight that I see here came,
A short time ago, to the king's court
While he was seated at dinner.
980 This maiden had come there the day before
To offer her service to the king.
She remained at the court in such a way
That she would serve as cup bearer,
984 And Gawain would protect her
From shameful or troublesome events.
Only a little while ago this knight—
Blinded by his pride—seized her from him.
988 Through the forest of Carlisle,
Gawain followed him all day long.
I saw him in the Perilous Cemetery
Where I was with him for some time,
992 Long enough for him to tell me the complete story—
How he had followed her all day.
I begged him politely to come
With me to rest for the night inside.

996   Mais il n'i vaut sans son destrier
       Venir i en nule maniere.
       Ne se vous avés m'amor ciere,
       Ne reins que je faire vous puisce,
1000   Gardés que bon ami vous truisce,   [7vb]
       Car une cose vous demant."
       Et cil li dist: "Je vous creant
       Quanques vous me vaurés requerre,
1004   Nis se c'estoit toute ma terre."
            "Sire," fait il, "vostre merci.
       De ceste pucele vous pri
       Que ma suer le gart anuit mais,
1008   Et le matin le rait en pais
       Li chevaliers qui l'amena:
       Mesire Gavains m'en pria
       Que fust anuit hors de sa garde."
1012   Et cil fierement le regarde,
       Puis li a dit: "Ce n'iert ja fait;
       Max cinc cens mile dehais ait
       Ki en tantes cors l'a sivie
1016   Et qui en fist tele estoutie
       Devant le roi a son mengier,
       Orains voiant maint chevalier,
       S'anuit le garde nus fors moi,
1020   Ne se jou ja le vous otroi
       Tant com je puisce estre sor piés."
       Li sire fu moult afaitiés,
       Qui li pria moult bonement
1024   Que il le baut sans matalent;
       La dame l'en pria aprés,
       Et toute la gent du palés,
       Que il l'otroit, si fera bien.
1028   Et cil respont: "Ce ne vaut rien;
       Je nel feroie por nul home."
       Li vaslés dist: "Ce est la some:
       Que se mon plaiscir n'en est fait
1032   Que je sui cil qui s'en revait
       A monsegnor Gavain arriere,
       Et dirai li que sa proiiere
       Ne puet estre par moi furnie.

996　　But there was no way he would
　　　Come here without his war horse.
　　　If you value my love,
　　　If anything I do pleases you,
1000　Acknowledge our friendship
　　　By granting me a request."
　　　And the lord replied, "I promise you
　　　Anything that you ask
1004　Even if it is all my land."
　　　　　"Sir," he said, "many thanks.
　　　I ask that you give this young woman
　　　To my sister to protect during the night
1008　And then return her in the morning
　　　To the knight who brought her.
　　　Milord Gawain asked this of me
　　　So that she'd be outside his guard tonight."
1012　The knight stared at the squire fiercely
　　　And then said, "This shall not be done!
　　　More than five hundred thousand curses!
　　　I have followed her to many courts.
1016　I committed this aggression
　　　Before the king at his table—
　　　Many knights observed this just a little while ago.
　　　And someone other than I should guard her tonight?
1020　I will never grant this to you,
　　　Not as long as I am alive."
　　　The lord had very good manners,
　　　And he begged very courteously
1024　That the knight give her over without ill will.
　　　The lady then also begged him,
　　　And all the nobles in the castle,
　　　To hand her over so that all would be well.
1028　But he replied: "It's of no use.
　　　I will not do this for anyone."
　　　The squire said, "That's that!
　　　If my request is not met,
1032　Then I am the one who will
　　　Go back to my lord Gawain
　　　And tell him that I was not able
　　　To fulfill his request.

1036 Il est plus bel que je li die,
     Quant jou en fin faire le dui,   [8ra]
     Et que je aille ariere a lui
     Por prendre o lui et bien et mal
1040 Qu'il me tenist por desloial."
         Quant li sires ot et entent
     Que cil adecertes l'enprent
     Et qu'il s'en veut aler ariere:
1044 "Amis," fait il, "se par proiiere
     N'en puet estre vostre bon fait,
     J'en ferai ançois un sorfait
     K'u mais isciés de ce castel.
1048 Amis," fait il, "ce est plus bel
     Que la me bailliés par amor,
     Si i arés gregneur honor,
     K'el vous soit par force tolue;
1052 Que ja ne vous sera rendue,
     Se on le vous taut par meslee,
     Et s'el m'est par amors livree
     En pais le rarés le matin."
1056 Cil set tres bien, ce est la fin,
     Que por droit nient s'en defforce
     Que rendre li estuet a force,
     Si qu'il n'en puet passer par el.
1060 "Sire," fait il, "en vostre ostel
     Me herbegai par bone foi.
     Or entreprendés trop vers moi,
     Qui dites que ja m'ert tolue,
1064 Ne ja ne me sera rendue,
     La pucele que je tant aim.
     De traïson i a un rain;
     Nus ne vous en porroit desfendre."
1068 "Amis, je vous ferai entendre,"
     Fait li sire, "qu'estre l'estuet
     Et qu'autrement estre ne puet,
     Se vous a raison entendés.
1072 La pucele que vous portés
     N'est pas vostre, ains l'avés toloite:
     Dont est raisons et fine et droite   [8rb]
     Que ne doit pas o vous coucier,

1036   It is better that I tell him,
Since I am finally obliged to do it,
And that I go back to him
To share good or bad fortune with him
1040   Than that he think me disloyal."
When the lord had heard that
The squire was without doubt undertaking this
And that he wanted to go back there,
1044   He said to him: "Friend, if by asking,
It is not possible to fulfill your wish,
Then I will use force today
Rather than have you leave the castle."
1048   "Friend," he said to the knight, "it is better
That you give in to me out of love,
Thus receiving great honor,
Than that she be carried off by force.
1052   If she is taken in battle,
She won't be returned to you.
But if she is given over freely,
You will have her peacefully in the morning."
1056   The knight knew very well that talk was over,
That it was no use to protest,
And that he had to hand her over,
And that there was no other way to proceed.
1060   "Sir," he said, "under your care
I lodged myself here in good faith.
Now you've gone too far against me
When you say that the young woman
1064   Whom I love so much will be taken
From me and not be returned.
There is something of treason here,
For which there can be no defense."
1068   "Friend, I will have you understand,"
Said the lord, "that this is the way it will be
And that it cannot be otherwise,
If you listen to reason.
1072   The young woman you have with you
Is not yours, for you have abducted her.
Thus it is reasonable, proper, and just
That she not be obligated to sleep with you.

1076   K'il a la hors un chevalier,
       Qui gist anuit a la capele
       Et vous suit por la damoisele,
       Si dist ce qu'il se conbatra
1080   Et que demain desraisnera
       Ke a tort en estes saisi.
       Et s'il le puet prover isi,
       Dont ariiés vous a grant tort
1084   De li ne joie ne deport.
       A grant tort ariiés eüe
       Joie ne soulas de sa drue,
       S'il le puet isi desraisnier."
1088   "Sire," ce dist le chevalier,
       "Il n'est pas par son dit prové;
       Bien m'eüst ataint et trouvé
       Ains que çaiens fusce venu,
1092   S'il i eüst son preu veü,
       Car j'esroie moult belement,
       Et le ceval n'estoit pas lent
       Sor quoi il m'aloit porsivant."
1096   "De droit nient m'alés plaidant,"
       Fait li sire, "ce est l'estrox;
       Je le prendrai ja voiant vox,
       U el m'ert par amors livree."
1100   Cil set moult bien que par meslee
       Ne la puet il mie desfendre,
       Si la veut mix par amors rendre
       K'estre laidis et perdre la.
1104   "Sire," fait il, "quant isi va
       Que rendre le m'estuet en fin,
       Quant je la rarai le matin,
       Jel souferrai a quel que paine."
1108   La dame le prent, si l'en mainne
       En sa canbre qui moult ert bele,
       Entre li et la damoisele,
       Et mangierent moult liement.   [8va]
1112   Li sires o toute sa jent
       Mangierent en la sale tuit,
       A grant joie et a grant deduit,
       Fors seulement le chevalier:

1076	There is a knight outside this castle
	Who is spending the night at the chapel
	And who is pursuing you on behalf of the maiden.
	He says that he will fight you
1080	And that tomorrow he will prove
	That her kidnapping was a crime.
	And if he is able to prove this,
	It would be very wrong
1084	For you to have sport or joy with her.
	You would have committed a great crime
	To have joy or solace in his friend,
	If he can prove his case this way."
1088	"Sir," the knight replied,
	"Saying it is not proving it.
	He could have easily caught up with me
	Before I came inside the castle
1092	If he had seen profit in it,
	For I travelled at an easy pace,
	And the horse with which he followed me
	Was not at all slow."
1096	"Your words are of no use,"
	Said the lord, "it is decided.
	I will take her now, right before your eyes,
	If she is not handed over freely."
1100	The knight knew very well that in battle
	He could never defend her.
	It was better to hand her over freely
	Than to be wounded and lose her.
1104	"Sir," he said, "if it must be,
	If, in the end, it's necessary to hand her over,
	Since I will receive her back in the morning,
	I will endure it grudgingly."
1108	The lady took her and led her
	Into her room, which was very beautiful.
	She and the young woman entered
	And ate there very happily.
1112	The lord and all his people
	Ate together in the hall
	With much good cheer and pleasure—
	All except for the proud knight.

1116   A celui desplaist le mangier
       Quant il n'i voit sa damoisele.
       Par le vile va la novele
       Ke Gavains estoit herbegiés,
1120   Puis que li solax ert couciés,
       La hors en l'Atre Perelox.
       Moult par en furent angousçox
       Clerc et borgois et chevalier;
1124   Tout le pule cort au mostier
       Priier Diu qu'il le gart de mort;
       La oïsciés un duel si fort
       Qu'il ne porroit estre conté.
1128   Li auquant sont as murs monté
       Por escouter que ce sera
       Et conment il esploitera.
           Mesire Gavains est assis
1132   Sor un tonbel de mabre bis,
       Entre le mur et le cancel.
       Tant par fu rice le tonbel
       Que je n'en os dire le taille,
1136   Car je dout moult que je n'i faille
       A deviser l'entailleüre,
       Por çou du deviser n'ai cure.
       Ne s'i fu pas sis longement,
1140   Que desous lui esmouvoir sent
       Contremont et sordre la lame.
       Mervelliés fu quant n'i vit ame
       Qui i abit ne tant ne quant;
1144   Et la lame se leva tant
       Que les piéz li ostent de tere;
       Il va un autre siege querre,
       Car cheli ne li gree pas.
1148   N'ot pas alé seul quatre pas   [8vb]
       Que le tonbel fu tout overt,
       Et qu'il i vit tout en apert
       Une damoisele gisant.
1152   Et el se lieve en son seant
       Tout voiant monsegnor Gavain,
       Et il leva sa destre main
       Por segnier son cief et son vis;

1116 The meal no longer pleased him
When he didn't see the young woman there.
The news spread throughout the town
That Gawain was about to spend the night
1120 (Since the sun had already gone down)
Outside in the Perilous Cemetery.
There was much anxiety
Among clerks and tradesmen and knights.
1124 Everyone ran to the church
To pray to God to protect him from death.
You could hear there more sorrow
Than can possibly be described.
1128 Some people climbed up on the castle walls
To listen to what would happen
And how Gawain would behave in battle.
Milord Gawain was seated
1132 On a tombstone of dark grey marble
Between the wall and the door of the church.
The tombstone was so richly carved
That I can't describe
1136 All the details.
I won't even dare try,
For I would undoubtedly fail.
He hadn't been sitting long
1140 When he felt the tombstone moving
Beneath him and pushing up.
He was very surprised,
For he couldn't see anyone around.
1144 The stone moved so much
That his feet left the earth.
He went to seek another seat,
For this one didn't agree with him.
1148 He hadn't gone four steps
When the tomb opened up completely,
And he saw a young woman
Laid out in full view.
1152 And she sat up
As Sir Gawain looked on.
He raised his right hand
To make the sign of the cross.

1156   Et nequedent, a son avis,
        Des l'ore primes qu'il fu né,
        Et qu'il sot counoistre biauté,
        N'ot il si tres bele veüe.
1160   Et fu moult ricement vestue,
        Mi partie de dous samis
        Qu'il en fu auques esbahis:
        L'une en fu vert, l'autre vermel.
1164   "Gavains," fait el, "moult me mervel
        Se vous avés paour de moi."
        "Damoisele," fait il, "je voi
        Çou que jou onques mais ne vi.
1168   Se un peu en sui esbahi,
        Il ne fait mie a mervellier:
        Il n'a si hardi cevalier
        El roiame le roi Artur
1172   Qui fust mie bien aseür,
        S'il vous eüst trouvé isi."
        "Sire," fait ele, "je vous di
        Que je sui cose de par Dé,
1176   Et Dix vous a ci amené
        Por jeter moi hors de prison.
        Je sai moult bien, se par vous non,
        N'iscisce ja mais a nul jor
1180   D'ire et de paine et de dolor,
        Mais j'en istrai anuit par vox."
        "Bele, de l'Atre Perillox
        Me dites," fait il, tout le voir,
1184   Car j'ai grant talent de savoir
        De cest non coument il l'ot primes;   [9ra]
        Si veul savoir de vous meïsmes
        Des quant et por quoi et coument
1188   Vous estes ci si soutiument."
            Ele respont: "Sire, mon pere
        Prist fenme aprés la mort ma mere
        Qui moult fu de lui au desus;
1192   Moult ert bele, mais j'ere plus,
        Si ot de moi moult grant envie.
        Par caraude et par sorcerie
        Et par traïson engigna:

1156　And yet, in his opinion,
　　　Never since the day he was born
　　　And had learned to recognize beauty,
　　　Had he seen anyone so beautiful.
1160　She was richly clothed
　　　In soft silk equally divided
　　　(This one thing surprised him),
　　　For half was green and the other half red.
1164　"Gawain," she said, "I am surprised
　　　That you are frightened of me."
　　　"My dear young woman," he replied, "I see
　　　What I have never seen before.
1168　If I am a little surprised,
　　　You shouldn't marvel:
　　　There is no knight so brave
　　　In all the realm of King Arthur,
1172　Who would be completely self-possessed
　　　If he found you here."
　　　"Sir," she said, "let me assure you
　　　That I am a creature of God
1176　And that God has led you here
　　　To release me from prison.
　　　I know very well, even if you don't,
　　　That I will never be released
1180　From this anger and pain and sorrow
　　　If I am not released by you tonight."
　　　"Beautiful one, tell me all about
　　　The Perilous Cemetery," he said,
1184　"For I am anxious to know
　　　How it got its name
　　　And to know about you—
　　　Since when, and why, and how it is that
1188　You are here in so solitary a place."
　　　　　She replied, "My father
　　　Took as wife, after the death of my mother,
　　　A woman of higher social rank than he.
1192　Beautiful as she was, I was even more so,
　　　And for this reason she was very jealous of me.
　　　By means of magic and witchcraft,
　　　She plotted treacherously.

1196   Sifaitement m'ensorcera
        Que j'en isci fors de mon sens;
        Foliant alai un lonc tans,
        Que jou ne soi que je fasoie.
1200   Seule erroie un jor une voie,
        Si encontrai, ce est la some,
        Un diable en sanlance d'ome.
        A raison me mist erranment:
1204   'Bele,' fait il, 'de cest torment
        Et de la grant enfermeté
        U vous avés lonc tans esté,
        Se vous voliés estre moie,
1208   Encor wi cest jor vous garroie.'
                "J'euc de garir moult grant talent,
        Si li craantai erranment
        A faire del tout son plaiscir,
1212   Et il mist painne a moi garir:
        Ainc puis n'oi touce de ce mal.
        Il me monta sor son ceval,
        Si m'aporta de si que ci.
1216   Des ice tans que je vous di,
        Ai puis esté ensanble o lui.
        Moult ai vescu a grant anui,
        Car trestout son plaisir faisoie
1220   Cascune nuit, et si gisoie
        Cascun jor seule en cest tonbel;
        Et neporquant quanque m'ert bel,   [9rb]
        A son sens et a son pooir
1224   Me faisoit il trestout avoir.
        Tout m'aconplisçoit mes a[viax]:
        De beles robes, de joi[ax],
        Et de viande, a m[on plaisir];
1228   Mais je v[ausisse miex morir]
        Qu'estre [soie, tant le haoie]
        Quan[t cascune nuit le veoie]
        Ve[nir si lait et si hideus].
1232   Por c'[est ci l'Atres Perilleus],
        Que c'ert [ci tox jors son ostel].
        Sire," [dist ele, "or n'i a el]:
        A lui co[mbatre vous cou]vient,

1196   Finally she bewitched me
        So that I lost my senses.
        I went about like a fool for a long time,
        So that I didn't know what I did.
1200   One day I wandered along a road
        And, this is the sum of it,
        I encountered the devil disguised as a man.
        He reasoned with me directly:
1204   'Fair one,' he said, 'you have been
        In this torment and afflicted
        By this infirmity for a long time.
        If you will be mine,
1208   I will cure you this very day.'
            "I had a great desire to be cured,
        So I immediately promised
        To do all he desired,
1212   And he undertook to cure me.
        I never again had an attack of madness.
        He made me get up on his horse
        And he brought me to this spot.
1216   Since this time I tell you about,
        I have been with him.
        This has been much to my sorrow,
        For I have had to do as he wished
1220   Each night, and lie helpless
        Each day alone in this tomb.
        And still he was good to me;
        According to his ability and sense of things
1224   He saw to it that I got everything,
        Anything my heart desired—
        Beautiful dresses, jewels,
        Food—whatever I wanted.
1228   But I would rather be dead
        Than live this way. I hate it
        When each night I see him coming—
        So ugly and so hideous.
1232   For it is here in the Perilous Cemetery
        That he takes his rest every day.
        Sir," she said, "now it has to be.
        You must battle him,

1236   Car je sai [de voir que il vi]ent
       Et qu'il n'est [mie lonc] de ci.
       Or ne soiiés mie esbahi;
       Aiiés en Diu bone esperance.
1240   Si vous avés bone creance,
       Ja mar le douterés de rien.
       La crois vous le conisciés bien,
       Dont je voi le signe lasus;
1244   Et quant vous onques serés plus
       Angouscex de vostre bataille,
       Regardés la sans nule faille,
       Reprenés ileuc vostre alainne,
1248   Et des deux pars de vostre painne
       Serés maintenant alegié.
       Se vous n'avés de moi pitié,
       Biax sire, si l'aiiés por vous;
1252   Car saciés bien tout a estrox
       Qu'il vous ocirra u vous lui,
       Ne ja mais n'ere hors d'anui,
       Si vous anuit ne m'en jetés.
1256   Biax dous sire, or vous atornés,
       Si montés sor vostre ceval,
       Car le traïtre desloial
       N'est pas long demie louee."   [9va]
1260   Et Gavains a sa teste armee,
       Si est u bon ceval monté.
       La pucele au cors acesmé
       De armer se haste et avance:
1264   Son escu li baille et sa lance.
       Estes vous le diable au mur:
       "Or soiés," fait ele, "aseür!"
       Ens est entrés par mi la porte:
1268   "Pute," fait il, "vous estes morte,
       Et vostre lechierres honnis.
       Vilainement ert departis
       A cort terme cest parlement;
1272   Mar vit le vostre acointement."
       Cele respont conme cortoise:
       "Certes," fait ele, "moult me poise
       Que onques fui vostre putain,

1236   For I know for certain that he will come
And that he is not far off.
Now don't be frightened.
Trust in God:

1240   If you have true faith,
You have no reason to worry about anything.
You know very well the power of the cross—
There is one over there.

1244   And if it ever happens
That you are hard-pressed in battle,
Don't fail to look at it.
Catch your breath again in this way,

1248   And your fatigue
Will then be relieved.
If you don't have pity for me,
Dear sir, then have it for your own sake.

1252   Know this for sure: that either
You will kill him or he will kill you.
I will never escape from this distress
Unless you deliver me from it tonight.

1256   Dear sweet sir, now prepare yourself
And mount your horse,
Because the foul traitor
Is but a half league away."

1260   So Gawain put on his helmet
And mounted his good horse.
The young woman hurried to arm
And ready him for battle.

1264   She handed him his lance and shield.
The devil was already at the wall.
"Now," she said, "be confident."
The devil entered in through the gate and said,

1268   "Whore, you're dead,
Along with your disgraceful lover.
This conversation will soon end
With unfortunate consequences.

1272   It was bad luck to have made your acquaintance."
She replied politely,
"Certainly," she said, "it weighs much
On me ever to have been your whore,

1276   Mais vés ci monsegnor Gavain,
        Qui moult est proisié et loé,
        Et j'ai bien ma creance en Dé
        Qu'il li sera anuit aidans,
1280   Si n'ere plus vostre soignans."
            Quant cil sot que ce Gavains fu,
        A mervelle en fu irascu,
        Car bien set que bien est prisiés.
1284   Lors est l'uns vers l'autre eslaisciés
        Tant com ceval porent randir,
        Si se fierent de tel aïr
        Des lances desox les mameles
1288   Qu'anbedex volent en asteles.
        Onques por çou ne s'aresterent:
        Si durement s'entrencontrerent
        Des cevax, des cors, des escus,
1292   K'anbedex sont entrabatus,
        Et ex et les cevax ensanble.
        Gavains de mautalent trestranble,
        Si est tantost en piés saillis,
1296   Et cil ne fu mie esbahis,   [9vb]
        Ains a mis le main a l'espee.
        A tant conmence la meslee;
        Onques hom si dure ne vit.
1300   Moult doute l'uns l'autre petit,
        Au sanlant que cascuns d'ex fait.
        Le deable les saus li vait,
        Sel fiert del brant en l'elme amont,
1304   K'en plusors lius li quasa et ront.
        Gavains fierement le reçoit;
        Bien li paie çou qu'il li doit,
        Car il le fiert tout a bandon:
1308   Cent caus li done en un randon
        Ains que l'assax fust departis.
        Moult par fu grans li fereïs.
            Li diables le fiert del brant,
1312   Amont desor l'elme luisant,
        Que le cercle l'en a rompu;
        Li caus glaçoie sor l'escu,
        Si l'en abat plus d'un quartier.

1276	But you see here Sir Gawain,
	Who is much praised and honored.
	And I have good faith in God
	That he will help me tonight
1280	So that I will no longer be your whore."
	When he heard that this was Gawain,
	He became very angry—it was amazing to behold.
	For he was aware that he had a great reputation.
1284	Then they turned one against the other
	As rapidly as their horses could gallop.
	They hit each other with such violence,
	Striking their lances against their breast-plates,
1288	So that both lances broke into pieces.
	This didn't stop them.
	They clashed so fiercely
	With horses, bodies, and shields
1292	That both of them, as well as their horses,
	Were thrown down to the ground.
	Gawain trembled with anger at his bad luck,
	But jumped up immediately onto his feet.
1296	The devil wasn't disconcerted either,
	But rather grabbed his sword in his hand.
	The fight began all over again;
	Never was a man so fierce in battle to be seen.
1300	Neither doubted the strength of the other,
	Judging from the way they acted.
	The devil used his sword to attack
	The top of Gawain's helmet so fiercely
1304	That it broke in several places.
	Gawain received the blow bravely;
	He paid him back well, just as he deserved,
	For he struck him without reserve.
1308	He gave him a hundred vigorous blows
	Before the fight was over.
	It was a very fierce battle.
	The devil hit him with his sword
1312	On top of his shining helmet,
	So that the band was broken.
	The blow glanced over his shield,
	Lopping off about a quarter of it.

1316   Gavains le fiert du brant d'acier,
       Si durement en l'elme amont,
       Les bones pieres que i sont,
       Esmeraudes, safir, topace,
1320   Abat devant lui en la place:
       N'i remaint ne or ne esmal
       Qu'il n'abate tout contreval.
       Li caus descent desor la hance;
1324   De la brogne qui si ert blance
       A abatu le destre pan.
       Anbedoi sont en grant ahan,
       En grant angousce et en grant paine,
1328   Car cascuns d'ex forment se paine
       De l'autre grever et laidir.
       Li diables ot grant aïr,
       Moult grant prouece et moult grant force:
1332   Gavain recule des qu'el porce,
       A l'entree de la capele.   [10ra]
       "Gavains," ço dist la damoisele,
       "Dont ne creés vous bien en Dé,
1336   Le gloriex de maïsté?
       Vés la le signe de la crois."
       Gavains a entendu la vois
       Et la parole a la mescine;
1340   Sore li cort de tel ravine
       Qu'il la reculé quinze piés.
       Moult par fu le deable iriés
       Quant voit que reüser l'estuet;
1344   Sore li cort a l'ains qu'il puet,
       Se li fait une autre envaïe.
       Desor le hiaume de Pavie
       Le fiert devers la destre part:
1348   De l'elme li abat le quart,
       Et des mailles de l'auberc cent.
       Li caus sor l'espaulle descent,
       Si qu'il l'a en dex lius navré;
1352   Ferant ferant l'en a mené,
       Tant qu'el porce l'a enbatu.
       Gavains tint le brant molu,
       Si se desfent au mix qu'il puet.

1316   Gawain, in return, gave him such a strong blow
On top of his helmet that
All the precious stones there—
Emeralds, sapphires, and topazes—
1320   Were knocked off.
Neither gold nor enamel was left;
He knocked it all to the ground.
The blow descended to his thigh
1324   So that he cut off the right side
Of his coat of mail.
Both were in great suffering,
Hard-pressed and in pain,
1328   For each tried as hard as possible
To do the other great injury and harm.
The devil was very angry,
Full of prowess and very strong.
1332   Gawain retreated to the porch
At the entrance to the chapel.
"Gawain," the young woman said to him,
"Don't you believe firmly in God,
1336   The most glorious Lord?
Look over there at the sign of the cross!"
Gawain heard the voice
And words of the young woman.
1340   He ran toward the devil with such violence
That he forced him back fifteen feet.
The devil became very angry
When he saw that he was losing ground.
1344   He ran toward Gawain, as soon as he could,
To make a new assault.
He hit him on his Pavian helmet
On the right-hand side,
1348   Cutting off a quarter of it and
Tearing off a hundred pieces of his coat of mail.
The blow descended to his shoulder
So that he cut him in two places.
1352   He slashed about with his sword so fiercely
That he forced Gawain back to the porch.
Gawain held the sword slackly
And defended himself as well as he could.

1356   Li diables les saus li muet,
        Si li a fait le tierc asaut;
        Li sans qui des plaies li saut
        L'a moult grevé et afoibli.
1360   Longement se conbat issi
        Et se desfent a quel que paine,
        Por peu qu'a son voloir nel manne
        Li diables qui grant force a,
1364   Ne mais que Gavains s'esforça
        Por la pucele qui ploroit.
        Et neporquant mestier li ot
        Ce qu'il ot adosé l'arvol;
1368   Qu'il ot en la teste et el col
        Et es espaulles mainte plaie.
        La pucele forment s'esmaie,   [10rb]
        Qui si afebloiier le voit:
1372   "Lasse," fait ele, "ce que doit
        Que deable a si grant vertu!
        A! bon chevalier, que fais tu?
        De la crois dont ne te sovient?"
1376   A Gavain sa force revient,
        Sa proece et son hardement:
        Sore li cort moult radement
        Quant il ot la crois regardee.
1380   Tel caup li done de l'espee
        Que a genox l'a abatu;
        De cief en cief li fent l'escu,
        Que les moitiés cieent a terre.
1384   Autre fois l'est alés requerre,
        Car il voit qu'i l'a moult grevé;
        Sor un tonbel l'a raüsé
        Qui ert deriere ses talons.
1388   Li tonbiax ert et grans et lons,
        Si l'a enpaint par de desus.
        Que vous en diroie je plus?
        Si durement par desus ciet
1392   Qu'il n'a pooir qu'il se reliet.
        Au caoir que l'aversier fist,
        Et au grant branle que il prist,
        Est le hiaume en terre ferus,

1356   The devil changed his attack
And began a third assault.
The blood that flowed from the wounds
Gave Gawain trouble and weakened him.

1360   Thus he fought for a long time
And defended himself with difficulty.
He was almost subdued by
The devil, who had great strength,

1364   But for the extra effort Gawain made
On account of the maiden who cried.
Nevertheless, he needed
To lean against the arcade.

1368   He had wounds on the head
And neck and shoulders.
The maiden was frightened
When she saw him weaken:

1372   "Alas!" she said, "is it possible
That the devil has such strength?
Ah, good knight, what are you doing?
Don't you remember the cross?"

1376   Gawain's strength returned,
As well as his bravery and hardiness.
He ran to attack his enemy quickly
Once he had looked upon the cross.

1380   He gave such a blow with his sword
That he knocked the devil to his knees.
From start to finish, his shield had defended him,
Although half of it had been cut to the ground.

1384   He needed to attack again,
For he saw that he had wounded him badly.
He was forced to retreat
To a tomb behind him.

1388   The tomb was large and long,
And Gawain pushed him over it.
What more can I say?
He fell on top of it so hard

1392   That he couldn't get up.
In the course of the devil's fall
And the great blow that he took,
His helmet was forced off onto the ground

1396   Si que li las en sont ronpus,
       Et qu'il vola loins en la place.
       Gavains en voit nue la face,
       Sel fiert du brant en mi le vis;
1400   Par desus les ex en a pris
       La face et demi le menton.
       Puis le refiert tout a bandon,
       Si qu'il en a la teste prise.
1404   Lors s'est la damoisele asise,
       Qui moult a grant peor eüe;
       Puis dist, "Iceste sorvenue
       Soit de Damediu beneoite.   [10va]
1408   Longement ai esté destroite,
       En grant angousce et en grant ire.
       Bien puet trestox li mondes dire
       Que c'est ci le bon chevalier,
1412   Et cil qui tox jors seut aidier
       As damoiseles au besoig."
       Bien ont oï l'estor de loig
       Et les asaus et les cembiax
1416   Cil qui estoient as cretiax;
       Bien sevent que l'un est vencu,
       Mais ne sevent li quex ce fu,
       S'ont de Gavain moult grant paor.
1420   Issi soufrirent dusqu'au jor
       En tel ire et en tel pensé.
       Et il a son cief desarmé,
       Si s'est couciés les la capele
1424   U devant a la damoisele.
           Tantost com il fu ajorné
       Et que le solel fu levé,
       Point li vallés a la capele.
1428   N'ot chevalier ne damoisele
       Ne borgois en tout le castel
       Ne cort aprés le damoisel
       Por monsegnor Gavain veoir,
1432   Si ont grant talent de savoir
       Com il ot la nuit esploitié.
       A grant mervelle furent lié
       Quant sain et sauf l'orent trové,

1396	So that the laces broke
	And it rolled far off from where he was.
	Gawain, seeing his face uncovered,
	Struck a direct hit with his sword.
1400	The blow landed above the eyes
	And cut through the face, splitting the chin.
	He renewed his attack vigorously
	Until he cut off his head.
1404	The young woman, who had been very afraid,
	Spoke from where she was seated:
	"The outcome in this event
	Is due to the Blessed Lady.
1408	I was ravished for a long time,
	To my great sorrow and anger.
	Now all the world can rightfully say
	That this is the *bon chevalier*.
1412	This is the one who knows best
	How to aid damsels in distress."
	All those on the parapets of the castle
	Who had been watching the battle from afar
1416	Had heard the assaults and attacks.
	They knew that only one had been victorious,
	But they didn't know which one.
	They had great fear for Gawain.
1420	Thus they suffered until daylight,
	Plagued by these emotions and thoughts.
	Gawain had taken off his helmet
	And gone to sleep in the chapel,
1424	While the young woman sat in front.
	Right at daybreak,
	Just as soon as the sun had risen,
	All the townspeople ran to the chapel.
1428	There wasn't a knight or maiden
	Or tradesman in all the castle
	Who didn't run out
	To see Sir Gawain,
1432	For they were eager to learn
	How he had fared during the night.
	What a miracle! They were so happy
	To find Gawain safe and sound.

1436   Et a mervelle ont esgardé
       Le diable qui ert ocis;
       Por çou qu'il gastoit le païs
       En ont grant joie demenee.
1440   La nouvele est partout alee
       Que le diable estoit destruit,
       Et si seüscent bien trestuit
       Que l'atre avoit son non perdu.
1444   Li chevaliers levés se fu,   [10vb]
       Si demanda sa damoisele,
       Quant il ot fait metre sa sele
       Et il se fu moult bien armés.
1448   Puis est el grant cemin entrés
       Qui le menra en son païs.
       Et Gavains a a raison mis
       Le damoisel qui a lui vint:
1452   "Biax amis," fait il, "que devint
       La pucele et le chevalier?"
       "Sire," fait il, "sor son destrier
       Estoit montés quant je vinc ça,
1456   Et je sai bien que il s'en va
       Le grant cemin en sa contree.
       Mais bien fu ersoir acievee
       La proiiere que me feïstes,
1460   Car tout issi com vous deïstes
       Le garda ma suer toute nuit,
       Puis le remist en son conduit
       Geui quant il se fu armés."
1464   "Dous amis," fait il, "or pensés
       Et de moi et de mon destrier,
       Que nous eüsçons a mangier,
       Si ert vostre bontés parfaite.
1468   Moult ai anuit male nuit traite,
       Si ne mengai des ier matin."
       Cil est montés sor son roncin,
       Qui est grant et fort et isnel,
1472   Si s'en va poignant au castel.
       Dex de ses vallés apela,
       Pain et vin assés lor bailla,
       A grant planté haste rostis,

1436	They marvelled at the sight
	Of the devil's corpse.
	Because he had ravaged their country,
	They displayed great joy at his defeat.
1440	The news spread quickly
	That the devil had been destroyed.
	They all realized
	That the cemetery had lost its name.
1444	The proud knight got up out of bed
	And asked for the young woman,
	As soon as he had had his horse saddled
	And he was fully armed.
1448	Then he started out on the highway
	That led to his own country.
	Meanwhile, Gawain turned to speak to
	The young man who had come out to him.
1452	"Dear friend," he asked, "what happened
	To the knight and the girl?"
	"Sir," he said, "he had mounted
	His war horse just as I was coming here,
1456	And I am sure that he is now
	Taking the highway to his home.
	But the request that you made of me
	Was completely fulfilled last night,
1460	For just as you requested,
	My sister guarded her all night,
	And he only got her back
	Today after he was armed."
1464	"Dear friend," Gawain replied, "now pay
	Some attention to me and my horse,
	So that we might have something to eat,
	And your generosity will be perfect.
1468	I have been through a bad night,
	And I haven't eaten since yesterday morning."
	The young man mounted his horse,
	A large, powerful, and fast one,
1472	And rode quickly to the castle.
	He called over two servants
	And gave them plenty of bread and wine,
	A big hunk of roasted meat,

1476   Et un pasté de dex pertris;
        Assés lor baila un et el,
        Blans doubliers et hanas et sel,
        Si lor bailla avainne et fain.
1480   Puis revint poignant a Gavain,
        Qui l'atendoit el cimentire.   [11ra]
        De ce n'i a il plus que dire,
        Mais qu'il mangierent liement.
1484   Gavains conmanda erranment
        A metre son frain et sa sele.
        "Sire," ce dist la damoisele,
        "Por Diu et por honor vous pri
1488   Que vous ne me laisciés ici,
        Car moult remanroie esgaree.
        Aler veul en vostre contree
        Ensanle o vous, s'il vous est bel."
1492   "Sire," ce dist le damoisel,
        "Menés ent la pucele et moi,
        Et g'irai por un palefroi,
        S'il vous plaist, que cevaucera;
1496   Car j'ai grant volenté pieça
        D'aler ent en vostre servise."
        "Amis dous, a vostre devise
        Veul jou," fait il, "qu'i soit tot fait."
1500   Et cil por un palefroi vait
        Vistement arriere au castel:
        Onques ne veïstes plus bel
        Ne plus cointement acesmé.
1504   Le palefroi a amené,
        Si est la pucele montee;
        Et Gavains a sa teste armee,
        Si est montés sor son ceval.
1508   Puis oirrent aprés le vassal
        Tout troi ensifaitierement.
        Cevaucié ont bien longement
        En tel guise com je vous di,
1512   Tant que vint aprés miedi.
            Adont virent le chevalier
        Bien loins devant ex cevaucier,
        Mais il l'ont bien recouneü

1476   And a pie made of two partridges.
      He gave them plenty of one thing and another—
      White napkins, cups, and salt—
      And, of course, oats and hay.
1480   Then they returned quickly to Gawain,
      Who awaited him at the cemetery.
      Of this there is no more to say,
      But that they ate happily.
1484   Gawain then quickly called for
      The saddle and harness to be put on his horse.
      "Sir," the young woman said,
      "For God's sake and my honor,
1488   I pray you not to leave me here,
      For this would leave me greatly troubled.
      I want to go to your country
      With you, if you would be so kind."
1492   "Sir," the young man said,
      "Take both me and the young woman
      And I will go get a palfrey,
      If it pleases you, for her to ride on.
1496   For a long time I have had a great desire
      To ride with you and be in your service."
      "Dear friend," Gawain replied,
      "All shall be done just as you wish."
1500   The young man went back quickly
      To the castle for a horse:
      Never have you seen a more beautiful one,
      Nor one so elegantly outfitted.
1504   He led the palfrey out,
      And the young woman mounted it.
      Gawain put on his helmet
      And mounted his own horse.
1508   Then, thus equipped, all three of them
      Rode out after the knight.
      They had been riding a long time
      In just the way I told you
1512   Until it was afternoon.
        Then they saw the knight
      Riding in the distance before them.
      But they easily recognized him

1516   Et au destrier et a l'escu,
        Qui ert d'une color vermel,
        Si reluist contre le solel.   [11rb]
        Si l'ont por çou mix avisé
1520   Qu'il l'avoit deriere jeté,
        Por la pucele qu'il portot.
        La damoisele grant duel ot
        Que Gavains trouva u sarcu;
1524   Plus devint vermelle de fu
        Quant ele sot que c'estoit il:
        "Sire," fait ele, "est çou cil
        A cui vous vous devés conbatre?
1528   Se troi l'asaloient u quatre
        Il aroient ains moult a faire
        Qu'il li peüscent riens forfaire.
        En Bretaigne n'a chevalier
1532   Plus outrecuidié ne plus fier,
        Ne plus douté en son païs;
        Maint bon chevalier a ocis
        Par sorfait et par estoutie.
1536   Si vous poés sans vilonie
        Et sans grant blasme retorner,
        Je vous os bien dire et loer
        Que vous laisciés ceste bataille.
1540   Onques ne feïstes sans faille
        Nule, neïs celi d'ersoir,
        Dont tant vous deüsciés doloir
        Com vous deveriés de cestui.
1544   Tant ai oï parler de lui,
        De sa force et de sa valor,
        Que jou en a moult grant paor."
        Et Gavains dist: "Ja Diu ne place
1548   Que je m'en fuie ensi de place
        Tant com soie ne sains ne vif,
        Ne qu'il ait ensi sans estrif
        La damoisele qu'il en porte."
1552   "Mix vaudroie estre," fait el, "morte,
        Que vous perdisciés devant moi
        Par force nis le petit doi,
        Car de dolor m'avés jetee,   [11va]

1516 By his war horse and shield
   That were of a red color
   And shining brightly in the sun.
   They were able to spot him
1520 Because he had put the shield behind him
   On account of the girl he carried.
   The other woman that Gawain had picked up
   From the coffin became very troubled.
1524 Her face turned red when she
   Realized who this knight was.
   "Sir," she said, "is this the one
   You are planning on fighting?
1528 Even if three or four went against him,
   They would have a hard time
   Doing him any harm.
   In all of Brittany there is no knight
1532 More presumptuous, nor cruel,
   Nor more feared in his country.
   He has killed many a good knight
   Through his pride and excess.
1536 If you can, without villainy
   Or shame, turn back now.
   I dare to speak frankly and counsel you
   To leave off this battle.
1540 Surely you could never have any battle,
   Not even the one last night,
   In which you would have to suffer
   As much as you will have to from this one.
1544 I have heard much talk about him,
   About his strength and his valor,
   So that I have great fear of him."
   And Gawain replied: "So help me God,
1548 I will never flee from this place
   As long as I am alive and kicking,
   Nor will he keep without challenge
   The young woman he has carried off."
1552 "I would rather," she said, "be dead
   Than see you lose through force
   So much as your little finger,
   For you have saved me from misery!

1556 Et je dout tant ceste meslee
   K'onques mais si grant paor n'oi.
   Sire, par le diable soi
   Qui il ert et de sa valor.
1560 Il a dusqu'a none de jor
   La force de trois chevaliers,
   Les plus hardis et les plus fiers
   Que on puist en nul liu trover;
1564 Quant le solel doit decliner,
   Des qu'il est none et en avant,
   Va un petit afebloiant.
   Petit et petit afoiblie
1568 Desi a l'ore de complie,
   Mais tox jors est fors et hardis.
   Ja ne sera si afoiblis,
   Ce saciés vous veraiement,
1572 Que il n'ait force et hardement
   Contre le mellor chevalier
   Que ost vers lui armes baillier.
     Une autre cose vous en di,
1576 Si savés bien si est ensi.
   Vostre mere si fu moult sage
   Auques vous dist de son corage;
   Je sai bien qu'ele fu faee,
1580 Si vous dist vostre destinee,
   Et vous acointa sans mentir
   Quanques vous devoit avenir.
   Moult vous proia que prex fuissiés,
1584 Que ja nul jor ne vesquissiés
   Ne seriiés vencus ne mors
   Par nul home qui tant fust fors,
   Ne mais que vous dist de cestui
1588 Que vous vous gardisciés de lui,
   Car el ne doutoit se lui non.
   Et je vous dirai ja son non,
   Si porrés mix par çou savoir
1592 Si je vous di mencongne u voir.   [11vb]
   Je sai bien qu'ele vous nouma,
   Et si vous dist et devisa
   Qu'il n'avoit si fel chevalier,

1556   I dread this battle so much
       That I have never before had so much fear.
       Sir, I know from the devil himself
       Who this knight is and of his valor.
1560   He has, until nightfall,
       The strength of three knights,
       The strongest and fiercest ones
       That can be found anywhere.
1564   When the sun begins to set,
       Just after the hour of nones,
       A weakening begins.
       Little by little he weakens
1568   Until the hour of compline
       But still remaining strong and hardy.
       He will never be so weakened—
       Know this for sure—
1572   That he doesn't have strength and vigor
       To combat the best knight
       Who dares to do battle against him.
          I'll tell you another thing,
1576   And you know very well that it is so:
       Your mother who was very wise
       Also spoke of his courage.
       I know that she was a fairy
1580   And told you about your destiny.
       She informed you truthfully
       Of things that would happen in the future.
       She begged you to be bold
1584   So that you would never be vanquished—
       Neither defeated nor killed—
       By any man, no matter how strong,
       Except for this one here
1588   Whom you should guard yourself against.
       For she had fear only of him.
       And I will tell you his name,
       So that you can judge more easily
1592   Whether I speak the truth or lie.
       I know that she told you his name
       And that she explained carefully
       That there is no knight so cruel,

1596 Si outrequidié ne si fier,
Ne plus fort en toute Bretaigne:
C'est Escanors de la Montaigne.
Itant vous dist el de cestui
1600 Que s'il vous couvenoit a lui
Conbatre, qu'ele ne savoit,
Ains ert en doute, qui vaintroit."
    "Bele," dist il, "c'est verité;
1604 Ensi com vous l'avés loé
Le me dist ele et devisa.
Mais ja Dix tant ne me herra
Que je m'en voisce arriere issi.
1608 Mix aim estre mors que honi,
Car la mors est tost trespassee,
Mais la honte a longe duree,
Car cascuns le dist et raconte;
1612 Et je ne porroie sans honte,
Ce veés vous bien, retorner.
Tant m'estuet aprés lui aler
Que il m'ocirra u jou lui."
1616 "Moult dout," fait ele, "vostre anui.
Et quant autrement ne puet estre,
Et vous savés ja tout sen estre
Et son errement et sa vie,
1620 Et savés bien qu'il afoiblie
A l'esconsement du soleil,
Se volés croire mon conseil,
Ja a lui ne prendrés meslee
1624 Desi que none soit passee."
    "Bele," fait il, "je vous kerrai:
Aprés none m'i conbatrai,
Si com vous le m'avés loé."
1628 Toute jor ont issi erré,
Tant qu'il vinrent a une haie.   [12ra]
Et cil qui point ne se delaie,
Qui grant pieça l'avoit passee,
1632 Fu entrés en une valee,
Si que Gavains en ot perdue
Une grant piece la veüe,
Et que il ne vit ne ne sot

1596   None so arrogant nor proud,
        None so strong in all of Brittany.
        This is Escanor of the Mountain.
        Finally she told you that
1600   If you meet up with this knight
        In battle, that she didn't know, for
        The outcome was undecided, who would win."
        "Fair one," he replied, "it's the truth.
1604   Just as you have sworn,
        So she explained it to me.
        But God does not hate me so much
        That I would retreat from here.
1608   I prefer death to dishonor,
        Since death is over with quickly;
        But dishonor lasts a long time,
        For everyone repeats the story.
1612   And I cannot turn back,
        You see, without dishonor.
        Thus I must go after him
        So that either he kills me or I kill him."
1616   "I dread very much," she said, "your struggle.
        Since it can't be otherwise,
        Since you now know of his nature
        And of his adventure and his life,
1620   And especially that he weakens
        At the setting of the sun,
        You will want to heed my counsel.
        Now do not engage him in battle
1624   Until it is past nones."
            "Fair one," he said, "I will do so.
        I will battle with him after nones,
        Just as you have advised me."
1628   All day long they travelled
        Until they came to a row of trees.
        And he who certainly wasn't dragging his feet
        Had travelled quite a distance
1632   And entered into a valley,
        So that Gawain had lost sight
        Of him for quite a while
        And he couldn't see or know

1636   Quel part li chevaliers errot.
         Lors se conmença a haster.
    Puis le vit devant lui errer
    Bien loins par mi une canpaigne.
1640   Il esgarda aval la plaigne,
    Si vit devant lui un castel:
    Onques si bien clos, ne si bel,
    Si rice, ne si bien assis,
1644   N'ot mais veü a son avis.
    Lors quida bien de verité,
    A ce que il ert avespré,
    Que li chevaliers qu'il sivoit
1648   U castel se herbegeroit;
    Si vit bien que por nul besoing,
    Tant estoit li chevalier loing,
    Ne l'ataindroit il ains l'ostel.
1652   "Vallet," dist il, "or n'i a el,
    Je voi bien que ce chevalier
    S'ira ja laiens herbegier,
    Et nous conment le porron faire?"
1656   Cil qui ert frans et debonaire
    Li respondi: "Sire, moult bien;
    Mar vous esmaierés de rien
    Tant que je soie sains ne vis.
1660   Cis castiax et tox li païs
    Et ceste grant forest fu moie.
    A une autre suer que j'avoie
    Dounai trestout en mariage
1664   A un chevalier preu et sage,
    Et le païs et la contree
    O ma seur qu'il a espousee.   [12rb]
    Si quit bien que cel chevalier
1668   S'ira ja laiens herbegier,
    Et nous irons ciés un borgois
    Qui est rice et sage et cortois,
    Qui fu hom son pere et le mien,
1672   Si nous herbegera moult bien.
    Car ce ne seroit mie bel
    Que nous alisçons u castel,
    Por nul besoing, prendre l'ostel

1636 Which direction the knight went.
       Then Gawain began to speed up
       Until he saw him travelling ahead
       Quite far away in the middle of a field.
1640 He looked across the plain
       And saw before him a castle.
       Never before had he seen one
       So well-defended, so beautiful,
1644 So wealthy, nor so well-placed.
       Now he thought for sure that,
       Because night was approaching,
       The knight he was pursuing
1648 Would seek hospitality there.
       He saw also that there was no way—
       So far off was the knight—to catch up
       With him before he reached the castle.
1652 "Young man," he said, "now it's a fact,
       I know for sure that this knight
       Will go inside there for lodging.
       And us? what can we do?"
1656 He who was generous and debonair
       Replied: "Sir, we'll do very well.
       You don't have to worry about anything
       As long as I am alive and healthy.
1660 The castle and all the countryside
       And this extensive forest are mine.
       Another sister whom I have
       I gave in marriage to a young knight—
1664 Hardy and wise—and gave as dower
       The countryside and the land
       With my sister whom he married.
       I believe that this knight
1668 Will go inside there to rest
       And we will go look up a merchant,
       Who is wealthy, smart, and polite,
       Who served both me and my father
1672 And who will provide for us well.
       This will certainly be better
       Than going to the castle,
       When there's no need, to spend the night

1676   Aveuc vostre anemi mortel."
            "Va donc," fait il, "sans demorier
        Faire l'ostel aparellier,
        Que delivre et bel le truisons."
1680   Li vaslés fiert des esperons
        Le ronci qui moult tost l'en porte.
        Lors vit entrer par mi la porte
        Le chevalier qu'il vont sivant.
1684   Il va les rues trespassant
        Tant qu'il est venus au segnor.
        "Cil Dix," fait il, "vous doinst honor,
        Biax sire, qui por nous sauver
1688   Se laisça en la crois pener."
        "Amis," fait il, "et Dix vous gart.
        Travellié estes, si est tart,
        Et je vous ferai sans dangier
1692   En ce castel bien herbegier,
        Car bien est tans de prendre ostel."
        "Sire," fait il, "je ne quier el,
        La vostre tres grande merci."
1696   Lors est un chevalier sailli
        Que la damoisele descent;
        Uns escuiers son ceval prent,
        Et doi le courent desarmer.
1700   Or m'estuet del vaslet parler,
        Qui est ciés le bourgois venu,
        Et quant le bourgois la veü
        Moult en a grant joie menee.   [12va]
1704   "Sire," fait il, "vostre jornee
        Est parfaite, çou saciés vous;
        Herbegiés estes a estrox.
        Ja mar proiier vous en ferés;
1708   Demain tout a loisir irés
        Veoir vostre suer u castel."
        "Sire," ce dist le damoisel,
        "Je sui herbegiés voirement,
1712   Mais or montés delivrement
        S'irons encontre un chevalier
        Que j'amain çaiens herbegier;
        Si li faites moult grant honor,

1676   With your mortal enemy."
           "Go then," Gawain said, "quickly,
      And arrange for our lodging,
      So that we will find it ready."
1680   The young man spurred his horse,
      Which carried him quickly to the gate.
      There he saw going through the entrance
      The knight whom they were following.
1684   He crossed through the streets
      Until he came to the lord of the castle.
      "May God," he said, "give you honor,
      Dear sir, He who allowed himself
1688   To hang on the cross for our salvation."
      "Friend," the lord replied, "may God protect you.
      You have travelled far, and it is late.
      And I can safely provide good
1692   Hospitality for you in this castle,
      For it is surely time you took a rest."
      "Sir," he said, "I seek no further.
      Many thanks to you."
1696   Then a knight jumped up
      To help the woman down from the horse.
      A squire took his horse,
      And others ran to disarm the knight.
1700   Now I must talk about the young man
      Who arrived at the home of the merchant.
      When the merchant saw him
      He was very happy.
1704   "Sir," he said, "your journey
      Is finished, this you know.
      Of course you will be given lodging.
      You never have to beg me to do this.
1708   Tomorrow you will go, at your leisure,
      To visit you sister in the castle."
      "Sir," replied the young man,
      "Assuredly I will lodge here.
1712   But now mount your horse quickly
      So that we can go meet a knight
      Whom I bring with me to lodge here.
      Do him great honor,

1716   Que onques son per ne mellor
        Ne fu nés en toute Bretaigne.
        Des les pors dusqu'en Alemainge
        N'est nus si bien enteciés;
1720   Si vous devés faire moult liés
        De çou que vous est avenue
        Si grans joie de sa venue."
                Moult en est li ostes joians.
1724   Tantost apele ses sergans,
        Si lor conmande a atorner
        Les seoirs, le fu, le souper
        Si delivrement et si bien
1728   C'on nel peüst blasmer de rien.
        Puis est montés sor son destrier,
        Qu'il ot grant et fort et legier,
        Si s'en est de la vile isçus.
1732   Et Gavains estoit ja venus
        Desi as portes du castel.
        Mervelles les apele bel
        Li borgois, qui o lui le maine
1736   En la soie maison demaine.
        Ens el palais le fist descendre.
        Il avoit fait tapis estendre
        Et coutes pointes u seoir,
1740   Si i mena Gavain seoir;   [12vb]
        Devant ex ert le fu moult grant.
        A tant acourent li sergant
        Por lui desarmer errament;
1744   Mervelles le sert bonement
        La damoisele o le cief bloi.
        "Or vous soufrés," fait il, "un poi:
        Je n'iere encor pas desarmés."
1748   Lors a son vallet apelé:
                "Amis," fait il, "va tost et cour
        La sus amont en cele tour,
        Et si fai tant par ton porcas
1752   Que cil n'ait joie ne soulas
        De la pucele que il maine.
        Por moie amor i met grant painne
        Que ta suer anuit mais le gart,

1716   For in all of Brittany neither his peer
    Nor his better has ever been born.
    From here to Germany
    You won't find anyone so fine.
1720   You ought to be very happy
    Because of what has happened
    And have great joy at his coming."
        The host was indeed very happy.
1724   He immediately called his servants
    And told them to arrange the seats,
    Start the fire and make dinner,
    So quickly and so well,
1728   That no one could complain about anything.
    Then he mounted his war horse—
    Which was big, strong, yet light-footed—
    And went out of the town.
1732   Meanwhile, Gawain had already arrived
    At the gate of the castle.
    The merchant addressed them politely
    And took them by the hand
1736   And brought them to his home.
    Inside the courtyard he had them dismount.
    He had tapestries and quilted
    Coverings spread out as seats,
1740   And he led Gawain over to them.
    In front of them the fire was roaring.
    The servants came running
    To help him take off his armor.
1744   A young blond woman
    Served amazingly well.
    "Wait a bit, please," said Gawain.
    "I don't yet want to be disarmed."
1748   Then he called over to the young man:
        "My friend," he said, "go quickly
    And run over there to the castle.
    Do what you can so that the knight
1752   Has neither joy nor solace
    From the young woman he leads around.
    For love of me, take pains to see
    That your sister guards her tonight,

1756   Et si di de la moie part
        Que s'il nel veut acreanter
        Que il n'i a fors du monter;
        Car je m'en conbatrai ançois
1760   C'anuit mais le gart sor mon pois."
        Li vallés vistement i cort.
        Alé s'en erent de la cort
        En la salle u il se seoient,
1764   Et quant li chevalier le voient
        Moult par l'ont tout bel apelé.
        Et Escanors l'a regardé,
        Si l'a moult bien recouneü,
1768   Puis dist: "Mal soiés vous venu,
        Sire fol gars mesafaitiés;
        Ja mais nul jor ne serai liés
        Des que de vous vengiés me soie.
1772   Se hors de çaiens vous tenoie,
        Je m'en vengeroie moult bien;
        Ke de m'amie maugré mien
        Ersoir departir me feïstes.
1776   Segnor," dist il, "ainc ne veïstes
        Si fol garçon ne si sorfait."   [13ra]
        Trestout lor a conté le plait,
        Com le soir devant l'ot servi,
1780   Et li sire li respondi:
        "Sire, ja Dix li fix Marie
        Ne vous doinst force ne baillie
        De lui enpirier ne grever."
1784   "Or laisçons," fait il, "çou ester,
        Qu'il morra encor a mes mains."
        Li vallés qui n'ert pas vilains
        Li respondi trestout en pais:
1788   "Sire," fait il, "je n'en puis mais
        Se me haés por cest mesfait."
        Fait il: "Segnor, de cel forfait
        Je m'en met en vo jugement,
1792   Se je fac le conmandement
        Monsegnor Gavain a qui sui,
        Et encor le ferai je wi,
        Que ja por lui ne le lairai.

1756	And for my sake tell the knight
	That if he does not agree to this
	He has no recourse but to remount—
	For I will fight him today
1760	Rather than let him guard her."
	The squire ran quickly over there.
	They had left the courtyard and gone
	Into the hall where they sat.
1764	And when the knights all saw him,
	They greeted him warmly.
	Escanor looked at him
	And recognized him right away.
1768	He said, "May evil come to you,
	You despicable fool!
	Not for one day will I be happy
	Until I have taken my revenge.
1772	If I could get you outside of here,
	I would easily have my revenge,
	Because you forced me to give up
	My *amie* last night.
1776	My lord," he said, "never before
	Have you seen such a foolish, proud boy."
	He told them all about the judgment
	Served up to him the night before.
1780	To this the lord replied:
	"Sir, may Jesus, the son of Mary,
	Never give you the power
	To annoy or harm this young man."
1784	"We'll let it be for now," he said,
	"For he will yet die by my hands."
	The young man, who was not rude,
	Replied quite calmly: "My lord,"
1788	He said, "I can't help it
	If you blame me for this misdeed.
	Lord, for this crime," he continued,
	"I place myself under your judgment:
1792	I was fulfilling the command
	Of Gawain, whom I serve.
	And I will do it again today;
	For his sake, I will not let it go.

1796 Segnor," fait il, "je vous dirai
   Porquoi cest estrif est monté."
   Lors a de cief en cief conté
   Conment il prist devant le roi
1800 La pucele par son derroi,
   Et conment Gavains l'a sivi,
   Et conment il se conbati
   A l'aversier el cimentire;
1804 Onques rien n'i laisça a dire
   Com il l'a suï toute jor.
   Lors mist a raison le segnor:
     "Sire," fait il, "je vous requier
1808 Que se vous m'avés de rien cier
   Que vous un don me creantois."
   "Par foi," fait il, "ce n'est pas drois
   Que je de rien vous escondie.
1812 Non ferai jou ja en ma vie
   De rien que je puisce aramir:
   Bien vous devroie a gré servir,   [13rb]
   Qui me dounastes le castel."
1816 "Sire," ce dist le damoisel,
   Mesire Gavains me proia
   De cele damoisele la
   Que ma suer le gart anuit mais,
1820 Si soit rendue tout en pais
   Le matin a cel chevalier;
   Et je vous veul forment proiier
   Que vous issi le faciés faire."
1824 Lors ne se pot Escanors taire,
   Qui la parole a entendue:
   "Veus me tu," dist il, "de ma drue
   Com ersoir faire departir?
1828 Mix vauroie orendroit morir
   Que ja mais tant com je vis soie
   Soit en garde fors en la moie.
   Sire," dist il, "se vous creés
1832 Ce garçon que vous la veés,
   Vous en arés honte et anui.
   Quant par vostre proiere sui
   Herbegiés en vostre maison,

1796   Sir," he said, "I will explain to you
Why this strife has arisen."
Then he told from start to finish
How, in front of the king, Escanor

1800   Had outrageously snatched up the girl
And how Gawain had followed him
And how Gawain had fought
With the devil at the cemetery.

1804   He told them all about how
Gawain had followed the knight the whole day.
Then he addressed the lord again:
    "Sir," he said, "I beg you,

1808   If you have any esteem for me at all,
That you grant me my request."
"In faith," the lord said, "it is not right
That I should refuse you anything.

1812   I will not fail, during my lifetime,
To do whatever I promise.
I ought to serve you with pleasure,
For you gave me this castle."

1816   "Sir," the young man replied,
"My lord Gawain made a request
Concerning this young woman here:
That my sister guard her tonight,

1820   On condition that she be returned
Peacefully in the morning to this knight.
I want to urge you most strongly
To see that this is accomplished."

1824   Now Escanor, who had heard this speech,
Could keep silent no longer.
"Do you really intend to have
My friend leave me just like last night?

1828   I would rather die right now
Than have her, while I am alive,
Be guarded by anyone other than me.
Sir," he said, "if you believe

1832   This boy whom you see here,
You will have shame and trouble from it.
When by your own request
I am given lodging in your home

1836   Se on m'i faisoit se bien non,
        Il vous seroit a mal torné."
        "Par foi," fait il, "il c'est verité.
        Jou meïsme vous herbegai,
1840   Mais au vallet acreantai
        Que je feroie sa proiiere.
        Or ne sai jou en quel maniere
        Le quel je doie mix laiscier."
1844   "Sire," ce dist le chevalier,
        "Ce est drois et fine raison
        Que vous gardés de traïson,
        Que vous en seriiés retés
1848   Se de rien i ere grevés
        Par vous ne par vostre seü.
        Se g'i avoie mal eü,
        Vilenie ni enconbrier,   [13va]
1852   Vous en ariés reprovier
        A tox les jors de vostre vie."
        Et le sire la li otrie,
        Et li dist qu'il soit aseür
1856   Que, se c'estoit le rois Artur,
        Ne li consentiroit il mie
        Que il li feïst vilenie
        Tant com il fust en son castel.
1860   "Amis," fait il au damoisel,
        "Je ne l'en pus pas dessaiscir,
        S'il nel veut de sen gré soufrir,
        Ne je ne doi por nule perte
1864   Faire traïson si aperte
        Por vous ne por vostre consel."
        "Par foi," fait il, "moult me mervel
        Que vous ne faites tout mon buen,
1868   Soit tors soit drois, ains que le suen;
        Et puis que faire nel volés,
        Li chevaliers est tox armés
        Qui porsuit por la damoisele.
1872   Encor n'osta ne frain ne sele,
        Si est la jus ciés un borgois,
        Si s'en conbatera einçois
        K'anuit mais sor son pois le gart.

1836 And you don't treat me well,
It will turn out badly for you."
"By my faith," he said, "it is true.
I myself offered you lodging.
1840 But to the young man I have promised
That I will fulfill his request.
Now I don't know how to decide
Which one I ought to ignore."
1844 "Sir," the knight replied to this,
"It is only right and reasonable
That you guard yourself from treason
And that you be restrained in this
1848 So that I will not be harmed
Either by you or by your men.
If I encounter evil here,
Or villainy or conflict,
1852 You will be reproached for it
All the days of your life."
And the lord granted him his *amie*
And said that he could rest assured
1856 That, even if it were King Arthur,
He would never allow anyone
To act villainously against him
As long as he was in his castle.
1860 "Friend," he said to the young man,
"I can't force him to give her up
If he won't allow it willingly.
Under no circumstance should I
1864 Commit such an obvious treason,
Not even on your account."
"In faith," he said, "I am very surprised
That you don't want to grant me my wish,
1868 Whether right or wrong, rather than his.
Since you don't want to do it, know
That the knight who is pursuing
This young woman is fully armed.
1872 He has not yet removed harness or saddle;
He is at the home of a merchant,
And he will battle with the knight
Tonight rather than have him guard her.

1876 Et je li di de soie part
     C'orendroit remont si s'atort,
     Car je sera en vostre cort,
     Ce saciés vous tout a estrox,
1880 La bataille par devant vous."
          Lors court por Gavain a l'ostel.
     Li sire dist: "Or n'i a el,
     Escanors, quant Gavains ça vient,
1884 A lui conbatre vous couvient;
     Mais je vous lo c'autrement aille:
     Laide seroit ceste bataille
     Et coustouse, s'ele ert par nuit;
1888 Trop seriés coustox, je cuit,   [13vb]
     Se ne la metés en respit."
     Et li chevalier li ont dit
     Que ce seroit grans vilenie;
1892 Il est plus bel qu'il baut s'amie
     En la garde a la dame wi mais,
     Et le matin le rait en pais.
          La dame meïsme l'en prie,
1896 Et si li creante et otrie
     Que loiaument li gardera,
     Et le matin le ravera.
     Greanté l'a a quel que paine;
1900 La dame le prent, si l'en maine
     En sa canbre dedens la tor,
     Si li a fait moult grant honor
     Conme de boire et de mengier
1904 Et de bel lit a li coucier.
     Li ostes, qui grant joie en a,
     Un de ses vallés apela:
     "Cor," dist il, "si di a Gavain
1908 Qu'il se herbert duqu'a demain,
     Que li chevaliers a livree
     La damoisele sans mellee
     En la garde a la dame wi mais."
1912 Et cil i cort tout demanois,
     Si est ciés le borgois venu;
     Monsegnor Gavain a veü
     Tout prest d'armes, et si devoit

1876 And I counsel him, for his part,
To remount quickly and get ready,
For there will be in your court—
You should know this without a doubt—
1880 A battle right here in front of you."
He ran then where Gawain was lodged.
The lord said, "It must be this way,
Escanor! When Gawain arrives here,
1884 You will have to fight him.
But I would have you do otherwise.
The battle will be ugly
And costly, and will be at night.
1888 I think it will be too costly
If you don't put it off."
And the knights also told him
That this would be a great outrage,
1892 That it would be better to leave
His *amie* under the lady's guard today,
But get her back in peace in the morning.
The lady of the castle begged this of him.
1896 And she promised him and swore
That she would guard her loyally
And give her back in the morning.
Reluctantly, the knight granted her this.
1900 The lady took the young woman and led her
Into her chamber within the tower.
She provided for her, with great honor,
Such things as food and drink
1904 And a good bed to sleep on.
The lord, who was very happy,
Called over one of his squires:
"Run," he said, "and tell Gawain
1908 That he can rest until morning,
That the knight has given up
The young woman, without fighting,
To the protection of my lady."
1912 The squire ran over there quickly
And came to the home of the merchant.
He saw Sir Gawain fully
Armed and ready to go

1916   Aler a la cort orendroit.
Cil li a dit k'i se demort,
Et k'il n'aille pas a la cort,
Mais toute la nuit se repost.

1920   "Amis," dist Gavains, "ains que j'ost
Mes armes, di moi verité,
S'Escanors a acreanté
Le mandement que je li fis."

1924   Et cil li dist: "Jel vous plevis
Qu'il l'a graé a mon segnor: [14ra]
Alee s'en est en la tour
O ma dame, si que jel vi."

1928   Gavains, qui pas ne l'en creï,
Qui mix en veut estre avoiié,
I a son vallet envoiié
Por savoir se c'ert verité

1932   Si conme cil li ot conté.
Li vallés s'en cort a le tor;
La damoisele et sa seror
Trova desor un lit seant,

1936   Puis s'en vint a l'ostel corant,
Si li a dit que c'ert bien voir.
A tant s'ala Gavains seoir,
Si l'ont maintenant desarmé.

1940   En main liu ot le vis hurté,
Si que li sans en ert saillis;
Si en ert un peu enlaidis
Que du sanc que de la suor.

1944   Li sires ot une seror,
Bele et courtoise et debounaire,
A qui il ot un baing fait faire
Por baignier monsegnor Gavain;

1948   Moult par l'ot bien fait et a plain,
Si qu'il ert ja tout apresté,
Si l'ont en la canbre mené,
Si l'ont baignié et costeï.

1952   Moult tres doucement l'a servi
Li suer a l'oste a son pooir,
Et si poés de fi savoir
Que cele qu'il ot amenee

1916   Immediately to the court.
        He told him he could put this off
        And not go to the court,
        But relax instead for the night.
1920   "My friend," said Gawain, "before I take off
        My armor, tell me truthfully
        Whether Escanor consented to
        The demand that I made."
1924   And the squire replied, "I guarantee
        That he granted this to my lord:
        She has gone to the tower
        With my lady—I saw her go."
1928   Gawain, who didn't fully believe it
        And wanted further verification,
        Sent the young man there
        To learn if this were true
1932   As it had been told to him.
        The young man ran to the tower:
        Both the young woman and his sister
        He found sitting on a bed.
1936   Then he ran back to the merchant's house
        And said that it was definitely true.
        Only then did Gawain go to sit down,
        And they now disarmed him.
1940   His face was wounded in many places,
        And the blood was spurting out.
        He was not a pretty sight
        What with the blood and his sweat.
1944   Their host had a sister,
        Beautiful, courteous, and good.
        He ordered her to prepare a bath
        For cleaning up Sir Gawain.
1948   She took care to prepare it well:
        And when it was all ready,
        They led him into the room,
        And they bathed him and dressed his wounds.
1952   The sister of the host, to the best
        Of her ability, served him very gently.
        And if you want to know what happened
        To the woman he had brought with him—

1956   S'est de lui servir moult penee.
        Quant baigniés fut tot a loisir,
        Et il s'en vaut du baing iscir,
        Lors li aporte par francise
1960   Li suer a l'oste une cemise
        Et unes braies de cainsil,
        Plus blances que n'est flors d'avril.   [14rb]
        Quant fu baigniés et atorné,
1964   Dont fu le mengier apresté.
                Lors a on l'iaue demandee.
        A aise les la ceminee
        Est assis mesire Gavain,
1968   Si fist devers sa destre main
        Seoir l'oste o la damoisele
        Qu'il amena de la capele;
        De l'autre part devers sa coste
1972   Fist seoir o la suer son oste
        Son vallet qu'il ainme forment.
        Puis orent moult plenierement
        Pain et vin et car et poison,
1976   Oisiax rostis et venison,
        Et quanques lor vint a plaisir:
        Moult les fist l'ostes bien servir
        A grant joie et a grant deduit.
1980   Moult orent grant planté de fruit.
                Tantost com il orent mengié,
        Por çou qu'il erent travellié,
        Firent les le feu son lit faire.
1984   Je ne vous porroie retraire
        L'onor que li bourgois li fist,
        Que moult durement s'entremist,
        Et cascuns d'ax a son pooir,
1988   De quanques il porent avoir.
        Ensi dormi et reposa.
        Et Escanors s'aparella
        Au matin quant il fu grant jor,
1992   Ke mout li desplaist le sejor.
        Moult li poise que de sa drue
        Avoit la saisine perdue
        Cele nuit et cele devant.

1956   Great effort was made to serve her too.
After Gawain had been bathed in leisure,
And he had gotten up out of the tub,
The sister of the host

1960   Brought him a shirt as a gift
And a pair of linen pants
Whiter than April flowers.
After he was bathed and dressed,

1964   A meal was prepared for him.
       Then the water was called for.
Gawain was seated comfortably
By the fireplace

1968   And on his right side were seated
The host and the woman
Whom he had led from the chapel.
On the other side were placed

1972   The sister of his host
And the squire Gawain held so dear.
Then they had their fill
Of bread and wine, meat and fish,

1976   Roasted birds and venison,
And whatever else they wished for.
The host had them served well
To their great joy and delight.

1980   They all had plenty to eat.
       As soon as they had eaten,
Because they were very tired,
They made up his bed near the fire.

1984   I cannot tell you about all
That the merchant did in his honor,
For it would take too long.
He and all of his servants

1988   Provided them whatever they needed.
Thus Gawain slept and was refreshed.
When it was daylight the next day,
Escanor got ready to leave,

1992   For the stay hadn't pleased him much.
It bothered him greatly that
He had lost hold of his *amie*
That night and the night before.

1996   Vistement l'arma un sergant,
      Si li mist son fran et sa sele;
      Il demanda sa damoisele,
      Et la dame li amena.   [14va]

2000   A Gavain la novela en va
      K'Escanors, qui point ne se targe,
      A ja pendu au col se targe,
      Si est pieça hors de la porte

2004   O la pucele qu'il en porte.
          Quant Gavains l'ot, moult li desplest;
      Vistement saut sus, si se vest,
      Si a ses armes demandees.

2008   Por çou k'el erent trop usees,
      Li a li borgois aporté,
      Ki moult le veut servir a gré,
      Hiaume a visiere de Senlis

2012   Et hauberc de çanbel faitis
      Et cauces blances et treslices:
      Onques ne veïstes si rices.
      Moult fu clere et trencant l'espee

2016   Qui aveuc li fu aportee,
      Et li escus nouiax et frois,
      Et si ert d'un moult rice orfrois
      La guige et toutes les enarmes.

2020   Onques Gavains si rices armes
      N'ot mais veü en son aé.
      Un ceval fort et desree,
      Roide et isnel et lanceïs,

2024   Le mellor de tout le païs,
      Li ont amené en la place.
      Et Gavains dist: "Ja Dix ne place
      Que cest service soit perdu;

2028   Et Dix me doinst force et vertu
      Et pooir qu'en tel liu vous truise
      Ke gueredoner le vous puisce,
      Que moult m'avés fait grant honor."

2032   "Sire," fait il, "je vous honor
      Por mon segnor que je ci voi,
      Et por çou que je quit et croi
      Que prodome estes et vaillant.

1996   A squire armed him quickly,
And he put on the bridle and saddle.
He asked for the young woman,
And the lady led her to him.

2000   The news came to Gawain
That Escanor was making no delay,
Had hung his shield on his neck,
And some time ago had left through the gate

2004   With the young woman on his horse.
       Gawain was displeased at this.
Quickly, he jumped up and got dressed
And asked for his armor.

2008   Because his was so mangled,
The merchant, who was eager to do
All he could to serve Gawain,
Brought him a visored helmet from Senlis,

2012   A hauberk made for jousting,
And leggings of closely woven white mail.
Never before have you seen such riches.
The sword that he brought him

2016   Was clean and sharp,
And the shield was brand new.
The suspenders and all the straps
Were richly embroidered.

2020   Never in his life had Gawain
Seen such elegant armor.
A horse—strong and spirited,
Rapid, light-footed, and eager—

2024   The best in the country,
Was led out to him.
And Gawain said, "May it never please God
That this service be forgotten,

2028   And may God give me the power and grace
And ability so that, if you ever find
Yourself in need, I can protect you,
For you have honored me greatly."

2032   "Sir," he replied, "I honor you
On account of my lord here
And because I believe firmly
That you are a good, brave man.

2036   Je ne vous sai aler offrant,   [14vb]
        Mais prenés çaiens sans dangier
        Quanques onques vous est mestier,
        Car tout vous met en abandon."
2040   "Moult a ci," fait il, "rice don.
        Je ne le vous osaise querre;
        Si ne quit que en nule terre
        Si grant honor mais faite fust
2044   A home k'on ne couneüst,
        Et j'en avoie bon mestier.
        Mais de l'espee et del destrier
        Ne veul je pas, vostre merci:
2048   Je l'ai grant et fort et hardi,
        Espee doree trencant.
        Moult par est le gueredon grant,
        Que je doi encor del sourplus.
2052   Armer m'estuet, qu'il n'i a plus;
        Moult me dout de trop demorer."
        Grant paine ont mis a lui armer
        Li vaslés et les damoiseles;
2056   A tant furent mises les seles,
        Puis ont les cevax amenés.
        Mesire Gavains est montés,
        Que onques estrier n'i requist,
2060   Et li vaslés son escu prist,
        Quant il fu montés, et sa lance.
        Li ostes le sert et avance,
        Qui a la pucele montee
2064   Qu'il orent o ex amenee,
        Si se misent tout a la voie;
        Et li bons ostes les convoie
        Tant que il vinrent dusqu'au bois.
2068   "Sire," dist il, "je m'en revois;
        A Diu soiiés vous conmandés."
        Lors est Gavains u bos entrés
        Tout li cemin k'Escanors oirre,
2072   Et il le recounut en oirre
        U il aloit baisant s'amie.   [15ra]
        Et mesire Gavains li crie,
        Qui consentir ne li veut plus:

2036   I don't know what more I can offer you,
        But don't hesitate to take from inside
        Whatever you have need of,
        For all is at your disposal."
2040   "How generous!" Gawain replied.
        "I wouldn't dare ask you!
        Never before in any land
        Has such honor been paid
2044   To a man people didn't know.
        And I have had good service,
        But I don't want to take the sword
        And war horse, thank you anyway.
2048   I have a large, strong horse
        And a sharp, gilt-edged sword.
        Your gift is so large that
        I will always be in your debt.
2052   I must get armed, for it's high time.
        I am afraid to delay any longer."
        The young man and the women
        Took great pains to arm him;
2056   Then they saddled the horses
        And afterwards led them out.
        Sir Gawain, who needed no stirrup,
        Mounted his horse,
2060   And the young man, once he was
        Mounted, took up his shield and his lance.
        The host came forth and served him:
        He helped the girl mount,
2064   The one they had brought with them,
        And they all started out on the road.
        Their good host rode with them
        Until they came to the woods.
2068   "Sir," he said, "I turn back here.
        I commend you to God."
        Then Gawain entered into the woods,
        Following the path that Escanor had taken,
2072   And he found him en route,
        Where he was kissing his friend.
        Sir Gawain, who would not allow this
        Any longer, cried out to him:

2076   "Vassal," fait il, "metés la jus!
        Trop l'avés longement portee;
        Ja plus ne l'arés sans meslee.
        Trop en avés esté saisi!"
2080   Et Escanors li respondi:
        "N'en blasmés nului se vous non;
        Car, par saint Lasdre d'Avalon,
        Bien m'eüsciés ataint des ier,
2084   Se trop n'est lent vostre destrier,
        Car je n'erroie fors le pas.
        Mais je ne quit ne ne croi pas
        Que ja par vous en soit enprise
2088   Vers moi bataille en nule guise.
        Je ne vous en depri de rien.
        Une cose saciés vous bien:
        Que jou tramis de mon païs
2092   La damoisele o le cler vis
        Toute seule a le cort le roi,
        Puis i alai par grant derroi
        Prendre la voiant maint baron,
2096   Por avoir raisnaule ocoison
        De conbatre moi contre vous."
        Et Gavains dist: "Ce est l'estrox;
        Ja en averés la meslee,
2100   Quant vous tant l'avés desirree."
            La damoisele iree estoit,
        Et li vaslés, por çou qu'il voit
        Que la bataille est si matin.
2104   "Sire," fait il, "en cest cemin
        N'ert pas ceste bataille bel.
        Je sai pres de ci un prael,
        Et une lande bele et grant,
2108   Si seroit moult plus avenant
        K'i alisciés, s'il vous plaisoit,
        Et jel jugeroie par droit   [15rb]
        Faire vostre bataille en pré.
2112   Trop vous seroit a mal torné,
        S'ele estoit ci en ces quarieres,
        En ces tais et en ces raiieres."
            Escanors dist: "C'est verité.

2076   "Vassal," he said, "let her down.
       You have carried her for too long.
       You will no longer keep her without battle.
       You've molested her for too long."

2080   And Escanor replied to him,
       "Don't blame anyone but yourself,
       For, by St. Lazarus of Avallon,
       You could have caught up with me yesterday,

2084   For your war horse is hardly slow,
       And I didn't wander from the path.
       But I don't believe for a minute
       That you have really undertaken

2088   To do battle with me.
       I won't deprive you for anything.
       One thing you know very well—
       That I sent the young woman

2092   With the bright face, completely
       Alone, from my country to the royal court;
       Then I went there to disrupt things
       And retake her in sight of many barons

2096   Simply in order to have occasion
       For fighting against you."
       And Gawain said, "It's decided!
       You will surely have the battle

2100   That you have desired for so long."
         The woman with Gawain was upset,
       As was the squire, for he saw
       That the battle would be too early.

2104   He said, "Sir, this road
       Is not a good place for this fight.
       I know a meadow near here,
       A wide and level area,

2108   And it would be to your advantage
       To go there, if you please.
       I think it will conform more to the rules
       To hold your battle in the meadow.

2112   You would be badly judged
       If the battle were fought here
       In this place full of ruts and mud."
         Escanor said, "This is the truth.

2116   Il n'ert ja par moi destorné,
       Se Gavains veut, que je n'i aille."
       Tox jors demoure la bataille,
       Sin a li vaslés joie grant.
2120   "Amis," font il, "va ore avant,
       Et nous te sivrons dusque la."
       Et cil en une sente entra,
       Si a tant par le bos alé
2124   Qu'il est en une lande entré
       Qui moult estoit et grande et bele.
       Lors descendi la damoisele
       Escanors sor l'onbre des carmes,
2128   Puis estraint entor soi ses armes;
       Et Gavains est aparelliés.
       Lors est l'uns vers l'autre eslaisciés,
       Et se sont se entreferus
2132   Que des espix croiscent les fus,
       Et qu'il volerent en tronçons;
       Ainc ne se murent des arçons.
              Quant Gavains ot sa lance fraite,
2136   Vistement a l'espee traite,
       Sel vait iriement requerre.
       "Gavains," dist il, "ens en ma terre,
       N'est pas coustume ne usage,
2140   S'uns chevaliers par son outrage
       A vers autre bataille prise,
       Ja n'i ara en nule guise
       Espee traite desi la
2144   Que li uns d'ex keüs sera;
       Ains s'entressaient au jouster,
       Et font des lances aporter,
       Et jostent tant, quoi qu'il lor griet,   [15va]
2148   Que li uns d'ex a terre ciet.
              "Ce dient cil de Normendie,
       Que si bele chevalerie
       N'a el siecle que de jouster.
2152   Faisons des lances aporter,
       S'ert plus bele nostre bataille.
       Prions cest vallet qu'il i aille,
       Ki a ronci fort et isnel,

2116   I will not stand in the way,
If Gawain wants me to go there."
The battle was deferred for the day,
To the great joy of the young man.

2120   "Friend," he said, "now go on before us.
And we will follow you there."
So this one entered onto a path
That went through the woods

2124   Until he arrived at a place
That was very open and beautiful.
Then Escanor helped the young woman
Dismount in the shade of some elm trees.

2128   Then he managed to arm himself,
And Gawain got himself ready.
Then they rushed toward one another,
And they clashed so hard

2132   That the handles of their lances broke
So that they flew into pieces.
Yet they each stayed in their saddles.
    Once Gawain had broken his lance,

2136   He quickly took up his sword
And turned angrily to attack.
"Gawain," he said, "in my country
It is not our custom or usage—

2140   If one knight contemptuously
Takes up battle against the other—
That he would ever, under any circumstance,
Experience a sword drawn against him

2144   If one of them had not fallen.
It is necessary to joust
And have lances brought to them,
And to joust, however long and hard,

2148   Until one of them falls to the ground.
    "The Normans say that there is
No more elegant chivalric deed
In all the world than jousting.

2152   Let us have lances brought
So that our battle will be more elegant.
Let us ask this squire, who has
A strong, fast horse,

2156   Vistement arriere au castel,
        Si nous aport un fais de lances."
        "Amis," font il, "car nous avances;
        Mervelles t'en saron bon gré."
2160   Et cil i est moult tost alé,
        Ki moult volentiers se travaille,
        Por çou que il veut la bataille
        Desi a none delaiier.
2164   Et cil s'alerent onbroiier
        Tant que li vallés s'en repaire,
        Qui moult a en soi grant contraire,
        Et qui moult a le cuer dolent.
2168   Et cil s'asisent erranment,
        Cascuns dalés sa damoisele;
        Son escu, son elme et sa sele
        Osta cascuns d'ex por laiscier
2172   Rafrescir soi et son destrier.
              Ensi se demourerent tant
        Que li vaslés revint poignant,
        Ki a sis lances aportees,
2176   Grosses et grandes et quarees,
        Ki moult li fissent grant rancune.
        Mais si tres longe en i ot une,
        Grosse et quarree de quartier,
2180   Qu'il n'avoit si prou chevalier,
        Si grant ne si fort ne si dur,
        El roiame le roi Artur,
        Ja tant ne se penast de poindre,
2184   Qu'il le peçoiast par ajoindre.   [15vb]
              Gavains les lances esgarda:
        D'une cose se porpensa
        Dont tox li mons le doit prisier.
2188   "Va," fait il, "a cel chevalier,
        Si li porte de moie part
        Ces sis lances, et si esgart
        Lex quex trois il en aime plus,
2192   Si m'en raporte le sorplus;
        Car je veul qu'il en ait li cois."
        Et cil par dejouste le bois
        I va poignant par une sente.

2156   To go quickly back to the castle
    And bring us a bunch of lances."
    "Friend," they asked, "do us this favor,
    And we will be very grateful."
2160   The squire was soon on his way;
    He was very glad to do this job
    Because he wanted the battle
    To be delayed until nones.
2164   The two knights went to rest in the shade
    Until the return of the young man,
    He who was in great conflict
    And much grieved in his heart.
2168   They quickly sat down,
    Each one beside his young woman.
    Each of them removed his shield,
    His helmet, and his saddle,
2172   To refresh himself and his horse.
        Thus they dallied until
    The squire returned at a good pace,
    Carrying six lances—
2176   Heavy, long, and well-shaped—
    That gave him much trouble to carry.
    One of them was so very long,
    Heavy and squared in quarters,
2180   That there was not such a hardy knight,
    None so big and strong and powerful
    In all of Arthur's kingdom,
    That, no matter how hard he tried,
2184   Could break it in battle.
        Gawain looked at the lances:
    He thought of something that
    Would make the whole world praise him.
2188   "Go," he said to the squire, "to that knight
    And on my behalf carry to him
    These six lances, and let him choose
    The three that he likes the best
2192   And carry back the rest to me.
    For I want him to have the first choice."
    So the young man took a path
    Along the side of the woods.

2196   Toutes les lances li presente
        De par Gavain en tel maniere
        Que les trois l'en renvoit arriere,
        Et les trois a cois en retiegne.
2200   Il ne veut pas, quoi qu'il aviegne,
        Car bien voit qu'il est pres de none,
        Se Dix la victore l'en done
        Ke par armes vaintre le puisce,
2204   Que cil nule occoison i truisce
        Ne qu'il die pas que ce fust
        Por çou que le cois en eüst
        Des lances, ains veut mix par tant
2208   Que Escanors coisisce avant.
            "Ahi, Gavains," fait Escanors,
        "Trestout ausi conme li ors
        Tox les autres metax sormonte,
2212   N'est il de nul chevalier conte,
        Ki ait bones taces fors vous.
        Moult par devés estre joiox,
        Ki tant avés honor et pris
2216   Que neïs a vos anemis
        En couvient bien par force dire.
        Je meïsme en ai grant ire
        De çou que onques porcaçai
2220   Ceste bataille que jou ai.
        Si nel di jou pas por doutance   [16ra]
        Mais qui destorne et desavance
        Chevalier si bien entecié
2224   S'en doit estre forment irié."
            Des lances les trois grosses prent,
        Et les autres au vallet rent.
        Si li prie forment et dit
2228   Que de soie part li mercit
        Gavain de son rice present,
        Et se ratort delivrement,
        Et mont et relaist sa ventaille,
2232   Et si reviengne a sa bataille.
        Grant cose a en faire l'estuet,
        Car nus d'ax laiscier ne le puet
        Sans blasme, des qu'i l'ont enpris.

2196   On Gawain's behalf, the squire presented
     All the lances in such a manner
     That Escanor kept the three best
     And sent back the other three.

2200   Gawain didn't want, no matter what happened
     (For he saw it was close to nones),
     To win on account of his armor,
     If God did grant him victory.

2204   He didn't want to take the chance
     That he would say that he had won
     Because he had had first choice
     Of arms. Thus it was better

2208   For Escanor to choose first.
       "Ah, Gawain," said Escanor,
     "Just as gold surpasses
     All the other metals,

2212   There is no one counted as a knight
     Who is more distinguished than you.
     You ought to be very happy,
     You who have such honor and esteem,

2216   For even your enemies
     Are forced to speak well of you.
     I am very annoyed at myself
     For having recently sought out

2220   This battle that I now face.
     I do not say this out of fear—
     For whoever engages a knight
     This well-qualified in battle

2224   Ought to be very troubled by it."
       He took the three largest lances
     And left the squire the other three.
     He begged him to express

2228   On his behalf his thanks
     To Gawain for this generous gift.
     He turned around quickly,
     Mounted his horse, let down his visor,

2232   And got ready for battle.
     Necessity is a difficult thing,
     For neither of them could now halt,
     Without blame, what they had undertaken.

2236   Li vallés s'en revint pensis,
        Ki de Gavain grant paour a,
        Et Gavains se reparella.
            Moult furent ambedoi vassal;
2240   Cascuns lait corre le ceval,
        Et se fierent en mi les pis
        Des lances, si que les esclis
        En volent en haut et en loins;
2244   Car il froiscierent dusqu'es poins.
        Puis a cascuns une autre prise,
        Et se ferirent en tel guise,
        Des lances desox les mameles,
2248   Qu'anbedex volent en asteles.
            Au daerain prist Escanors
        Sa grant lance, c'ert ses trasors,
        Et son estoi que il ot fait:
2252   De li quide il entresait,
        Por çou que valoit autres quatre,
        Par sa force Gavain abatre.
        Et Gavains la soie reprent,
2256   Si laiscent corre vistement
        Li uns vers l'autre le destrier.
        Escanors le feri premier,   [16rb]
        Por le longor que sa lance ot,
2260   Mais onques froiscier ne le pot,
        N'il ne pot abatre Gavain,
        Si en fu moult de corox plain.
        Et Gavains se tint si tres bien,
2264   Onques ne desgrea de rien,
        Ains li est volee des poins
        En mi le pré la lance loins,
        Si qu'el caï sor un boison.
2268   Gavains le feri a bandon
        Desous le boucle de l'escu,
        Qu'estroé li a et fendu,
        Si que sa lance peçoia;
2272   Onques de point ne desgrea.
        Vistement ont lor tor repris,
        Et s'entrevienent vis a vis.
            Quant Gavains traite l'espee,

2236 The squire returned heavy-hearted,
Because he feared for Gawain,
And Gawain was preparing for battle.
    Both of them were brave knights;
2240 Each let his horse run
And struck each other so hard
With lances that the splinters
Flew about far and wide,
2244 For they broke off right at the handle.
They each took up another and,
Holding the lances beneath their breasts,
Struck each other in such a way
2248 That both lances flew into pieces.
    For the final pass, Escanor took up
His big lance, his treasure
That he had held in reserve.
2252 He was quite certain,
Because it was equal to four others,
That he could beat Gawain with it.
And Gawain took up his lance,
2256 And they let their horses run fast
The one against the other.
Escanor had the first hit
Because his lance was longer,
2260 But it did not break anything
Nor knock down Gawain,
And because of this he was very angry.
And Gawain held up very well;
2264 He wasn't harmed by anything.
Then Escanor's lance flew from his fist
Far away into the meadow
Until it fell into a bush.
2268 Gawain struck him with vigor
On the boss of the shield,
Making a hole and splitting it
So that his lance pierced it.
2272 Still he was not harmed.
Quickly they turned around
And attacked face to face.
    When Gawain had picked up his sword,

2276   Vistement vint a la meslee,
        Sel fiert par mi le hiame amont;
        Et cil si tres bien li respont
        Que Gavains moult s'en mervella.
2280   Moult par fu dure et moult dura
        La bataille des deus vassax:
        Des escus, des cors, des cevax,
        Se sont mainte fois encontré,
2284   Mais il erent si bien armé,
        Et lor auberc si fort estoient,
        Ke peu mesfaire se pooient.
                A monsegnor Gavain avint,
2288   A une fois que a lui vint
        Por lui grever et asaillir,
        Qu'il le feri par tel aïr,
        Amont sor le hiaume luisant,
2292   Que contreval glaça le brant,
        Si descendi desor l'escu:
        Des qu'en la boucle l'a fendu,
        Si qu'il n'en pot son brant ravoir.   [16va]
2296   Et cil par force et par pooir
        Se parti tantost de Gavain,
        Se li fist voler de la main
        La bone espee que il tint,
2300   Dont a Gavain grant ire avint.
                Se Gavains douta la meslee
        Quant il ot perdue s'espee,
        Nus hom ne s'en doit mervellier.
2304   Il esperone le destrier,
        Par devant Escanor se lance,
        Et saisi vistement la lance
        Qui ert caïe a Escanor.
2308   Il ne le dounast por tout l'or
        Qui soit desi en Antioce.
        Le bon destrier ariere broce,
        Si retorne a loi de hardi,
2312   Por requerre son anemi.
        Endementiers qu'il le requiert,
        Se porpensa se il le fiert
        Sor le hiame u sor l'escu,

2276   Quickly he started fighting
        And hit high on Escanor's helmet;
        He in turn responded so fiercely
        That Gawain was amazed.
2280   The battle between the two knights
        Was fierce and lasted a long time:
        Their shields, bodies, and horses
        Clashed many a time;
2284   But they were so well-armed,
        And their chain mail so strong,
        That they couldn't harm one another.
            It happened to Gawain
2288   That one time he was able
        To press the attack so hard
        And strike Escanor with such force,
        Glancing on top of the helmet,
2292   That his blade slid down
        And descended onto the shield:
        He sliced it through to the boss,
        So that he couldn't retrieve the sword.
2296   Escanor, with a burst of strength and ability,
        Parted so quickly from Gawain
        That he forced the good sword
        Gawain held to fly from his hand,
2300   Which made Gawain very angry.
            If Gawain dreaded the battle
        Now that he had lost his sword,
        No one should be surprised.
2304   He spurred his war horse
        And sprang in front of Escanor
        And quickly seized the lance
        That had been thrown by him.
2308   He wouldn't have parted with it
        For all the gold from here to Antioch.
        He spurred his war horse back
        And turned again fiercely
2312   To attack his enemy.
        During the time this took,
        He thought of this: if he hit him
        Upon his helmet or his shield,

2316   A ce qu'il a si grant vertu,
        Que sa lance peçoiera
        U que des puins li volera,
        Si n'ert ja, conment qu'il en ciee,
2320   Que durement ne l'en mesciee.
        Car a escient set et voit,
        Se sa lance perdue avoit,
        Qu'il ne porroit arme trouver
2324   A desfendre u a prover,
        Dont il peüst faire nul bien.
        Lors se porpense d'une rien,
        Qu'il ne li puet faire nul mal,
2328   S'il ne fiert par mi le ceval.
            Lors esperone le destrier,
        Et cil qui tint le branc d'acier
        La moult fierement atendu.
2332   Gavains a le ceval feru   [16vb]
        A l'encontrer par mi le pis,
        Si que li fers en est saillis
        Par mi le senestre costé.
2336   Lors s'est d'Escanor acosté.
        Au caoir que li cevax fist,
        Par le bort de l'escu le prist,
        Si li a del col erracié,
2340   Si en a son brant fors sacié.
            Moult fu cil iriés quant il voit
        Son ceval mort et lui caoit.
        Moult vistement en piés resaut:
2344   "Gavains," dist il, "por cest asaut
        Ne sui je pas ne mors ne pris,
        Si en estes de vostre pris
        Vers moi durement enpirié.
2348   O moi serés parex a pié,
        Se le brant d'acier ne me faut."
        Gavains set bien se il l'assaut,
        A ce qu'il est et grant et fort,
2352   Ja li ara son ceval mort;
        Mix le veut il requerre a pié,
        Car durement seroit irié
        S'il veoit mort le Gringalet.

2316   They were so very strong
   That his lance would break
   Or fly out from his hands;
   Whichever way it happened,
2320   It would turn out badly for him.
   For certainly he understood well
   That, if he lost this lance,
   He wouldn't be able to find
2324   Another weapon for defense or attack,
   And the outcome would be bad.
   He could think of no way
   That he could do him harm
2328   Unless it was through the horse itself.
      Then he spurred his war horse;
   And the one who held the steel sword
   Waited for him very bravely.
2332   Gawain struck the horse
   In order to hit the breast
   So that the iron sprang out
   Through the left side.
2336   Then he came up alongside Escanor.
   As the horse began to fall,
   He grabbed him by the side of the shield
   And pulled him from the horse's neck
2340   And snatched away his sword.
      Escanor was very angry when he saw
   That his horse had fallen and was dead.
   He quickly got up on his feet:
2344   "Gawain," he said, "because of this attack
   I am neither dead nor captured,
   But your reputation, as I
   See it, has gone down greatly.
2348   You will soon be like me on foot
   If my sword does not fail me."
   Gawain knew that if he attacked him—
   Because he was so huge and strong—
2352   His horse would soon be dead.
   He would rather fight on foot,
   For he would be very angry
   If he saw Gringalet dead.

2356   Poignant s'en vint a son vaslet;
       Tout de son gré est descendu,
       Son ceval li baille et l'escu
       Qu'il ot a Escanor toloit,
2360   Puis revint arriere toute droit
       El pré u Escanors l'atent.
       Et cil plus de demi arpent
       Vait encontre les menus saus.
2364   La veïsciés moult durs assaus
       Menuement reconmencier,
       Et sous les espees d'acier
       Fauser moult souvent les haubers;
2368   Tout devienent vermax les fers,
       Qui plus erent blanc d'une flor.   [17ra]
       La peüsciés moult dur estor
       Entre les dex vassax veoir,
2372   Car saciés de tout son pooir
       Grieve l'uns l'autre et enconbre.
       Li damoisiax qui ert en l'onbre
       Et les puceles font grant duel.
2376   "Lasse," fait cascune, "mon wel
       Seroie jou orendroit morte."
       A mervelle se desconforte
       Cele qu'Escanors amena.
2380   Por le grant paour que ele a
       Caï a la terre pasmee,
       Et quant ele fu relevee,
       Si conmença un duel a faire
2384   Conme de crier et de braire.
       "Lasse," fait ele, "maleüree,
       Se je en estrange contree
       Pert si faitierement ensi
2388   Mon soulas, mon cuer, mon ami,
       Dont i ving jou en mal endroit.
       J'ai oï dire, et si est droit,
       Que de sorfait ne vint nus biens.
2392   Li tors est mon ami et miens;
          "Car il estoit en son païs
       Rices manans et poëstis,
       Et jou de tout bien aaisie.

2356 Quickly he rode over to the young man
And, of his own free will, dismounted;
He handed over his horse and the shield
That he had taken away from Escanor.
2360 Then he went straight back
To the meadow where Escanor waited.
And this one rushed to attack him
From more than half an acre away.
2364 There you could see many fierce attacks
Start up over and over again,
And under the steel swords
The chain mail broke often.
2368 The metal that was once as white
As a flower was now blood red.
There you could see a hard-fought
Battle between the two knights.
2372 Know that each tried his hardest
To hurt and beat the other.
The young man over in the shade
And the young women complained bitterly.
2376 "Alas," each said, "if I had my wish,
I would die on the spot."
The one whom Escanor had been
Leading around was strangely upset,
2380 And because of the great fear she had,
She fainted onto the ground.
And when she had been revived,
She started to make her complaint,
2384 Accompanied by weeping and crying:
"Alas," she said, "sorrow to me
If I, in a foreign land,
Lose in this manner
2388 My solace, my heart, my friend,
With whom I came here for no good!
I have heard said, and it is true,
That nothing good ever came of excess.
2392 Both my friend and I are at fault.
    "Because he was, in his country,
Very rich and powerful,
I led a life full of ease.

2396   Si fui par sorfait envoie
Toute seule a le cort le roi,
Puis vint mes amis aprés moi
Prendre moi, voiant maint baron,
2400   Por avoir raisnable ocoison
De conbatre soi a Gavain.
Il cuidoit estre bien certain,
Se il Gavain vaintre peüst,
2404   Que en tout le siecle n'eüst
Chevalier qui l'osast atendre."
Li dex celi n'est mie mendre   [17rb]
A la pucele o le cief bloi,
2408   Que moult avoit corox en soi,
Que Gavains prist el cimentire:
"Lasse," fait ele, "ne sai que dire,
Se je en tel guise pert ci
2412   Le bon chevalier, le hardi,
Qui m'a jetee de tel painne,
Et qui a tel honor me mainne
Ensamble o lui en sa contree.
2416   Lasse, dolante, et esgaree,
Remandrai ci a grant martyre."
Et li damoisiax par grant ire
Ront ses caviax et crie et brait:
2420   Onques si grant duel ne fu fait
Par seul trois gens com il demainent.
Et li doi chevalier se painent
D'ex ocirre, c'est grant damage.
2424   Mais Gavains a grant avantage,
Por l'escu qui au col li pent;
Et neporquant bien se deffent
Escanors qui nel doute mie,
2428   Par sanblant, vaillant une alie.
      Gavains irïement li vint;
De la bone espee qu'il tint
Desus le hiaume le feri,
2432   Si qu'il li tranca et fendi
Tox les las que les lui el pré
Est le hiaume en terre volé;
Puis le refiert tout derecief.

2396   Out of arrogance, I was sent
       All alone to the court of the king;
       Then my friend followed after me,
       To seize me, in full view of the barons,
2400   In order to have an excuse
       To fight himself with Gawain.
       He was convinced that,
       If he could beat Gawain,
2404   There would be, in all the world,
       No knight who would dare to confront him."
       The second of the two women—
       The blond whom Gawain had taken
2408   From the cemetery—was full
       Of anger and complained no less:
       "Alas," she said, "what is to say
       If I lose in this manner
2412   The brave *bon chevalier*,
       Who saved me from such suffering,
       And who takes me, with such honor,
       With him into his country?
2416   Alas, sorrowing and troubled,
       I await a martyr's death."
       As for the young man, in his anguish
       He tore his hair, cried out, and wept.
2420   Never before has such great sorrow
       Been expressed by only three people.
       Meanwhile, the two knights strained to kill
       Each other. It was a great shame!
2424   But Gawain had a big advantage
       Because of the shield hanging from his neck.
       Nevertheless, Escanor, who seemed
       To fear nothing, fought valiantly
2428   And defended himself well.
           Gawain attacked him fiercely.
       With the good sword that he held,
       He struck him on top of his helmet
2432   So that he split it and burst
       All the laces: the helmet flew off
       Onto the ground in the meadow.
       Then he struck again eagerly;

2436   Cil se deffent a moult grant grief,
        Et neporquant tel coup li done
        Sor le hiaume, que tout l'estone,
        Si que li caus est descendus
2440   Si durement desor l'escu
        Qu'il l'i abati dusqu'au heut.
        Escanors, qui forment se deut,
        Et qui mais ne s'a dont deffendre,   [17va]
2444   Merci li crie et se veut rendre,
        Mais Gavains ne le veut reçoivre,
        Qu'il crient qu'il nel veulle deçoivre,
        Por çou qu'il li ert mescaoit;
2448   Et crient se de lui revenoit
        El desus, que ne l'oceïst,
        Por çou que sa mere li dist
        Que ja ne doutast se lui non.
2452   Ce l'en a mis en soupeçon,
        Et tant le het dedens son cuer
        K'il ne souferroit a nul fuer
        K'il li escapast vif ne sain.
2456   Lors le feri trestout de plain
        A descouvert par mi le vis.
        Par desus les ex en a pris
        Tout le nés et l'une des faces;
2460   Del caup i parurent les traces;
        Des qu'es espaules l'a fendu.
        A cel caup l'a mort abatu.
             Lors i vint le vaslet pognant,
2464   Et cele, grant joie menant,
        Que Gavains o lui amena.
        Et cele grant duel demena
        Qu'Escanors avoit amenee,
2468   Mais que Gavains l'a confortee,
        Ki por li corut eranment.
        Moult par li prie doucement
        Qu'ele l'oublit si se confort:
2472   "Bele," fait it, "se je l'ai mort,
        Ne me doit estre en mal retrait,
        Car ç'a esté par son sorfait,
        Ki vous esmut de sa contree

2436 Escanor had trouble defending himself.
Nevertheless, he struck such a blow
On Gawain's helmet that he was quite stunned;
The blow came down so hard
2440 Onto the shield that the point
Of the blade almost touched him.
Escanor, who was in great distress
And who had no defense,
2444 Cried for mercy and wished to give up.
But Gawain didn't want to accept,
For they cried that he shouldn't be deceived,
Because Escanor was intent on doing him harm.
2448 He believed that, if Escanor got
The upper hand again, he would kill him,
For his mother had said that
He should fear no one else.
2452 It was this that made him suspicious.
Such hatred had he in his heart
That he would not, at any price,
Allow him to escape safe and sound.
2456 Thus he attacked with full force,
His head uncovered and face visible.
The blow hit over the eyes,
Taking off the nose and one of his cheeks,
2460 Even cutting into the neck along the way.
It split him down to the shoulders.
With this blow he was struck dead.
     The squire ran up quickly
2464 Along with the young woman—very joyous—
Whom Gawain had led there with him.
And she whom Escanor had led there
Displayed only great sorrow;
2468 But Gawain went over quickly
In order to comfort her.
Gently he begged her
To forget him and be comforted.
2472 "Fair one," he said, "if I have killed him,
The deed should not bring me reproach;
For it was caused by his pride,
Which brought you from his country

2476   Por porcacier ceste mesllee.
        Mais de çou soiiés toute certe
        Bien vous restoerai la perte,
        Se volés croire mon consel.
2480   De nule rien ne me mervel   [17vb]
        Se vous avés ire et pesance,
        Mais de ce soiiés a fiance
        Que je vous en menrai o moi
2484   A grant joie a la cort le roi,
        Si i arés a grant honor
        A vostre cois dru u segnor,
        Le quel que vous vaurés eslire.
2488   "Sire," dist ele, "n'i a que dire;
        Fait ert vostre conmandement.
        Quant en vostre merci me rent,
        Faites ent tant a cief de tor
2492   Que prou i aie et vous honor."
               Lors s'aparellement de l'errer.
        La damoisele fait monter
        Que Gavains o lui amena
2496   Sor un bon palefroi qu'ele a.
        Gavains monta sor son destrier,
        Et le vaslet, qui ert legier,
        Et qui moult volentiers le fist,
2500   Le damoisele Escanor prist
        De devant lui sor le roncin.
        A tant se mettent au cemin.
        Lors le mena le damoisel
2504   Herbegier au premier castel,
        U il orent ostel moult rice,
        Car li sire n'estoit pas nice,
        Qui d'ex grant joie demena
2508   Por le vaslet quis amena,
        Si rot grant joie de Gavain.
        Le chevalier n'ert pas vilain,
        Ki fist au matin atorner,
2512   Quant il vit qu'il durent monter,
        Un palefroi moult ricement,
        Tout en ert fres l'acesmement,
        Li lorains, li frains, et la sele,

2476 In order to pick this fight.
Rather know for certain,
That the loss will be made up to you,
If you want to take my advice.
2480 It wouldn't surprise me at all
If you are angry and sorrowful,
But be assured about this:
That I will be very happy
2484 To take you with me to the royal court,
And you will be honored there;
You will have friend or husband,
Whichever you wish to choose."
2488 "Sir," she said, "what can I say?
I will do as you command.
I place myself in your hands.
Act in such a way that in the end
2492 I have profit and you honor."
Then they got ready to ride.
Gawain helped the young woman
Whom he had brought with him
2496 Mount the good palfrey that she had.
Gawain got up on his war horse,
And the young man, who was slight,
And who volunteered to do so,
2500 Placed Escanor's companion
Before him on his horse.
Thus they started out on the road.
The young man led them to the nearest
2504 Castle to rest for the night,
Where they found luxurious lodging,
For its lord was no fool:
He was very happy to see them
2508 Because of the squire leading them
And especially because of Gawain.
This knight was no dolt:
When morning began to break
2512 And he saw that they were ready to mount,
He prepared for them a valuable palfrey—
All freshly ornamented were
Reins, harness, and saddle.

2516   Sel dona a la damoisele
      Que cil portoit sor le roncin.   [18ra]
      A tant se mettent au cemin.
          Or oirre moult Gavains plus bel,
2520   Qu'o lui porte le damoisel
      Son escu, son elme, et sa lance.
      Gavains, qui de l'errer s'avance,
      Tant crut et hasta sa jornee
2524   Qu'il aproca de sa contree.
      Une gaudine aprés un bruel
      Trespassa, tant que de Carduel
      A set petites liues vint.
2528   Une aventure li avint
      Ileuc, que je ne doi pas taire:
      Car il oï crier et braire
      Une pucele a grant besoing,
2532   Et ert en la forest si loing
      K'a grant paine en oï le cri.
      "Vaslet," fait il, "as tu oï
      Que j'ai oï?" Et cil respont,
2536   Et les damoiseles si font,
      Qu'eles l'ont pieça entendu.
      Et Gavains a lors respondu:
          "Par foi," fait il, "je ne lairoie,
2540   Por rien el monde que je voie,
      Que je n'aille a li por savoir
      Quele ocoison el puet avoir
      De plourer qui si se demente,
2544   Et je quit bien que ceste sente
      Me menra trestout droit a li.
      Vallet, et tu m'atendes ci,
      Entre toi et ces damoiseles,
2548   Tant que je sace ces noveles,
      Por quoi ele est en tel esmai.
      Et quant je le voir en sarai
      Je revenrai ici tout droit,
2552   Et saces que c'ert orendroit,
      S'autre ocoison ne me detient.
      Biax amis, et se ce avient   [18rb]
      Que je tele aventure truisse

2516   This he gave to the young woman
        Whom the young man had carried on his horse.
        Then they set out on the road.
           Now Gawain travelled in greater comfort,

2520   For the young man carried
        His shield, his helmet, and his lance.
        Gawain, who pressed ahead,
        Moved so quickly that

2524   He soon approached his own country.
        After some brushwood, he passed through
        A forest, until he came within
        Seven leagues of Carlisle.

2528   Something happened there that
        I cannot pass over silently.
        He heard—crying and weeping—
        A maiden in distress.

2532   She was so far into the forest
        That he could barely hear her cry.
        "Young man," he said, "did you hear
        What I heard?" And he, along with

2536   The young women, replied that they
        Had heard it for some time.
        And Gawain said then to them:
           "By my faith, I can't leave this,

2540   Not for anything in the world;
        I have to go find out
        What reason she could have
        For crying—she who laments so.

2544   I know quite well that this path
        Will lead me straight to her.
        Young man, wait for me here,
        You and the young women,

2548   While I go for information about
        Why she is in such distress.
        As soon as I have found out,
        I will come straight back.

2552   This I will do without delay
        As long as nothing else detains me.
        And, dear friend, if it should happen
        That I find such an adventure

2556 Que bien tost revenir ne puisse,
     Trestout ce grant cemin tenras,
     Droit a Carduel, et si diras
     A la roïne de par moi
2560 Que ces puceles li envoi.
     Et si li di de moie part
     Que por le moie amor les gart,
     Et bel les apiaut et honort
2564 Tant que je venrai a la cort.
     Et s'el te demande nouveles
     Ne te toi, ne des damoiseles,
     Qui ele sont, bien porras dire."
2568 "Volentiers," fait li vaslés, "sire;
     Ja de mot menti ne l'en ert."
     Et Gavains des esperons fiert
     Le Gringalet cele part droit
2572 U la pucele oïe avoit.
           Quant il ot une piece alé
     Et il ot un tertre avalé,
     Si a la pucele veüe.
2576 De la robe qu'ele ot vestue,
     Ki tant ert avenant et bele,
     De son lorain et de sa sele,
     Del palefroi qui si ert rice,
2580 Si com le conte le m'afice,
     Ki plus ert blanc que nule flor,
     De son frain et de son ator,
     Ki trestout vauroit deviser
2584 Et bien i vauroit aviser,
     N'a si bon clerc dusqu'a Paris,
     Ja tant n'i metroit son avis,
     K'il en deïst por nule painne
2588 Tout le voir en une semainne,
     K'il n'i trespassast quoi que soit.
     Mesire Gavains tres bien voit
     Que nus hom ne li faisoit mal.   [18va]
2592 Il esperone le ceval,
     Si est venus tout droit a li:
     "Cil Dix," fait il, "qui ne menti,
     Bele, vous doinst joie et honor.

2556 That I am not able to return quickly,
   Then lead everyone straight ahead
   On the highway to Carlisle and say
   To the queen, on my behalf,
2560 That I send her these young women.
   And ask her on my behalf
   If she will guard them, for love of me,
   And welcome them and honor them
2564 Until I come to the court.
   And if she asks for information
   About you or the young women—
   Who they are—you're free to tell her."
2568 "Gladly, sir," said the young man,
   "I will speak only the truth."
   Gawain spurred his horse Gringalet
   To gallop straight to where
2572 He had heard the maiden's cry.
     When he had gone a little way
   And had descended a hill,
   He saw the young woman.
2576 Of the robe she wore,
   So becoming and beautiful,
   Of the harness and saddle
   Of her palfrey that was so elegant
2580 (My story tells me that
   It was whiter than any flower),
   Of the bridle and of her attire,
   There is no clerk from here to Paris
2584 Who would want to describe it all
   And take account of everything.
   No matter how hard he might try,
   There's none who could, without great effort,
2588 Tell everything, even if he had a week,
   Without leaving out something.
   Sir Gawain saw clearly that
   No one was doing her any harm;
2592 He spurred his horse
   And came up straight in front of her:
   "In the name of God, who never lies,
   Fair one, may He grant you joy and honor.

2596   L'ocoison de vostre dolor,
       Por quoi vous faites dol si grant,
       Vous requier et pri et demant
       Ke me dites, s'il ne vous poise."
2600   Cele qui ert france et cortoise
       Li respont: "Sire, volentiers.
       Sire," fait ele, "uns chevaliers,
       Biax et prox et cortois et sage,
2604   Ki m'amena en cest boscage,
       M'amoit par amors et je lui.
       L'ocoison de mon grant anui
       Vous conterai: jewi matin,
2608   Quant nous alion ce cemin,
       Entre moi et mon ami cier,
       Si oïmes un duel moult fier
       K'une pucele demenot.
2612   Ensi li fist, ensi li plot,
       Que en cel cemin me laisça;
       Le bai de Gascogne eslaisça
       Por aler l'aventure querre.
2616   En ceste piece ci de terre
       Me rouva que je l'atendisse,
       Mais ains que de li departisse,
       Me bailla un sien esprevier,
2620   K'il amoit plus et tenoit cier
       Que rien en ceste siecle vivant.
       Bien savoie qu'il l'amoit tant
       Com il pooit plus amer rien,
2624   Fors seul mon cors; si me dist bien
       Que sor toute rien li gardasse.
       Et jou conme caitive et lasse
       De grant folie m'entremis:
2628   L'esprevier a disner enpris,   [18vb]
       Ki d'oisiax moult petit savoie.
       Endementiers que jel paissoie
       D'un oiselet qu'il avoit pris,
2632   Li espreviers, qui ert assis
       Sor mon puig, si m'est escapés.
       Mes amis en sera dervés
       Quant il venra; si sui traïe,

2596 I ask and pray you to tell me
The reason for your sadness.
Tell me, if you please,
Why you are in such great grief."

2600 She who was courteous and candid
Replied: "Gladly, sir."
And she continued, "A knight, sir,
Handsome and brave, courteous and wise,

2604 Led me into this grove.
He's in love with me and I with him.
I will tell you the reason for
My great sorrow: this morning

2608 As we travelled along this road,
Both my dear friend and I
Heard a terrible scream
Coming from a young girl.

2612 Thus he did as he pleased
And left me on this highway.
He let run his Gascon bay
In order to seek this adventure.

2616 Right here on this very spot
He asked me to wait for him,
But before I parted from him
He gave me one of his sparrow hawks,

2620 One that he loves more and holds dearer
Than anything else living in this world.
I know very well that he loves it
More than he loves anything else,

2624 Except for my body. And he told me
I should guard it against everything.
And I—wretched and unfortunate one!—
Undertook something very foolish.

2628 I, who know little about birds,
Tried to feed the sparrow hawk.
While I was feeding him
A little bird that he had captured,

2632 The sparrow hawk, who was perched
On my finger, escaped from me.
My friend will be out of his mind
When he comes back; I have betrayed him

2636 Par mescaance et par folie.
     "Jel counois tant a orgellox,
     A felon et a estorçox,
     Que je dout que ja mais ne m'aint;
2640 Et je n'ai ki l'oisel reclaint,
     S'uns autres ne s'en entremet."
     Et Gavains li dist et pramet
     Que son esprevier li rendra,
2644 Ne de li ne se partira
     Desi qu'ele en soit resaisie.
     La damoisele l'en mercie,
     Qui de la pramesse a grant joie:
2648 "Sire," fait ele, "Dix vous en cie
     Ke l'esprevier puisciés reprendre;
     Car se vous le me poés rendre,
     Dont m'arés vous toute garie,
2652 N'il n'ert ja mais jor de ma vie
     Que seul del dire ne vous aim."
     "Bailliés moi," fait il, "le reclaim
     S'irai l'esprevier apeler."
2656 Moult s'entremet du reclamer
     L'oisel, qui siet el caisne haut;
     Mais nule cose ne li vaut,
     Car il ne fait sanblant ne ciere.
2660 Il vait avant et puis ariere,
     Mais tout içou ne li vaut rien,
     Et de çou li va auques bien
     Que l'esprevier pas ne s'eslongne,
2664 K'il est ataciés a la longne.
     Quant il voit que rien ne li monte,   [19ra]
     Moult vistement el caisne monte,
     Ne mais qu'il fu ains dearmés.
2668 Quant il fu u caisne montés,
          A tant es vous le chevalier.
     Les armés vit et le destrier,
     Si a demandé qui il sont:
2672 "Au mellor chevalier del mont,"
     Fait la pucele, "et au plus prox:
     Bien les en os aatir tox,
     Fors vous seul, que je n'i met pas."

2636 Through bad luck and folly.
"I know he is so proud,
So cruel, and so brutal
That I fear he will no longer love me.
2640 I have no one to get the bird back,
No one who will undertake this for me."
And Gawain spoke to her and promised
That he would get the sparrow hawk back
2644 And that he would not leave her
Until it was recaptured.
The young woman thanked him
And was very happy with his pledge.
2648 "Sir," she said, "may God help you
To recover the sparrow hawk,
For if you can get it back for me,
You will have rescued me.
2652 There will not be a day in my life
That I don't express my thanks."
"Tell me," he said, "his call
So I can retrieve the sparrow hawk."
2656 He tried hard to recapture
The bird that sat high up in an oak tree.
But nothing worked, for Gawain didn't
Seem familiar or dear to him.
2660 Gawain moved forwards and backwards,
But all counted for nothing.
The only good thing in all this
Was that the sparrow hawk couldn't fly off,
2664 For he was attached to a string.
When Gawain saw that nothing would move it,
He climbed quickly into the tree,
But not without disarming himself first
2668 Before he climbed the oak tree.
Just then the knight returned,
Saw the armor and the war horse,
And asked whom they belonged to.
2672 "To the best knight in the world,"
Said the young woman, "and the most brave:
I venture to compare him to all
I have ever met, except for you."

2676 Conté li a eneslespas
     Com il l'avoit ileuc trouvee,
     Seule, pensive, et esplouree,
     Por la perte de l'esprevier.
2680 Lors li respont le chevalier:
     "Pute," fait il, "vous i mentés.
     N'est pas l'afaire issi alés;
     Moult va autrement la besoigne.
2684 Je sai moult bien com cil s'eslongne,
     Qui sa barate veut couvrir.
     Cuidés me vous por fol tenir,
     Et mencoigne prover a voir?
2688 Je puis a escient savoir,
     Car maintes fois l'ai esprové,
     Ke moult a tost fenme trouvé
     Qu'ele doit dire a son besoing."
2692 Por mon conte que je n'aloing,
     Ne veul lor barate descrire.
     Assés m'en avés oï dire
     En autres lius, si m'en tairai.
2696 Mais li chevaliers sans delai
     Prist le palefroi par le frain,
     Et le ceval a l'autre main
     Que Gavains avoit amené.
2700 Puis est vers celi retorné,
     Et li dist qu'en sa conpaignie
     N'iert el ja mais jor de sa vie: [19rb]
     Ileuc le laira toute seule.
2704 Ja mais nel servira de boule;
     Trop l'en a servi longement,
     N'onques mais si apertement
     Son barat ne seut ne ne vit.
2708 Et mesire Gavains li dit:
          "Sire," dist il, "ne cuidiés mie
     Que jou por vostre vilenie
     Venisce ça; n'onques n'avint;
2712 Onques seulement ne me vint
     En corage ni en porpens.
     Ja n'arai tant perdu de sens
     Que jou tel outrage requiere.

2676 Then she told him immediately
About how he had found her here,
Alone, melancholy, and weeping,
Because of the loss of the sparrow hawk.

2680 To this the knight replied:
"Whore," he said, "you lie about this!
This is not how the affair went;
The distress went very differently.

2684 I see clearly how this one runs off,
He who wants to cover up his treachery.
Do you think I am a fool?
That I'll accept a lie for the truth?

2688 I can know this much for sure,
For many times I have proved it:
A woman is quick to find words
To escape from a tight place."

2692 So that my story not grow too long,
I won't describe women's tricks.
You have heard me speak of them
Elsewhere, so I will keep silent.

2696 But the knight, without delay,
Took up the reins of the palfrey,
As well as, with his other hand,
The horse Gawain had brought there.

2700 Then he returned to the woman,
And he told her she was no longer
His companion, not for another day in his life:
He would abandon her there all alone.

2704 She would no longer serve him with deceit;
She had already done this for too long.
But never before had he so clearly
Known or seen her trickery.

2708 Now Sir Gawain spoke to him:
"Sir," he said, "don't believe
For a minute that I would come
To dishonor you; this would never happen.

2712 No such idea or intention
Ever came to me.
I haven't totally lost my senses
So as to seek to commit such an insult.

2716 Or oiiés de çou ma proiiere:
Ke en prengiés mon escondit,
Et je juerai sans respit,
Quant vous plaira, moult volentiers,
2720 Moi vintisme de chevaliers,
Ke je vostre honte ne quis,
Ne jou parole ne li dis,
Se vous l'aviiés toute oïe,
2724 Dont el fust par vous enhaïe."
Et li chevaliers li a dit:
"Ja n'en prendrai vostre escondit;
Moult pris poi vostre sairement.
2728 Je sai moult bien conment cil ment
Qui de tel barate s'essoigne."
A tant o les cevax s'eslongne,
Si qu'il ne sorent qu'il devint;
2732 Et mesire Gavains revint
A la damoisele au cler vis
Quant il ot l'esprvier repris,
Si la doucement confortee:
2736 "Or ne soiiés mie effree,
Ma damoisele," fait icil
Qui d'autres homes valoit mil
Por amor, honor, et francise.   [19va]
2740 "Çou saciés bien que sans faintise
Avrés mon consel et m'aïe,
Ne ja mais nul jor de ma vie
Ne vous gerpira duqu'a tant
2744 Que ce soit par vostre conmant
Por aventure qui m'aviegne."
"Sire," fait el, "Dix vous maintiegne
Et gart d'autre mesaventure;
2748 Car saciés de ceste aventure
Ai je grant ire et grant dolor,
Car por bien faire et por honor
Vous est issi mesavenu:
2752 Vous n'estiés a moi venu
Fors por moi conforter de m'ire."
"Bele," fait il, "n'i a que dire;
Del desconforter n'i a rien.

2716   Now listen to what I beg of you:
Accept my justification
And I will swear—if you wish,
Immediately and of my own free will,

2720   Before twenty knights, including myself—
That I never sought to shame you,
That I said nothing to her
That you couldn't have overheard,

2724   Nothing that would merit your hatred."
And the knight replied to him:
"I will not accept your explanation;
You take your oath very lightly.

2728   I know too well how this one lies
To escape from such a trick."
And so he went off with the horses
So that they didn't know what happened to him.

2732   And Sir Gawain returned
To the young woman with the pretty face,
After he had recovered the sparrow hawk,
And comforted her gently.

2736   "Now don't be frightened,
Young lady," said he who was worth
A thousand times more than other men
In love, honor, and generosity.

2740   "Know for sure that without hesitation
You will have my counsel and my aid
And that not even one day of my life
Will it be lacking, unless

2744   It be by your command,
Whatever happens to me."
"Sir," she said, "may God protect you
And guard you from any other misadventure.

2748   For you know that I have had
Great upset and sorrow from this one.
You came to do good deeds or earn honor
And have encountered much trouble.

2752   You would not have come to me
Except to comfort me in my distress."
"Fair one," he said, "there's little to say;
It is no use to be distressed.

2756 Une fois mal et autre bien
      Couvient a prodome avenir,
      Ne ja ne li doit souvenir,
      S'il puet autre fois honor faire,
2760 Que por çou s'en doie retraire."
          Quant Gavains ot prises ses armes,
      Qui gisoient desox les carmes,
      D'iluec s'en part, plus ne sejorne,
2764 O la damoisele s'en torne.
      Ne set quel part ne en quel terre
      Aventure veut aler querre,
      Si ne set ne conment ne queles;
2768 Mais volentiers les queïst teles,
      S'il onques faire le peüst,
      Que il l'aventure seüst
      U le chevalier est alé
2772 Ki son ceval en a mené.
      De ce est en moult grant porpens.
      Lors conmença uns si lais tens,
      De noif et de pluie et de gresle,
2776 Ki tout caoient pelle et mesle,   [19vb]
      Tounoille, foudre, et espars,
      Ki caoient de toutes pars,
      Si qu'il ne set que faire puiscent,
2780 Ne de quel part plus pres il truiscent
      Castel ne borc ne herbegage;
      Car seulement un ermitage
      N'a il en toute le forest.
2784 "Sire," dist ele, "si vous plest,
      Je vi orains sor cest cemin,
      Par u je ving jewi matin,
      Pres de ci une crois couverte;
2788 Et se nous poions sans perte
      Desi a le crois parvenir,
      Encor porrions bien garir
      A l'aïe del creator."
2792 "Bele," fait il, "il n'i a tor
      Fors d'aler delivrement."
      A la crois vinrent erranment,
      Si s'i mucierent anbedui.

2756   A little bad and a little good
Come to every good man.
It is not worth remembering.
If he can obtain honor another time,
2760   It is this he ought to recall."
        When Gawain had picked up his armor
That was stretched out under the trees,
Then he left that place, lingering no longer.
2764   And the sparrow-hawk woman left with him.
He didn't know where or in what country,
But he wanted to go seek adventure,
And he didn't know how or what kind.
2768   But he would gladly seek such exploits,
If he could ever do it,
That would let him know
Where the knight had gone
2772   Who had led his horse away.
He had much worry because of this.
Then the weather suddenly turned bad;
Snow and rain and hail,
2776   All fell thick and fast.
Thunder, flashes and bolts of
Lightning fell everywhere,
So that they didn't know what to do.
2780   Nowhere around could they find
Castle, fortress, or lodging.
There wasn't even a hermitage
Anywhere in all of the forest.
2784   "Sir," the woman said, "if you please,
I saw a while ago on this road,
Along which I came this morning,
A covered cross near here;
2788   And if we can without harm
Get as far as the cross,
We will also be protected
Through the help of our Savior."
2792   "Fair one," he said, "there is nothing
To do but to go there quickly."
They came to the cross shortly thereafter,
And they both huddled together there.

2796   Moult i soufrirent grant anui,
        Entre la pucele et Gavain;
        Car toute nuit dusqu'au demain
        Dura cele tormente isi,
2800   Ne nus d'ex d'ileuques n'isi,
        N'il n'i mangierent ne ne burent.
        A la nue terre se jurent,
        N'il n'i orent nule rien plus.
2804   Je ne vous di rien du sorplus,
        Si i orent autre delit,
        Mais itant vous di que lor lit
        Fu moult durs et mesaaisiés.
2808   L'orés, qui n'ert pas acoisiés,
        Lor fist grant mal et grant contraire;
        Et Gavains, qui ne pot plus faire,
        A la pucele de soulas,
2812   Le tint toute nuit en ses bras,   [20ra]
        Si que il jut devers l'oré,
        Et si tint son escu doré
        Detriés son dos por le tormente,
2816   Ki si le destraint et tormente.
        Et si a l'esprevier assis
        Que il avoit u caisne pris
        Amont sor le las de la crois,
2820   Si orent cavé un destois,
        K'il n'i orent autre cousin.
        En tel guise dusqu'au matin
        Soufrirent, et quant il fu jor,
2824   Par le plaisir au creator
        Si fist bel tans et cler et pur.
        Et li niés au bon roi Artur
        Fu forment iriés et pensis;
2828   Moult par se tint a entrepris
        De la pucele qui fain a.
        C'est li tiers jors que ne menja,
        N'il n'en puet prendre nul conroi;
2832   Mais la grant paour et l'effroi
        K'ele a eü du grant orage
        Li taut de mengier le corage,
        Se qu'ele a le fain oubliee.

2796	They both suffered greatly there,
	Both the young woman and Gawain;
	For all night long until the morning
	The storm lasted,
2800	So that they couldn't leave there,
	Nor could they eat or drink.
	They lay down on the bare earth,
	For they didn't have anything else.
2804	I'll say nothing more about whether
	They had other pleasures there.
	But this much I will say: their bed
	Was very hard and uncomfortable.
2808	The storm, which had not let up,
	Made things hard and difficult for them.
	And Gawain, who was not able to do
	Anything more to comfort the girl,
2812	Held her the whole night in his arms,
	So that he lay on the windy side
	And placed his gilded shield
	Over his back against the storm
2816	That harassed and plagued them so.
	And the sparrow hawk that he had
	Recovered from the oak tree sat
	On the cross, tied with a leash.
2820	Thus they were housed in a sort of cave,
	For that was all the comfort they had.
	In this manner they suffered
	Until morning, and when day broke,
2824	Thanks to the grace of God, the weather
	Became beautiful, clear, and bright.
	And the nephew of good King Arthur
	Was very troubled and thoughtful.
2828	He had to do something
	For the young woman who was hungry.
	It was her third day without food,
	And he couldn't offer her anything.
2832	But the great fear and anguish
	Caused by the storm had
	Staved off the desire to eat,
	So that she had forgotten her hunger.

2836   "Bele," fait il, "que vous agree,
Que vous plaist il que nous façons?
Ja consel ne secors n'arons
Por demorer ci en cest bois."

2840   "Sire," fait ele, "a vostre cois;
Je ferai tout vostre plaiscir.
Mais je ne sai le quel coisir,
Le sejorner u le mouvoir;

2844   Car nous n'avons nul estovoir
Par quoi nous puisçons sejorner,
Et tel mal me fera l'esrer
Que je ne sai le quel en prendre."

2848   "Pucele," fait il, "a l'atendre,
Voi jou nostre grant enconbrier."
A tant es vous un cevalier   [20rb]
Qui le cemin venoit vers ex.

2852   Li chevaliers n'ert mie sex,
Qui bien paroit pro et vassal,
Ains faisoit mener un ceval
A un escuier devant lui.

2856   Ensanble le virent andui,
Entre Gavain et la pucele;
Et il wida tantost la sele
Del palefroi quant il les vit.

2860   A soi meïsme l'avoit dit
K'il ont d'aïe grant mestier,
Et si pense que d'ax aidier,
Por çou qu'il sanlent bone gent,

2864   Seroit moult grant afaitement,
Et c'on lor face aucun secors.
Vers eus torna trestout le cors,
A l'ançois que il onques puet;

2868   Et mesire Gavains s'esmuet,
Et la pucele, contre lui,
Si le saluent anbedui.
     Cil bonement les resalue:

2872   "Biax sire, de vostre venue,"
Fait Gavains, "nous ert grans mestiers."
"Dites moi," fait li chevaliers,
"Si vous plaist, conment vous errés,

2836   "Fair one," he said, "what is
       Your pleasure? What should we do?
       I suggest that there is no advantage
       In staying here in this forest."
2840   "Sir," she said, "you choose;
       I'll do whatever you say.
       I don't know how to decide
       Whether to stay or to move on.
2844   For we have no supplies
       That would enable us to stay;
       Yet it is much trouble to move,
       So I don't know which to choose."
2848   "Young lady," he said, "I see
       Greater problems in staying here."
       Just then a knight could be seen
       Who came toward them on the road.
2852   The knight, who seemed prudent and loyal,
       Was by no means alone,
       For he had a horse led
       By a squire riding before him.
2856   They both saw him at the same time,
       Both Gawain and the young woman.
       The knight quickly jumped from the saddle
       Of his horse, when he saw them.
2860   He had said to himself that
       They were in great need of aid,
       And so he thought he would help them,
       For they seemed like noble people,
2864   And it would be a good deed
       To give them some aid.
       He moved toward them
       As quickly as he could;
2868   Sir Gawain and the young woman
       Moved toward him,
       And so they both greeted him.
            He returned their greeting politely.
2872   "Dear sir," Gawain said,
       "Of your arrival we have had great need."
       "Tell me," the knight said,
       "If you please, how you came here,

2876   Ki vous estes et dont venés,
Et u avés anuit geü,
Et s'avés mengié ne beü
Puis qu'entrastes en la forest,
2880   Et si me dites, se vous plest,
U vous avés enpris ceste oirre."
Et Gavains li respont en oirre,
Si li a ensi raconté
2884   Com je vous ai ici conté;
Et cil qui bien fu ensegniés
S'est de la mervelle segniés
Que si lor est mesavenu.   [20va]
2888   "Des que je sui a vous venu,
Et vous m'avés conté vostre estre,
De mix," fait il, "vous en doit estre.
Je vous aiderai se je puis,
2892   Mais un don vous demant et ruis,
Ançois que vous aiiés men don,
Que me dongniés un gueredon
Au jor que je demanderai."
2896   Et Gavains dist: "Jel vous donrai
Volentiers a vostre plaiscir,
Ne mais que jel puisce aramir."
      Cil li a dit: "Ne cuidiés mie
2900   Que je face tel vilonie
Que je don vous demant por rien
Que ne puisciés aramir bien,
Que ce seroit trop grant forfait."
2904   Et Gavains dist: "Don ert il fait
Quant vous issi le demandés."
Et cil dist: "Dont me conmandés
Tout en travers vostre plaisir.
2908   Cel mien ceval poés saisir
Aveuc vostre oex, car jel vous doig.
Bien ai veü vostre besoing,
Dont vous estes moult esmaiiés,
2912   Por çou me plaist que vous l'aiiés;
Et veul que ceste damoisele,
Ki me sanle cortois et bele,
Ait por le besoig que je voi

2876 Who you are and where you come from,
Where you have spent the night,
And if you have eaten or drunk
Since you entered into the forest.
2880 And tell me also, if you please,
Why you chose this route."
And Gawain quickly replied,
And he told everything just as
2884 I have told the story to you.
And the knight, who was well brought up,
Crossed himself in wonder
At the misadventures they had had.
2888 "Because I have come to you
And you have told me all your affairs,
Everything ought to," he said, "get better.
I will help you if I can,
2892 But I have something to ask of you.
Give me your word today
That you will grant me a boon
On the day that I ask you for it."
2896 And Gawain said: "I will gladly
Give you whatever you wish
As long as I am able to arrange it."
The other one replied, "Don't think
2900 That I am such a villain
That I would make a request lightly
Or one that you could not fulfill,
For that would be a great crime."
2904 And Gawain said, "What needs to be done
Will be done when you ask for it."
The knight replied: "Then command me
To do whatever you please.
2908 You may even take my horse
For your use, for I give it to you.
I have certainly noticed your needs,
For you are in a very weakened state;
2912 Thus it pleases me if I can be of aid.
I want this young woman,
Who seems very noble and beautiful,
To have, for I can see she needs it,

2916 De moie part ce palefroi,
   Ensi com il est atornés.
   Il m'ert moult bien gueredonés
   A mon besoig, et en liu mis,
2920 Des que vous le m'avés promis;
   Je ne vous en redout de rien."
   Et Gavains dist: "Vous dites bien;
   Je vous en rent cinc cens mercis.
2924 Ne devés pas estre escondis,   [20vb]
   Quant si bel don m'avés doné,
   K'il ne vous soit gueredoné;
   Se j'en pooie en liu venir,
2928 Vous i porrés bien avenir."
   Fait soi li chevaliers par tans:
   "Et je sai bien que a nul sens
   Ne remanra, se jel demant,
2932 Que je n'aie mon couvenant.
   Mais je requier, s'il ne dessiet,
   A la pucele qui la siet,
   Et vous, que j'en veul moult priier
2936 Que me doigniés cel esprevier
   Que je voi sor cel las seoir,
   En atente de mix avoir:
   Moult me sanleroit le don grant.
2940 Savés por quoi jel vous demant?
   Se je ja mais vous reveoie,
   Et l'esprevier o moi avoie,
   Par çou vous ramenberriiés
2944 K'un guerredon me deveriés:
     "Por çou le vous ai demandé."
   Et Gavains a lors conmandé
   A la pucele que li baut:
2948 "Sire," fait il, "se Dix me saut,
   Se je peüsce autre conroi,
   Pour le grant bien que en vous voi,
   Prendre de vous en nule guise,
2952 G'i eüsce grant paine mise;
   Mais saciés bien que je ne puis."
   Et Gavains dist: "Je ne vous ruis
   Nule riens plus que fait m'avés."

2916 This palfrey as a gift from me,
Completely equipped as it is.
I will be well-rewarded in return,
When and where I need it,

2920 For you have promised it to me.
I have no doubt about this."
And Gawain said, "You speak well;
I thank you five hundred times over.

2924 Nor ought you to be refused,
After you have given me such a gift,
Whatever you might ask from me.
If I am able to get there,

2928 You'll be able to see it happen."
In his turn, the knight replied:
"And I certainly know that nothing
Will keep you from fulfilling,

2932 When I ask for it, this covenant.
May I be so bold as to ask
You and the young woman seated there
For something I want very much:

2936 That you give me this sparrow hawk
That I see sitting there on its leash.
I await a greater boon later.
This would seem to me a great gift.

2940 Do you know why I ask for it?
If I ever meet you again,
And I have the sparrow hawk with me,
Then you will be able to remember

2944 That you owe me my request.
"This is why I have asked for it."
And Gawain thus commanded
The young woman to give it to him.

2948 "Sir," he replied, "so help me God,
If I could offer anything else,
Because I see how virtuous you are,
I would go to the greatest effort

2952 To do so and not take anything in return;
But you may be sure that I'm not able to."
And Gawain said, "I want nothing
More from you than what you have done."

2956   Et cil li dist: "Vous ne savés
Qui je sui, ne ja ne sarés
Desi a tant que vous arés
Pooir de mon guerredon rendre."
2960   Lors fist son escuier descendre,
Conme sages et bien apris;   [21ra]
Et quant il ot d'ex congié pris,
Si est montés sor son roncin.
2964   Ariere trestout le cemin
A par mi la forest tenu,
Ensi com il estoit venu.
            Gavains a pris le palefroi,
2968   U il avoit moult rice agroi,
Conme de lorain et de sele,
Si a montee la pucele,
Et il est u ceval montés.
2972   Puis s'apensa des grans bontés
Ke li chevaliers li a faites.
Par maintes fois les a retraites
Et porpensees en son cuer,
2976   Et si doute que en nul fuer,
Ce l'en a fait moult esmaiier.
Ne l'en puist a son gré paiier,
Ensi conme li est avis.
2980   Et la damoisele au cler vis
Est en grant joie et en grant hait
Del secors que Dix li a fait;
Car moult estoient esmaiié,
2984   Mais or sont il bien avoiié,
De bons cevax bien atorné.
Lors s'en sont ensanle torné,
Et oirrent une voie plaine,
2988   Si com aventure les maine.
En tel guise com je vous di
Oirrent dusqu'aprés miedi,
K'il n'ont ne mengié ne beü;
2992   Lors ont un chevalier veü,
Armé moult bien et moult a droit,
Qui venoit vers ex trestout droit.
Li chevaliers lor dist en haut:

2956 And he replied, "You do not know
Who I am, nor will you know
Until the time you are able
To grant me my request."
2960 Then he had his squire dismount
Like a wise and well-trained man;
And when he had taken his leave,
He mounted his own horse.
2964 He went back down the road
That went through the forest
The same way that he had come.
    Gawain took the reins of the palfrey,
2968 Which was very richly decked out,
Complete with saddle and harness,
And he helped the girl up
And then mounted his own horse.
2972 He thought again of the many gifts
That the knight had given him.
Many times he recalled them
And thought about them in his heart.
2976 And he feared that, not for any price—
And this bothered him greatly—
Would he be able to repay him
The way that he wanted to.
2980 And the pretty young woman
Was very happy and hopeful
Because of this rescue God had granted.
For they had been at their wits' end,
2984 But now they were well-provided for
With this beautifully adorned horse.
So they both turned around
And followed a level road
2988 To wherever chance would lead them.
In this way, just as I have told you,
They travelled until after noon,
And still they hadn't eaten or drunk a thing.
2992 Just then they saw a knight,
Well-armed, well-decked out,
Who was coming straight toward them.
The knight shouted out to them:

2996 "Biax sire," fait il, "Dix vous saut,
Et vostre bele conpaignie."
"Chevalier, Dix vous beneïe,"   [21rb]
Fait Gavains, "et vous doinst honor.
3000 Ensi ai erré toute jor,
Ne sai quel part, par aventure."
Et cil respondi a droiture,
Ançois que il li laist plus dire:
3004 "Dites moi," fait il, "biax dox sire,
Vostre non, s'a plaisir vous vient;
S'il vous plaist, savoir me couvient
Ki vous estes et dont venés:
3008 Vous me sanlés gens esgarés,
Et qu'en cest bos avés geü.
Moult i avés anuit eü,
S'il est issi, mauvais ostel:
3012 N'i eüstes ne pain ne sel,
Vin ne poisçon, ne autre rien.
Je m'en sui aperceüs bien
Que vous peüst mestier avoir.
3016 Se vous eüsciés tout l'avoir
C'onques eut le rice Soudain,
N'eüsciés vous por tout un pain,
Ne un tout seul hanap de vin."
3020 "Vous estes," fait Gavains, "devin;
Ensi nous est il avenu."
Et cil qui ert a ex venu
Li dist: "Frans chevaliers, itex
3024 Ne fu pas ersoir mes ostex;
Ains me vant bien k'une pucele,
La plus cortoise et la plus bele
Ki soit desqu'au porce de Rome,
3028 Et si est fille a si haut home
Tant qu'ele est dame du castel,
Me fist ersoir tout le plus bel
C'onques nul chevalier eüst:
3032 Car nule rien qui me pleüst
Ne me fu desdit ne veé."
"Moult fustes dont mix areé,"
Fait li Gavains, "que je ne fui: [21va]

2996   "Dear sir," he said, "may God save you
         And your beautiful companion."
         "Knight, may God bless you,"
         Replied Gawain, "and give you honor.
3000   I have been travelling all day,
         Nor do I know where by chance I've come."
         And the knight responded quickly
         Before he could say anything more:
3004   "Tell me," he said, "my dear sir,
         Your name, if you please.
         If you will, let me know
         Who you are and where you come from.
3008   You seem like someone troubled
         And who has spent the night in the forest.
         If this is true, you have had
         Poor lodging there last night.
3012   You would not have had bread or salt,
         Wine, fish, or any other thing
         (I know this all too well),
         Nor could you have had a meal.
3016   Even if you had had all
         The wealth of a rich sultan,
         You would not have had a loaf of bread
         Nor a single cup of wine."
3020   "You are," replied Gawain, "a soothsayer.
         Just so did it happen to us."
         And he who had approached them
         Said to them: "Noble knight, such
3024   Has not been my lodging last night.
         Thus I can boast about a girl,
         The most courteous and beautiful
         From here to the gates of Rome,
3028   Daughter of such a noble man
         That she is lady of the castle,
         Who did everything last night better
         Than ever a knight has experienced.
3032   Nothing that could bring pleasure
         Was refused or denied me."
         "You have had everything much better,"
         Said Gawain, "than I had it.

3036 Nous n'eümes ne ier ne wi,
     Entre moi et ceste pucele,
     Qui vausist pas une cenele,
     De rien que on peüst mengier."
3040 "Biax sire," fait le chevalier,
     "Je vous pramet bien et otroi
     Que ains que vous partés de moi,
     Ja mar en serés esmaiiés,
3044 Serés vous moult bien avoiiés
     D'avoir ostel et bel et cointe.
     Je weul moult estre vostre acointe
     Et en vostre conmandement;
3048 Mais or oiiés premierement,
     Ançois que vous aiiés del mien,
     Conment je vinc primes a bien.
          "Biax dox sire, il avint jadis,
3052 Bien a passé cinc ans u sis,
     Quant j'estoie encor jovencel,
     Aprentis d'armes et novel,
     Que je amai une pucele,
3056 La plus cortoise et la plus bele
     Qui soit desi a Carlion.
     Hardi me fist conme lion
     Amors qui en ses las me mist;
3060 Cortois et enprenant me fist,
     Tant que je le requis d'amor.
     Pensis li mostrai ma clamor
     Au plus sagement que je poi.
3064 Ele prisa mes dis moult poi,
     Et se seut en moult grant despit;
     Porquant si m'en quist un respit,
     Et dist que s'en porpenseroit,
3068 Et quant ele me reverroit
     Si m'en respondroit son plaisir.
     Je ne voil pas longes soufrir,
     Ains le revinc veoir par tens,
3072 Et si li priai del porpens   [21vb]
     Et del respons qu'ele dut faire,
     Conme cortoise et debonaire,
     Me respondist sa volenté.

3036 Neither yesterday nor today
Have we, neither I nor this girl,
Had so much as the fruit of a wild rose,
Nor anything else to eat."

3040 "Dear sir," said the knight,
"I promise you truly that
Before you have parted from me—
Don't be troubled any longer—

3044 You will be on your way to
Good, elegant lodging.
I want to be your friend
And to be in your service.

3048 But now hear first of all,
Before you have help from me,
How I came to such good luck.
"My dear sir, once upon a time,

3052 More than five or six years ago,
When I was still a young man,
Newly apprenticed in arms,
I loved a young woman—

3056 The most courteous and beautiful
From here to Camelot.
Love, who caught me on his leash,
Made me as hardy as a lion.

3060 He made me so noble and bold
That I begged love of her.
Deeply troubled, I revealed my pain
To her as wisely as I could.

3064 She took what I had to say lightly
And answered me disdainfully.
Nevertheless, as a sop to me,
She said she would think about it,

3068 And when she saw me again,
Would tell me what she wanted.
I didn't want to suffer long,
So I returned to her a little later

3072 And begged her consideration
And the response she had promised—
That courteously and nobly she should
Tell me what she desired.

3076 Quant je me fui moult dementé,
     Et ma mesestance contee,
     Ele ne fu pas esgaree
     De respondre raisnablement,
3080 Et me prouva moult vistement
     A buens et a verais ses dis.
     Ainc ne furent par moi desdis,
     Car je vi bien que c'ert raison,
3084 N'el ne querroit fors ocoison
     Par quoi je m'en fuisce tornés.
     'Amis,' dist ele, 'se vos m'amés,
     Et vostre parole est certaine,
3088 Que por moi soiiés en tel paine
     Com vous m'avés dit et conté,
     Dont sai je bien de verité
     Ke vous ne querrés pas ma honte.
3092 Il n'a fil a si rice conte
     En Gales ni en Engletere
     Ki m'osast proiier ne requerre
     Que je l'amasse en tel maniere,
3096 Que je feïsse sa proiiere,
     Ne qu'il eüst por nul porcas,
     De moi ne joie ne soulas,
     Neïs seulement d'un baisier,
3100 Devant la qu'il fust chevalier.
     Et se vous el me querriés
     Dont sai je bien que vauriiés
     Veoir ma honte apertement;
3104 Mais je vous di seürement
     Que se vous estes chevalier
     Et je vous oi d'armes prissier,
     Si que le pule bien en die,
3108 Ke je devenrai vostre amie.
     Ja mar en douterés de rien.   [22ra]
     Aseürés en serés bien
     Ançois que vous partés de moi:
3112 Par cest anelet de mon doi,
     A ceste esmeraudete fine,
     Vous fas de m'amor la saisine,
     En tel guise com je devis.

3076 When I told her how depressed I was
     And spoke of my sad state,
     She did not trouble herself
     To reply reasonably;
3080 She countered very quickly
     With good and truthful arguments.
     I did not argue with her,
     For I saw clearly that she was right
3084 And that she would seek the first excuse
     For getting rid of me.
     'Friend,' she said, 'if you love me
     And speak truly when you say that,
3088 On my account, you are in such pain,
     As you have recounted,
     Then I know very well
     That you won't seek to shame me.
3092 There isn't a son of such a rich count
     In all of Gaul or England
     Who would dare to beg or ask
     That I would love him in this way
3096 Or fulfill his request;
     For he would have no reward from me,
     Neither joy nor solace,
     Not even a kiss,
3100 Before he had become a knight.
     And if you seek this from me now,
     I can be sure that you want—
     Obviously—to see me dishonored.
3104 I tell you with certainty
     That when you are a knight
     And I hear you praised for feats of arms,
     And people speak well of them,
3108 Then I will become your friend.
     Now you need have no doubt about it.
     You may be well assured of it
     Before you part from me.
3112 This ring from my finger,
     With this fine emerald,
     Will be a sign of love to you,
     According to the rules I stated.

3116 Et si vous di, biax dox amis,
      Que je vous fas tel convenant
      Ke vous ne me querrés avant,
      Car saciés que par le sorplus
3120 Perderiés le mains et le plus.'
         "Moult fui liés quant je tant en oi.
      De li pris çou que prendre en poi,
      Car l'anel del doi li sacai;
3124 Par l'anel d'amor atacai,
      Et par le don qu'ele me fist.
      Et la damoisele me dist
      Moult doucement au departir
3128 Ke se je voloie joïr
      De li, ne de sa druerie,
      Que d'orguel et de vilonnie
      Me gardaisce, et de tout sorfait;
3132 Et je li dis que c'ert bien fait
      Quant ele l'avoit conmandé.
      Et quant j'euc congié demandé
      Si m'en alai en mon païs.
3136 Par mon pere et par mes amis
      Euc armes dedens la quinsainne;
      Et saciés que je mis grant paine
      A porcacier pris et honor.
3140 Tant fis que la gent de l'onor,
      Et li jone et li cenu,
      Distrent qu'il n'avoient veü
      Onques mais a un chevalier
3144 En tant de terme porcacier
      Si grant pris com j'avoie fait.
      Je ne vous puis pas cascun fait   [21rb]
      Ne cascune ouvre raconter,
3148 Mais bien vous os dire et conter
      Que j'en soufri maint grant ahan.
      Et quant ce vint au cief de l'an,
      Si revinc a ma damoisele,
3152 Si li ramenbrai la querele
      Et le couvent qu'ele me fist;
      Et la damoisele me dist
      Que j'avoie trop entrepris:

3116	And I say to you, dear sweet friend,
	That I make this agreement
	So that you don't pursue me beforehand.
	Know that, through such excess,
3120	You will lose everything.'
	"I was very happy when I heard this.
	I took from her what I was able to take,
	For she took off the ring from her finger:
3124	I was attached to love by the ring
	And by the gift that she made.
	And the young woman said to me,
	Very sweetly, in leaving,
3128	That if I wished to take joy
	In her or in her friendship,
	I should guard myself from pride
	And from villainy and every sort of excess.
3132	And I told her this would be done,
	Whatever she had commanded.
	Then I asked permission to leave,
	And I returned to my own country.
3136	With the help of my father and friends,
	I was dubbed a knight within five days.
	Know that I took great pains
	To pursue fame and honor,
3140	So much so that all the noble people,
	Both the young and the old,
	Said they had never before seen
	Any other knight
3144	Obtain in such a short time
	So much fame as I had.
	I cannot tell you every deed
	Nor every good work I accomplished,
3148	But I can certainly tell you
	That I suffered many a great trial.
	And when it came to the end of a year,
	I returned to the young woman
3152	And reminded her of our talk
	And the agreement she had made.
	And the woman said that
	I had asked too much of her.

3156   N'estoie pas de si grant pris,
De tel los ne de tel bonté,
Que je deüsce estre monté
D'avoir la si tres tost conquise.

3160   Et se je euc grant paine mise,
Le premier an, a querre pris,
Saciés de voir que je i mis
En l'autre aprés tes quatre tans;

3164   Et quant vint au cief de deus ans,
Si revinc a m'amie arriere,
Si li ramanbrai ma proiire,
Et le convent qu'ele me fist.

3168   Et la damoisele me dist
Que je querroie grant sorfait:
N'avoie pas d'armes tant fait
K'encor le deüsce requerre.

3172   Le tierc an alai men pris querre,
Si que tout mon pooir i mis;
N'onques n'oï de nul païs
Parler ne de nule contree

3176   U il eüs nule asanlee
De guere ne de tornoiier
Que je n'i fusce le premier,
Por çou que g'i peüsce ataindre;

3180   N'onques encor ne me soi faindre
D'estre cortois et honerable.
Que vous feroie longe fable?
Tant fui dedens cel an prisiés   [22va]

3184   Si cortois et se envoisiés,
Si biax et si prox et si gens,
Et tant amés de toutes gens
Par tout u j'ere couneü,

3188   Encore est il moult bien seü,
Car la parole en ert trop grant,
Si fas que vilain qui m'en vant,
Mais por le voir que je vous cont

3192   De cief en cief le vous racont,
Si com l'aventure m'avint.
Et quant au cief de trois ans vint,
Si revinc arriere a m'amie;

3156 I was not of such great renown,
Nor of such fame or excellence,
That I ought to aspire
To have conquered her so quickly.

3160 And if I had taken great pains,
The first year, to acquire fame,
Then certainly I would take
Four times as much in the next year.

3164 And when, at the end of two years,
I came back to my friend
And reminded her of my request
And the agreement she had made,

3168 The young woman replied
That I suffered from pride:
I hadn't accomplished such great
Feats of arms that I had earned her.

3172 In the third year of seeking fame,
I put all my effort into it:
There wasn't a land
Where you couldn't hear me spoken of,

3176 No country where people gathered
For war or a tournament
Where I wasn't the first in valor,
If I had the chance to do it.

3180 Nor did I ever fail
To be courtly and honorable.
Why should I make a long story of it?
I was judged during this year

3184 So courteous and so ardent,
So handsome, so brave, and so noble,
And so loved by everyone
Everywhere—by all who knew me.

3188 It is still very well-known,
For much talk went around.
But it would be crude of me to brag.
It is only to tell you the truth

3192 That I have told from start to finish
The details of what happened to me.
And when the end of three years came,
I returned to my friend.

3196 Dis li que de sa druerie
     M'avoit saisi par un anel,
     Si n'estoit pas seant ne bel
     Que plus le me contretenist.
3200 Et la damoisele me dist
     Que je disoie bien raison:
     N'i avoit que une acoison
     Que bien ne la deüsce avoir.
3204 A escient pooit savoir,
     Tant l'en avoit le monde dit,
     N'i avoit mais nul contredit
     Que d'armes si grant pris n'eüsce
3208 Que par droit avoir le deüsce;
     Mais encor i ot une essoine.
     Puis me dist: 'Ce vous en eslogne;
     Une cose vous nuist vers moi:
3212 La trecerie que je voi
     Par tout le monde conmunal;
     Car tant sont trestout desloial
     Que cascuns qui a cief en trait,
3216 Et de s'amie ses bons fait,
     Je n'en voi nesun trestout sous
     Que des que il en est saoul
     Que tantost autre ne requiere.'
3220 Puis me dist qu'en itel maniere   [22vb]
     Ne me voloit ele pas amer:
     En travers me voloit clamer
     A estre siens s'ele estoit moie;
3224 Ja de li saisine m'aroie
     Desi qu'ele en fust bien seüre.
     Et je respondi a droiture
          "Ja mar en douteroit de rien:
3228 Je l'en aseüroie bien
     Par sairement u par fiance.
     Ele dist que par tel seürtance
     Ne seroit el ja aseür;
3232 Le neveu au bon roi Artu,
     Gavain le prou et l'ensegnié,
     Ki tant est amé et prisié,
     Voloit qu'en plege li livrasse.

3196   I said that she had assured me
Of her friendship by means of a ring,
And that it would not be fitting nor good
To deny me any longer.

3200   And the young woman said to me
That I spoke reasonably.
There was only one thing
Keeping me from having her.

3204   She knew with certainty—
So much had the world spoken of it
That it wasn't possible to deny—
I had such great fame in battle

3208   That I ought by rights to have her.
But she still had one concern.
Then she said: 'There's something that holds me back;
One thing speaks against you in my eyes.

3212   I see the treachery committed
By everyone around and about;
For they are all so disloyal
That anyone who reaches his goal

3216   And takes his pleasure in his *amie*—
I don't see a single one among them
Who, as soon as he is satisfied,
Doesn't run off to another.'

3220   Then she told me that she didn't want
To love in such a manner.
On the contrary, she wanted to claim me
To be entirely hers if she would be mine.

3224   I would not have possession of her
Until she was completely assured.
And I straightway replied
    "That she should not fear anything.

3228   I would assure her perfectly
By word of honor or taking an oath.
She said that such an assurance
Would not be enough to satisfy her.

3232   She wanted the nephew of King Arthur,
Gawain the brave and well-mannered,
Who was so loved and praised by all,
To deliver a pledge to her.

3236   Oiiés com el fu fole et lasse
        Et dolante et maleüree;
        Car par trestoute le contree
        Ert seü qu'il estoit ocis.
3240   Et je demaintenant li dis,
        Qui dire pas ne li voloie
        Sa mort, que pas nel counissoie,
        Si ne sai s'il me plegeroit
3244   Quant de rien ne me counisoit."
            Quant Gavains oï ces noveles,
        Du vallet et des damoiseles
        Li resouvint donques a primes.
3248   "'Non fac jou,' dist el, 'jou meïsmes,
        Ki en plege le vous demant;
        Quoi que je face a en avant,
        Nel conois or fors d'oïr dire.
3252   Mais a tout le mont l'oi eslire
        Que c'est tot li mix enteciés,
        Li plus loiax, li plus prisiés,
        Li plus prox et li plus raisnable
3256   Qui soit de la Reonde Table.
            "'Quant il est tant loiax et prox,   [23ra]
        Et je l'oi aficer a tox
        Ne nus ne l'ose contredire,
3260   Nis cil qui de lui ont envire
        Ne s'osent de rien entremetre,
        Bien m'os donc en son plege metre,
        Se vous issi le me livrés,
3264   Car se vous ne l'en delivrés
        Bien sai qu'il s'en deliverra
        Et vostre cors me liverra,
        S'il vous ataint, volliés u non,
3268   Car il est de si grant renon,
        Si cortois et si bien apris.
        Se vous avés vers moi mespris,
        Ne entrepris de nule riens,
3272   Tant est loiax que je sai bien,
        Se par vous en plege l'avoie,
        Et je me meïsce a la voie
        D'aler l'en a la cort semondre,

3236   Listen to how foolish and miserable,
      Unhappy and unfortunate, she was;
      For it was known throughout the world
      That Gawain had been killed.
3240   And I, who didn't want to tell her
      About his death, said to her
      That, since he didn't know me,
      I didn't know if he would pledge
3244   Himself to someone he didn't know."
       When Gawain heard this news,
      He remembered for the first time
      The young man and the young women.
3248   "'Nor do I,' she said, 'know him myself,
      I who demand this pledge of you.
      No matter what happens in the future,
      Right now I don't know him except through hearsay.
3252   But I have heard from all parts of the world
      That he is the most qualified,
      The most loyal, the most valued,
      The most brave, the most reasonable
3256   Of all the knights of the Round Table.
      "'Because he is so loyal and brave
      (And I have heard it affirmed by all
      Without any contradiction;
3260   Not even those who are envious
      Of him dare to start up anything),
      I will place myself under his protection,
      If you approve.
3264   For, unless you prevent this,
      I know that he will fulfill his pledge
      And turn you over to me
      If he catches you, like it or not;
3268   For he is of such great fame,
      So courteous, and so well-mannered,
      That, if you have mistreated me,
      Or failed to undertake something,
3272   His loyalty is well-known:
      If he is your bondsman,
      And I must set out on the road
      To summon him from the court,

3276 K'il m'en venroit çaiens repondre,
Et conme pleges contenir;
Et se il vous pooit tenir
Par force tant vous destraindroit
3280 K'amender le vous covendroit.
         "'En sa loiauté tant me fi,
Que jel recevrai bien de ci,
Je nel quier ja aler avant.'
3284 Et je li dis: 'Jel vous creant,'
Qui bien savoie qu'il ert mort.
Ensi fumes a un acort,
Entre moi et ma damoisele.
3288 Or fu ma parole plus bele
Quant ele m'ot tel couvenant.
Ke vous iroie jou contant?
Ersoir premere fois m'avint
3292 Que ma besoigne a droit point vint,
Et que je jui ensanble o li."
Et Gavains lors li respondi: [23rb]
"Dites moi dont u vous alés:
3296 Savoir weul, quant vous tant valés,
Et vous avés si bele amie,
Por quoi l'avés se tost guerpie."
         Cil li dist: "Jel vous dirai bien.
3300 Veoir vois la plus bele rien
Qui soit de ci desi qu'as Tors:
Priie l'ai lonc tans d'amors,
Si me doit wi cest jor respondre."
3304 "Bien vous doit ore Dix confondre,"
Fait Gavains, "et si di que fax,
Car laidement avés or sax
A la pucele son servise.
3308 Vous l'avés novelement conquisse,
Et si l'avés trois ans proiie,
Et c'est la premiere foïe
K'ox en avés eü vos buens,
3312 Si devés estre trestox suens
Par le counvent que li feïstes,
Si qu'a vostre dit li meïstes
En plege le bon chevalier;

3276 Then I am sure he would respond
And behave as one pledged to me.
And he would be able to hold you
By force until he convinced you
3280 That it was necessary to make amends.
    "'I am so sure of his loyalty
That I will accept his guarantee
Without seeking him out in advance.'
3284 And I said to her: 'I promise you,'
Knowing well that he was dead.
We struck an accord,
The young woman and I.
3288 Our speech became more pleasant
As soon as this agreement was reached.
What more can I tell you?
Yesterday evening was the first time
3292 That my desires were satisfied
And that I spent the night with her."
And Gawain replied to him,
"Tell me where you are going.
3296 I want to know why, if you are so valued
And have such a beautiful friend,
You have abandoned her so quickly."
    This one replied, "I'll be glad to tell you.
3300 I am going to see the most beautiful one
There is between here and Tours.
I have begged her for love for a long time,
And so she is supposed to reply today."
3304 "May God confound you," said Gawain,
"Even if I speak foolishly.
For you have repaid your young woman
Meanly for her service.
3308 You have just now conquered her,
After three years of courting.
It's the first time
That you have had your reward.
3312 And you ought to be entirely hers,
According to the bond you made with her
And that you told me was guaranteed
By the *bon chevalier*.

3316   Or alés un autre proiier.
        Ci ne voi je mot de raison,
        Car vous n'avés nule ocoison
        Par quoi enhaïr le doiiés:
3320   Por Diu vous pri que vous soiiés
        Vers la damoisele loiax.
        Cil qui sont treceor et fax
        Vers celes qui ne lor meffont
3324   Fuscent or tout segnié el front,
        Pleüst a Diu le tout poisçant;
        Car il en a par le mont tant
        Qu'i font as loiax grant contraire."
3328   Et cil dist: "Qu'avés vous a faire
        De moi ne de ma damoisele?
        Cele est tant avenans et bele,
        Si cointe et si noble et si sage,   [23va]
3332   Et si est de si haut parage,
        Qui me doit faire mon respons,
        Ke trestout les plus haus barons
        Qui soient desi a la mer
3336   Metroient paine a li amer.
              "Li autre m'a tant travellié,
        Tant en ai pensé et vellié,
        Si m'a rendu mon gueredon,
3340   Et el m'a de s'amor fait don;
        Je l'ai moult tres bien deservie,
        Car tant l'ai amé et servie,
        Et tant ai a çou entendu,
3344   Qu'el ne m'aroit oan rendu
        De mon service la moitié.
        Et quant je ai tant esploitié
        Ke jou qui ai en painne esté
3348   En ai sor li la poesté
        De faire li corox avoir,
        Li veul issi faire savoir
        L'anui que j'ai por li soufert:
3352   Tel merite a qui issi sert."
              Gavains li dist: "Gentil franc honme,
        Por tox les sains c'on prie a Rome,
        N'entreprendre ja vers li tant,

3316   Yet now you go to seek another.
        I see no reason in this,
        For there is no occasion
        For you to hate her.
3320   I pray you in the name of God
        To be loyal to this young woman.
        As for those who are false and cheating
        To lovers who make no affront:
3324   May it please God the Almighty
        To mark them on their brows
        With a sign of infamy! For there are so many
        In the world who are disloyal."
3328   And the knight replied: "What have you
        Got to do with me and my woman?
        She is so charming and beautiful,
        So elegant, noble, and wise,
3332   And she is of such high lineage,
        She who must reply to me today,
        That all the noblest barons
        Who live from here to the sea
3336   Are love-sick for her.
            "The other one made me work so hard
        That I had troubled thoughts and sleepless nights
        Before she gave me my reward
3340   And made a gift of her love.
        I certainly deserved her,
        For I loved her and served her so much
        And waited for her so long
3344   That she couldn't possibly
        Return the half of it.
        And when I had succeeded—
        I who had been in such pain—
3348   In having her in my power
        And could express my anger,
        I let her know just what
        I had suffered: I gave her
3352   Just what she deserved."
            Gawain replied, "Be a gentleman!
        For all the saints revered in Rome,
        Do not treat her this way,

3356   Ains li tenés son convenant,
        Si ferés bien et que cortois.
        Il n'a sou ciel si rice rois,
        Se il avoit vers li tant fait,
3360   Que ce ne fust trop grant forfait,
        Se il le deguerpissoit si."
        Et li chevaliers respondi:
        "De nient vous oi entremetre.
3364   Je ne vous en veul rien prometre
        Que moult bien tenir ne vous velle.
        Il me plaist moult qu'ele s'en duelle,
        Quant ele m'a tel anui fait;
3368   Et ce est la some del plait,   [23vb]
        Je n'en feroie rien por vous."
        Et Gavains dist: "Ce est l'estrox.
        J'amai tant monsegnor Gavain
3372   Ke je feroie que vilain
        Se je soufroie qu'il eüst
        Reproce la u mes cors fust,
        Ne se il a mort u a vie
3376   Estoit retés de vilenie.
                "Quant vous por raison ne por bien
        N'en volés faire nule rien,
        Ne por moi qui tant vous en pri,
3380   Une cose de voir vous di:
        Quant vous volés tant entreprendre,
        Il vous couvient de moi deffendre."
        Et cil respont: "Or sui jou pris.
3384   Moult m'avés de legier conquis,
        Ki quidiés que je rien en face
        Ne por vous ne por vo manace."
                Que vous en diroie je plus?
3388   Lors se traient un poi en sus;
        Bien s'acesmerent les vassax,
        Et laiscent corre les cevax,
        Se se fierent par tel angousce
3392   Que l'une et l'autre lance frousce.
        Mais quant li uns ot l'autre outré,
        Il se sont si entrencontré,
        Car il vinrent si radement,

3356 But rather hold to your agreement,
Act like a good and courteous knight.
Not even the most powerful
King on earth could treat her thus
3360 Without committing a great crime
If he abandoned her like this."
And the knight replied:
"Don't mix in this affair.
3364 I don't want to promise you anything
That I don't intend to do.
I'd much rather make her suffer
For the suffering she caused me.
3368 And this is the sum of it:
I'm not going to do anything for you."
And Gawain said, "Then it's decided.
I love Sir Gawain so much
3372 That I would be a villain
If I allowed him to be
Reproached in my presence—
Whether he is dead or alive—
3376 If he was accused of villainy.
"If you don't want to listen—
Neither out of good sense nor fairness,
Nor because I ask it of you—
3380 Then I have just one thing to say:
If you persist in undertaking this,
Then you will have to fight me."
And he replied, "Now you've got me!
3384 You've conquered me so easily!
Do you think I'd back off
From you or your threats?"
What more can I say?
3388 Each one drew back a little;
They armed themselves well
And then let their horses gallop.
They clashed so violently
3392 That both their lances broke.
But when they had passed each other,
They turned around right away
And came at each other so quickly—

3396   Et se li livres ne me ment,
        Il se sont si entreferus
        Des cevax, des cors, des escus,
        Ke il et li ceval caïrent.
3400   Et li chevalier sus salirent.
        Tantost com Gavains sus sali,
        Radement et bien asali
        Le chevalier l'espee traite;
3404   Tele envaïe li a faite
        Ke cil en est tox esmaiiés;   [24ra]
        Neporquant bien li a paiiés
        De tox ses caus les gueredons.
3408   Nes a pas receüs en dons,
        Ains li a bien gueridonés;
        Car tes set vins l'en a donés
        Dont uns autres moult s'esmaiast,
3412   Ki en tel guise li paiast.
        Neporquant mesire Gavain
        L'outra d'armes au daerain,
        Si que cil ne se pot deffendre.
3416   Mais quant il vaut s'espee rendre,
        Mesire Gavains li dist lors
        Que ja s'espee ne son cors
        Ne recevra en tel maniere,
3420   K'il ne vaut onques sa proïiere
        Orains por nule painne oïr.
        Mais s'il a talent de joïr
        Ne de son cors ne de s'onor,
3424   Tenir li convenra l'amor
        K'a la damoisele a pramisse.
        Et se li dist qu'en itel guisse
        Conme lui et li convendroit,
3428   Quant en sa prison li rendroit,
        L'en feroit il la seürté.
        Et cil qui ert d'armes outré
        Li respont: "Volentiers, biau sire."
3432   "Dont vous couvient vostre non dire,"
        Fait Gavains, "que savoir le veul
        Por conter cest ouvre a Carduel."
        Et cil dist: "J'ai non Espinogre.

3396   If my source doesn't lie—
That they crashed together fiercely—
Horses, bodies, and shields—
And both riders and horses fell.

3400   The knights jumped up from the ground.
As soon as Gawain was on his feet,
He drew his sword and quickly
And fiercely assailed the knight.

3404   He attacked so violently
That the knight was taken aback;
Nevertheless, he repaid him well
For all of his blows.

3408   He did not receive them as a gift
Without giving back a gift in kind.
For he gave him one hundred and forty blows,
Which would have defeated anyone

3412   Else who was paid in this way.
Nevertheless, Sir Gawain
Finally exhausted his adversary,
So that he couldn't defend himself.

3416   But when he went to give up his sword,
Sir Gawain said to him that
He would not receive either
His sword or his body this way:

3420   Not until he accepted the request
That he had ignored a minute ago.
But if he wanted to continue
To enjoy his life and honor,

3424   He should hold to the love
He had promised the young woman.
And if he said that
He would hold to their agreement,

3428   He would release him
In return for his guarantee.
And he who had been defeated
Replied, "With pleasure, dear sir."

3432   "Please tell me your name,"
Said Gawain; "I want to know it
So that I can tell this story at Camelot."
And he replied, "My name is Espinogre.

3436 En tout le roiame de Logre
Ne quidoie je pas trouver
Ki me peüst d'armes outrer;
Et si est de Wi men sornon.
3440 Or me dites le vostre non,
Et de quel terre estes venu;
Car s'il m'est issi avenu   [24rb]
Ke hom qui ne soit de grant pris
3444 M'ait a armes vencu ne pris,
Por que m'amie dire l'oie,
Ja mais a nul jor n'arai joie.
Et s'il m'est issi encontré
3448 Ke miudre de moi m'ait outré,
Mendre en ert mon corox et m'ire."
"Je ne vous puis le mien non dire,"
Fait Gavains, "que je l'ai perdu,
3452 Si ne sai ki le m'a tolu."
        "Or le me couvient aler querre,
Mais ne sai u ne en quel terre;
Si vous couvient o moi venir
3456 Et, se vous volés, contenir
A mon plaiscir et a mon gré."
Et cil li respont: "Jel vous gré
Que jou irai moult volentiers,
3460 Conme cil qui est vostre entiers,
Et que par droit avés conquis."
"Quant nous l'aron," fait Gavains, "quis
Et nous dex arons tant ouvré
3464 Que nous aron mon non trouvé,
Jel vous dirai eneslespas.
Et saciés bien, n'en doutés pas,
Jel vous met bien el covenant,
3468 Que je vous ferai entretant,
Se je puis, bele conpaignie.
Onques en toute vostre vie
Chevalier tant ne se pena,
3472 Plus bele ne la vous mena."
        Li chevaliers sans contredit,
Tout issi que Gavains ot dit,
A la parole creantee;

3436   In all the realm of Logres,
       I don't believe I could find
       Anyone who could defeat me in arms.
       My name comes from the land of Wi.
3440   Now tell me your name
       And from what country you come.
       For if it has happened to me
       That I have been defeated and captured
3444   By a man little known for his valor,
       Then my friend will hear of it and
       I'll never again find joy.
       And if it has happened that
3448   I have been defeated by someone better than I,
       Then my annoyance and anger will be less."
       "I can't tell you my name,"
       Said Gawain, "for I lost it,
3452   And I don't know who took it from me.
          "Now I must go seek it,
       But I do not know where to look for it.
       And you ought to come with me,
3456   And, if you wish, to act
       According to my will and pleasure."
       And the knight replied, "I am
       Very happy to go with you
3460   And to be entirely in your command,
       For it is your right by conquest."
       "If, during our search," said Gawain,
       "We work together in such a way
3464   That we succeed in finding my name,
       I will tell it to you immediately.
       Know this for sure, have no doubt!
       I will hold to this agreement
3468   And will, if I can, provide you
       A good companion in the meantime.
       Never in all your life will you find
       A knight who puts himself to such pains
3472   Or behaves better toward you."
          The knight, without debate,
       Believed completely
       What Gawain had said.

3476 Et Gavains reçut lors s'espee
      Par le couvent que il ont fait:
      K'il doit adrecier le meffait
      Si com li contes est contés.   [24va]
3480 Lors sont sor lor cevax montés,
      Ki les ex erent estraiiers.
      Puis les mena li chevaliers
      Au castel dont il ert partis.
3484 Trestox et les fais et les dis
      A la damoisele conterent:
      En quel guise il s'entrencontrerent,
      Com cil sen conte li conta,
3488 Et com li estris tant monta
      K'en la forest se conbatirent;
      Et coment il s'entrabatirent,
      Conme la concorde fu faite.
3492 En itel guise les afaite
      Gavains, qui fist, sans demorer,
      Ileuc au chevalier jurer
      Que ja mais en toute sa vie
3496 Par amor ne par drüerie
      N'amera fenme se li non.
      Lors veut cele savoir son non,
      Mais il li dist: "Ce ne puet estre,"
3500 Car il set ja tant de sen estre
      K'il nel puet a nule rien dire.
      Et cele li dist: "Biax dox sire,
      Vous qui n'avés pas vostre non,
3504 Bien sai que moult estes prodom,
      Et que forment vous doi amer.
      Bien sai, s'il m'esteüst clamer
      A Gavain de cest chevalier
3508 Ke moult par fust men droit plenier,
      Quant onques parler n'en oï,
      Nonques mes amis ne joï
      De nule amor fors de la moie,
3512 Ne mais qu'il ert entrés en voie
      D'aler une autre porcacier.
      Or le m'a ci cest chevalier
      Por la soie amor ramené.

3476   And Gawain gave him back his sword,
According to the agreement they had made.
Thus he could rectify his misdeed,
Of which we have heard tell in the story.

3480   They mounted their horses
That were wandering nearby.
The knight led them to the castle
From which he had just parted.

3484   They told the young woman
Everything they had done and said:
How they had encountered each other,
How the young man had told his story,

3488   How their argument grew so that
They fought one another in the forest,
How he had been defeated,
How the accord had been reached.

3492   In such a way, Gawain arranged
Things so that he had the knight
Promise, without hesitating,
That never in all his life,

3496   Neither as lover nor as friend,
Would he love any woman but her.
Then she wanted to know his name,
But he said to her, "It cannot be."

3500   For he knew at least this much about him—
That he couldn't tell anyone his name.
So she said to him, "My dear sir,
You who have no name,

3504   I am sure you are a good man
And that I ought to love you very much.
I know that, if I had complained
To Gawain about this knight, it would have been

3508   Very hard to claim my rights—
I had never heard talk of this,
And my friend had never enjoyed
Any love except for my own,

3512   Although he had started on the path
Of chasing after another.
Now this other knight, for love of Gawain,
Has brought my friend back to me.

3516   Tant l'a a armes demené   [24vb]
       K'il m'a çaiens son cors rendu,
       Et si li a moult cier vendu
       Le fol pensé qu'il ot enpris.
3520   Moult par est Gavains de grant pris,
       S'en doit a Diu mercis et grés
       Ke tant est prissiés et amés. "
              La pucele prist a droiture,
3524   Ki grant joie a de l'aventure,
       Lor escus, et ses fist descendre;
       Puis fist ses vallés moult entendre
       A ex honerer et servir.
3528   Grant painne mist a deservir
       La bonté que Gavains li fist,
       Ki en aventure se mist
       Por faire li son dru avoir.
3532   Le castel, l'ostel, et l'avoir
       Li a tout mis en abandon,
       Si li prie par gueredon
       K'il en face conme del suen.
3536   Moult orent ostel bel et buen,
       Et moult furent la nuit a aise;
       Car quanque cuident que lor plaise
       Fu fait, qu'onques n'i ot essoigne.
3540   Mais por mon conte que n'aloigne,
       Ne voil aconter tox lor mes
       De beles cars, de poisçons fres,
       Et de venisons et d'oisiax,
3544   Dont li services fu moult biax,
       Et d'autres mes a grant plenté,
       Ki ci ne seront pas conté,
       De vin de diverse maniere.
3548   Mais plus valut la bele ciere
       Que la damoisele lor fist,
       Ke le sien a bandon lor mist,
       Q'a lor volenté en preïscent,
3552   Ke quatorze mes ne feïscent.
              Que vous iroie jou contant?   [24bisra]
       La damoisele lor fist tant
       Com el pot plus joie et honor.

3516 Through battle, he forced him
To turn himself over to me
So that he has dearly bought
The foolish idea he had pursued.
3520 Certainly Gawain is of great renown
And one ought to give praise to God
That he is so valued and loved."
Right away, the young woman,
3524 Who was most happy about this event,
Took their shields and had them dismount.
Then she told the servants to wait on them
With great honor and to serve them.
3528 She took great pains to deserve
The generosity Gawain had shown her
In undertaking this adventure
To restore her friend to her.
3532 Her castle, home, and goods—
She put all at his disposal
And begged him as compensation
To treat them as his own.
3536 They had very good lodging
And spent the night at their ease.
Everything imaginable was done
For their pleasure, whatever was needed.
3540 But so that my story isn't too long,
I don't want to list all the dishes
Of tasty meats, of fresh fish,
Or of the venison and game birds,
3544 Which they were served so well,
Or of other dishes aplenty—
Nor will anything be said
Of the many varieties of wine.
3548 But the reception the young woman
Provided was of greater value:
She placed all that was hers before them:
If they had asked for it,
3552 They would have had fourteen courses.
Have I now satisfied you?
The young woman provided them
As much joy and honor as possible.

3556   Et l'endemain, quant il fu jor,
       Li doi chevalier se leverent;
       Delivrement et bien s'armerent,
       Puis se sont a la voie mis.
3560   Et la damoisele au cler vis,
       Cele qui ert o eus venue,
       A o ex sa voie tenue,
       Et lor oste a Diu conmanderent.
3564   Arriere en la forest entrerent
       Par u il vinrent cele part;
       Et se fortune nes depart
       Ja mes nul jor ne fineront,
3568   Si com il dient, ains iront
       Amont et aval par la terre,
       U qu'il soit le Gringalet querre.
       Et quant il l'aront si bien quis
3572   K'il l'aront par armes conquis,
       S'iront querre les damoiseles,
       Celes qui discent les nouveles
       A Gavain qu'il estoit ocis.
3576   Si ont devisé et enquis
       Aprés queront cex qui a tort
       Se sont vanté que il l'ont mort;
       Et quant il trovés les aront
3580   Par armes lor contrediront
       C'onques mort ne reçut par ex,
       Et si se conbatront as dex,
       Et puis au tierc, s'il est trouvés.
3584   Et quant il les ara prouvés
       Si dist que il Gavain querra,
       Et que moult bien le trovera,
       Car bien set qu'il est devenus.
3588   Quant au plain furent revenus,
       Devisant lor oirre et lor oeuvre,
       Es vous que del bois lor descuevre   [24b*i*srb]
       Un chevalier en une lande.
3592   Des le mer dusques en Islande
       N'en ert nus si bien atornés;
       Rades, isniax, et sejornés
       Ert li cevax u il seoit.

3556 And the next day, when it was daylight,
The two knights got up.
They armed themselves quickly and fully,
Then went on their way.
3560 And the pretty young woman,
The one who had come with them,
Set out on the way with them,
And they commended their hostess to God.
3564 They went back into the forest
From which they had come.
Unless fortune would separate them,
They would never ever stop,
3568 They said, until they searched
High and low across the earth
To seek out where Gringalet might be.
And when they knew for sure
3572 That they had recaptured him,
Then they would go seek the young women,
Those who had told the news
To Gawain that he had been killed.
3576 And they had arranged and agreed
That afterwards they would seek those who
Had wrongfully bragged that they had killed him.
And when they had found them
3580 They would challenge them to deny
That they had killed him.
And after they had fought these two,
They would fight the third, if he was found.
3584 And once he had exposed their lies,
He without a name said he would seek Gawain
And that he would find him easily,
For he knew what had become of him.
3588 When they had reached the open countryside,
While planning their route and actions,
They saw a knight emerge
From the woods onto the heath.
3592 From the sea to Iceland
One couldn't find another so well-equipped:
The horse on which he sat
Was light-footed, quick, and well-fed.

3596 Li chevaliers pas ne veoit
     Les deus chevaliers qui venoient.
     A mervelle li avenoient
     Toutes les armes qu'il portot.
3600 Cauces de fer caucies ot
     Plus blances que n'est nus argens,
     Et il ert biax et grans et gens,
     Et bien paroit delivre et prox;
3604 Et saciés que il ot desox
     Son hauberc un porpoint vestu,
     Couvert d'un moult rice boufu.
          Son hauberc ert safré menu,
3608 Et si ert a plus cier tenu,
     De tox çax qui veü l'avoient,
     Que les cauces de fer n'estoient:
     Moult ert fort et legier et cler.
3612 Et si avoit cote a armer
     D'un paile de Constentinoble,
     Et sa çainture ert cointe et noble
     K'il ot desus sa cote çainte;
3616 Car s'amie ne s'ert pas fainte,
     Ki envoïe li avoit,
     A faire les oeuvres a droit,
     De caviax et d'or et de soie.
3620 Anuis seroit, se je voloie
     Tout deviser de cief en cief,
     Seul de l'elme qu'il ot el cief
     Et del cercle et de la visiere.
3624 Sor le hiaume ot une baniere
     De ses armes moult bien taillie,
     Que s'amie li ot baillie
     Et donee par drüerie.   [24b*i*va]
3628 Son ceval ert de Lombardie,
     Fort et isnel et tost alant.
     Et saciés qu'il ot en talant,
     S'il puet ses anemis trouver,
3632 Que il vaura ja esprover
     Et veoir son rice corage.
     Lors li fist son rice bernage,
     Qui a bien le faisoit entendre,

3596   The knight could not see
        The two knights who approached him.
        They looked with wonder at
        Each piece of armor he carried.
3600   The shoes of iron that he had
        Were whiter than new gold,
        And he was big, beautiful, noble,
        And he seemed to be generous and brave.
3604   And know that he was dressed under
        His chain mail with a doublet of
        Very elegantly embroidered silk.
           His chain mail was tightly knit,
3608   And it was judged of greater value
        By all those who saw it
        Than his shoes of iron:
        It was very strong and light and bright.
3612   And over his mail he wore a tunic
        Of silk from Constantinople.
        And the belt that he had around
        His tunic was elegant and noble.
3616   For his friend didn't hold back—
        The one who had sent it to him—
        From doing her work properly
        With threads of gold and silk.
3620   It would be tiresome if I wanted
        To describe everything from top to bottom—
        So I'll describe only the helmet on his head
        And its ring and its visor.
3624   On top of his helmet he had a banner
        Beautifully embroidered with his arms
        That his *amie* had given to him
        And granted him out of friendship.
3628   His horse was from Lombardy,
        Strong and frisky and fast.
        And know that he had no other desire
        Than to locate his enemies
3632   So he could prove his ability
        And demonstrate his great courage.
        Thus his noble bearing made him—
        In expectation of good conduct—

3636 L'escu par les enarmes prendre;
     Si mist la lance sox l'aisele,
     Et s'afica dedens la sele,
     Puis a son ceval porficié.
3640 A saciés qu'il ot aficié
     Son col d'un cointe fremal d'or;
     Et si avoit pendu un cor
     A son col dedens son escu.
3644 L'escu de geules couvert fu,
     A un lion ranpant d'ermine.
     En sa grosse lance fraisnine
     Avoit un gonfanon pendant;
3648 Si a çaint le plus rice brant
     De tout le roiame de Logre.
     Entre Gavain et Espinogre,
     Moult bonement esgardé l'ont.
3652 Li chevaliers dont je vous cont
     Venoit grant joie demenant,
     Et un sonnet d'amors cantant
     K'avoit nouvelement apris.
3656 Lors a par les enarmes pris
     Son escu et sa lance ensanle;
     En mi le camp, si com moi sanle,
     A tout jeté par mautalent.
3660 Et saciés qu'il ot en talent
     De conmencier un duel a faire,
     Come de crier et de braire
     Et de ferir ses poins ensanle,
3664 Si qu'a tox qui l'esgardent sanle   [24bisvb]
     Qu'il ait grant talent d'estre mort,
     Sans ce qu'il eüst nul confort
     Conme ne fenme li feïst.
3668 Son escu et sa lance prist,
     Si s'est estraint et porficié,
     Si a son ceval eslaiscié
     Moult radement lance alongie.
3672 Si a sa cançon conmencie,
     Dont il avoit deus vers cantés.
     "Est cil chevaliers encantés,"
     Fait Gavains, "qui si se contient?"

3636   Take up his shield by the straps.
       He placed the lance under his arm
       And attached it inside the saddle
       And dug his spurs into his horse.
3640   And know that he had attached
       At his neck an elegant clasp of gold
       And he had hung a heart
       From his neck under his shield.
3644   The shield was covered with his arms—
       Gules with a rampant lion of ermine.
       From his long lance of ash
       Hung a war flag.
3648   And around his waist was the most magnificent
       Sword in all the realm of Logres.
       Both Gawain and Espinogre
       Looked at him with great pleasure.
3652   The knight I just told you about
       Approached exuding great joy
       And singing a love song
       That he had just learned.
3656   Suddenly he took up his shield
       By the straps, together with his lance,
       And threw them down in anger,
       So it seemed, onto the middle of the field.
3660   And know that he was of a mind
       To give himself over to sorrow,
       By crying out and shouting
       And wringing his hands
3664   So that to all who looked at him
       It seemed he wanted to be dead,
       Without being able to be comforted
       Either by man or by woman.
3668   Then he took up his shield and lance
       And grasped them and dug his spurs in
       So that he let his horse gallop
       Very fast, his lance at the ready.
3672   And he picked up his song again
       Where he had left off after two verses.
       "Is this knight enchanted," asked Gawain,
       "That he behaves so strangely?"

3676   Et cil la lance que il tient
       Et l'escu rejeté a la terre.
       "Alas!" fait il, "tant je vois querre
       Ceste aventure a grant mescief."
3680   Ses dex conmence de requief
       Si fort que nul qui le veïst
       Ne fust que pitié n'en preïst.
             Quant i l'ot longement mené,
3684   A guise d'ome mal sené,
       Tout de recief reprist ses armes,
       L'escu saisi par les enarmes,
       Si ra son ceval porficié,
3688   Et le sonet qu'il ot laiscié
       Reconmença lués a canter.
       "Bien me puis," fait Gavains, "vanter
       Ke j'ai veü mainte aventure,
3692   N'onques mais en ceste mesure
       Ne vi chevalier contenir.
       Je ne me porroie tenir
       Que je n'aille a lui por enquerre
3696   Dont il vient et que il va querre."
             Vers lui poignent par mi la lande.
       Mesire Gavains li demande,
       Mais qu'i l'ot saluéançois
3700   Conme debounaire et cortois,
       Que il li die, se lui plaist,   [25ra]
       Dont cele joie et ce duel naist
       K'i li voit ensanle mener.
3704   Car il se porroit bien pener
       De querre tant com terre dure
       Ains qu'il trovast tele aventure;
       Et por çou li requiert et prie
3708   Que l'acoison del duel li die
       Et de la joie qu'il demaine.
       "Sire," fait il, "por nule painne
       Qui ci me devroit acorer
3712   Ne poroie je demourer,
       N'o vous tant longement ci estre
       Que dit vous eüsce mon estre,
       Dont je vieg ne quel part je vois.

3676 Then the knight again threw down on the ground
The lance that he held and his shield.
"Alas," he said, "soon I must seek
An adventure that will bring me sorrow."
3680 His sorrow began once more,
So strong that no one who saw him
Could fail to have pity on him.
When he had gone on this way a long time,
3684 Seemingly like a madman,
Once again he took up his arms,
Seizing the shield by the straps
And digging his spurs into his horse,
3688 And he began once again
The song that he had left off singing.
"I certainly can brag," said Gawain,
That I have seen many an adventure,
3692 But never before have I seen
A knight behave so uncontrollably.
I can't restrain myself
From going up to him to inquire
3696 Where he is coming from and what he seeks."
The two spurred their horses across the plain.
Sir Gawain asked him, but not before
He had first greeted him
3700 Courteously and debonairly,
If he would tell him, if he pleased,
The reason for this joy and sadness
That he had seen him display.
3704 For he could make the effort
To search to the ends of the earth
Before he found such an adventure.
Thus he asked and begged the knight
3708 To tell him the reason for his sorrow
And also for the joy that he displayed.
"Sir," he said, "on account of the pain
That would afflict me,
3712 I could not stay here
And rest with you long enough
For me to tell you who I am,
Whence I come, or where I go.

3716 Car a un gué dehors ce bois,
      Ki est plus de cinc lües loing,
      M'estuet ja estre a grant besoig.
      Mais itant de voir vous en di,
3720 Se jou n'i sui ains mïedi
      Que jou arai le tout perdu,
      Si vauroie estre mix feru
      De deus espix par mi le cors."
3724 Et Gavains li respondi lors:
          "Sire," dist il, "si vous plaissoit,
      Je sui ci qui o vous iroit
      Cele part u vous iriiés
3728 Tant que devisé m'ariiés
      Et vostre duel et vostre joie.
      Moult ai grant talent que je l'oie,
      Por savoir cele grant mervelle."
3732 Et cil de dire s'aparelle,
      Tout en alant; oiiés le conte,
      Si com li chevaliers le conte.
          "Sire," dist il, "jadis avint
3736 Que ciés un grant rice home vint
      Un mien sires a cui jou ere.
      Moult nous i fist on bele ciere,   [25rb]
      Et moult eümes bel hostel,
3740 Je n'uc onques puis autretel,
      Ce saciés vous veraiement;
      Et se je de rien vous en ment
      Si soie jou honis ancui,
3744 Si vous di je bien que je sui,
      Qui a vous m'en avou si fort,
      En grant aventure de mort.
          "Moult fist li sire grant honor
3748 Et grant feste de mon segnor
      Et de cex ki vinrent o lui.
      Quant vint au mengier, assis fui,
      Ki du segnor estoie acointe,
3752 O sa fille, ki moult fu cointe
      Et cortoise et bien acesmee;
      N'avoit si bele en la contree.
      J'ere adont chevalier nouvel;

3716   For there is a ford outside this wood
       That is more than five leagues distant,
       Where it is very urgent that I be.
       I can only tell you truly that
3720   If I am not there by noon
       I will have lost everything;
       I would prefer to be struck
       By two lances in the middle of my body."
3724   And Gawain replied to him thus:
       "Sir," he said, "if you please,
       I am someone who will go with you
       This distance that you travel
3728   While you tell me about
       Both your sorrow and your joy.
       I have a great desire to hear about it,
       To know about this wondrous thing."
3732   And the knight got ready to speak
       While riding forth; listen to the story,
       Just as the knight told it.
       "Sir," he said, "once upon a time
3736   It happened that my lord, to whom
       I am bound, stayed with a very powerful man.
       We were welcomed courteously
       And provided with excellent lodging,
3740   Such as I have never had since;
       This you should truly understand.
       If I should lie about anything,
       Let me be shamed immediately.
3744   And yet I tell you truly that I—
       Who have confessed so much to you—
       Am engaged in a deadly adventure.
       "The lord arranged all with great honor
3748   And much festivity for my lord
       And for all those who came with him.
       When it was time to eat, I was seated
       As one who was close to my lord,
3752   Beside his daughter, who was gracious,
       Courteous, and elegantly dressed.
       There was none so beautiful in the land.
       I was then a young knight;

3756   Tant parlai seanment et bel,
        Et tant fu ma proiiere bele
        Et plaissans a la damoisele,
        Ki de grant biauté ert granie,
3760   Que me dona sa drüerie.
        Je le plevi et ele moi
        Que tox jors mais en bone foi,
        Sans barat de fause traïne,
3764   Durast nostre amors enterine,
        Si qu'el n'ameroit puis se moi non.
        Je li refis autretel don,
        Ke je fors li n'en ameroie.
3768   A escient jurer porroie
        K'encor dure l'amor ensi,
        C'onques nus de nous n'en isci,
        Ne ne fausa de couvenant.
3772   En tel sens dura l'amors tant
        K'a une fois nous mesavint:
        Je ne sai conment ce avint,
        Dont ce sortit ne dont ce mut,   [25va]
3776   Ne mais sa mere s'aperçut
        Et qu'ele sot bien qu'ele m'amot.
        A grant mervelle li desplot.
            "Or l'a gardee si por moi
3780   Que ne peut puis prendre conroi
        Que je parlaisse ensanble a li;
        Si a bien deus ans et demi
        Qu'ele est por moi issi gardee.
3784   Or l'a requisse et demandee
        Uns rices hom de cest païs;
        Par le consel de ses amis
        Et par le porcas d'un sien frere,
3788   Li a creantee li pere,
        Si l'en doit mener wi cest jor.
        Et el en a si grant dolor
        A poi qu'ele n'est morte d'ire,
3792   Mais el ne l'ose contredire,
        Car son pere l'a conmandé;
        Si m'a priveement mandé
        Qu'ele en ert wi cest jor menee.

3756   I spoke politely and well,
          And I was able to phrase my request
          So pleasingly to the young woman,
          Who was graced with such beauty,
3760   That she gave me her friendship.
          I pledged to her and she to me
          That forever and in good faith,
          Without trickery or betrayal,
3764   Our perfect love would last forever,
          And she would love no one but me.
          I in turn pledged to her
          That I would love no one else.
3768   I can swear with certainty
          That our love endures and
          That neither of us
          Betrayed this agreement.
3772   In this manner, the affair lasted
          Until one day a mischance occurred.
          I don't know how it happened,
          What its cause or source was,
3776   But her mother perceived that
          She was in love with me.
          She was most displeased.
            "Now she guarded her so closely
3780   That I could not find occasion
          To talk together with her.
          For two and a half years,
          She was kept from me like this.
3784   Then a powerful lord of that country
          Made inquiry and asked for her hand;
          With the help of his friends
          And a payment by his brother,
3788   She was promised to him,
          And the lord is to take her away this very day.
          And she has such great sorrow
          That she is close to death.
3792   But she didn't dare to oppose
          That which her father had commanded.
          She had privately announced to me
          That she would be leaving today.

3796   La joie que j'ai demenee,
        Que veïstes premierement,
        Je vous di bien seurement
        Ke ce est por çou que jou sai
3800   Que jou ja endroit le verrai;
        Et le duel que je fac aprés,
        Je le fac por çou que ja mes
        Ne le verrai, sin a tele ire
3804   Que jel ne porroie a rien dire,
        Si vaudroie mix estre mort.
        Et aprés si me reconfort,
        Por seul itant que je bien sai
3808   Que jou ja endroit le ferai
        Si tres bien par devant ses ex
        Que nus nel porroit faire mix.
        Car quant je verrai ja lor gent
3812   Je les ferrai si durement,   [25vb]
        Et tant serai prox et seür,
        Que nus fors le bon roi Artu,
        Que je n'i met pas et Gavain—
3816   Si fas que fol et que vilain
        Qui m'en vant, mais itant vous di
        Ke tant serai prox et hardi
        Que nul chevalier fors ces dex,
3820   Ki a tant fust asanblé sex,
        Nel feroit si bien por ses ix,
        Ke jou nel face encore mix.
            "Si grant duel ai que cil l'en mainne,
3824   Que nus ne porroit la grant painne
        Ne le fais d'armes endurer,
        Tant conme je porrai durer,
        Que je souferrai por li ja.
3828   Si me plaist moult que le verra;
        Car nus hom que le devroit pendre
        Ne porroit, s'il n'amoit, enprendre
        Le fais d'armes que cil enprent
3832   Quant amors le tient et esprent.
            "L'autre duel que je fac aprés,
        Se le fac grant je n'en puis mais,
        Car j'ai un moult grief fais enpris;

3796   The joy that I have displayed,
That you saw at first,
I tell you certainly,
Is on this account: that I know
3800   That I will soon see her.
And the sorrow that I showed afterwards
Was because I never again
Will see her. I have such grief
3804   That I can speak no more about it;
I would rather be dead.
And afterwards if I found comfort,
It was only because I knew
3808   That I would soon behave
So well in front of her eyes
That no one could do better.
For when I see those people
3812   I will make things difficult for them.
I will be so brave and hardy
Like no one except for the good King Arthur,
Whom I have never met, and Gawain—
3816   I act foolishly and rudely
To brag this way. But I tell you
That I will be so brave and hardy
That no knight, other than these two,
3820   Of all those who know how to do battle,
Could do so well before her eyes
That I wouldn't acquit myself better.
    "I have great sorrow to see her carried off;
3824   No one else could endure such great pain
Or such feats of arms
As I am getting ready for,
I who will suffer pain now for her sake.
3828   And it pleases me greatly that I will see her.
For no man required to endure it
Could, if he didn't love, take up
The feats of arms that he, whom
3832   Love holds and embraces, undertakes.
    "The other sorrow I showed afterwards
Was because I might fail at this great task,
For I have undertaken a very dangerous thing.

3836   Que chevaliers prox et hardis
       A aveuc le chevalier vint.
       Ce me dist cil qui a moi vint
       Et qui l'uevre me reconta,
3840   Et se me dist qu'il les conta
       A l'oiscir, ains qu'il partist d'ex.
       Or sai de voir, quant je sui sex,
       Et j'ai enpris si grant outrage,
3844   Ke je porcas mon grant damage.
       Encor me dist çou li mesages,
       Ki moult estoit cortois et sages,
       Que il les vit moult bien armés.
3848   Or oiiés, se vous nel savés,
       Por qu'il sont armé si tres bien.   [26ra]
       C'on ne puet celer nule rien.
       Ains est auques l'uevre seüe:
3852   Que la damoisele est ma drue,
       Et que je l'aim par drüerie.
       Si doutent ma grant estoutie
       Por çou qu'il sevent que je l'aim;
3856   Et por le droit que je i claim
       Se doutent, et ne gardent l'eure
       K'a un mal pas les core seure.
       Bien en peüscent estre en dute,
3860   Se j'eüsce une bone route.
          "Car tantost com je le veïsse
       Isi grant calenge i meïsse
       Que bien parust qu'ele fust moie;
3864   Et ja soit çou que je seul soie,
       Si vous di jou, conment qu'il ciee,
       Ke ele ert moult bien calengie.
       Si sai moult bien, quoi que jou die,
3868   Que jou n'en souferroie mie;
       N'onques ne fu nul chevalier,
       Neïs Rollant et Olivier,
       Ki peüst soufrir tel estor,
3872   Que il n'en fust au cief del tor,
       Se mervelle n'est, mort u pris.
       Mais je l'ai en tel guise enpris
       Que c'est la fin, u j'en morrai

3836	The knight has twenty brave
	And hardy knights with him.
	This I was told by one who came to me
	And told me about the whole affair.
3840	He told me that he had counted them
	Upon leaving, before he parted from them.
	Now I know for sure that, if I am alone,
	I have undertaken too great a challenge
3844	And will gain only great harm.
	The messenger also told me,
	One who is courteous and wise,
	That he had seen them heavily armed.
3848	Now listen, if you don't already know,
	Why they are so well armed.
	It is impossible to hide anything.
	Thus the whole affair is known:
3852	That the young woman is my friend,
	That I am bound to her in love.
	Thus they fear a furious attack
	Because they know that I love her;
3856	They are afraid because I have
	A just claim to her; they fear the moment
	When I attack them in a narrow place.
	They certainly ought to be afraid,
3860	If I had good troops with me.
		"For as soon as I see her
	I will make such a challenge
	That they will surely know she is mine.
3864	But I know that because I am alone,
	I assure you, that whatever happens,
	She will be fiercely defended.
	I know perfectly well, this I tell you,
3868	That I will not survive this battle.
	There has never been another knight—
	Not even Roland or Oliver—
	Who could endure such a battle
3872	Without being, in the final analysis,
	Short of a miracle, killed or captured.
	But I've taken it on this way
	And this is it—either I die

3876 U jou m'amie rescourrai."
          "Espinogre," fait lors Gavain,
     "Moult est le chevalier vilain
     Et outragex, qui autre voit
3880 D'amor en si tres grant destroit,
     Si nel secort a grant besoing."
     "Sire," fait il, "pas ne m'essoing,
     Se vous en volés entremetre,
3884 Que men pooir n'i wuelle metre;
     Car je sui vostres par raison,
     N'il n'i puet avoir ocoison   [26rb]
     De quanque vous vaurés enprendre
3888 Ke bien n'en welle mon fais prendre.
     Ja n'en serai vers vous escis."
     Lors li ont anbedui pramis
     K'a cel besoig li aideront;
3892 Et li chevaliers lor respont:
          "Segnor," fait il, "les vos mercis.
     Se mes outrages vous ai dis
     Que j'ai enpris par ma sotie,
3896 Conparer ne les devés mie;
     Ne jou de çou ne vous requier,
     Se jou mon grant outrage quier
     Dont jou ne me puis departir,
3900 Ke vous pas i doiiés partir.
     Car ce seroit moult grans damage
     Se nus de vous par mon outrage,
     Que j'ai par ma folie enpris,
3904 Ert de ceste oeuvre mort ne pris."
          Quant ç'oï monsegnor Gavain,
     Qui de grant francisse estoit plain,
     Lors l'en est moult grans pités prise;
3908 Ke il set bien que par francise
     Les ensengne il et escuse,
     Et lor secours por çou refuse
     K'il crient qu'o lui lor en mescie.
3912 "Sire," font il, "conment qu'il cie,
     Quant nous l'avons issi enpris,
     Nous en serons u mort u pris,
     U nous vous rendrons vostre amie."

3876   Or I rescue my friend."
            "Espinogre," Gawain then said,
        "He is a vile, proud knight
        Who would see another in such
3880   A tight fix because of love
        And not help him in his great need."
        "Milord," Espinogre replied, "I won't hesitate,
        If you want to get involved,
3884   To do all I can to help.
        For I am by rights yours.
        There will never be an occasion,
        No matter what you undertake,
3888   When I fail to take my part.
        I will never be unwilling."
        Then they both promised to aid
        The love-sick knight in this time of need.
3892   And the knight then responded:
            "Milords," he said, "I thank you.
        If I have told you of the extremes
        I have been led to by my folly,
3896   It was not so that you should pay.
        I do not ask this of you—
        I seek out my great challenge
        From which I cannot escape,
3900   And you ought not to take part.
        For this would be a terrible shame
        If either of you, through my excess
        That I have undertaken out of folly,
3904   Were killed or captured in this affair."
            When Sir Gawain heard this,
        He who was so full of generosity
        Was seized by intense pity.
3908   He knew that it was out of generosity
        That he talked thus and excused them.
        For this reason he refused the help
        Of them who wanted to battle with him.
3912   "Sir," Gawain said, "no matter what happens,
        We have already undertaken this:
        Either we will be killed or captured,
        Or we will hand over your friend to you."

3916 Li chevaliers les en mercie,
     Qui a mervelle s'esjoï
     De la pramesse qu'il oï:
     "Segnor," fait il, "Dix vous en oie
3920 Que rendre me pusciés ma joie,
     Dont j'ai esté lonc tans en paine.
     Cil qui d'onor faire se paine
     Dix li refait au cief del tor   [26va]
3924 A son besoig joie et honor;
     N'il n'ert ja tant desavoiiés
     Que il ne soit tost avoiés,
     Car Dix le secort et avoie."
3928 Lors se sont tot mis a la voie
     Por aler en ceste besogne.
     "Sire, se ja Dix bien me dogne,"
     Fait la damoisele a Gavain,
3932 "Il m'est prise si tres grant fain
     Ke me verrés ja erragier
     Se je n'ai moult tost a mangier.
     Si vous di tot seürement
3936 Que se je n'ai delivrement
     Une piece de pain au mains,
     Que je mengerai ja mes mains,
     C'onques rien si grant fain n'en ot."
3940 A Gavain mervelles desplot
     Quant il oï ceste novele.
     Lors a dit a la damoisele:
          "Bele," fait il, "por Diu merci!
3944 Nous ne porrions trouver ci
     Riens el monde por nul avoir
     Qui nous peüst mestier avoir;
     Et vous savés que par raison
3948 Ne puet avoir nule ocoison,
     K'il nous couvient andex aidier
     Orendoit a cel chevalier.
     Car nous li avon couvenant,
3952 Si ne seroit mie avenant,
     Quant convenencié li avon,
     K'a ce besoing li falison:
     Ki ensi fali li aroit,

3916 The knight expressed his thanks to them—
He was overjoyed about
The promise he had just heard.
"Milord," he said, "may God hear you
3920 So that you can bring me happiness,
For I have been in pain for a long time.
He who gives himself pains for honor
Will be repaid by God in the end
3924 With joy and honor as he deserves.
Neither will he be so cast off
That he would not be soon comforted,
For God keeps him and protects him."
3928 So they proceeded on their way
To the impending event.
"So help me God,"
Said the young woman to Gawain,
3932 "I have been seized by such great hunger
That I will be at my wits' end
If I do not soon have something to eat.
I tell you most assuredly that,
3936 If I don't immediately get
Hold of a piece of bread,
I will eat my own hands.
No one has ever had such great hunger."
3940 Gawain was very displeased
When he heard this news
And said to the young woman:
"Fair one, may God have mercy!
3944 We can't find anything here—
There's nothing in the world to be had
That we could possibly eat.
And you know perfectly well
3948 That there is no time for this
Since it is necessary for us both
To help this knight immediately.
For we've made an agreement with him
3952 And it would be very bad if,
After having made this promise,
We should fail him in this need.
Whoever would fail in this,

3956 Des que le pule le saroit,
     La reproce en seroit toudis.
     Gardés que ne me soit de pis,
     Et que n'i aie deshonor,
3960 Por le francise et por l'onor   [26vb]
     Que vous avés en moi trové.
     Tox jors vous seroit reprové
     Ceste ouvre, s'il estoit seü
3964 Ke vous li eüsciés neü.
         "Je vous pri qu'il ne vous desplaise,
     Et que soufrés vostre mesaise
     Tant que ceste euvre soit passee."
3968 "Je n'iere tant fole provee,"
     Fait ele, "que je par men gré
     Ceste parole si vous gré,
     Et que je tox jors mix ne veulle
3972 Autrui anui, qui que s'en duelle,
     Et cui qu'il desplaisse de rien,
     Que je ne vauroie le mien.
     Ne cuidiés pas que je me faigne,
3976 Et que li fains ne me destragne
     Gregnor que je ne die encor.
     Ki me donroit cinc cens mars d'or
     Por soufrir dusque vers midi,
3980 Sor ma loiauté le vous di
     Ne porroie je soufrir mie;
     Et ce sera grans vilenie,
     Quant je sui ci en vostre garde,
3984 Se g'i muir par vostre mesgarde.
         "Sire," fait ele, "je vous di
     Que j'ai autrefois esté ci,
     Si vi ci devant un castel,
3988 Un petit outre ce vaucel,
     Il n'i a pas liue et demie.
     Onques en toute vostre vie,
     De beles tors, de rices sales,
3992 En Engleterre ni en Gales,
     N'en veïstes seulement sis
     Qui si fuscent a droit assis."
     Mais j'ai aillors m'entente mise

3956   As soon as it was known,
Would be reproached forever.
Take care that things not get worse for me
And that I am not dishonored here;
3960   Take into account the generosity
And honor that you have found.
You would be reproached forever
If it were known that you had
3964   Interfered in this affair.
     "I beg you not to be displeased
And that you put up with your discomfort
Until after this affair is over."
3968   "I will not be so foolish,"
She said, "that I will voluntarily
Agree with what you desire.
I will always prefer the annoyance
3972   Of others, no matter who suffers,
No matter what their displeasure,
Than that I could wish my own.
Don't think that I feign hunger
3976   Or that hunger doesn't oppress me
More than I can ever say.
Even if someone would give me
Five hundred gold coins to wait
3980   Until noon, I swear to you that
I would never be able to endure it.
And it will be a great villainy
If, while under your protection,
3984   I die of neglect."
     "Sir," she continued, "I tell you
That I have been here before
And have seen a castle right up ahead,
3988   Just beyond this little valley,
Barely a league and a half away.
Never in all your life
Have you seen such beautiful towers,
3992   Such rich rooms; not more than six
Either in England or in Gaul
Are so well put together."
But it is not my intention

3996   Que a dire vous la devise
Si com cele le devisa;   [27ra]
Car ele dist et reconta
Moult tres bien, quanques ele i vit,
4000   Et si li a conté et dit
K'il siet dedens un plaisceïs,
Et que li castiax est garnis
De quanque il couvient a prodome.
4004   "Li asnes ciet par la sorsomme,"
Fait Gavains, "ç'ai oï retraire;
Mais or voi qu'il le m'estuet fare,
Et k'o vous aler m'en couvient,
4008   Quant issi a plaiscir vous vient."
      Salemons dist en un sien livre
Que cil n'est pas del tot delivre
Ki conpaignie a fenme prent;
4012   Que cil qu'ele tient et souprent,
Puis qu'il est soupris de s'amor,
Moult a de quoi faire clamor,
S'il avoit seul itant de cuer
4016   Qu'il s'en osast plaindre a nus fuer;
Mais nus ne s'en ose clamer.
Et cil qui plus couvient amer,
Et qui plus est d'amor en paine,
4020   Et cil qui tox jors plus s'en painne
De servir le a volenté,
Et plus en est entalenté,
Et plus lor fait bien et honor,
4024   Plus s'en repent au cief de tor.
      A autre ouvre li cuers me tire;
Revenir wel a ma matire,
Car assés ai de fenmes dit,
4028   N'il n'i a mais nul contredit
Qu'il en i ait se petit non
Qui ne soient de tel renon.
      "Espinogres," fait Gavains lors,
4032   "Or m'est bel ke avés deus cors.
Cascuns de vous en a un buen:
Sonés le vostre et il le suen   [27rb]
Tant que on l'oie quatre mos,

3996	To tell you everything
	That she described;
	For she spoke and told
	At great length what she had seen;
4000	She told him further
	That the castle lay inside a palisade
	And that it was outfitted
	Appropriately for a gentleman.
4004	"The ass crumbles under too heavy a load,"
	Replied Gawain; "that I have heard said.
	But I see now that I have to do this;
	It is necessary for me to go with you,
4008	If this is what will bring you pleasure."
	Solomon says in his book
	That he is no longer free
	Who holds company with a woman.
4012	For he whom she clings to and catches up
	Unawares, as soon as he is completely
	Enamored, has much cause to lament,
	If he only has enough heart
4016	To dare to complain in any way;
	But no one ever dares to complain.
	Those who are most driven to love
	And who take the greatest pains to love
4020	And who are always engaged
	In serving her at will,
	Those who are most full of ardor
	And do her the most honor and good,
4024	They repent the most in the end.
	But my heart draws me elsewhere;
	I want to return to my subject,
	For I have said enough about women.
4028	No one will contradict me
	If I say there are few among them
	Who do not have such a reputation.
	"Espinogre," said Gawain then,
4032	"It is good that you have Cadrés.
	Each of you has a job.
	You attend to yours and he to his,
	And before either has heard four words,

4036   Et je vous suirrai les galos,
           Des que j'arai tant esploitié
           Ke la pucele ara mengié.
           Mais ains m'estuet tant porcacier
4040   Que la pucele ait a mengier
           Ke jou face nule autre rien."
           "Nous le veon," fait il, "moult bien
           Que ne puet pas autrement estre."
4044   Lors tornent un peu a senestre,
           Entre Gavain et la pucele,
           Si errerent une sentele
           Tant qu'il sont au castel venu,
4048   Ki n'ert pas clos de pel agu,
           Mais de haut mur et de fossé.
           Si ot un grant bos adossé,
           Et un plaiseïs tout entor,
4052   Ki clooit le baile et la tor,
           Si qu'il n'i ot fors une entree.
           La pucele est laiens entree,
           Ki bien counisçoit le païs;
4056   Et cil qui n'en ert pas naïs,
           Ne nul honme n'i counissoit,
           Entra par la porte tout droit,
           Si ala vers le tor amont.
4060   Tout a ceval passa le pont,
           Sans ce que nul home veïst
           Ki de rien li contredeïst.
              La pucele remest defors,
4064   Et cil qui sans non estoit lors
           Entra tantost dedens la sale.
           Un doublier qui n'ert mie sale,
           Mais blanc que sor la glace nois,
4068   Vit estendu desor un dois.
           Une coupe ot desus d'or fin
           Toute plainne de moult bon vin.
           Flans, gastiax, gaufres et pastés,   [27va]
4072   Poivre caut i vit et lardés
           Dedens une blance escuele;
           Et si vit une damoisele
           Ki au disner estoit assise;

4036 I will follow you at a gallop
As soon as I have seen to it
That the young woman has eaten.
But now it is necessary for me to search for
4040 Something for the woman to eat;
I can't do anything else."
"We will do it," Espinogre replied,
"For it cannot be otherwise."
4044 Gawain and the young woman
Turned a little to the left;
They rode along a narrow path
Until they came to a castle
4048 That was not enclosed with sharp stakes
But with a high wall and moat.
And next to it was a big woods
And a hedged-in area all around
4052 That circled the enclosure and the tower
So that there was only one entrance.
The young woman entered there,
She who was familiar with the place.
4056 And he who had not been born there
And didn't know anyone
Entered straight through the gate
And went up toward the tower.
4060 Still on his horse, he passed over the bridge
Without seeing anyone
Who interfered in any way.
The young woman stayed outside,
4064 And he who was still without a name
Entered quickly inside the hall.
He saw a tablecloth that was not dirty
But rather white as new snow
4068 Spread out over a dais.
There was a goblet on it of fine gold
Filled with very good wine.
He saw there tarts, cakes, waffles,
4072 And meat pies, well-seasoned dressing,
And, inside a white bowl, pieces of meat.
And he saw a young woman
Who was seated at the table.

4076 Et se biauté puet sans francise
   Nule damoisele amender,
   Dont se puet ele bien vanter
   C'onques Nature ne pot faire
4080 Plus bele, s'ele fust debonaire,
   Mais tant ert orgelloxe et cointe
   Que nus qui de lui fust acointe
   N'en peüst bien dire a nul fuer.
4084 On aime le cors quant u cuer
   A cortoisie et loiauté,
   Si vous di bien par verité
   K'en orguel a moult malvais oste:
4088 Biautés qui a orguel s'acoste
   Est en maint liu toute perdue.
   Et li chevaliers le salue
   Moult bonement, si li demande
4092 Que li doinse de sa viande.
    "Or entendés," fait il, "pucele:
   La hors a une damoisele,
   Tout a ceval en cele cort;
4096 Et se on tost ne le secort,
   Et on a mengier ne li porte,
   Ja mais n'istra de cele porte,
   Ains sera morte sans retor.
4100 Ele esta devant cele tor;
   Ele vous prie par francise,
   Par guerredon et par servise,
   Que vous m'aidés a cest besong."
4104 "Sire, se je ja rien vous dong,
   Dont soie je," fait ele, "honie;
   Ains me sanle grant estoutie,
   Si estes moult outrecuidié
4108 Quant vous seulement ce cuidiés   [27vb]
   Que je doie por vous rien faire.
   N'estes pas de si grant afaire
   Que seul penser le deüsciés.
4112 Malvais apel i eüsciés
   Se mes frere fuscent ci tox,
   Dont jou ai set hardis et prox;
   Mais il sont en cele forest."

4076   If any woman could improve
        Upon beauty without noble actions,
        Then she could easily boast
        That Nature had never made
4080   Anyone more beautiful—if she had been gracious.
        But she was so proud and conceited
        That no one who knew her
        Could speak well of her in any way.
4084   One loves the body when courtesy
        And loyalty accompany the heart.
        I tell you truly that pride
        Has many a bad follower:
4088   Beauty that joins up with pride
        Has lost her advantage.
        The knight greeted her graciously
        And asked her if
4092   She would give him some food.
           "Now listen, my dear," he said,
        "Outside is a young woman
        Sitting on horseback in the courtyard;
4096   And if someone doesn't help her soon
        And carry some food to her to eat,
        She will never leave the entryway.
        She would rather die than go away.
4100   She is down below this tower;
        She asks that you—generous,
        Noble, and helpful—
        Aid me in this distress."
4104   "Sir, I would be ashamed
        If I gave you anything!
        What audacity,
        What presumption,
4108   For you to think that
        I would do something for you!
        You are not so important
        As even to think of it.
4112   You would be called to task
        By all my brothers—
        I have seven hardy and brave ones,
        But they are off in this forest."

4116   "Pucele," fait il, "si vous plest
        Ke je por un moult petit don
        Vous doie un bien grant gueredon,
        Il ert moult bien gueredonés,
4120   Se vous seulement me donés
        Un seul gastel et un pasté."
        "N'ert pas issi le mien gasté,"
        Fait la pucele, "par mon cief."
4124   "Ja n'en venrés issi a cief,"
        Fait uns nains qui devant li sert.
        "On dist que ses paroles pert
        Souventes fois qui cort a ciens.
4128   Ja n'esploiterés vers li riens,
        Je connois moult bien sa maniere,
        Par francise ne par proiiere;
        Mais par orguel et par sorfait
4132   Erent tot vostre plaiscir fait.
              "Dites moi, qui en cort hantés,
        N'est par orguel orguex dontés?
        Metés orguel encontre orguel:
4136   Jel vous lo ensi et sel weul,
        Quant vous avés si grant besoig.
        La viande n'est mie loig.
        S'en poés a grant plenté prendre."
4140   "On doit moult douter a mesprendre,
        Et je crienbroie trop mesfaire;
        Sel voloie si en pais faire,"
        Fait cil sans non, "se je peüsce,
4144   Que jou sen mal gré n'en eüsce."
        "Ce n'iert," fait soi li nains, "ja mes."   [28ra]
        Et il est lors alés plus prés,
        Si prist un pasté et un pain,
4148   Et un lardé a l'autre main,
        Dont l'escuele ert toute plainne.
        Et li nains par le frain l'en mainne
        A la pucele qui l'atent.
4152   Et il la viande li rent;
        Si li prie de soi haster,
        Car n'ert loiscirs de sejorner:
        Grans mestiers ert qu'il se hastast,

4116   "My dear," Gawain said, "if you wish
That I, for this very small gift,
Grant you a very large reward,
Then I will repay you well
4120   If you only give me
A little cake or meat pie."
"None of my food will be wasted,"
Said the girl, "over my dead body."
4124   "You will not succeed this way,"
Said a dwarf who served her.
"It is said that he who runs from dogs
Often loses his speech.
4128   You will accomplish nothing with her,
For I know her manners very well.
Not by generosity nor by prayers,
Only through brashness and force
4132   Will all your wishes be met.
    "Tell me, you who hang around the court,
Is not pride repaid with pride?
Place pride against pride:
4136   Thus I advise you to do
When you have such great need.
The meat is right before you.
Take as much as you want."
4140   "One ought to hesitate to misbehave,
And I fear making a bad mistake.
I prefer to do things peacefully,"
Said the knight without a name, "if I can,
4144   So as not to bring about resentment."
"This can never be so," said the dwarf.
So Gawain went up closer
And took a meat pie and bread,
4148   And, in the other hand, a piece
Of meat, of which the bowl was full.
The dwarf took up the reins and led him
To the young woman who waited outside.
4152   He gave the meat to the young woman
And asked her to hurry,
For he was not free to stay long:
He had great need for haste,

4156   Et grans besoins que il alast
       A la rescouse au chevalier
       A cui il doit en oirre aidier,
       Si com li a en couvenant.
4160   Et cele li dist maintenant:
            "Sire," dist el, "se Dix me voie,
       Je serai moult tost a la voie
       O vous, mais il m'estuet penser
4164   Ançois de ma vie tenser,
       Dont j'ai en grant espreuve esté.
       Cest mangier qui ert apresté
       M'a rendu a estrox la vie.
4168   Nel tenés pas a vilonie
       De mes grans besoins amentoivre:
       Il m'esteüst avoir a boire.
       Je sui de si grant soi souprise,
4172   Qui des jewi matin m'est prise,
       Que je ne le puis endurer;
       Si ne porroie pas durer
       Longement se je ne bevoie.
4176   Et j'ere moult tost a la voie
       O vous, des que j'ara beü."
       Lors est cil sans non esmeü,
       Que n'i estut autre proiiere,
4180   Si revient en la sale arriere.
       Puis vait au dois la coupe prendre;
       Mais quant il i vaut la main tendre,   [28rb]
       Cele qui ert au dois asisse
4184   A ains de lui la coupe prise,
       Si li a moult fierement dit:
       "On i meïst ja contredit,
       Et u vin et en la viande,
4188   Si cil qui sont en cele lande
       Et en cel bois en lor deduit
       Fuscent ens en la sale tuit.
            "Mais or m'avés sole trouvee,
4192   Si avés sor moi esprovee
       Vostre proece: grant honor
       Vous est a faire deshonor
       A une seule damoisele."

4156 And it was urgent that he get to
The rescue of the knight
Whom he ought to be rushing
To help, as he had promised.

4160 The young woman spoke to him now:
"Sir," she said, "as God is my witness,
I will soon be on the way
With you, but it is also necessary

4164 To think first of preserving my health,
Which has never before been so tested.
This food that was prepared
Has certainly saved my life.

4168 Don't chalk it up to malice
If I remind you of my great need:
I must have something to drink.
I have been prey to such a great thirst

4172 That has plagued me since this morning
That I cannot endure it any longer.
I won't be able to last
Very long, if I don't drink something.

4176 I will quickly be on the road
With you as soon as I have drunk something."
He who was without a name was astonished,
But without being asked again,

4180 He went back into the hall.
He went to the dais to pick up the cup.
But when he stretched out his hand,
She who was seated at the table

4184 Took the cup from him
And spoke to him very angrily:
"One would not defy me
By taking wine and meat

4188 If they who are in the countryside
And seeking pleasure in the woods
Were all here in the hall.
"But now you have found me alone,

4192 And you have used me to prove
Your valor: great honor
You'll have for dishonoring
An unprotected woman!"

4196   Et le nains par ire l'apele,
      Si li dist: "Sire chevalier,
      Ja n'arés de li sans dangier
      Vaillant un seul quartié de pain."
4200   Cil prist la coupe ens en sa main,
      Vuelle u ne welle, si l'en porte
      Celi qui l'atent a la porte.
      Et l'autre qui siet a la table
4204   Li dist: "N'estes pas bien raisnable,
      Sire vassal, ne bien apris,
      Qui ci avés sor son pois pris
      Mon mengier. Se cil fust en vie
4208   Dont tout le monde avoit envie
      Por le bien qui en lui estoit,
      J'en eüsce encor moult haut droit.
      Ahi! Mors, tant par es costoxe,
4212   Felenesse et contralioxe,
      Que ja n'espargneras prodome:
      N'a damoisele duqu'a Rome,
      Ne de la duques en Espaigne
4216   Ki esgaree n'en remagne.
      Ahi! Ahi!" dist el, "Gavain,
      Ne fust pas traite de ma main
      Ma coupe, se vous fuisciés vis,   [28va]
4220   Ne mon mengier devant moi pris;
        "Je n'en eüsce nul regart.
      Or n'est il mais qui nos drois gart,
      Ne qui i mete contençon."
4224   Cil qui n'ot soig de sa tençon
      A au nain la coupe livree;
      Et cele qui s'ert delivree
      Et de la viande et del vin
4228   Se rest o lui mise au cemin.
      Il n'ont mie granment alé,
      Puis qu'il ont le pont avalé,
      K'il ont trouvé le chevalier
4232   Qui li ot doné le destrier
      A la crois, et le palefroi
      A tout le sele et tout l'agroi,
      Dont il avoit moult grant besong.

4196   And the dwarf spoke to her angrily.
Then he said: "Sir Knight,
You will not get anything from her
Willingly, not even a little bread."
4200   And he picked up the cup in his hand,
Like it or not, and carried it
To the one who waited at the gate.
And she who sat at the table
4204   Said: "You are not very sensible,
Vassal, nor very well-mannered,
You who have taken my food against
My wishes; if he were alive,
4208   He who was envied by all the world
For the goodness that was within him,
I would have prompt justice for this.
Alas, Death, you who are so costly,
4212   Thieving, and disloyal,
You never spare a good man;
There is no woman from here to Rome
Nor back through all of Spain
4216   Who is not left distraught.
Alas, alas," she said, "Gawain,
This cup would not have been taken
From my hand if you were alive,
4220   Nor my food taken away from me.
    "I would have faced no danger;
But now there is no one to guard
Our rights or offer a challenge."
4224   He who had no care for her defense
Gave the cup to the dwarf,
And she who had been given
The meat and the wine
4228   Set out with him on the road.
They hadn't gone very far;
They had just reached the bridge
When they met the knight
4232   Who had given them the war horse
Back at the crossroad—as well as
The palfrey with saddle and harness—
For which there had been great need.

4236   Si tint l'esprevier sor son poing
        K'i li avoit ileuc donné;
        Et si estoit si bien armé,
        Et si a droit, qu'en nule terre
4240   Plus acesmé n'esteüst querre.
        Il le salue, si li quiert,
        Com cil qui a besoig le quiert,
        C'or li rende le gueredon;
4244   Et si li amentoit le don
        Dont li gueredons est deüs;
        Et s'il n'est orendroit rendus,
        Et il veut tant ne quant atendre,
4248   Ja mais n'ara pooir de rendre.
        "Si vous dirai," fait il, "por quoi:
        Ce castel est lassus tout quoi;
        Il n'i a orendroit nului
4252   Qui faire vous peüst anui.
        Li chevaliers de laiens tuit
        Sont en cel bos en lor deduit,
        J'en sai tres gewi la novele;
4256   Et laiens a une pucele,   [28va]
        Dedens cel castel enfremee,
        Que j'ai plus de trois ans amee;
        Si vous pri que le me dounois."
4260   "Par foi," fait il, "ce est bien drois
        Que vous l'aiiés, se onques puis;
        Et se je el castel le truis,
        Ja m'en trouverés tout loial."
4264   Lors torne arriere le ceval,
        Si revint arriere en le sale.
        Et cele qui forment le male
        Par parole et moult le maudit,
4268   Li a moult estoutement dit
        Que mal i soit il retornés.
        Et il est lors vers li alés,
        Si l'a par le destre bras prise;
4272   Puis si l'a devant lui asise
        Sor son ceval, puis si s'en torne.
        En la sale plus ne sejorne.
        Et cele qui tenrement pleure

4236 He held on his finger the sparrow hawk
    That had been given him there.
    He was so well-armed, in such a
    Befitting way, that one couldn't
4240 Find anyone so fashionable on earth.
    He greeted Gawain and asked him,
    Like someone who needed help,
    To make good on his promise.
4244 He reminded Gawain of the boon
    That he was obliged to fulfill.
    If he didn't acquit himself at once
    Or delayed the least bit,
4248 He would never again have the chance.
    "And I will tell you," he said, "why.
    This castle is defenseless.
    Right now there is no one
4252 Who can make trouble for you.
    All the knights from there
    Are sporting in the woods.
    I have just learned this news.
4256 And shut up inside this castle
    Is a young woman whom I have loved
    For more than three years.
    I ask you to deliver her to me."
4260 "By my faith," said Gawain, "it is
    Certainly proper that you should have her;
    If I can find her in the castle,
    Then you will find me completely loyal."
4264 Then he turned his horse back
    And went back into the hall.
    And she, who spoke so badly
    Of him and cursed him so,
4268 Told him very rudely that
    His return was a bad thing.
    And he rode up to her
    And grabbed her by the right arm;
4272 Then he seated her before him
    On his horse and turned back.
    No one else remained in the hall.
    And she, weeping pitifully,

4276   Le maldist, et si prie et eure
        Que Dix mal entente li doigne;
        Et quant ele voit qu'ele esloigne,
        Et qu'ele est ja hors de la porte,
4280   A mervelle se desconforte.
        Lors tort ses poins et brait et crie,
        Et dist en haut: "Aïe! aïe!
            "Lasse," fait ele, "tant Dix me het.
4284   Ainmi lasse, que or nel set
        Mon frere le prox Codrovain?
        Ahi! ahi!" dist ele, "Gavain,
        Tant avons de vous grant damage:
4288   Ja ne fust pensé cest outrage,
        Cest grant orguel et cest sorfait
        Ke cis chevaliers m'a ci fait,
        Se vous fuisciés sain et delivre."
4292   Et il toutes voies le livre
        Et tent a celui qui tant l'ainme;   [29ra]
        Et ele tot adés reclainme,]
        Et si afice çou et jure
4296   Que ja ceste grant desmesure
        Ne fust faite, se il vis fust.
        Uns siens frere, qui a un fust
        Estoit lors afustés por traire,
4300   Oï la damoisele braire:
        A grant paine l'a tresoïe.
        Et la pucele autre fois crie;
        Il ne set quoi, car trop est loing,
4304   Mais bien entent qu'el a besoing.
        C'ert Codrovain qui reclamoit.
        Et li chevaliers qui l'amoit,
        Qui or la tient en sa baillie,
4308   Li a dit: "Bele douce amie,
        Je sui Ragidel de l'Angarde,
        Et puis c'or estes en ma garde
        Moult en devés grant joie avoir.
4312   A escient poés savoir
        Que je sui ci li vostre amis.
        Ja m'avés vous tox jors pramis
        Que vous n'amiés rien fors moi.

4276 Cursed him and called on God
      To give him bad luck.
      Seeing that she was being carried off
      And that she was already at the gate,
4280 She lamented her plight even more.
      She wrung her hands, cried, screamed,
      And called out, "Help! Help!
            "Alas, that God should so despise me!
4284 How sad that my brother, the proud
      Codrovain, doesn't know about this!
      Alas! Alas!" she said, "Gawain,
      We have so much sorrow on your account:
4288 If you were alive and free,
      I wouldn't have to suffer this outrage,
      This great arrogance and insolence
      That this knight commits against me."
4292 And he took her straight back
      And handed her over to him who loved her.
      And she continued to complain,
      To allege and swear that this
4296 Outrageous act couldn't have been
      Accomplished if Gawain were alive.
      One of her brothers, who was posted
      Behind a tree, ready to shoot his bow,
4300 Heard the young woman cry out.
      It was hard to hear her clearly.
      And the young woman cried out again;
      He didn't know what she said, for she was far away,
4304 But he understood that she needed help.
      This was Codrovain whom she called for.
      And the knight who loved her,
      Who now held her in his guard,
4308 Said to her, "Beautiful, sweet friend,
      I am Ragidel of Angarde,
      And because you are now in my protection,
      You ought to express great joy.
4312 You can be certain
      That I am your friend.
      You have always declared
      That you loved no one other than me.

4316 Se on vous croit par vostre foi,
      Que j'en ai de vostre main destre,
      Dont en doi jou aseür estre."
      Quant la damoisele l'oï,
4320 A mervelle s'en esjoï.
           Dont a dit: "Sire chevalier,
      A qui je veai mon mengier,
      Je vous en dois gage en merci,
4324 Et de ceste oeuvre vous merci,
      Car moult m'avés a gré païe.
      C'estoie or forment esmaïe,
      Moult dolante et moult esgaree;
4328 Car je quidoie estre livree
      A honme que je pas n'amasse.
      Ja mais a nul jor ne manjasse   [29rb]
      S'il me fust issi avenu.
4332 Bien soit cel chevalier venu
      Ki si m'a wi païe a gré.
      Jou afi volentiers et gré,
      Se lui plaist, que a vous me doigne,
4336 Et si li proi qu'il me pardoigne,
      Et que il pas ne prenge a pris
      Çou que tant ai vers lui mespris."
           "Bele," fait il, "jel vous pardoig.
4340 Mais tant i a que je vous doig
      A ce chevalier que vous tient,
      Ma damoisele, et si couvient
      Que de çou que je vous ai fait,
4344 Car je sai bien que j'ai mesfait,
      Que me pardonés le mal gré."
      "Sire," fait ele, "jel vous gré."
           Ses freres qui oïe l'ot,
4348 A l'ançois que il onques pot,
      Est venus au castel poignant.
      En la cort trova un sergant,
      Si li demande qui faisoit
4352 La noise que oïe avoit;
      Et cil sans nule demoree
      Li a la verité contee:
      Onques ne l'en menti de riens.

4316   If one can trust your pledge,
Which you gave me with your right hand,
Then I ought to be given assurance."
When the young woman heard this,
4320   She was extremely joyful.
       Then she said, "Sir Knight,
You to whom I refused my food,
Now I am obligated to you.
4324   I thank you for this deed,
For you have paid me generously.
I was just now very upset,
Very sorrowful and distraught,
4328   Because I thought I'd be handed over
To a man I didn't love at all.
I would never have eaten again
If this had happened to me.
4332   Blessed be the arrival of this knight
Who has repaid me so generously.
And I consent willingly,
If it please him, that he gives me to you.
4336   I pray that he will forgive me
And that he will not hold a grudge
For my bad behavior toward him."
       "Fair one," Gawain said, "I pardon you.
4340   But it remains for me to give you
To this knight who holds you,
My dear woman; moreover, I must
Ask you to pardon me as well
4344   For what I have done—
For I know that I misbehaved."
       "Sir," she said, "I grant you this."
       The brother, who had heard her cry,
4348   Came galloping up to the castle
As quickly as he could.
In the court he found a servant
And asked him who had made
4352   The noise that he had heard.
And without delay he told
The truth of the matter;
He didn't lie about anything.

4356   "Or n'est mie cis païs miens,"
        Fait il, "se il l'en mainne issi."
        Eranment d'une estable issi
        Moult vistement un sien vallet,
4360   Si li tramist le Gringalet,
        Si li mist le frain et le sele.
        Puis monta en une torele,
        Qui ert desus le maistre porte;
4364   Moult delivrement li aporte
        Son escu, s'espee, et sa lance.
        Et il hors del baile se lance
        Des qu'il fu montés el destrier,   [29va]
4368   K'il estoit icel chevalier
        Qui laisça Gavain o s'amie
        U bois par sa grant jalousie,
        Et qui lor cevax en mena.
4372   De l'esploitier tant se pena,
        Puis qu'il fu du castel isçus,
        K'il a les chevaliers veüs,
        Et les damoisseles ensanble;
4376   Et se il ja nes desasanble,
        Et il ne depart cele route
        Et desconfist vistement toute,
        A çou qu'il est chevaliers buens
4380   Et li cris du païs est suens,
        Il ne se prisse un angevain.
        Cil sans non l'oï le cemin
        Venir poignant par mi un val,
4384   Et quant il counut le ceval
        Qui li chevaliers cevaucoit,
        Onques isi grant joïe n'ot.
        D'angousce rien ne li enquiert,
4388   Mais hardiement le requiert,
        Et cil lait corre contre lui,
        Si s'entrefierent anbedui.
            Li chevalier le fiert avant,
4392   El quartier de l'escu devant,
        Que sa lance en asteles vole,
        Com se ce fust une ventvole.
        Cil sans non l'a aprés feru,

4356 "Now this country is no longer mine,"
He said, "if he leads her away like this."
Quickly he called one of his servants
To come forth from the stable
4360 And bring him his horse, Gringalet,
And harness and saddle him up.
He got on the horse from a mounting block
That was near the main gate.
4364 A servant quickly brought him
His shield, his sword, and his lance.
As soon as he had mounted his war horse,
He rushed beyond the palisade:
4368 He was the very same knight
Who—because of his intense jealousy—
Had left Gawain with his friend
In the woods and taken their horses away.
4372 He pushed himself so hard,
After issuing from the castle,
That he soon saw the knights
And the young women together.
4376 And if he doesn't break them up,
And force them to disband
And go their separate ways,
Then he who is a good knight
4380 And to whom the land's fame belongs,
Won't be worth a bean.
He without a name heard him on the road,
Riding quickly through a valley,
4384 And when he recognized the horse
That the knight was riding,
He had never been so happy.
In his anger, he didn't ask questions,
4388 But went right to battle;
Codrovain rushed toward him,
And they clashed against one another.
   The knight hit Gawain first,
4392 Striking a portion of his shield in front,
So that his lance flew into pieces,
Like a thing fluttering in the breeze.
He without a name hit him next

4396   Desox le boucle de l'escu,
        Com cil qui ne l'espargne point,
        Que l'escu li a au bras goint,
        Et le bras au costé li serre;
4400   Tout estendu le porte a terre.
        Puis a mis le main a l'espee;
        La teste li eüst caupee,
        Quant la damoisele li prie
4404   Et requiert que pas ne l'ocie: [29vb]
            "Sire," dist ele, "ce m'est vis
        Que se vous l'aviiés ocis
        Ja mais nul jor joïe n'aroie."
4408   Et li chevaliers li otroie
        Et dist qu'il fera tout son buen,
        Par si que il face le suen.
            "Sire," dist Codrovain le Rox,
4412   "Tant a prouece et bien en vox,
        Francise et debounaireté,
        Que ne devés estre reté
        De rien nule que m'aiiés fait,
4416   Que ç'a esté par mon sorfait;
        Et por çou otroi bien et gré
        A faire tout le vostre gré."
            "Sire," dist il, "vostre merci.
4420   A ceste damoisele ci
        Vous pri c'ox pardounés vostre ire;
        Et si vous veul encor plus dire,
        Dont je vous veul forment priier,
4424   Ke welliés que ce chevalier
        Ait par vostre otroi vostre suer,
        Car il l'ainme de tout sen cuer,
        Et je quit bien qu'ele aime lui;
4428   Et si vous acordés andui
        Entre vous et la vostre amie,
        Sans rancune et sans vilonnie.
        Jel vous ofri des avant ier,
4432   Quant je montai por l'esprevier,
        Ke je sor sains vous juerroie
        Moult volentiers que je n'avoie
        A la pucele cose dite,

4396   Under the boss of his shield,
Like someone who didn't want to spare him:
He forced the shield up against his arms
So that he was pressed to one side

4400   And thrown down on the ground.
Then Gawain picked up his sword;
He was about to cut off his head,
When the young woman spoke up

4404   And begged that he not kill him.
      "Sir," she said, "it's evident
That if you kill him
I will never again have joy."

4408   And the knight granted this to her
And said that he would follow her wishes
If the knight would promise the same.
      "Sir," said Codrovain the Red,

4412   "You are so full of prowess and goodness,
Generosity and gentility,
That you ought not to be blamed
For anything that you have done to me,

4416   For it was all because of my pride.
For this reason I agree willingly
And with pleasure to do all that you wish."
      "Sir, " Gawain replied, "I thank you.

4420   I ask that you set aside your anger
Toward this young woman here.
And I want to ask something else of you,
For which I beg you most earnestly:

4424   That you agree to grant
Your sister to this knight,
For he loves her with all his heart.
And I believe that she loves him as well.

4428   And you should both make peace—
That is, you and your friend here,
Without rancor or villainy.
Two days ago I proposed,

4432   When I climbed up for the sparrow hawk,
That I would swear by the saints,
Of my own free will, that I had said
Nothing to this young woman

4436   Se j'ere renclus u ermite,
        Le plus saint et le plus prodome
        Ki soit de ci desi qu'a Rome,
        Dont je fusce reté de rien."
4440   "Je vous en croi," fait il, "moult bien
        K'ains n'en fu mot par vous parlé."   [30ra]
        Ensi com il fu porparlé
        Et la cose fu devisee,
4444   Fu la concorde creantee.
            Lors a repris le Gringalet
        Cil sans non, qu'i n'i eüst ret
        Ja mais sans nule contençon,
4448   Et se li fist del sien le don;
        Si vous di je bien que li suens
        Estoit assés et biax et buens.
        Si frere, que la noise oïrent,
4452   Tantost des esperons ferirent,
        Si passerent tertres et vaus:
        N'espargnent mie lor cevaus,
        K'il n'ont pas trouvés lens ne frains,
4456   Ains esperonent qui ains ains.
        Puis ont demandees noveles,
        Ançois qu'il ostascent les seles,
        A un vaslet qu'il ont trouvé.
4460   Cil a qui il l'orent rouvé
        Lor dist ensi com il avinrent,
        Et il lors en la sale vinrent,
        Si ont lor armes demandees.
4464   Cil qui el furent conmandees
        Lor livra; il se sont armé,
        Puis sont es bons cevax monté
        Et sont isçu par grant desroi.
4468   Et jurent que se c'ert le roi
        Ki eüst enpris tel sorfait
        Si seroit il de lui tot fait
        En tel guise qu'il en morroit,
4472   Que rien garantir nel porroit.
        Ne targa gaires qu'il les voient;
        Lors se porficent et desroient,
        Si ont les lances alongies,

4436 For which I could be blamed,
   Not even if I were a recluse or a hermit,
   The most saintly and most Christian
   Who could be found from here to Rome."
4440 "I am completely convinced," he replied,
   "That you didn't say a word."
   Thus, just as Gawain had proposed,
   Everything was accomplished,
4444 And peace was established.
     The knight without a name took back
   Gringalet without delay
   And without any protest,
4448 And made a gift of his horse to Codrovain;
   And I can assure you that Gawain's
   Was beautiful and good enough.
   Codrovain's brothers, who had heard the noise,
4452 Quickly spurred their horses
   And rode through hills and valleys,
   Not sparing their horses,
   Which didn't feel the reins
4456 And galloped like never before.
   Then, without removing their saddles,
   The brothers asked for news
   From a servant they encountered.
4460 This one to whom they made inquiries
   Told them what had happened.
   They went into the hall
   And ordered their arms be brought out.
4464 Those who were commanded to do so
   Brought them out; the brothers armed themselves,
   And then mounted their good horses
   And rushed out in great anger.
4468 They swore that, even if it were the king
   Himself who had committed this outrage,
   They would deal with him
   In such a way that he would die
4472 And nothing could protect him.
   It wasn't long before they saw the others.
   They spurred their horses and advanced,
   Their lances were extended,

4476 Et les enarmes enpongnies
Des escus, por corre lor seure.
Codrovains li Rous en is l'eure, [30rb]
Ki lors ert u ceval montés,
4480 Laist corre, sis a encontrés,
Si lor a moult fierement dit:
S'un d'ex ert par ex desconfit,
Ke ja mais un n'en ameroit.
4484 Et si jure que il feroit
Por ex çou c'onques ne fist nus;
Car se cil en faisoient plus,
Il se torneroit ja vers eus
4488 Et se conbateroit por ex.
    "Segnor," dist il, "or entendés.
Je ai deus chevaliers trouvés,
Prox et cortois et ensegniés,
4492 Et cil de ça est tant prissiés,
Ki a a moi cangié ceval,
Tant l'ai trouvé prou et loial
Ke nus ne vous diroit por rien
4496 Seulement le moitié del bien
Ke on porroit trouver en lui."
Mais ce est traval et anui
De reconter vous tout le conte
4500 Si com Codrovain le reconte,
Com il ert en caisne monté;
Si lor avoit dit et conté
Com il i ot l'esprevier pris
4504 Et com il l'i avoit soupris.
De cief en cief lor conte l'uevre;
Puis lor dist aprés et descuevre
Com il a faite le concorde.
4508 Tant lor a dit qu'il les acorde
Et que l'uevre fu creantee
Ensi com ele ert devisee.
    Lors l'ont proiié de remanoir,
4512 Et qu'il s'en voist a lor manoir
Ensanble o ex, et s'en soit sire.
Et il lor conmença a dire
Moult bonement, qu'il ne pot estre; [30va]

4476 And they had seized the straps
Of their shields, ready to engage them.
Codrovain the Red,
Who was already mounted on his horse,
4480 Rode up to meet them
And spoke very forcefully to them:
If one of his party was harmed by them,
He would never love them again.
4484 And he swore that he would do
To them what had never been done before:
For if they made another move,
He would turn against them
4488 And battle on the other side.
        "Lords," he said, "now listen:
I have found two knights,
Brave, courteous, and well-mannered,
4492 And this one here, who has exchanged
Horses with me, is especially praiseworthy.
I have found him so brave and loyal
That I can't begin to tell you
4496 Half of all the goodness
That one can find in him."
But this is hard work and boring
To retell the entire story
4500 Exactly as Codrovain told it.
Thus he spoke and told them
How Gawain had been in the oak tree
And how he had taken the sparrow hawk
4504 And how he had surprised him.
From beginning to end he told the story.
Then he spoke some more and revealed
How they had made an agreement.
4508 He spoke until he got them to agree
That the affair should be concluded
Just as it had been arranged.
        Then they asked Gawain to stay
4512 And to go back to the manor
With them and be treated royally.
And Gawain began to tell them,
Very graciously, that he could not:

4516 Car il lasça or sor senestre
  Un chevalier deus liues loig
  Ki d'aïe a moult grant besoig.
   Lors li a l'uevre recontee,
4520 Ensi com cil li ot contee
  Ki aloit rescorre s'amie;
  Et il jurent qu'il n'ira mie
  Se il ne vont ensanble o lui.
4524 Et il lor dist: "Segnor, je cui
  Que j'ai ici trop sejorné;
  Mix me vendroit estre acoré,
  Quant je li ai couvenancié,
4528 K'il ne fust par moi avancié,
  Car j'en seroie en fin traïs.
  Si vous en renc grés et mercis
  De çou que vous m'avés offert,
4532 Et il vous sera bien soufert
  K'ox i venrés ensanble o moi.
  Et je vous pramet et otroi,
  S'o moi vous i plaist a venir,
4536 K'a vostre me poés tenir."
   Il li pramettent qu'il iront
  Et s'aficent que il feront
  Tout lor pooir de la rescoxe.
4540 Codrovains a la Teste Roxe
  Li dist: "Sire, ne vous poist mie,
  Je menrai ariere m'amie,
  Et se Ragidiax le m'otroie
4544 J'en menrai la soie et la moie,
  Car eles n'ont o nous que faire.
  Et ce pas ne li doit desplaire,
  Se je l'en main, car je vous di,
4548 Et loiaument le vous afi,
  Que bien l'en ert tenu le don,
  Et tantost que nous revendron
  Je li rendrai sans contredit."
4552 Puis lor a divisé et dit   [30vb]
  Qu'il n'a en la forest trestor,
  Sentele ne adreceor
  K'il ne sace, et qu'il les suirra

4516   For he had left, two leagues away,
        On the left-hand side, a knight
        Who was in dire need of help.
           He laid out the whole affair
4520   Just as it had been told to him
        By the one who was rescuing his friend.
        And they swore they would go nowhere
        Except together with him.
4524   And he said, "Lords, I believe
        That I have already stayed too long.
        I would be most upset if,
        After having struck a deal with him,
4528   He were not aided by me:
        I would be a true traitor!
        I am very pleased and thankful
        By what you have offered me.
4532   It will be much appreciated
        If you go there together with me.
        I give you my assurance,
        If it pleases you to come with me,
4536   That I will be obligated to you."
           They promised him that they would go,
        And they affirmed that they would do
        All in their power toward the rescue.
4540   Codrovain with the Red Hair
        Said to him, "If you don't mind,
        I will lead my friend back,
        And, if Ragidel agrees,
4544   I will also lead his young woman back,
        For they have no business with us.
        And this step ought not to displease him,
        If I lead her away, for I tell you
4548   And loyally affirm it to you
        That she will be given back to him.
        As soon as we have returned,
        I will turn her over without a fuss."
4552   Then he continued to say that
        There was in all the forest no shortcut,
        No winding path, nor crossroad
        That he didn't know and that he would

4556   Tantost com il armés sera;
        Mais ains sera d'armes garnis,
        Car, s'il en estoit desgarnis
        La endroit en si grant afaire,
4560   U tel besoins ert de bien faire,
        Ja mais nul jor joie n'aroit
        De la honte qu'il en aroit.
            Cil s'en retorne et cil s'en vont,
4564   En tel guise com je vous cont,
        De bien faire tout abrievé.
        De ce a moi pas n'estrivés
        C'or ne soit cil sans non a aise,
4568   Et k'a mervelle ne li plaise,
        K'il a porcacié tel gent
        Dont le porcas est bel et gent,
        Ki tant est bien aparellie
4572   Et de bien faire encoragie.
        Ensi sox les elmes enclins
        Trespassent sentes et cemins
        Et erroient les grans galos,
4576   Tant qu'il ont trovés les esclos,
        Par mi une lande, des dex
        Qui cevaucoient devant ex;
        Serreement oirrent aprés.
4580   Entre Espinogre et Cadrés,
        Qui erroient plus que le pas,
        Estoient ja venu au pas,
        U il atendent la venue
4584   Du chevalier et de sa drue.
           Saciés bien que Cadrés ot non,
        Bon chevalier et de grant non,
        Cil a qui cele ouvre apendoit.
4588   En itel maniere atendoit,
        Et Espinogres aveuc lui: [31ra]
        N'estoient encore qu'il dui
        Quant il ont la route veüe.
4592   Et cil qui conduisoit sa drue
        Est li premiers entrés el pas.
        Cadrés lait corre eneslespas,
        Tant com cevax li pot randir,

4556   Catch up as soon as he was armed.
        But first he would go get new arms,
        For if he were caught off-guard,
        Unprepared, in such an important event,
4560   Where his good deeds were greatly needed,
        He would never enjoy another happy day
        On account of the shame he would have.
          So he turned back, and the others went on,
4564   Just in the way I have told you,
        All geared up for great deeds.
        Now don't try to tell me that
        He without a name wasn't happy
4568   Or that he wasn't very pleased
        That he had acquired such people—
        So beautiful and noble—
        Who were completely ready
4572   And eager to do good deeds.
        Thus, with their helmets lowered,
        They travelled along roads and paths;
        They went at great speed
4576   Until they found the footprints
        On the ground of the two
        Who had galloped ahead.
        The others followed after in tight ranks.
4580   Espinogre and Cadrés,
        Who had ridden ahead very fast,
        Had already come to a narrow place
        Where they awaited the arrival
4584   Of the knight and his friend.
          Be assured that Cadrés was his name,
        A *bon chevalier* of great renown,
        He to whom this affair pertains.
4588   They waited in this manner,
        Espinogre alongside him.
        There were still just two of them
        When they saw the party coming.
4592   And the one who led his friend
        Was the first to enter the pass.
        Cadrés let his horse run
        As fast as a horse can gallop,

4596   Si l'a feru par tel aïr
        En l'escu en la boucle amont
        K'il l'abati tout en un mont,
        Lui et le ceval tot ensanble.
4600   Et Espinogres, ce me sanble,
        A si l'autre aprés feru
        Que du ceval l'a abatu
        Tot envers en une sentele
4604   Devant les piés a la pucele.
            Dont les escrie durement,
        Si retorne menuement,
        Et fiert et de lance et d'espee.
4608   Onques mais ne fu tex meslee
        Par seul dex chevaliers souferte
        Sans enconbrier d'ax ne sans perte.
        Moult soufrirent d'armes grans fais;
4612   Et si vous di que onques mais
        A dex chevaliers çou n'avint
        K'il fuscent asanblé a vint
        D'un tel fais d'armes sostenir
4616   K'un mal pas a force tenir
        Que nus des vint passer n'i puet.
        Cadrés trop hardiement muet,
        Si a fait un trop rice encontre,
4620   Et fiert le premier qu'il encontre
        El pis entre les deus mameles,
        Ke sa lance vole en asteles.
        Cil kaï jus tout a un frois;
4624   Et fiert un autre del retrois
        Si grant caup par mi le visiere
        K'il l'abat sor l'arçon derriere,   [31rb]
        De son ceval si qu'il caïst,
4628   S'uns escuiers ne le tenist.
        Ne fu pas jetés li tronçons,
        Ains a feru des esperons,
        Si fiert le tierc et puis le quart.
4632   Et Espinogres de sa part
        Ne li doit de bien faire rien.
        Cascuns d'ex le fait si tres bien
        Ke li autre s'en esbahiscent;

4596　And he struck him in such a way
　　　High on the boss of the shield
　　　That he knocked down both at once,
　　　Both rider and horse together.
4600　And Espinogre, so it appears to me,
　　　Struck the one who followed
　　　So that he knocked him from his horse
　　　Onto the middle of the path
4604　Right at the feet of the maiden.
　　　　　He challenged the others rudely
　　　And turned quickly to the charge,
　　　Striking with both lance and sword.
4608　Never before was there such a battle
　　　Caused by only two knights
　　　In which neither was harmed nor lost.
　　　They endured great feats of arms.
4612　And I tell you again that never before
　　　Has such a thing happened to two knights:
　　　That they could encounter twenty knights
　　　And survive such feats of arms
4616　And hold their position so well
　　　That none of the twenty could pass through.
　　　Cadrés exerted himself very bravely
　　　And had a very profitable encounter;
4620　He hit the first knight he met
　　　Right in the middle of the chest,
　　　So that his lance broke into pieces.
　　　That one fell down with one blow.
4624　With the stump he struck another one
　　　With such a terrible blow on the visor that
　　　He pushed him back on top of the saddlebow
　　　So that he fell from his horse,
4628　And no squire could hold him.
　　　Without throwing away the stump,
　　　Cadrés struck with renewed energy
　　　A third and then a fourth knight.
4632　Espinogre, for his part,
　　　Didn't let the enemy accomplish anything.
　　　Each of them fought so well
　　　That his adversaries stood amazed.

4636 Neporquant si se ravertiscent,
     Si se tienent moult a honi
     De çou qu'il ont esté laidi
     Par deus chevaliers seulement.
4640 Car il quident seürement
     Ke il n'i ait un seul des vint,
     Nes le pior qui o ex vint,
     S'il trovast orains un de cex,
4644 Si fuscent cors a cors par ex,
     K'il nel cuidast ocirre u prendre,
     Que ja ne se peüst deffendre.
     Por la vergongne qu'il en ont
4648 Du grant anui que cil lor font
     Ont tout ensanle un poindre pris,
     Si ont sor ex le pas porpris,
     Si que deguerpir lor couvint.
4652 A Espinogre lors souvint
     De çou que ses conpains li dist
     Ançois que de lui departist.
          Lors a pris son cor si le sone,
4656 Si que tox li bos en resone,
     Et cil qui sivent l'ont oï.
     Cil sans non moult s'en esjoï,
     K'il a au corner entendu
4660 Que il se sont bien deffendu,
     Et que tant se porront tenir
     K'il i porra a tans venir.
     Lors a feru des esperons,   [31va]
4664 Si a dit a ses conpaignons:
          "Segnor," dist il, "or en venés,
     Car a cel cor qu'oï avés,
     Sone uns de cex qui nous atendent,
4668 Ki a grant anui se deffendent."
     Lors laiscent les cevax aler.
     Quant vint a un tertre avaler
     Si ont les chevaliers veüs:
4672 Espinogre ert au frain tenus,
     Si ert trestoute la meslee
     El val desor lui arestee.
          Cadrés a bien recouneü

4636   Nevertheless, they pulled themselves together:
They would be terribly ashamed
If they were defeated
By only two knights.
4640   For they were convinced that
There wasn't a single one of the twenty,
Even if he were the worst of them,
Who, if he now met one of them
4644   And engaged in single combat,
Would not easily kill or capture him
So that he could no longer defend himself.
On account of the shame of it
4648   And their great worry at the prospect,
They regathered for the attack.
They regained their position at the pass,
And the other two had to retreat.
4652   And Espinogre remembered
What his companions had said to him
Before they departed from him.
      So he took up his horn and sounded it
4656   So that it resounded throughout the woods
And those who followed heard it.
The knight without a name rejoiced
At hearing the horn sounded,
4660   Knowing that they had defended
Themselves well and held off the enemy
So that he could arrive in time.
He dug in his spurs
4664   And said to his companions:
      "Milords," he said, "let's hurry!
For by this horn that you have heard
One of those who awaits us calls,
4668   And he's having trouble defending himself."
Then they let their horses gallop.
Just as they were about to descend a hill,
They saw the two knights.
4672   Espinogre was being held by the bridle
And was hounded by knights circled
All around him in the little valley.
      Cadrés easily recognized

4676   Celui sans non, qu'il a veü
       Qui li vient aidier sans faintise,
       La lance sox l'aisele mise;
       Et li autre qui aprés vienent
4680   Les lances alongies tienent,
       Si ont les escus enbraciés,
       D'adier les tox encoragiés.
          Quant il ont veü lor secors
4684   Ki en poi d'eure lor est sors,
       Moult par en ont grant joie eüe;
       Por lor force qui ert creüe
       A cascuns jetee la main,
4688   Si prist un autre par le frain.
          Cil sans non hardiement muet,
       Tant com cevax rendre li puet,
       Si se fiert en la gregnor presse,
4692   Ke forment s'angousce et apresse
       De lor chevaliers retenir.
       S'en fiert si un en son venir,
       D'une lance qui moult ert forte,
4696   K'a terre du ceval le porte.
       Et li autre qui aprés vienent
       Les lances alongies tienent;
       De tex i ot quin abatirent
4700   Les chevaliers qu'il en ferirent.   [31vb]
       Moult hardiement les requissent;
       Par force a la voie les missent,
       Ferant ferant en lor venue,
4704   K'onques regne n'i ot tenue.
       Por un petit qu'il ne passerent
       Outre le pas; les entasserent
       Par force et par armes tox vint,
4708   Si que d'ex tans d'onor avint,
       De ce qu'il sont avant venus,
       K'il ont deus des lor retenus.
       Prison les fissent fiancier;
4712   Puis se painent d'ex avancier,
       Si se revont mesler a ex.
       Bien aidierent li huit as dex
       K'il troverent si enconbrés,

4676 The knight without a name and realized
      That he was eager to come to his aid,
      His lance set under his armpit.
      The others who followed him
4680 Also had their lances extended,
      And they had their shields in their arms,
      Ready to help the others.
          When they saw that help
4684 Had arrived at the hour of their need,
      The two knights were overcome with joy;
      Encouraged by these forces,
      Each extended his hand
4688 And grabbed another by the bridle.
          He without a name pressed forward bravely,
      As fast as his horse could go,
      Into the thick of the battle,
4692 Very anxious to bring
      The knights under his control.
      At his arrival, he struck one
      With a lance that was very strong
4696 And threw him from his horse onto the ground.
      And the others who followed him
      Moved forward with extended lances.
      Of these there were five who fought
4700 The knights whom they laid into.
      They attacked most forcefully,
      Pushing them back along the road,
      Slashing about at their approach
4704 So that no one could hold onto his reins.
      Shortly thereafter they regained
      The pass; they forced by virtue
      Of their arms all twenty to regroup,
4708 And they gained much honor
      Because of this charge,
      For they captured two there
      And made them their prisoners.
4712 Then they pressed their attack
      And returned to battle the others.
      The other eight provided much help
      To the two who were hard-pressed,

4716   Et si ont cex desbaretés.
        Et quant li fuiant au pas vinrent,
        A l'entree lor frains retinrent.
        Puis ont arriere regardé,
4720   Si ont veü et esgardé
        Ke cil que caçoient n'estoient
        Que seul dis, et si ne veoient,
        Si garderent et lonc et pres,
4724   Nul secors qui venist aprés.
        Moult se tienent a entrepris,
        Si ont lor hardement repris,
        Ses requierent hardïement;
4728   Et se li livres ne me ment
        U je trovai le conte escrit,
        Onques nus chevaliers ne vit
        Si buen estor de tant de gent,
4732   Car se cil vinrent radement,
        Li dis qui preu et hardi erent
        Hardiement les encontrerent.
        La ot desus l'erbe nouvele
4736   Maint trox de lance et mainte astele,
        Et maint chevalier pris au frain.   [32ra]
        Cadrés, qui n'ot pas le cuer vain,
        Ki grant piece s'estoit pris garde
4740   Et voit s'amie qui l'esgarde,
        Point le ceval de grant aïr
        Et vait celui au frain saisir
        Ki le jor prendre le devoit.
4744   Et cil sans non, qui tot çou voit,
        Ki avoit brisie sa lance,
        Broce le ceval, si se lance
        Entre lui et les chevaliers.
4748   Lors esperonent les destriers
        Si conpaignon qui erent pres,
        Si se sont tout lancié aprés,
        Si ont les chevaliers forclos.
4752   Ne lor ont pas torné le dos
        Si conpaignon, qui bien veoient
        Que lor segnor forclos avoient
        Si anemi qui son frain tienent:

4716 And they forced the others to flee.
And when those in retreat came to
The narrow pass, they slowed down.
Then they looked back
4720 And saw quite clearly that,
Of those who hadn't been thrown down,
There were only ten left; they realized,
Looking about far and wide,
4724 That no other help was arriving.
So they returned to their enterprise
And picked up the fight again
And attacked forcefully.
4728 And if the book in which I found
My story written doesn't lie,
No knight had ever before seen
Such a skirmish with such good noblemen.
4732 For just as these men attacked forcefully,
So did the ten brave and valiant knights
Return the attack vigorously.
On the new grass lay many
4736 Stumps and broken pieces of lances,
And many knights captured.
Cadrés, whose heart was not empty,
And who had, for a long time, taken note
4740 And seen his friend watching him,
Set his horse in motion
And seized by the bridle
Her to whom he had a right that day.
4744 And he without a name, who saw this,
And who had broken his lance,
Spurred his horse and lunged between
Cadrés and his adversaries.
4748 His companions who were nearby
Spurred their war horses
And rushed forward after him
And turned back the knights.
4752 His companions did not turn their
Backs, for they saw clearly
That the enemy had encircled
Their lord and had seized the bridle.

4756 Hardiement desqu'a lui vienent
   Por lui delivrer et secorre.
   Grant painne ont mis a lui rescorre,
   Mais il n'en peuent traire a cief;
4760 Et Cadrés li ot ja du cief
   Li hiaume osté et esracié,
   Sil tint par le col enbracié,
   Com cil qui moult savoit de gerre,
4764 Si se laisça glacier a terre.
    Quant Cadrés a terre le tint,
   Prison fiancier li couvint,
   Car del deffendre n'i ot point.
4768 Bien fu l'estors en icel point
   Com vous m'oés conter et dire,
   Car cil qui se dervoient d'ire
   De lor segnor qu'il voient pris
4772 L'ont moult hardiement enpris
   A faire por lui delivrer:
   Mix se veulent o lui livrer   [32rb]
   K'en prison l'en maint Cadrés si.
4776 Este vous que du bos issi
   Cadrovain le Rox, qui venoit
   Si durement com il pooit.
    Radement entra en l'estor,
4780 Si fiert un chevalier des lor
   Tel caup que lui et le destrier
   Fist a le terre trebucier.
   Oseement outre se lance
4784 Si fiert del retrox de le lance
   Un des autres qu'il encontra
   Si qu'a peu qu'il ne l'effronta:
   A terre tox pasmés caï.
4788 Cadrovain le tierc renvaï,
   Si qu'il li a caupé le pong,
   Et qu'il vola el camp bien loig
   De l'espee que il tenoit.
4792 Cil qui veoient qu'il venoit
   Si outrajeusement vers ex
   Ne cuident pas que il soit sex,
   Ains cuident bien qu'aprés lui viegnent

4756 They rushed forward in a flurry
   To deliver him and save him.
   They tried hard to rescue him,
   But in the end they didn't succeed;
4760 For by now Cadrés had knocked off
   And torn the helmet from his head
   And held him by the neck,
   Like someone who knew much about war,
4764 And let him slip to the ground.
    When Cadrés had him on the ground,
   He made him pledge himself a prisoner,
   For he couldn't possibly defend himself.
4768 The battle proceeded exactly
   As you have heard me tell it.
   For they who were wild with anger
   To see their lord captured
4772 Vigorously undertook all
   They could to rescue him.
   They preferred to give themselves up
   Than that Cadrés keep him in prison.
4776 Just at this moment Codrovain
   The Red came forth from the forest
   Riding as fast as he could.
    He rushed into the battle
4780 And hit one knight there with such a
   Blow that he made him and his war horse
   Stumble to the ground.
   With daring, he lunged farther
4784 And, with the butt of his lance, hit
   One of the other opponents
   So that he had little response:
   He fell to the ground unconscious.
4788 Codrovain took on a third one
   And chopped off his hand;
   It flew onto the field far away
   From the sword it had held.
4792 Those who saw that he advanced
   So outrageously toward them
   Couldn't believe he was alone;
   They thought surely that there followed

4796   Si grans gens que ja les retiegnent,
        Et que nul escaper n'en puisse
        Por ce que on el camp le truisce.
        Auques lor est li cuers faillis,
4800   Si quident estre mal baillis,
        Se cil en vienent el desus.
        De la deffense n'i ot plus:
        Lor segnor ont el camp laiscié,
4804   Si s'en va cascuns eslaiscié
        Tant com il puet del ceval traire.
        Et cil sans non, qui voloit faire
        La bonté qu'il avoit enprise,
4808   A la damoisele au frain prise,
        Ki gaires ne s'est deffendue,
        Si l'a lués a Cadrés rendue.
           Or a Cadrés joie trop grant,   [32va]
4812   Car s'amie qu'il aime tant,
        Et qui tant est bele et cortoise,
        A rescouse par sa prooise,
        Et du chevalier qu'il a pris,
4816   Ki avoit sor son pois enpris
        A mener la en sa contree.
        Moult a bone aïe trouvee,
        Ki si li a couvent tenu.
4820   Lors sont li set frere venu,
        Ki cacié orent longement
        Cex qui s'en vont vilainnement.
        Moult li ont tout priié et quis,
4824   Quant il orent son estre enquis,
        K'il sejornast ensanble o ex.
        Et il lor dist que par ex dex,
        Par son cors et par l'Espinogre,
4828   Par tout le roiame de Logre
        Sera tant l'aventure quise
        K'il ont devisee et enprise
        K'en aucun liu le troveront.
4832   Et quant il trovee l'aront,
        Si lor pramet que sans trestor
        Sera par ileuc son retor,
        Et qu'il en fin ne se movra

4796   A great troop that would capture them
And that no one would escape
If he were found on the field.
Thus their hearts failed them,
4800   For they believed their position bad
If the enemy had the upper hand.
There was no more chance for defense;
They left their lord on the field,
4804   And each one fled as fast as he
Could push his horse to go.
And he without a name, who wanted
To finish the good deed he had undertaken,
4808   Grasped the bridle of the maiden's horse,
Which was no longer defended,
And handed her over to Cadrés.
Now Cadrés was extremely happy:
4812   For he had rescued, through his prowess,
His friend—whom he loved so much
And who was beautiful and courteous—
From the knight he had captured,
4816   He who had tried by using force
To take her away into his country.
He had found those who held to their
Promise to him to be of great aid.
4820   Then the seven brothers rode up,
They who had chased for a long time
Those who fled from there shamefully.
After they had asked about his condition,
4824   They requested him most eagerly
To come and stay with them.
He replied that both of them,
Both he and Espinogre,
4828   Followed an adventure
Through all the kingdom of Logres
That they had planned and undertaken
And that some place they would find it.
4832   And when they found it,
They promised that without delay
They would return by way of them
And that in the end he would not

4836   Al revenir, si lor dira
        Son contenement et son estre;
        Car il ne porroit por rien estre
        Que son estre lor fust conté
4840   Desi qu'il ait son non trové
        Et l'aventure que il quiert.
        Cascuns li prie et li requiert
        Ke il le laist aler o lui;
4844   Et il s'afice que il dui,
        Il ne puet estre autrement fait,
        Ne le tiegnent mie a sorfait,
        N'a orguel ni a vilonie,
4848   Il iront sans plus conpaignie.   [32vb]
        Puis lor a priié, ce me sanle,
        Ke il sejornent tot ensanle
        Et k'al castel Codrovain soient
4852   Sejornant, tant qu'il le revoient
        Et qu'il oient parler de lui;
        Car moult grant joie et grant anui
        Set de voir que il li afiert,
4856   A l'aventure que il quiert,
        A soufrir ains que il revignent.
        Por çou lor prie qu'il se tignent
        Ensanble tant qu'il le revoient;
4860   Et il bonement li otroient
        K'en tel maniere l'atendront.
        Mais moult lor poise qu'il ne vont
        Ensanble o lui, s'il li pleüst;
4864   Car se il nul besoig eüst,
        Moult li aidascent volentiers.
        A tant se part des chevaliers
        Gavains, et va querre son non
4868   Entre lui et son conpaignon.
            Entre Cadrés et Ragidel
        Ensanble alerent au castel,
        Et zCodrovains les i mena,
4872   Ki d'ex grant joie demena,
        Et qui moult grant honor lor fist;
        Et cascuns des freres i mist
        Son pooir qu'il n'i fali rien

4836	Go away without telling them
	Who he was and what he was about.
	For it was not possible
	To tell them who he was
4840	Until he had found his name
	And the adventure that he sought.
	Each one begged him and insisted
	That he be allowed to go with them;
4844	But he assured them it must be so—
	That it couldn't be otherwise—
	They shouldn't consider him presumptuous,
	Nor proud, nor villainous,
4848	If they would go without companions.
	Then he asked the others, so it seems,
	That they would stay together and
	Spend some time at Codrovain's castle
4852	Until they returned
	Or until they heard talk of them.
	For he was quite sure that both
	Great joy and sorrow were promised to him
4856	Through the adventure that he sought,
	And sure to be endured before he returned.
	For this reason Gawain asked that they stay
	Together until he and Espinogre returned.
4860	And they happily granted it to him—
	They would wait for him this way.
	But it weighed heavily on them
	That they couldn't go with him.
4864	For if there were any need,
	They would gladly volunteer to help.
	Thereupon Gawain parted from
	The knights and went to seek his name,
4868	He and his companion, that is.
	Both Cadrés and Ragidel
	Went together to the castle,
	And Codrovain led them there,
4872	Expressing great joy to them
	And doing much to honor them.
	Each of the brothers did everything
	In his power to see that nothing failed

4876   A faire lor honor et bien.
        Moult orent envoisié sejor;
        Car onques ne passa nul jor
        Ke cascuns d'ex ne fust a cois
4880   D'aler en riviere u en bois.
        A lor plaiscir pooient faire
        U corre as ciens u aler traire;
        Car li sire ert moult poëstis,
4884   Et saciés bien que ses païs
        Estoit aaisiés de tox biens.   [33ra]
        Moult i avoit oisiax et ciens,
        Lïemiers, saietes et ars,
4888   Rivieres et forés et pars,
        Ki tot lor est abandoné.
        Et le don qui estoit doné
        A Ragidel, qu'il averoit
4892   S'amie quant il revenroit,
        Li fu tenu moult loiaument.
        Or me restuet dire conment
        Cil qui aloit por son non querre
4896   En aventure par la terre
        Puet traire a cief de son afaire.
        Je ne vous porroie retraire
        Com il ala ne com il vint,
4900   Ne mais que un jor li avint
        K'il erroit par mi un boscage,
        Et qu'il trova un ermitage,
        Et que de l'ermitage isçoit
4904   Uns chevaliers qui i avoit
        La messe a l'ermite escoutee.
        Si ot une cape afublee
        D'escarlate a penne d'ermine,
4908   Orlee d'une sebeline:
        A cel tans n'i avoit pas mances.
        Si ot cemisse et braies blances,
        A la guise galesce ouvrees;
4912   S'ot une cauces decaupees
        Desus uns esperons dorés
        Qui moult estoient bien ouvrés.
        Et saciés que le chevalier

4876 To honor them or assure their well-being.
       They had a most joyous visit,
       For not a day passed by in which
       Each of them hadn't the choice to ride
4880 Along the river or in the woods.
       They could do as they liked,
       To hunt with hounds or bow and arrow.
       For the lord was very wealthy,
4884 And—be sure of this—his country
       Was endowed with great resources.
       There was an abundance of birds and dogs,
       Bloodhounds, arrows and bows,
4888 Rivers and forests and parks—
       All was available to them.
       As to the promise that had been made
       To Ragidel—that he would have
4892 His friend when he returned—
       It was held to faithfully.
       Now I want to stop and tell how
       He who went to seek his name
4896 On an adventure across the land
       Could bring about the end of this matter.
       I can't tell you all about
       How he came and went,
4900 Only that one day it happened,
       As he wandered through a grove,
       That he found a hermitage,
       And that from the hermitage emerged
4904 A knight, who had just heard
       A mass conducted by the hermit.
       And he wore a scarlet cape
       Lined with ermine
4908 And hemmed in sable
       (At that time they didn't wear sleeves);
       His shirt and breeches were white,
       Worked in the French manner;
4912 He wore notched stockings
       And golden spurs over them
       That were finely constructed.
       And you may be sure that the knight

4916   Seoit sor un moult bon destrier,
        Tox dessarmés, l'espee çainte;
        Si ot une pucele atainte
        Ki moult ert avenans et bele,
4920   Si li contoit une nouvele
        Ki ert el païs avenue.
        Et cil bonement le salue   [33rb]
        Ki de son non mie n'avoit.
4924   "Sire," dist il, "Dix vous avoit
        De çou que vous alés querrant."
        Puis li a dit: "Je vous demant,
        S'il vous plaist, que vous me donés
4928   Un don, qu'ensanble o moi venés
        Entre vous et cel chevalier
        Wi mais deduire et herbegier,
        Et vous arés ostel si buen
4932   Com s'il estoit u vostre u suen,
        Car il ert a vostre devise."
        "Sire," fait il, "je ai enprise
        Une aventure que je quier;
4936   Por çou si vous pri et requier
        K'il ne vous poist se je n'i vois:
        Par castiax, par viles, par bois,
        Le querrai tant qu'ele ert trovee."
4940   "Chevalier, s'il ne vous agree,"
        Fait il, "a prendre mon ostel,
        Dont vous pri jou et requier d'el;
        Et de çou que je vous veul dire
4944   Ne me devés vous escondire
        K'il n'i eüst grant mesproison."
        "Sans laideté et traïson,"
        Fait il, "quant vous tant me proiiés,
4948   Vous en ert li dons otroiiés."
        Et cil respont: "Vostre merci.
        J'ai un castel moult prés de ci,
        Un petit outre ce vaucel,
4952   Si i est orendroit moult bel
        Mon disner prest et atorné;
        Vous n'en serés pas destorné
        Le trait d'un arc de vostre voie,

4916 Was seated on a very fine war horse.
   He was unarmed, except for a sword.
   And he had met a young girl
   Who was beautiful and gracious;
4920 He was telling her a story
   That had taken place in his country.
   And he greeted courteously
   The knight who had no name.
4924 "Sir," he said, "God grant that
   You find what you are searching for."
   Then he added, "I beg you,
   If you please, that you grant me
4928 A boon: that you come with me today,
   Both you and your companion,
   For diversion and lodging.
   You will have as good a stay
4932 As if you were in your own home,
   For everything is at your disposal."
   "Sir," he replied, "I have undertaken
   An adventure that I'm pursuing;
4936 For this reason I ask and pray
   That it not trouble you if I don't come.
   I will seek through castles, villages,
   And woods until I have found it."
4940 "Knight," he said, "if you don't agree
   To accept my hospitality,
   Then I beg and require it of you:
   Because I want to speak to you.
4944 You ought not to refuse,
   For it would be a great misdeed."
   "When you ask me this way," Gawain said,
   "You will certainly be granted it,
4948 Without insult or treason."
   And the lord replied, "Thank you.
   I have a castle near here,
   A little beyond this valley;
4952 Right now my dinner has been
   Prepared and set on the table;
   You will not be detoured farther
   Than the length of a shot of an arrow,

4956   Et por çou que je vostres soie
        Vous pri que vous sans demorer
        I vegniés aveuc moi disner."
        Et il li dist: "Jel vous otroi."   [33va]
4960   A tant s'en tornerent tout troi,
        Si sont dusqu'au castel venu.
        Ançois qu'il fuscent descendu,
        Estoient ja les tables mises,
4964   Et li sergant avoient prises
        Les touailes et les bacins.
        Les doubliers, li pains, et li vins
        Fu tost aparelliés et mis.
4968   Puis si sont au disner assis,
        Des que l'iaue lor fu dounee,
        K'il n'i ot autre demoree;
        Et saciés bien que li mengiers
4972   Fu biax et rices et pleniers,
        Et l'iement donés et pris.
        Quant il orent longement sis,
        Cil qui sire ert de le maison
4976   Mist ses deus ostes a raison:
            "Segnor," fait il, "je vous veul dire
        La dolor et l'anui et l'ire
        K'avenue est novelement,
4980   Dont tout le mont ert en torment,
        Quant il sera par tout seü.
        J'ere l'autre soir esmeü
        Por aler en un mien afaire,
4984   Se on peüst celer et taire
        Ce que je vous veul ci conter,
        Nus hom nel deüst reconter,
        Mais l'uevre est ja par tout seüe,
4988   K'el ne porroit estre teüe.
        Ce poise moi que on le set.
        Ahi! Dix, tant fortune het
        Les dames et les damoiseles!
4992   Quant eles saront ces noveles
        Ke vous m'orrés ja ci conter,
        Moult s'en porront desconforter.
        Car cil en cui Dix avoit mise

4956   And because I am at your disposal
I ask that you without delaying
Come with me to dinner."
And Gawain replied, "I grant you this."
4960   And so all three of them turned
From there and went to the castle.
Before they had dismounted,
The tables had been set up,
4964   And the servants had brought
The towels and the basins.
Table covers, bread, and wine
Were quickly prepared and set out.
4968   Then, as soon as the water was brought around,
They sat down to dinner—
There was no other delay.
And be assured that the food
4972   Was elegant, exquisite, and plentiful,
And served and cleared with pleasure.
After they had been sitting a long time,
He who was lord of the manor
4976   Addressed his two guests as follows:
      "Milords," he said, "I want to tell you
About the sorrow, trouble, and anger
That I experienced recently,
4980   On which account all the world would be
In torment if it became known.
I was on my way the other night
To take care of one of my affairs:
4984   If one could hide and keep silent
What I am about to tell you,
Then no man ought to repeat it;
But the affair is already known by all;
4988   It can't possibly be suppressed.
That it is known weighs heavily on me.
Alas! God! That fortune should so hate
The ladies and the young women!
4992   When they learn this news
That you will hear me tell you,
They will be extremely upset.
For he in whom God has placed

4996 Loiauté, prouece, et francise,   [33vb]
      K'il avoit fait cortois et sage,
      Sans vilounie et sans outrage,
      Sans orguel et sans desmesure
5000 (Il n'avoit de nul sorfait cure,
      Ains amoit honor et raison)
      Est mors par mauvaise ocoison.
      Et quant je tant vous en ai dit,
5004 Savoir poés sans contredit
      Dont la mesaventure sort.
      Quant on le sara a la cort,
      Moult en ara le rois grant ire.
5008 Alas! qui li osera dire
      Del bon chevalier c'on a mort
      Et decaupé a si grant tort?
      C'est son neveu dont je vous cont."
5012 "Ostes, por tox les sains du mont,"
      Fait cil sans non, "que savés vous?"
      "Jel sai bien," dist cel, "a estrox."
      "Et vous coument?" "Jel vous dirai,
5016 Ke ja de mot n'en mentirai.
           "Je voloie aler l'autre soir
      En deduit por mes bos veoir.
      Quant je dui de ma porte iscir,
5020 Si vi trois chevaliers venir,
      Moult bien armés sor lor destriers;
      Vers moi vint poignant li premiers,
      Tox seus par mi une quarriere,
5024 Et si laisça les deus arriere.
      Il me salua et je lui;
      Aprés me dist: 'Sire, je cui
      Ke estes de cest ostel sire;
5028 Por çou vous proiier et dire,
      Si serai vostre a tox jors mais,
      Ke vous me herbegiés wi mais.'
      Et je li dis: 'Jel vous otroi.'
5032 Lors s'en vint çaiens aveuc moi   [34ra]
      Li chevaliers, sel descendimes,
      Et jel desarmai jou meïsmes;
      Puis fis en sauf ses armes metre,

4996   Loyalty, bravery, and generosity,
Who has acted with courtesy and wisdom,
Without villainy or provocation,
Without pride and without excess
5000   (He had no need to be cured of pride,
For he always loved honor and reason),
This one died in a bad accident.
And when I have told you all about it,
5004   You will know without a doubt
The cause of this misadventure.
When one learns of this at court,
The king is going to be very angry.
5008   Alas! Who will dare to tell him
That the *bon chevalier* has been murdered
And chopped up so badly into pieces?
It is his nephew of whom I speak."
5012   "Host, in the name of all the saints,"
Said he without a name, "what do you know?"
"Of this I know a great deal," the host answered.
"How do you know this?" asked Gawain. "I will tell
5016   You without a single false word," replied the host.
       "The other night, I wanted to go
For pleasure to look around the woods.
I was about to leave the gate
5020   When I saw three knights approaching
On their war horses, very well-armed.
The first one came toward me,
All alone, along a paved road,
5024   Leaving the other two behind.
He greeted me and I him;
Then he said to me, 'Sir, I think
You are lord of this castle;
5028   Thus, I would like to ask you—
I will be forever after obliged—
That you give me lodging tonight.'
And I said to him, 'I grant you this.'
5032   Then the knight came inside with me;
We helped him dismount,
And I myself disarmed him.
Then I had his armor put in a safe place

5036   Et fis mes vallés entremetre
         De son ceval mettre a estable.
         Mais se je fusce bien raisnable,
         Bien ensegniés et bien cortois,
5040   J'eüsce demandé ançois
         Ki il ert et dont il venoit,
         Et kele aventure il querroit.
         Car puis que je herbegié l'oi,
5044   Et je le mal et l'anui soi
         Ke il ert alés porkacier,
         Je nel poi de çaiens cacier
         Ne jeter de ma maison fors.
5048   Lors vint çaiens a tout un cors
         Uns des chevaliers qui sivoit;
         Li autres, qui aprés venoit,
         Portoit les membres et le teste,
5052   Si en demenoit moult grant feste
         Et grant joïe de l'aventure.
         Je li demandai a droiture
         Ki ert li mors que il portoit,
5056   Dont si grant joïe demenoit,
         Et por coi l'avoient ocis.
         'J'avoie,' dist li uns, 'pramis
         La teste a une moie amie.'
5060   'Et je, si Dix me beneïe,'
         Dist l'autres, 'la moie le cors.'
         Et je lor redemandai lors
         L'ocoison por quoi il l'avoient
5064   Ensi ocis com il disoient.
         Lors me conmença l'uns un conte,
         Dont jou ai duel et ire et honte
         De reconter le a nul home."
5068   "Ostes, por tox les sains de Rome,"
         Fait cil sans non, "dites le moi,
         Car je vous di en bone foi   [34rb]
         C'est l'aventure que je quier;
5072   Por çou si vous pri et requier
         Ke vous m'en contés tout le voir."
         "Jel vous ferai moult bien savoir,"
         Fait li ostes, "n'en doutés ja,

5036   And had my servants undertake
       To put his horse in the stable.
       But if I had been more reasonable,
       Better trained, and more courteous,
5040   I would have asked first
       Who he was and where he came from
       And what kind of adventure he sought.
       For after I had lodged him
5044   And learned of the evil and grief
       That he had been pursuing,
       I could no longer chase him away
       Or throw him out of my home.
5048   One of the knights who followed
       Came inside with a body;
       The other who followed after
       Carried the limbs and head,
5052   And they displayed very great joy
       And celebrated this adventure.
       I at once asked who
       The dead person they carried was,
5056   About whose death they showed such joy,
       And why they had killed him.
       'I have,' said one of them, 'promised
       The head to my *amie.*'
5060   'And I, if God grant it me,'
       Said the other, 'promised mine the body.'
       And I then asked again about
       The reason for having killed him
5064   In the way they described.
       At this, one of them began a story
       Which I have sorrow, anger, and shame
       To retell to any person."
5068   "Host, in the name of all the saints of Rome,"
       Said he without a name, "tell me this story,
       For I say to you in all good faith,
       This is the very adventure I seek;
5072   For this reason I ask and require
       That you tell me the whole truth."
       "I would have you know everything,"
       Said the host, "have no fear about this,

5076 Si conme cil le me conta.
      "Li doi des chevaliers prioient
      Dex damoiseles qu'il amoient,
      K'a grant mervelle estoient beles.
5080 Trois ans priierent les puceles,
      Si c'onques rien n'i esploitierent;
      Un jor avint qu'i les prierent
      Moult bonement de tox lor cuers.
5084 Les damoiseles erent suers,
      Et li chevalier conpaignon.
      Li ainsnee dist que le don
      De s'amor avoit ja doné,
5088 Si n'ert pas le chevalier né
      Par quoi il fust ja retoloit;
      Car tant ert biax et tant valoit
      Cil cui ele donoit s'amor
5092 Ke ja n'ameroit a nul jor
      Nul chevalier se celui non.
      Lors li demanda cil son non
      Ki se dervoit de duel et d'ire.
5096 'Jel puis bien en toutes cors dire,
      K'il est tant et dit et només
      Que ne puet estre en cort celés;
      Car çou est monsegnor Gavain,
5100 Cui li cortois et li vilain,
      Et cil qui sont par tout le mont,
      Loent sor tox ceus qui i sont.'
      Li autres enquist maintenant
5104 A celi cui il amoit tant
      Le sien cuer et le sien pensé.
      'Mon cuer en est bien porpensé,'
      Dist ele, 'Ja n'en doutés rien.   [34va]
5108 Je ne sai pas nomer le mien,
      Ki il est ne quant jel ferai;
      Mais une cose de voir sai,
      Si l'avés vous tres bien oï,
5112 Ke ma suer a fait son ami
      De monsegnor Gavain sans faille,
      Si ne gart l'ore qu'ele i aille
      A la cort le roi por li querre,

5076 Just as he told it to me.
   "Two of the knights pursued two
  Young women whom they loved,
  Who were marvelously beautiful.
5080 For three years they courted the maidens
  And never had anything to show for it.
  It happened that one day they pleaded
  Very urgently with all their hearts.
5084 The young women were sisters,
  And the knights were friends.
  The older one said that the gift
  Of her love had already been given
5088 And there was no knight alive
  Who could force him away,
  For he to whom she had given her love
  Was so handsome and so esteemed
5092 That she would never love
  Any knight but this one.
  Then he who was mad with anguish
  And anger asked her his name.
5096 'I can say it in every court:
  He is so well-spoken-of and renowned
  That in no court can it be hidden;
  For it is Sir Gawain whom all—
5100 Whether nobleman or peasant
  Or any other in all the world—
  Praise more than any other.'
  The other knight now inquired
5104 Of her whom he loved with
  All his heart and mind.
  'My heart is preoccupied,'
  She said, 'have no doubt about it.
5108 I am not in a position to name mine,
  Say who he is, or when I met him;
  But I know one thing truly,
  And you have heard it clearly:
5112 My sister has definitely
  Made Sir Gawain her friend.
  At any hour she might go
  To the court of the king to seek him

5116   Por sa drüerie requerre,
       Et je irai ensanble o li.
       Une cose de voir vous di,
       Que se me suer ne li agree,
5120   Ensi com ele si est dounee,
       Ke je meïsme m'i donrai
       En tel guise que j'amerai
       Un chevalier par son consel;
5124   Et c'ert le Chevalier Vermel
       De qui je ferai mon ami.
       Et saciés bien que je vous di
       Del bon chevalier, del seür,
5128   Ki a la cort le roi Artur
       Vint antan estre chevalier,
       Ki les armes et le destrier
       Conquist par son cors seulement,
5132   Desarmés, par grant hardement,
       Et li rois Artus li dona
       Del chevalier qui en porta
       Sa coupe d'or de devant lui.'
5136   Moult furent angousçox li dui
       Qui les puceles requerroient;
       Puis lor discent que il estoient
       Mellor chevalier que cil n'erent.
5140   Et les damoiseles jurerent
       Que se lor dis n'estoit provés,
       Et qu'il se fuscent esprovés
       Cors a cors par lor deus escus,
5144   Si qu'il les eüscent vencus,   [34vb]
       Ke ja mais nul n'en ameroient;
       Et se il issi nel faisoient
       Dedens un terme qui fust cort,
5148   Eles iroient a la cort.
           "Et cil discent, 'Se nous vencons,
       Qui tant proïes vous avons,
       Dont n'arons nous vos drüeries?'
5152   'En fin devenrons vos amies,'
       Disent eles, 'quant ce sera,
       Mais ja se Dix plaist n'avenra,
       Car ce seroit trop grant damage.'

5116 And make demands on his friendship,
And I would go with her.
I tell you one thing plainly:
That if he accepts my sister,

5120 As soon as she is given to him,
Then I will give myself there,
In this sense, that I will only love
A knight with his counsel.

5124 And this will be the Red Knight
Whom I shall make my friend.
You can be sure that I speak
Of the good knight, the reliable one,

5128 Who came last year to the court
Of King Arthur to be made a knight,
Who conquers arms and horse
With his body alone, without

5132 Arms, through his great bravery.
King Arthur gave him armor
Taken from the knight who had carried off
His golden cup from under his nose.'

5136 The two who pursued the young women
Were very full of sorrow;
Then they said that they were better
Knights than the other two.

5140 And the young women swore that
If their boast were not proven
And they weren't tested
In single combat, shield against shield,

5144 And they weren't victorious,
They would never ever love them.
And if they didn't accomplish this
In a short space of time,

5148 They would go to the court.
      "And these knights asked, 'If we win,
We who have pursued you so long,
Will we have you as our friends?'

5152 'In the end, we will become your friends,'
The women replied, 'if it happens so.
But may it please God not to happen so,
For it would be a very great shame.'

5156 Par tel sorfait et par tel rage
      S'esmurent cil por Gavain querre;
      Tant errerent par ceste terre,
          "Un jor avint qu'il l'encontrerent.
5160 Seul et desarmé le troverent
      Cil qui querroient por ocire;
      C'est damages qu'il l'estuet dire:
      Sa deffense rien ne valut.
5164 Par itel ocoison morut
      Li niés le roi, ce saciés bien.
      Onques n'oi si grant duel de rien,
      Ne ja mais ne quit qu'il me viegne
5168 Si grant dolor por riens qu'aviegne.
          "Quant il fu issi avenu,
      Et cil furent çaiens venu
      Ki tout l'avoient depecié,
5172 Le destre bras, qu'il ot trencié,
      Lor demandai, sel me dounerent;
      A tout le sorplus s'en alerent
      Par matinet en lor païs.
5176 Et saciés bien que il ert mis,
      Se je puis vivre longement,
      Si bien en or et en argent,
      Se li orfevres ne se faint,
5180 Onques nus bras a nul cors saint   [35ra]
      Ne fu mais se ricement mis.
      Je l'ai bien voué et promis,
      Et je m'en doi bien entremetre
5184 De faire le ricement mettre,
      Car li prodom fist moult d'onor
      As chevaliers de ci entor,
      Si devroit bien cascuns entendre
5188 Ki en porroit gueredon rendre."
          "Biax dox ostes," fait cis sans non,
      "Por Diu et por sa raençon,
      Counoisciés vous bien Gavain?"
5192 "Je vous mosterrai ja sa main,"
      Fait li ostes, "se Dix me voie."
      Maintenant por le main envoie,
      Ki en un coffre ert enfremee,

5156   Greatly insulted and filled with rage,
    The two left to go seek Gawain;
    They wandered all over the earth.
        "One day it happened that they met him;
5160   They found him alone and unarmed,
    The very one they sought to kill.
    It is a shame that I must say it.
    His defense was of no use.
5164   By these means the nephew
    Of King Arthur died, you may be sure.
    Never have I had such great sorrow,
    Nor do I think that ever again
5168   Such great sorrow will happen to me.
        "After this had occurred,
    And they had come inside,
    They who had cut up the body,
5172   I asked for the right arm that they
    Had cut off, and they gave it to me.
    With all the rest they left
    In the morning for their own country.
5176   And know that the arm will be preserved,
    Artfully encased in gold and silver—
    If I can live long enough and
    If the goldsmith holds out.
5180   Never before has the arm of any saint
    Been preserved so richly.
    I have taken vows and promised this;
    And well I ought to undertake to have
5184   This elegant reliquary made,
    For the good man brought much honor
    To knights all around here.
    Each one of them ought to exert himself
5188   To pay him proper respect."
        "My dear host," said he without a name,
    "In the name of God and redemption,
    Did you know Gawain well?"
5192   "I will show you his hand,"
    Said the host, "so help me God."
    Now he sent for the hand
    That was enclosed in a chest

5196 D'un drap de soie envolepee.
     Et quant le bras fu hors isçu,
     Ki estoit envox d'un boufu,
     A mervelle l'ont esgardé;
5200 Puis ont priié qu'il soit gardé
     A honor, tant qu'il soit seü
     Ki li cors ert dont li bras fu.
        Il lor respont qu'isi ert il:
5204 Ja rien de lui n'ert tenu vil,
     La u il soit, ne bras ne main;
     Car bien set que c'est de Gavain,
     Si doit estre moult cier tenu.
5208 Et cil qui ert sans non venu
     Li dist: "Sire, se Dix me gart,
     Ja mar de çou arés regart:
     Je vi, n'a pas quart jor, Gavain
5212 Vers Carduel out delivre et sain,
     Si aloit aventure querre.
     Or vous veul proiier et requerre,
     Par amor et par guerredon,
5216 Ke me creantés un seul don,
     Et je ne vous querrai sorfait."
     "Dont ert il," fait li ostes, "fait,   [35rb]
     Par si que je faire le puisce."
5220 "Ensengniés me dont u je truisce
     Ces qui ensi se sont vanté
     K'ont monsegnor Gavain maté,
     Et que il par ex reçut mort.
5224 Et saciés bien que il ont tort,
  a   C'onques par aus mort ne reçut.
  b   Voirs est c'uns chevaliers morut,
  c   Que seul et desarmé troverent;
  d   Et saciés bien qu'il en ouvrerent
     Moult laidement quant il l'ocissent,
     Sans çou que nul mot ne li dissent,
     Ne qu'il n'avoit d'ex nul regart.
5228 N'a sous ciel home qui n'esgart,
     Ki en lui ot sens et raison,
     Ki l'ociscent en traïson:
     Fu ce prouece s'il l'ocissent?

5196 And wrapped in a silk cloth.
And when the arm was brought out,
Covered with a fine cloth,
They looked at it in wonder.
5200 Then they asked that it be guarded
With honor until it was certain
Whose body the arm came from.
    The host replied that this would be done;
5204 No part of Gawain would be dishonored,
Whatever it be, neither arm nor hand;
For he was sure that this was from Gawain
And so ought to be held very dear.
5208 And he who had arrived without a name
Said to him: "Sir, may God protect me,
You have acted in error in this affair:
I saw, not four days ago, Gawain
5212 Near Carlisle quite alive and healthy,
On his way to seek adventure.
Now I want to ask and require—
Out of love and service—
5216 That you grant me a single favor,
And I will not ask anything unreasonable."
"Consider it done," the host replied,
"As long as it is in my power to do it."
5220 "Tell me then where I can find
Those who have bragged so much,
Saying that they had vanquished Gawain
And that he had been killed by them.
5224 You can be certain that they are wrong
a   For he was never killed by them.
b   It is true that a knight, whom they
c   Found alone and unarmed, is dead.
d   You can be certain that they behaved
Very badly when they killed him—
Without saying a word to him,
Without his even being aware of them.
5228 There isn't a man on earth, who has
Any sense or reason, who wouldn't conclude
That they had killed him treacherously.
Where is the prowess in killing him?

5232   Aprés se vanterent et dissent
      K'il avoient Gavain ocis.
      Je l'ai ja mainte fois enquis,
      N'onques encor ne peuc savoir
5236   Del chevalier, por nul avoir,
      Son non, ne de quel terre il fu,
      Fors qu'il portoit un tel escu
      Conme mesire Gavains porte."
5240   A mervelle se reconforte
      Li ostes, qui ot tex noveles
      Ki moult li sont plaisans et beles.
      Puis dist: "Sire, se Dix me voie,
5244   Je vous metrai bien en le voie,
      Moult volentiers, quant vous vaurois,
      Et ce est bien raisons et drois
      Ke de çou vous doie avoiier.
5248   Je vous vaurai ja convoiier
      Tant que je vous avoierai;
      Et por çou vous convoierai
      Ke jou vous mosterai la voie."
5252   Maintenant del tout les avoie
      Et de lor nons et de lor terre,
      De quanques il vaurent enquerre.
      "Sire," dist il, "veïstes vous   [35va]
5256   Onques le Faé Orgellox?
      Je ne sai mie bien son non,
      Mais je sai bien que son sornon
      Si est de la Roce Faee:
5260   Ensi est sa vile apelee.
      Li uns d'ex est ensi noumés,
      Et li autres est apelés
      Par tout Goumerés sans Mesure."
5264   "De cestui sornon n'ai jou cure,"
      Fait cil sans non, "qu'il n'est pas buens."
      "Et il est bien par raison suens,"
      Fait li ostes, "qu'il est assés
5268   Orgellox et desmesurés,
      Et si ai jou malement dit:
      Je meïsme i met contredit,
      Si est il bien dit et prouvés

5232   Afterwards they bragged and claimed
That they had killed Gawain.
I have inquired many times,
And I have not yet been able to learn
5236   Anything about this knight, no matter what—
Not his name, nor of what country he came,
Unless he carried a shield like
The one that Sir Gawain carries."
5240   The host was wonderfully comforted,
He who received such news
That was very pleasant and good.
Then he said, "If God protects me,
5244   I will put you securely on the path,
Very willingly, if you want this.
It is reasonable and quite right
That I should conduct you.
5248   I would like to accompany you
So that I can put you on the path.
For this reason I will accompany you
So that I can show you the way."
5252   Now he told them all about the knights,
Their names and their country,
Whatever they wanted to ask about.
     "Sir," he said, "have you never met
5256   The Proud Magician?
I never learned his name;
I only know his surname
And that he comes from Fairy Rock;
5260   Thus is his town called.
The first of them is called this,
And the other is called
By everyone Gomeret Without Measure."
5264   "I don't care much for his surname," said
He without a name; "it suggests nothing good."
"And it's his name for good reason,"
Said the host, "for he is arrogant
5268   Enough and full of excess,
But I express myself poorly:
I must contradict myself,
For it is always said and often proven

5272 K'onques nus trop ne fu d'assés.
Le tiers ne sai je pas qui fu,
Ne mais qu'il ert o ex venu;
Ce li oï dire et retraire
5276 K'il n'i ala por nul mal faire,
Fors por tenir ex conpaignie."
"Ot la saisine de s'amie,
Biax dox ostes," fait cil sans non,
5280 "Nus d'ax dex par cest ocoison?"
"Nenil," dist il, "ce me fu dit,
K'eles i miscent contredit,
Et si dissent a lor amis
5284 Ke il lor avoient pramis
Le cors Gavain u mort u vif,
Si ot entr'ex moult grant estrif,
Car les damoiseles disoient
5288 Ke autre fois veü l'avoient,
Et ce n'ert mie illeuc son cors.
Et li chevalier dissent lors
Ke se ert et sel prouveroient;
5292 Car as marciés crier feroient,   [35vb]
Par tox les castiax du païs,
K'il avoient Gavain ocis,
Et se nus osoit ce desdire
5296 K'il feroient crier et dire,
K'il seroient prest du prouver.
Si ne porent encor trouver
Ki i meïst nul contredit.
5300 Et de ces dex qui ce ont dit
N'i a il nul qui moult ne vaille,
Si veulent prouver par bataille.
    "Or est la cose alee tant,
5304 S'aucuns ne vient demain avant
Ki pruisse que ce n'est pas voir,
En fin lor convenra avoir
Les puceles sans nul delai.
5308 Eles en sont en tel esmai,
De ce que ne puent trouver
Ke çou lor ost a faus prouver
Ne par bataille contredire,

5272   That 'enough' has never meant 'too much.'
I don't know who the third one was,
Unless he came with the others.
I have heard said of him, and I repeat it,
5276   That he went there without bad intent,
But merely to accompany them."
"My dear host, did either one of the two
Obtain his lover as the result
5280   Of this affair?" asked he without a name.
"Not at all!" he replied. "According to what
Was told me, they broke their promise,
And they said to their friends
5284   That they had promised them
Gawain's body dead or alive.
There was great strife between them,
For the young women said that they
5288   Had seen Gawain another time
And that this couldn't be his body.
And the knights replied to them
That this was he and that they would prove it.
5292   They would let it be cried out in markets
Throughout all the castles of the land
That they had killed Gawain;
And, if anyone dared contradict them,
5296   In this which they had proclaimed,
They would be ready to prove it in battle.
They still cannot find
Anyone to challenge them.
5300   And of these two it is said that there
Have never been more valiant ones
Who wanted to prove themselves in battle.
      "Now the thing has gone this far:
5304   If no one arrives before tomorrow
Who can prove that this is not true,
Then they finally will obtain
The young women without delay.
5308   The women are very upset
Because they cannot find anyone
Who dares to prove the two knights false
Or to challenge them in battle—

5312   K'a poi que ne sont mortes d'ire.
        Savés por quoi eles s'esmaient?
        El doutent trop que cil nes aient
        En tel guisse com je vous cont.
5316   Si dient bien que s'ocirront,
        S'il les ont par ceste raison,
        Car eles erent ocoison
        Ke Gavains fu par eles mort:
5320   Eles n'avroient ja confort."
                "Oste," dist il, "ne vous anuit:
        Porron nous tant errer anuit
        Et demain dusqu'a mïedi?
5324   Une cose de voir vous di,
        Si nel di je pas por vantance:
        Se Damedix tant nous avance
        Ke demain a tans i vegnon,
5328   Je ai talent que nous venjon
        Le grant forfait que il ont dit.   [36ra]
        Nous dui i metrons contredit
        A armes; conment que il aille,
5332   Ne puet remaindre sans bataille."
                Lors dist li ostes: "Ce me sanle,
        Vous ne trouverés pas ensanle
        Les chevaliers que vous querés.
5336   Se par armes les conquerés,
        Dont vous avés ceste ouvre enprise,
        Moult avrés grant honor conquise.
        Se ne faites trop grant demeure,
5340   Vous i venrés moult bien a eures.
        Et si vous dirai bien conment
        Goumerés sans Mesure atent.
        Il a son pavellon tendu,
5344   Si a longement atendu
        Por cest afaire en une lande;
        Si enquiert ileuc et demande
        Savoir se nus vauroit desdire
5348   Ce qu'il a fait crier et dire:
        Ke par ex dex est Gavains mors.
        Tant est prox et hardis et fors
        K'il ne trouve qui l'en desdie,

5312   Thus they are nearly dead from distress.
        Do you know what troubles them most?
        They very much doubt that the knights earned them
        In the manner I related to you.
5316   And they say that they will kill themselves
        If the knights win them with this proof,
        For they furnished the occasion
        By which Gawain was killed;
5320   They will never have consolation."
            "Host," Gawain said, "don't be annoyed:
        Could we ride there tonight
        And all day tomorrow until noon?
5324   One bit of truth I want to say,
        And I don't say it to brag:
        If the Lord God helps us
        So that we arrive there tomorrow on time,
5328   I want to take revenge for
        The great evil deed that they have claimed.
        The two of us will meet this challenge
        In battle; whatever happens,
5332   This affair cannot rest without battle."
            The host replied: "It seems to me
        That you will not find in one place
        The knights that you seek.
5336   If you conquer them through armed battle,
        In this job you have undertaken,
        You will have achieved great honor.
        If you don't delay too long,
5340   You will arrive there in plenty of time.
        And I will tell you exactly how
        Gomeret Without Measure waits.
        He has pitched his pavilion,
5344   And he has been waiting a long time
        In a meadow because of this affair.
        Over there, he continually asks
        Around to learn if anyone wants to debate
5348   What he has had proclaimed:
        That Gawain was killed by the two of them.
        He is so brave, hardy, and strong
        That he doesn't find anyone to debate this,

5352   Si quide avoir demain s'amie.
        Li Feés Orgellox atent
    A son castel tout ensement
    Por savoir se ja venroit nus
5356   Ki de ceste oeuvre feïst plus
    Et qui ossast vers lui enprendre
    U a prouver u a deffendre
    Ce qu'il dist, qu'il a mort Gavain.
5360   S'aucuns ne vient avant demain
    Ki par armes l'en contredie
    En fin ara la soie amie."
    Lors se leverent del mengier;
5364   Puis monta cascuns u destrier
    Et si se missent a la voie.
    Et li ostes tant les convoie,   [36rb]
    Conme cortois et ensegniés,
5368   K'il lor a moult bien ensegniés
    Del païs trestox les assens,
    K'il n'i fauroient a nul sens
    A trover çou qu'il vont querant.
5372   Et quant il orent erré tant
    Ke li ostes retorner dut,
    Espinogres lors s'aperçut
    K'il avoient forment mespris,
5376   Si s'en tient moult a entrepris,
    Si le dist a son conpaignon,
    Ke il n'orent enquis son non.
        Lors l'ont moult bel a raison mis:
5380   "Sire, nous soumes vos amis,
    Et ce est bien raisons et drois,
    Ke bien avés a ceste fois
    Deservi que nous le soion.
5384   Biax dox ostes, si vos prion
    Ke vostres nons nous soit nonmés.
    Prodoume estes et renomés,
    Si amon vostre acointement,
5388   Et saciés bien seürement,
    Ja mar en serés en doutance
    Ke nous en la vostre acointance
    Somes tous et sans contredit."

5352   And he thinks he'll have rights to his *amie* tomorrow.
        The Proud Magician waits
        At his castle in the same manner
        To learn if anyone will come
5356   Who wants to become involved in this affair
        And who dares to challenge him
        Either to prove or defend
        What he claims, namely, that he has killed Gawain.
5360   And if no one arrives before tomorrow
        Who challenges him in battle about this,
        Then finally he will obtain his *amie*."
        At this, they got up from the table.
5364   Then each one mounted his war horse,
        And thus they set out on the way.
        And the host escorted them for a while,
        As was courteous and proper,
5368   And he instructed them very well
        In the landmarks throughout the countryside,
        So that they couldn't fail
        To find those whom they were seeking.
5372   And when they had ridden so far
        That the host had to turn back,
        Espinogre realized then
        That they had made a bad mistake,
5376   And feeling very embarrassed,
        He pointed out to his companion
        That they had not asked their host's name.
        Then, very politely, they spoke to him:
5380   "Sir, we are your friends,
        And this is reasonable and proper,
        For you have on this occasion
        Certainly deserved that we be such.
5384   Dear sweet host, we ask you
        That your name be revealed to us.
        You are a good man and respected,
        And we value your friendship;
5388   And you know with great certainty,
        You need never be in doubt about it,
        That we are completely and without exception
        Devoted to friendship with you."

5392   "J'ai a non Tristrans qui ne rit;
        Ja," fait il, "celer ne le quier.
        Segnor, si vous pri et requier,
        Par amor et par gueredon,
5396   Ke vous me creantés un don:
        Et je ne vous requerrai mie
        Ne outrage ne vilenie,
        Ja mar de çou paour arois."
5400   "Par foi," fait il, "ce est bien drois
        Ke nous façons vostre plaissir;
        Bien nous devés a vos tenir
        Tous jors mais des ore en avant."   [36va]
5404   "Segnor," fait il, "je vous demant,
        Par gueredon et par amor,
        Ke par ci soit vostre retor.
        Je nel sai, ne vous ne savés,
5408   De l'aventure que querés
        Ke vous en est a avenir;
        Mais savoir weul au revenir
        Conment vous ert de cest afaire.
5412   Tout me conterés au repaire,
        Ki vous estes ne de quel terre,
        Et l'ocoison qui vous fait querre
        L'aventure que vous querés.
5416   Se par armes cex conquerés
        Que vous avés longement quis,
        Moult par arés grant pris conquis."
                Bounement li ont otroiié.
5420   Quant assés les ot convoiié,
        Si revient li ostes arriere;
        Et cil oirrent en tel maniere
        Conme li ostes lor ot dit.
5424   Tant errerent que li uns vit
        En un val une bele tor,
        Qui estoit a un vavasor;
        Moult estoit rices li porpris,
5428   Et li sires moult poëstis
        Et moult prodom cui il estoit.
        A son contenement paroit
        K'il estoit de moult grant pooir.

5392 "My name is Tristan Who Never Smiles.
  I don't seek to hide it," he said.
  "My lords, I ask and demand of you
  That you grant me a boon,
5396 Out of love and service.
  I will not require anything
  Outrageous or villainous;
  Have no fear of this."
5400 "By my faith," he said, "it is certainly right
  That we do whatever you wish.
  We ought to be at your service
  Henceforth and forevermore."
5404 "My lords," Tristan replied, "I ask you,
  In service and in love,
  That your return be by way of here.
  I don't know, nor do you know,
5408 What the outcome of this adventure
  That you seek will be.
  But I want to know upon your return
  How you made out in this affair.
5412 You will tell me everything upon return—
  Who you are, from what country you come,
  And what made you seek the adventure
  That you are pursuing.
5416 If, in battle, you subdue these knights
  Whom you have sought for so long,
  You will have acquired a very great reputation."
   They gladly granted him this.
5420 When he had conducted them far enough,
  The host turned back.
  And the two went in the direction
  That the host had told them to go.
5424 They rode until one of them saw
  A beautiful tower in a valley
  That belonged to a vavasor.
  The estate was very prosperous,
5428 And the lord to whom it belonged
  Was powerful and full of valor.
  From his maintenance of things it appeared
  That he was of very great authority.

5432 La se herbegierent le soir
     Andoi ciés le bon vavasor;
     Si grant joie et si grant honor
     Li face Dix com il lor fist.
5436 Moult se jua, et moult lor dist
     De ses aventures la nuit,
     Et il a lui, si com je cuit,
     Reconterent assés des lor.
5440 Et l'endemain, quant il fu jor   [36vb]
     Et on ot armés les vassax,
     Si monterent sor lor cevax.
     Et quant il orent congié pris,
5444 Si se sont a la voie mis;
     Puis oirent un cemin ferré.
     N'orent mie granment erré,
     K'il ert encore assés matin,
5448 K'il trouverent un forc cemin.
     Si com Tristrans conté lor ot;
     Et li uns des cemins aloit,
     Si com Tristrans dit lor avoit,
5452 La u Goumerés atendoit,
     Et li autres au castel vait
     U li Orgellox crier fait
     Ke il a mort Gavain sans faille,
5456 Si quide le jor sans bataille
     Estre de s'amie saissis.
     Lors ont entr'ex un ju partis,
     Et si le parti cil sans non
5460 Bonement a son conpaignon:
     "Sire," dist il, "vous coisirés:
     L'un de ces deus cemins irés
     Por vostre besongne furnir,
5464 Et quant venra au revenir,
     Se Dix nous done si ouvrer
     Que par armes puisçon prover
     K'il ont menti de cest afaire,
5468 Ciés Tristran ert nostre repaire.
     Et cil quiançois i venra
     Son conpaignon i atendra,
     Tant qu'il oie parler de lui."

5432 The two of them stayed the night there
With the good vavasor.
May God give him as great joy and honor
As he rendered unto them there.
5436 That night he enjoyed himself
And told them much about his adventures;
And to him, so I think,
They told a number of theirs.
5440 And the next day, at daybreak,
Once the men were armed,
They mounted their horses.
When they had taken leave,
5444 They set out on their way.
They travelled along a paved road:
They hadn't gone very far on it,
For it was still early morning,
5448 When they came to a fork in the road,
Just as Tristan had told them.
And one of the roads led,
Just as Tristan had said to them,
5452 Up to where Gomeret waited,
And the other went to the castle
Where the Proud One had had it proclaimed
That he, without a doubt, had killed Gawain;
5456 He thought he would gain possession
Of his *amie* that day without a fight.
Then they had to part from one another,
And he without a name
5460 Spoke freely to his companion.
"Sir," Gawain said, "please choose.
You follow one of these two roads
To fulfill your task,
5464 And when you come back,
If God grants you this,
And you are able to prove in battle
That he has lied in this affair,
5468 Then let us return to Tristan.
And he who arrives there first
Will wait there for his companion,
Until he hears news of him."

5472   "Quant je," fait Espinogres, "sui
      A cois d'une de ces deus voies,
      Et faire l'estuet toutes voies,
      Si qu'il ne puet autrement estre,
5476   Je irai cesti a senestre,
      Ki me menra a Goumeret."   [37ra]
      "Et je en ceste autre me met,"
      Fait cil sans non, "si vous conmant
5480   Au gloriox le roi poisçant,
      Ki vous gart de honte et de mal."
      Lors broce cascuns le ceval,
      Si oirrent moult grant aleüre.
5484   Et Espinogres a droiture
      N'ot pas demie liue alee,
      K'il a une forest trouvee.
      Puis oirre longement issi
5488   C'onques de la forest n'issi,
      Tant qu'il a trouvee la lande
      U Goumerés est qu'il demande,
      Si com la parole est contee
5492   (Por noient seroit recontee,
      Car ele est bien dite et oïe),
      Si quide bien avoir s'amie
      Sans contredit que nus i mette.
5496   Ne quide que nus s'entremete
      De prendre contre lui desraisne
      Et quoi que il si se desraisne,
      Et il dist ses rices paroles,
5500   Si orgellousses et si foles,
      Com vous avés oï conter
      (Nes couvient mie reconter,
      Car assés bien vous en souvient),
5504   Estes vous qu'Espinogres vient.
          Cortoisement li dist en pais:
      "Dans chevaliers, ne dites mais
      Ke vous aiiés Gavain ocis:
5508   Vilainement avés mespris
      De ce que le desistes onques."
      "Sire vassal, et por quoi donques,"
      Fait Goumerés, "quant je di voir,

5472 "If I have," said Espinogre,
"The choice of one of these two ways,
And it is necessary to cover both routes,
And it can't be otherwise,
5476 Then I will follow the left-hand road
That will lead me to Gomeret."
"And I will set out on the other one,"
Said he without a name; "I commend you
5480 To the glory of the Lord God,
Who guards you from shame and evil."
At that each one spurred his horse
And set off at great speed.
5484 And straight ahead,
Not half a league away,
Espinogre came upon a forest.
He rode a long time in there,
5488 Without emerging from the forest,
Until he found the meadow
Where Gomeret was claiming justice,
As has already been told
5492 (There is no reason to retell it,
For it has been well told and heard):
He was sure he would have his *amie*
Without contradiction from anyone there.
5496 He didn't believe that anyone
Would dare to take issue with him.
And however he rambled on
And made elaborate speeches—
5500 So proud and foolish—
As you have heard tell
(It is not appropriate to retell them,
For you remember well enough),
5504 In short, Espinogre arrived.
      He spoke courteously in peace:
"Sir Knight, never say again
That you have killed Gawain.
5508 You have acted villainously
In not ceasing to say this."
"Sir Vassal," said Gomeret,
"Why shouldn't I, when I speak the truth,

5512   Ne l'os je bien faire savoir?"
       "Nenil," dist il, "onques n'avint.
       Il s'en conbatroit a tes vint,   [37rb]
       L'un aprés l'autre, com vous estes,
5516   Si trenceroit a tox les testes."
       Et Goumerés respondi lors:
       "Par foi," fait il, "j'en ai le cors,
       Mais il n'i a ne bras ne quisse,
5520   Et si sui tox pres que je pruisse
       Ke je l'ai et que li Faés
       En a les menbres aportés."
          Espinogres lors respondi:
5524   "Apertement avés menti.
       Je sui pres que je l'en deffende,
       Et que mort u pris vous en rende
       Ains que g'isce de ceste lande."
5528   Et Goumerés tantost demande
       Ses armes, et on li aporte
       Cauces de fer a maille forte,
       Plus blances qu'argens esmerés;
5532   Puis fu li haubers aportés,
       Fors et legiers, clers et trellis,
       Et hiaume qui fu de Senlis;
       Toute ert noire l'autre armeüre.
5536   Quant armés fu a sa droture,
       Il n'i a fait plus de demoure;
       Son ceval ert plus noir que moure,
       Et quant il se fu bien armés,
5540   Sor le bon ceval est montés,
       Tox pres de prouver erranment
       Çou dont li autres le desment.
       N'avoit entr'ex tertre ne vaus;
5544   Il laiscent corre les cevax
       Tant com cascuns li pot aler,
       Si se ferirent au joster
       Si grans caus par mi les escus
5548   K'estroés les ont et fendus:
       Outre fissent passer les fers,
       Sis assissent sor les haubers,
       K'il ont trouvé tenans et fors.   [37va]

5512 Dare to let it be clearly known?"
"It's false," he replied, "it never happened.
He could battle twenty of the like
Of you, one after the other,
5516 And cut off all their heads."
And Gomeret then replied:
"By my faith," he said, "I have the body,
Although it has neither arms nor legs,
5520 And I am quite ready to prove
That I have it and that the Magician
Has carried off the limbs."
Then Espinogre replied to this:
5524 "You have clearly lied.
I am prepared to defend this claim,
And turn you over dead or alive
Before I depart from this country."
5528 And Gomeret quickly called for
His armor, and he was brought
Iron leggings made of strong chain mail,
Brighter than pure gold;
5532 Then his hauberk was brought—
Strong and light, shining and tightly knit—
And a helmet that he had from Senlis;
The rest of the armor was black.
5536 When he was properly armed,
He didn't delay any longer.
His horse was blacker than a blackberry,
And when he was completely armed,
5540 He mounted his good horse,
Quite ready to prove immediately
What his opponent denied.
There was neither hill nor vale between them.
5544 They let their horses gallop,
Each one as fast as he could.
In the joust, they struck one another
With such a tremendous blow on their shields
5548 That they pierced and split them.
The lance heads passed through
And came to rest on the hauberks,
Which they found tough and strong.

5552 Si se fierent de tel esfors,
     Et par tel ire, des espiés,
     K'il n'i remest ceval en piés.
     Et de ce nes doit nus blasmer,
5556 Quant les cevax estut verser,
     S'il caïrent o les destriers;
     Guerpir lor couvint les estriers.
     Si sont tantost en piés sailli,
5560 Si a li uns l'autre asailli
     Moult tost et moult seürement.
     Et saciés bien certeinement
     Que nus qui esgardast l'estor
5564 N'en couneüst l'apeleor:
     Cascuns apeleor se fait.
     Espinogres les saus li vait
     Sel fiert et refiert a bandon:
5568 Cent caus li doune en un randon.
     Et cil qui de rien ne s'esmaie
     Hardïement li rent et paie
     Tox les caus qu'il li a donés.
5572 Frais est li hiaumes et quassés,
     Et tox detrenchiés li haubers;
     Nes garirent ne fus ne fers
     Ke li sans en cent lius n'en saille.
5576 Tant par fu fiere la bataille
     Ke nus ne vous seüst a dire
     Ki est le mieudre ne li pire;
     Mais saciés qu'en itel maniere
5580 Dura la bataille si fiere,
     Des qu'a ore de mïedi,
     K'il se furent forment laidi.
     Quant li estors ot tant duré,
5584 Et il orent tant enduré
     K'il orent lor elmes fendus,
     Et lor haubers tox deronpus,
     Et que par mi li sans en saut,
5588 Et c'on le voit vermel et caut,   [37vb]
          A le parfin issi avint
     Ke Goumerés les saus li vint,
     Si le feri si de l'espee

5552 They struck one another with such force
And with such anger with their lances
That their horses could not rest.
No one can blame either of these two
5556 If their horses tumbled
And they fell down with them;
The squires had to rescue them.
And they quickly jumped to their feet
5560 And attacked one another
Very rapidly and forcefully.
And you may be quite sure
That no one who watched this battle
5564 Could distinguish who started the fight.
Each one behaved like the aggressor.
Espinogre rushed toward him,
Attacking and reattacking without restraint.
5568 He gave him a hundred blows in a row.
And his opponent, unfazed by anything,
Held up bravely and repaid
All the blows he was given.
5572 The helmet was broken
And the hauberk completely cut up.
Neither wood nor iron could protect them
From the blood spurting in a hundred places.
5576 The battle was so very fierce
That no one could say
Who was the best or the worst.
But know that in just such a manner
5580 The battle lasted this violently
Until the hour of noon,
So that they were both very badly wounded.
When the battle had lasted this long,
5584 And they had endured so much
That their helmets were torn up
And their hauberks all broken,
And the blood spurted forth
5588 So that one could see it bright red and warm.
    Then in the end it happened
That Gomeret rushed at his opponent
And struck him so hard with his sword

5592 Ke ele est en l'escu coulee,
     Ce m'est avis, pié et demi.
     A peu ne li trencha par mi,
     Car il i feri par grant force.
5596 Au retraire tire et s'esforce,
     Mais ains qu'il l'eüst a soi traite,
     Fu l'espee les le heut fraite,
     Si que li puins et l'entrecor,
5600 Ki estoit adoubés a or,
     Li remest en la main sans plus.
     Et Espinogres li cort sus,
     Sel fiert et refiert par grant ire.
5604 Et Goumerés li prist a dire:
     "Sire," dist il, "or n'i a plus;
     Ne soiiés pas mal el desus.
     Quant je ne m'ai de quoi deffendre,
5608 Par estovoir me couvient rendre:
     Je me met en vostre merchi."
     Et Espinogres respondi
     Moult francement: "Et jel creant;
5612 Mais ce ert par tel couvenant
     Que vous en venrés aveuc moi
     Orendroit a la cort le roi,
     Si vous metrés en sa prison,
5616 Et counistrés la mesproison
     Del chevalier que oceistes.
     Kar saciés que vous mespresistes,
     Ki desistes que c'ert Gavain;
5620 Que fort et bien delivre et sain,
     Ce saciés de voir, le verrés
     A la cort quant vous i venrés."
     Et Goumerés issi l'otroie.
5624 A tant se metent a la voie
     Quant il orent lor cevax pris.   [38ra]
     Et cil sans non, qui ot enpris
     A querre l'Orgellox Faé,
5628 A tant cevaucié et erré
     K'il est venus a son castel,
     U il faisoit tout de nouvel
     Crier moult hautement son ban

5592   That it plunged through the shield,
       I would guess, about a foot and a half.
       He nearly cut all the way through,
       For he struck there with great force.
5596   He tried hard to pull out the sword,
       But before he could pull it toward him,
       It broke off at the hilt
       So that nothing more remained in his hand
5600   But the pommel and guard
       That were decorated in gold.
       And Espinogre set upon him,
       And attacked and reattacked furiously.
5604   And Gomeret addressed him:
       "Sir," he said, "that's it!
       Don't act badly in victory.
       When I have nothing to defend
5608   Myself with, I am forced to concede.
       I give myself up to your mercy."
       And Espinogre replied
       Very generously: "I grant it;
5612   But only if it is agreed
       That you will come with me
       Right now to the court of the king,
       Make yourself his prisoner,
5616   And learn about the crime
       Against the knight whom you killed.
       Know that you have committed a fault
       When you said that he was Gawain;
5620   That he is alive and well and strong,
       This you will see—know this truly—
       When you arrive at the court."
       And Gomeret granted all this.
5624   Then they set out on their way
       As soon as they had recovered their horses.
       And he without a name, who had undertaken
       To search for the Proud Magician,
5628   Had thus galloped and travelled
       Until he had arrived at his castle,
       Where he let be cried out once again
       Very arrogantly his proclamation,

5632   En tel guise conme Tristran,
        Li cortois chevaliers, li dist.
        Et il tantost le contredist,
        Sans çou c'onques n'i dist outrage:
5636   "Chevaliers," dist il, "grant damage
        Seroit, se il estoit ocis,
        K'il n'a de rien vers vous mespris,
        Ne vers autre, ç'ai oï dire.
5640   Onques ne fu en si grant ire
        Ke il por çou plus tost feïst
        Un outrage que on veïst,
        Que nus hom le peüst veoir.
5644   N'estes mie de grant savoir
        Ki vous vantastes de tel cose.
        Je sui cil qui desdire l'ose,
        Et qui par armes prouverai
5648   K'il est vis et sel mosterai."
              Li Faés lors li respondi:
        "Je proverai çou que je di
        A cui que il doie desplaire."
5652   Lors fist avant ses armes traire
        Si s'est moult vistement armés.
        Moult fu cointes et acesmés
        Quant il fu montés el destrier.
5656   Il n'avoit sous ciel chevalier,
        Se son grant tort ne li neüst,
        Que il bien vaintre ne deüst.
        Grant cerne ont fait la gent menue.
5660   Lors n'i ot plus regne tenue
        N'il n'i ot de manechier point;
        Cascuns d'eus le sien ceval point,   [38rb]
        Tant com il pot plus esploitier.
5664   Li Faés le feri premier
        Del bon espiel en mi le pis,
        K'il en fist voler les esclis.
        Cil sans non le feri aprés,
5668   K'il trenche de l'escu les ais,
        Si qu'il fist le hauberc fauser.
        Par mi l'espaule fist passer
        Jusqu'as doiles le bon espié,

5632   In the very way that Tristan,
The courteous knight, had told him.
And Gawain quickly challenged it,
Without speaking immoderately:

5636   "Knight," he said, "it would be
A great loss if Gawain had been killed,
For he never did anything wrong to you,
Nor against anyone else, that I have heard;

5640   Never was he so angered
That he would on this account
Commit such an evident crime,
Which no one could witness to.

5644   You are certainly not very smart
If you brag about such a thing.
I am the one who dares to challenge it,
And who will prove it in battle

5648   And show you that he is alive."
      The Magician then replied to him:
"I will prove what I say,
No matter whom it may offend."

5652   Then he had his armor brought out
And was very quickly armed.
He was very elegant and ornate
When he climbed up on his war horse.

5656   If he hadn't been the one at fault,
There wouldn't be a knight on earth,
Whom he couldn't easily overcome.
The less important people gathered in a great circle.

5660   Then the knights held back no longer;
There was no more menacing.
Each of them spurred his horse
And attacked as hard as he could.

5664   The Magician struck the first blow
With his lance in the middle of the chest
And caused the wood to splinter.
He without a name struck next

5668   And cut the wooden part of the shield
So that it caused the hauberk to break.
He made the good lance pass through
The shoulder up to the casing

5672   Si qu'il en parut bien plain pié
         Et plus encor devers le dos.
         Tout trenche fust et fer et os,
         Si l'enpaint par si grant vertu
5676   K'il a tout ensanle abatu
         En un mont lui et le destrier.
         Lors mist le main au brant d'acier,
         Sel vait ireement requerre;
5680   Et cil qui gissoit a la terre,
         Moult bleciés, li dist erranment:
         "Sire chevalier, je me rent.
         Quant si preu et si fort vous truis,
5684   Vers vous deffendre ne me puis;
         Je me met en vostre merchi."
         Et cil sans non li respondi
         Moult volentiers: "Et je vous praing;
5688   Mais tant vous di jou et apraing,
         Ains que jou vous voille reçoivre,
         Je n'ai talent de vous deçoivre,
         Que vous vendrés aveuques moi
5692   En prison a la cort le roi,
         Si menrés o vous vostre amie.
         Et se li rois la vous otrie
         Vous l'arés, et saciés de voir
5696   Ke vous ne la poés avoir
         S'au roi de nule rien desplaist."
         Et li chevaliers lors se taist:
         Ceste parole moult li grieve.   [38va]
5700   Et cil sans non l'espee lieve,
         Si fait de lui ferir sanlant;
         Et cil qui bleciés estoit tant
         K'il n'a pooir de lui deffendre
5704   Li va la soie espee rendre.
         "A! chevalier," fait il, "merci.
         Faites tant que je vous merci,
         Et que je soie vostres quites
5708   De ceste oeuvre que vous me dites.
         Se je perdoie issi m'amie,
         Je perdroie a estrox la vie,
         Car je n'aim riens el siecle tant.

5672   So that it cut through a full foot
Or more toward the back.
It cut everything—wood, iron, bone.
He attacked with such vigor
5676   That he struck down both together—
Both the knight and the war horse.
Then he picked up in his hand a steel sword
And angrily sought battle again.
5680   And he who had slipped to the ground,
Badly wounded, spoke quickly:
"Sir Knight, I surrender:
Because I find you so hardy and strong,
5684   I cannot defend myself against you,
And I render myself up to your mercy."
And he without a name replied
Graciously: "I accept your surrender.
5688   But I want to inform you fully,
Before I take you into my custody—
For I have no desire to deceive you—
That you will come with me
5692   As a prisoner to the court of the king,
And you will bring your friend with you.
And if the king grants it to you,
You will have her, and know for certain
5696   That you can have her only
If it brings no displeasure to the king."
And the knight was silent:
This speech gave him great sorrow.
5700   And he without a name raised his sword
And made as if to strike him.
And he who was so wounded that
He wasn't able to defend himself
5704   Handed over his own sword.
"Ah, Knight!" he said, "thank you.
Act so that I can thank you
And so that I am freed by you
5708   From this task that you spoke to me about.
If I would lose my *amie* this way,
I would certainly lose my life,
For I love nothing else on earth so much.

5712 Tant par vous voi prox et vaillant,
      Si ensegnié et si cortois,
      Car je sai de voir que li rois
      Le me rendra, se l'en priiés."
5716 "Chevalier, ne vous esmaiiés,"
      Fait cil sans non, que a amie,
      Ce saciés, ne faurés vous mie."
      Moult en a cil grant joie eüe.
5720 Lors atorne soi et sa drue,
      Et si fist sa plaie atorner;
      Puis s'en veut a la cort aler
      O le chevalier qui la pris.
5724 Lors l'a moult bel a raison mis,
      La u erroient le cemin.
      "Biau sire," fait il, "je devin,
      Ne sai se ma pensee est fine,
5728 Mais mes cuers ensi le devine,
      Au sanlant que je pens et voi,
      Vous estes de la gen le roi.
      Por çou vous pri, s'il pooit estre,
5732 Ke vous me desisciés vostre estre,
      Tant que j'en fusce bien certains."
      "Par foi," fait il, "je sui Gavains.
      Ja mon non ne vous ert celé
5736 Puis que j'ai par armes prouvé   [38vb]
      Ke je sui delivres et sains.
      Anïex seroie et vilains,
      Se jou a vous ni a autrui
5740 Celoie je mais qui je sui,
      Des que par terre ait tant esté
      Que je ai mon non recouvré
      Que j'avoie piecha perdu,
5744 Il doit estre par tout seü;
      Le grant orguel qu'aviés fait,
      Il doit estre par tout retrait
      Que feïstes au chevalier,
5748 Qu'el bois l'alastes detrenchier,
      Puis en aportastes le cors.
      Moult ains que del bois fuissiés fors,
      Crevastes ambedeus les eus

5712 I see that you are full of prowess, valiant,
So well-brought-up and courteous,
That I know certainly that the king
Will give her to me if you ask it of him."

5716 "Knight, don't be frightened,"
Said he without a name; "as to your friend,
Be assured, I won't fail you."
The Magician took great joy in this.

5720 Then he and his beloved got themselves
Ready and fixed up his wound;
Then he wanted to depart for the court
With the knight who had captured him.

5724 Thereupon he began to talk to him
Graciously as they travelled along.
"Dear sir," he said, "I suspect,
Not from any subtlety of reasoning,

5728 But because my heart tells me thus,
From what I perceive and observe,
That you come from the royal line.
For this reason I ask you, if you can,

5732 To tell me who you are,
So that I might be very certain."
"By my faith," he said, "I am Gawain.
My name need not be hidden now

5736 That I have proven in battle
That I am alive and well.
I would be behaving badly
If I, from you or anyone else,

5740 Ever hid who I am.
Having been all over the earth
Until I recovered my name,
Which I had lost for a time,

5744 It is right that it be known by all.
The great crime that you committed
Ought to be told about everywhere:
What you did to the knight,

5748 How you cut him up into pieces in the woods,
Then afterwards carried off the body.
Before you had left the woods,
You pierced both the eyes

5752   Au vallet qui n'estoit pas seus:
       Il avoit o lui trois puceles,
       Qui moult erent gentes et beles,
       Qui molt demenoient grant doel.
5756   Chascune d'eles a son woel
       Morist iloeques en la place;
       Tainte et persie avoit la face,
       Tant avoit chascune ploré.
5760   Quant je oi le duel escouté,
       Si ving a eles tout errant.
       Puis vi devant eles gisant
       Uns damoisel qui moult ert gent,
5764   Mais moult li estoit malement,
       Car on li avoit de novel
       Les eus tolois fors del cervel.
       Quant jel vi si mal atorné
5768   Qu'il ot andeus les ex crevés,
       Si cuidai de voir sans doutance
       Que trestoute la doliance
       Qu'eles menoient fust por lui.
5772   La grant ire et le grant anui
       Le grant doel qu'eles demenoient   [39ra]
       Demandai por quoi le faissoient.
       La premiere respont errant:
5776   "Sire, un chevalier molt vaillant
       Avons ci veü detrenchier;
       Onc ne li peümes aidier."
       Je demandai cui il estoit,
5780   Et l'autre si me responnoit
       Que ce ert messire Gavains
       Qui ici erroit trestous sains,
       Mais n'i avoit hauberc vestu,
5784   Ne nule arme fors son escu
       Et une lance solement.
       Ensi ert eschaitiement,
       Qu'il n'ot serjant ni escuier.
5788   Puis li vindrent dui chevalier
       Armés sor deus destriers d'Espaingne
       A travers par une champaigne
       Tant qu'il l'atainstrent en cel val.

5752 Of the young man who wasn't alone.
     He had with him three young women,
     Who were gracious and beautiful,
     Who cried out in great sorrow.
5756 Each one of them, in her sorrow,
     Wanted to die on the spot;
     Pale and colorless was each one's face,
     So much had each one wept.
5760 When I heard the weeping,
     I quickly rode up to them.
     Then I saw stretched out before them
     A young man who was very noble,
5764 But very badly injured;
     For someone had recently pulled
     His eyes out of the sockets.
     When I saw him so badly disposed of
5768 That he had both his eyes put out,
     I had no reason to doubt
     That all the grief
     They showed was for him.
5772 I asked for an explanation of
     The great anger, the great pain,
     And the great sorrow they displayed.
     The first replied right away:
5776 'Sir, we have seen a most valiant
     Knight cut up into pieces,
     Without ever being able to help him.'
     I asked who it was,
5780 And the other one told me
     That it was Sir Gawain
     Who rode about safe and sound,
     But without being clothed in his hauberk
5784 And with no arms except merely
     His shield and his lance.
     Thus he was poorly equipped,
     For he had neither servant nor squire.
5788 Then there came toward him two armed
     Knights on two Spanish war horses,
     Who rode across the plain
     Until they reached this valley.

5792   Lors laissent corre le cheval
        Pour lui ochirre et detrenchier;
        Puis conmenchierent a hucier:
        "Estés, estés, sire vassal."
5796   Cil s'arestut tout a estal,
        Qui tenoit sa lance en sa main.
        Li uns li dist en haut: "Gavain,
        Vous n'en irois en fin sans faille."
5800   A tant conmencha la bataille,
        Qui n'estoit mie paringal;
        Li cuivert felon desloial
        Ont detrenchié Gavain et mort.
5804   O fust a droit o fust a tort,
        I ala cel vallet courant,
        Qui moult estoit preus et vaillant,
        Que il cuida Gavain aidier;
5808   Mais ne li pot avoir mestier,
        Que il estoit ja decaupés.
        Li vallés ot les ex crevés,   [39rb]
        Pour ce ke aidier li cuida.
5812   Uns chevaliers le cors troussa
        Sour un destrier; par mi l'arbroie
        Se mistrent errant a la voie,
        S'i s'en vont moult grant aleüre.
5816   Et je lor pramis a droiture
        Que le vallet seroit vengié;
        Tornai m'en, quant j'oi pris congié,
        Que je n'i fui pas coneüs.
5820   Je vous ai tant quis et seüs
        Que j'ai sour vos la poesté
        Qu'il sera molt bien amendé,
        Le grant outrage et le desroi.
5824   Vous quidastes que ce fust moi
        Quant vos feïstes le mesfet."
        "Par foi, biau sire, autrement vet,"
        Respont li Orguelleus Faé.
5828   De chief en chief li a conté
        L'acoison por quoi el fu faite:
        "Ne doit estre en tel mal retraite,
        Puis qu'ele puet estre amendee.

5792   They let their horses run at full speed
In order to kill and dismember him.
Then they began to cry out,
'Stop! Stop! Sir Vassal!'

5796   He stopped immediately,
Holding his lance in his hand.
The one knight cried out, 'Gawain,
You will not get away this time!'

5800   Thereupon he began the fight;
It was hardly a fight between equals.
The dastard, treacherous criminals
Killed and dismembered Gawain.

5804   Whether rightly or foolishly,
This young man, who was brave
And valiant, came running up
For he thought he could aid Gawain;

5808   But he was unable to offer help,
For they had already cut him up.
The young man had his eyes pierced
Because he thought he could help.

5812   One knight tied up the body
On his war horse; they started out
On their way through the woods,
Galloping away at great speed.

5816   And I at once promised them
That the young man would be avenged.
I turned away, after I had taken my leave,
Without making myself known.

5820   I have searched for you so long
So that I would have power over you
And all might be properly rectified—
This great crime and treacherous act.

5824   You believed I was the victim
When you committed this crime."
"By my faith, dear sir, it happened differently,"
Replied the Proud Magician.

5828   From start to finish, he recounted
The circumstances of what had happened.
"It ought not to be told so badly,
Since it can be corrected.

5832 Voiant cels de vostre contree,
Vous renderai cel chevalier,
Et ses armes et son destrier,
Tout sain si com onques fu plus.

5836 Et si vous di por voir que nus
Ne vit onques encor plus cler
Que cil dont je vous oi conter
Fera, des que j'avrai tant fet

5840 Qu'aval le vis li avrai trait
Tant solement ma destre main,
Si sera tout gari et sain."
Gavains li dist: "Dous amis chier,

5844 S'or pooie tant esploitier
Que li vallés ses eus eüst
Et qu'au chevalier ne neüst
La traïson ke vous feïstes,   [39va]

5848 Encor porriés estre quites,
A ce que je vous aiderai."
"N'en soiés vos ja en esmai,
    "Sire," fait l'Orguelleus Faé,

5852 "Que onkes en sit grant santé
Ne fu encor li chevaliers,
Ne li vallés, biau sire chiers,
Com a la court le vous rendrai;

5856 De ce ne soiés en esmai."
        Ensi tindrent parlant lor voie,
Tant que il vindrent a la voie
Iloec endroit ou il parti

5860 D'Espinogre, son bon ami;
Si descendent iloec a pié,
Par un cemin qui ert forchié.
Lors i vint poignant sans demeure,

5864 Sor un noir ceval plus que meure,
Un chevalier grant aleüre.
Son destrier ert a desmesure
Isniax; qui voir en vaudroit dire,

5868 On ne porroit pas tel eslire
En la terre le roi Artus.
Le chevalier ert molt seürs:
Il estoit si armé sans faille

5832   In the presence of your countrymen,
       I will turn over this knight to you,
       Along with his armor and war horse,
       Safe and sound as never before.
5836   And I assure you truly that no one
       Will see more clearly
       Than this one whom I've heard you speak of,
       As soon as I have done the following:
5840   After I have waved my right hand
       In a simple gesture before his face,
       He will be completely cured and well."
       Gawain replied, "Dear sweet friend,
5844   If now I could succeed in this—
       That the young man regains his sight
       And the knight doesn't resent
       The treason you committed,
5848   Then you will have made satisfaction:
       In this endeavor I will help you."
       "Don't be upset about it,
           "Sir," said the Proud Magician,
5852   "The knight will never before
       Have been in such good health,
       Nor the young man either, dear sweet sir,
       As that in which I will present them at court;
5856   Don't be at all worried."
           Talking thus, they continued on their way
       Until they came to the very place
       Along the way where he had parted
5860   From Espinogre, his good friend.
       They dismounted and went on foot,
       Along a road that was forked.
       Then there came quickly riding toward them,
5864   On a horse blacker than a blackberry,
       A knight who rode at top speed.
       His war horse was faster than the wind;
       Whoever saw him would have to say
5868   That one couldn't find his equal
       In all of Arthur's land.
       The knight was very well-protected:
       He was so thoroughly armed

5872   Ne cremoit pas une maaille
        Caup d'espee ne de nule arme.
        Il est descendus sous un charme,
        Pour son destrier cengler estroit.
5876   Li Orguelleus Faés le voit,
        Si dist Gavain tout erranment:
        "Sire," dist il, "mon escient,
        Com je voi la un chevalier,
5880   Veés com cengle son destrier
        Et lace son elme gemé,
        Saciés bien qu'il a en pensé
        A faire vous aucun hontage.
5884   Je voel estre en vostre homage,   [39vb]
        S'irai vostre message querre,
        Dont il vient et que il va querre."
        Que que cil parloit a Gavain,
5888   Es vous venir par mi un plain
        Deus chevaliers molt bien armés,
        De toutes armes acesmés;
        Si paroit bien a lor escus
5892   Que forment s'erent combatus:
        Il erent tuit covert de sanc.
        Li uns sist sor un destrier blanc,
        Et li autres sist sour un sor.
5896   Cil avoit non Gomeret Mor;
        Molt estoit chevalier vaillant.
        Espinogres aloit devant,
        Qui sour le blanc destrier seoit.
5900   Et li noirs chevaliers le voit,
        Si com venoient traversant.
        Lors monte el bon destrier corant,
        S'enbrace l'escu et la lance;
5904   D'esperoner vers els s'avance,
        Si broce pour els encontrer.
        A Espinogre vait jouster.
        Quant cil le vit ver lui apoindre,
5908   Iriement vait a lui joindre.
        Sans parler et sans desfiances,
        Fierent es escus de lor lances
        Et li escu perchent et croissent;

5872 That he didn't have to fear anything—
Whether a blow from a sword or any other weapon.
He dismounted by an elm tree
So that he could tie up his horse.
5876 The Proud Magician saw him
And said quickly to Gawain,
"Sir," he said, "to my way of thinking,
When I see a knight there
5880 Tying up his war horse by a rope
And unlacing his jeweled helmet,
You can be certain he has no thought
Of acting dishonorably against you.
5884 I would like to be in your service,
And I will go seek news for you—
Where he comes from and where he is headed."
While this one spoke to Gawain,
5888 There approached from across a plain
Two very heavily armed knights,
All their arms ornamented;
It was quite apparent from their shields
5892 That they had just been in battle,
For they were all covered with blood.
One sat on a white horse,
And the other sat on a chestnut one.
5896 His name was Gomeret the Moor;
He was a very valiant knight;
Espinogre rode in front,
Sitting on the white war horse.
5900 And the black knight saw them
As they came riding up.
Then he mounted his good charger
And picked up his shield and lance
5904 And started to gallop toward them
And spurred his horse to the encounter.
He went to joust with Espinogre.
When this one saw him moving toward him,
5908 He quickly got ready to engage him.
Without speaking and without challenges,
They struck their shields with their lances,
And the shields gave way and broke.

5912 Nule de lor lances ne froissent,
      Que trop erent roides et fors,
      Et cil l'empaint de tel esfors,
      Volsist Espinogres ou non,
5916 Que il l'abati el sablon.
      De sen poindre a son cop repris:
      Fiert Gomeret en l'escu bis,
      Que par la crupe del destrier
5920 Le fait a terre trebuchier.
      Puis a saisi les deus chevaus,   [40ra]
      Si a guerpi les deus vassaus,
      Si s'en revient toute la voie
5924 Vers les deus qui sont en l'ombroie,
      Qui l'avoient piecha veü.
      Le ceval blanc ot couneü
      Mesire Gavains le courtois,
5928 Si sot bien trestout demanois
      Que ce estoit son compaignon
      Que cil abati el sablon.
      Il s'estoit pris au bon destrier
5932 Pour aler au noir chevalier
      Jouster, qui par grant demesure
      Aloit tout sol querre aventure;
      Car il ne quidoit pas que fust
5936 Nus hom qui de prouece eüst
[1]   Qui de lui se peüst desfendre: [A 75rc]
      Ne quide pas les cevals rendre
      Par nul chevalier qui soit nés.
[4]   "Sire," dist l'Orguillos Faés,
      "Je li dirai qu'il viengne a vos;
      Et se il est si orguillous
      Que n'i veulle venir por moi,   [75va]
[8]   Je vos jur et afi par foi
      Qu'il ne puet passer sans bataille.
      Ma bone espee qui bien taille
      Li enbatrai ens el cervel.
[12] Je vos proi que il vos soit bel
      Que je par vostre gré i voisse."
      Moult durement cil s'en envoisse;
      Qu'il estoit costume a cel jor

5912	Neither of their lances broke,
	For they were solid and strong.
	The black knight struck with such force
	That, whether Espinogre liked it or not,
5916	He knocked him down onto the ground.
	He took up the attack once again:
	He struck Gomeret on his grey shield
	So that he caused him to fall back
5920	Over the rump of his horse onto the ground.
	Then he seized the two horses
	And abandoned the two vassals
	And turned back toward the path
5924	That led to the two in the shade
	Who had watched him for a long time.
	Sir Gawain the courteous
	Recognized the white horse
5928	And immediately knew for certain
	That this was his companion
	Who had been thrown to the ground.
	He was about to grab his good war horse
5932	To go joust with the black knight,
	Who, in his great arrogance,
	Was seeking adventure all alone.
	For he couldn't believe that there was
5936	Any man so valiant that he
[1]	Could not defend himself against him.
	He didn't expect to turn over the horses
	To any knight living on earth.
[4]	"Sir," said the Proud Magician,
	"I will speak to him who would approach you;
	And if he is so arrogant
	That he doesn't want to return with me,
[8]	I swear to you and affirm by my faith
	That he will not pass by without a fight.
	My good sword that cuts so well
	Will strike him on the head.
[12]	I beg that it may be pleasing to you
	To allow me to go there."
	With much distress, Gawain sent him off.
	It was the custom in that day

[16]   S'uns chevaliers en un estor
        Venoit por joster ne por poindre
        N'en doit que un seus a lui jondre,
        Et se doi i vienent ensanble
[20]   Il serroient, si com moi sanble,
        Trestot recreant et honni:
        Ja mais ne serroient servi
        En cort a roi, s'il ert seü.
[24]   Por ce s'est premiers esmeü
        Por joster au chevalier noir;
        Mais il cuidoit a son espoir
        Que cil le tenist a beubant.
[28]   A tant s'en part sor le bauçant,
        Si point droit a noir chevalier,
        Et cil qui n'ot soig de tencier
        Repoint a lui grant aleüre.
[32]   L'Orguillous par grant desmesure
        Le fiert primes sor l'escu noir,
        Si vos di bien a mon espoir
        Se la lance ne fust brissie
[36]   Qu'il eüst la sele widie;
        Mais sa lance brise erranment.
        Et cil si com il vient corant
        L'avoit feru sor l'escu paint;
[40]   Del bien ferir pas ne se faint,
        Car mervelles ert aïrous.
        L'escu li perça a estrous,
        Et l'auberc a tot desronpu,
[44]   Mais un porpoint qu'il ot vestu,
        Qui fu fais par moult grant maistrie,
        Li a le jor sauvé la vie.
        Et neporquant par tel vertu
[48]   L'avoit del cheval abatu
        Qu'il li desjointa le braic destre.
        Ilueuc ne vaut pas longes estre,
        Ains le laissa demaintenant,
[52]   S'en mena le destrier corant.
        Les Espinogre et Gomerés
        En a avuecques lui menés;
        A tant s'en parti, si s'en vait.

[16] That if, in a battle, one knight
Came up to joust or attack,
Only one adversary must meet him;
And if two attacked together,
[20] They would be, so it seems to me,
Totally villainous and shameful.
They would never be allowed
To serve the king, if it were known.
[24] For this reason, the Proud Magician moved first
To joust with the black knight.
But he also worried that
Gawain would think him presumptuous.
[28] Thereupon he leapt on his horse
And rode straight to the black knight,
And he in turn, who had no care for talk,
Galloped toward him at great speed.
[32] The Proud Magician, in a rash move,
Struck him first on his black shield,
And I tell you truly that,
If his lance hadn't broken,
[36] He would have been thrown from the saddle.
But his lance broke at once.
And he who was attacking him
Struck him on his painted shield.
[40] He didn't hold back from striking hard,
For he was incredibly angry.
He pierced through the shield,
And the hauberk was badly broken up,
[44] But a doublet that he wore
That was very cleverly made
Saved his life that day.
Nonetheless, he struck him
[48] From his horse with such force
That he dislocated the Magician's right arm.
He didn't want to stay there long,
So he immediately left,
[52] Leading away his fast war horse.
He took with him as well
Those belonging to Espinogre and Gomeret,
And thus he departed.

[56]   A Gavain mervelles desplaist
         Quant li Orguillous fu ceüs;
         Il est au Gringalet venus,
         Si monte par l'estrier senestre   [N1 40ra]
         Et prist sa lance a la main destre.
         Puis dist a l'amie au Faé:
5940   "Damoisele de grant biauté,
         Vous remaindrois ci sans esmai,
         Sous cest ormel que je chi voi,
         Et g'irai vostre ami aidier,
5944   Et si li rendrai son destrier,
         Que cel chevalier la en mainne.
         Je soufferrai ains molt grant paine
         Que il l'en maint, se Diex me gart."
5948   Sous l'ormel la laist, si s'em part,
         Si vient a lui par mi la lande.
         Li noirs chevaliers li demande
         Qui cele damoisele estoit:
5952   "Sire," fait il, "se vous plaisoit,
         Ele seroit et moie et vostre."
         "Ja, par Saint Pol le bon apostre,
         N'i avrois part avoeques moi."
5956   Gavains li dist: "Sir, par foi,   [40rb]
         Vous requier et pri par franchise,
         Par guerredon et par servise,
         Que me rendois cel blanc destrier,
5960   Et puis celui au chevalier
         Que abatistes en la lande.
         La damoisele le vos mande
         Que vous li rendés par amor,
5964   Si ert cortoisie et hounor.
         Sire, encor vos revoel priier
         Que me rendois l'autre destrier,
         Si m'avrois dont grant honor faite;
5968   L'onor ert en tel lieu retraite
         Ou il vous orra maint prodome."
         "Par trestous les consaus de Rome,"
         Fait soi li chevaliers hidous,
5972   "Vilains estes et ennuious.
         Vous m'avés tel cose requise

[56]   Gawain was very displeased
       When the Proud One was thrown.
       He came up to Gringalet
       And mounted with the left stirrup
       And took his lance in his right hand.
       Then he said to the Magician's *amie*:
5940   "Young woman, you of such great beauty,
       You should remain here unafraid
       Under this elm tree that I see here,
       And I will go to aid your friend
5944   And return to him the war horse
       That this knight has led away.
       I would rather suffer great pain
       Than that he take it away, God willing."
5948   He left her under the elm tree and departed,
       And rode toward him across the plain.
       The black knight asked him
       Who the young woman was:
5952   "Sir," he said, "if it please you,
       She can be both yours and mine."
       "By St. Paul the Good Apostle," replied Gawain,
       "You will not share with me!"
5956   Gawain continued: "Sir, by my faith,
       I require and demand that you,
       Out of generosity, service,
       And duty, return the white war horse
5960   And also the horse of the knight
       You knocked down on the ground.
       The young woman also asks that
       You do this out of charity—
5964   It would be courteous and honorable.
       Sir, I want to ask again in addition
       That you return the other war horse,
       If you would do me a great honor.
5968   Your honorable nature will be talked about
       Where many a rich man will hear of it."
       "By all the councils of Rome,"
       Replied the evil knight,
5972   "You are villainous and rude.
       You require such a thing of me

Je nel feroie en nule guise,
Pour vos ne por vostre priere.
5976   Ja nes avrois en tel maniere.
Mais tant sachiés, dans chevaliers,
Que se vous li volés aidier,
O moi vos convendra conbatre
5980   Ou je les en menrai tous quatre,
S'ert li vostre en la conpaignie.
Et si en merrai vostre amie
Que je voi la desous cel orme,
5984   Si avrois sollers en la forme
O les autres les ont eüs
Qu'iloec gisent tout estendus,
Si serais tous quatre assamblés."
5988   Lors dist Gavains: "Vous me samblés
Molt faus et de molt male chiere,
Si sai tres bien que par priiere
Ne m'en feriés vos rien plus;
5992   Mais se de vos vieng au dessus,   [40va]
Je les quit bien trestous vengier."
"Laissiés ester le manechier,"
Fait le noir chevalier, "vassal,
5996   Si nous conbatons parigal:
Il n'a ichi que vous et moi;
Li autre sont tuit en reqoi
Qui la gisent tuit abaubi.
6000   Or sachiés que je vos desfi."
Sans nesun point de demorance
Prent cascun l'escu et la lanche,
Si se fierent par tel angoisse
6004   Que l'une lance et l'autre froisse
Sor les escus devant les pis;
Volent des lances les esclis.
Quant cascuns a sa lance fraite,
6008   Vistement a l'espee traite,
Si conmencent lor envaïe,
Qui molt sevent de l'escremie
Et molt orent de hardement.
6012   Cil qui ert noir com arrement
Vait ferir monsegnor Gavain

That I could never do—
Not for you nor for your polite speech.
5976   You will never have them!
But mark this well, Sir Knight,
If you want to render aid to her,
You will have to fight with me,
5980   Or I will lead away all four horses
And yours will be one of them.
And I will also carry off your friend
Whom I see there under the elm tree.
5984   You will be in the same position
That the others have been placed in
Who are lying there on the ground—
All four of you will be together."
5988   Then Gawain said, "I see that you are
Very false and of an evil temper,
And I see very well that, by asking nicely,
I won't get any further.
5992   But if I succeed in conquering you,
I guarantee they'll be well-avenged."
"Let be your menacing, vassal!"
Said the black knight,
5996   "For we will fight nonetheless;
There's only you and me here.
The others are all resting,
For they lie there completely defeated.
6000   Now mark how I defy you!"
Without any further delay,
Each took up his shield and lance
And attacked with such force
6004   That both lances broke
On the shields covering their chests:
Fragments of the lances flew about.
After each had broken his lance,
6008   He quickly grabbed his sword
And began the attack again.
They were both excellent swordsmen,
And they were both very brave.
6012   He who was as black as India ink
Went to strike Sir Gawain

Amont sor le hiaume de plain:
Tout le fent jusqu'el cercle d'or.
6016   Li cols descent desus la cor
De l'escu a sinnople taint.
Et cil de tel aïr l'empaint
Qu'ambedui li ceval caïrent.
6020   Li dui chevalier sus saillirent.
Gavains sailli sus vistement:
De lui vengier olt grant talent.
Sore li keut par grant vertu,
6024   Et celui rest vers lui couru;
Li uns d'els velt l'autre empirier.   [40vb]
Mais Gavains pour le coup vengier
Que celui li avoit douné
6028   L'en a resouse la bonté.
Il l'a feru tout a bandon,
A escremie de tel ton,
Sus en l'iaume el coing amont,
6032   Que tout li trencha en roont.
Jusqu'al chapelier l'a fendu:
A poi qu'i ne l'a abatu.
Li nois chevaliers li passa,
6036   Tout l'escu li trenche et quassa;
Si vint li cols de tel vertu,
Quant il fu parti de l'escu,
Qu'il trencha le pan del hauberc,
6040   Et el braiel li fist un merc,
Qu'il li embati plaine paume
En mi la place sor le hiaume.
S'il l'eüst droit aconseü,
6044   Je cuit qu'il l'eüst abatu.
Et Gavains ne resorti pas,
Ains vait vers lui plus que le pas,
Sel fiert sor le hiaume a bandon.
6048   O l'espee li met un son
Amont sor le hiaume forbi;
Et cil la molt bien recuelli
Qui savoit toute la mestrie:
6052   Ne crient nus de chevalerie.
Il fiert Gavain par grant outrage

Full force on top of his helmet:
He broke it up to the circle of gold.
6016 The blow descended to the corner
Of his tinted green shield.
And Gawain struck with such force
That both horses fell down.
6020 The two knights jumped to their feet.
Gawain was on his feet sooner;
He was anxious to have his revenge.
He struck the black knight forcefully,
6024 And he in turn attacked Gawain.
Each wanted to do the other great harm.
But Gawain, in order to take revenge
For the blow that had been given him,
6028 Paid him back in full measure.
He struck him with such force
And skill in using his sword
On the corner of his helmet
6032 That he made a hole in it.
He struck through to the bare head.
He very nearly struck him down.
The black knight slipped by,
6036 Striking and breaking Gawain's shield.
His blow was so forceful
That he not only cut the shield in half,
But also struck off a piece of his hauberk
6040 And made a mark on his belt;
He hit him with full force
In the center of his helmet.
If he had attacked him face to face,
6044 I think he would have struck him down.
But Gawain did not flinch;
He quickly moved toward his adversary
And struck him hard on the helmet.
6048 His sword rang out as it struck
The top of his helmet.
His opponent, a skillful fighter,
Defended himself well.
6052 He feared no one in the art of chivalry.
He struck Gawain with a terrible blow

Sor l'escu; li fait tel damage
Que il li trencha maintenant
6056   Cent mailles de l'auberc luisant,
Et que de la cote a armer
Li fist contreval devaler
Bon plain pié jusqu'a la chainture.
6060   Molt fu bele cele aventure   [41ra]
Quant ne li a le cors trenchié,
Tant est le brant escoulorgié
Par entre l'aissele et l'escu.
6064   Et Gavains a lui referu
Par grant ire sor l'escu noir.
Nus hom qui le poïst veoir
N'en seüst dire le meillour.
6068   Jusc'au vespre que faut le jour,
Se conbatent issi sans faille
Que le miudre de la bataille
N'en sorent eslire li troi
6072   Qui erent a pié en l'aunoi.
Vindrent vers els grant aleüre.
Et cil qui jusqu'a la chainture
L'avoit tout desarmé errant
6076   Li dist: "Franc chevalier vaillant,
Ai je garde de cil troi
Qui vienent ci armé sour moi?"
Gavains li dist isnelepas:
6080   "Par foi, amis, ce n'est pas gas,
Bien loiaument le vous plevis,
N'en i a nul si mes amis,
S'il vos adesoit sor mon pois,
6084   Je nel ferisse demanois:
Ja ne me sera reprouvé."
Lors avoit dit et conmandé
As trois qu'il s'en traient ariere;
6088   Et cil le font en tel maniere
Si com Gavains le conmanda.
Onques nus d'els mot ne souna,
Por riens que il lor avenist.
6092   Et li noirs chevaliers lor dist:
"Vassal," fait il, "je loeroie

On his shield; he did such damage
That he instantly cut off

6056 A hundred pieces of glistening mail
And, in slicing through, made a large piece fall
From his coat of arms
At least a foot down to the belt.

6060 It was a lucky thing that
Gawain's body was not cut up,
Such was the blow that lodged
Between his armpit and shield.

6064 And Gawain struck back
Very angrily on the black shield.
No person able to watch this
Would be able to say who fought better.

6068 Until vespers, at the end of the day,
They fought thus without weakening.
They fought so well that the three
Who sat at the base of the trees

6072 Weren't able to say who was better.
These three quickly ran toward them.
And he who had divested Gawain
Of his armor down to his waist

6076 Said at once: "Noble, valiant knight,
Must I protect myself from these three
Who approach me armed this way?"
Gawain immediately replied:

6080 "By my faith, friend, this is no joke.
I pledge you this in all loyalty,
There's no one I'll count my friend,
Who, if he touches you against my wishes,

6084 I would not challenge in battle.
There will be no reproach in this for me."
Then he spoke to them and commanded that
The three should retreat;

6088 And they acted in the very way
That Gawain had asked them to.
Not one of them uttered a word
About anything that happened to them.

6092 And the black knight then said:
"Vassal," he said, "I swear to you

         Que vos meïssiés a la voie,
         Tout sain et tout sauf o ces trois,
6096   Et ces quatre cevaus norois
         Me laississois tout quitement,   [41rb]
         Et cele pucele ensement
         Qui vos atent sous cel ormel,
6100   Si vos sera mils et plus bel,
         Qu'os avrois salve vostre vie."
         Dist Gavains: "Molt oi grant folie
         Que vos dites, se Dix me saut;
6104   Se ceste espee ne me faut,
         Je vos movrai tel contenchon,
         Ains que moi et vos departon,
         Qu'avrai la dame et les chevaus."
6108   Lors s'entrevienent les vassaus,
         Si fierement, par tele angoisse,
         Qu'ançois que l'un l'autre connoisse
         Se sont il molt forment grevé.
6112   Gavains li a un coup douné,
         Amont sor le hiaume vergié,
         Que l'espee li a trenchié
         L'iaume; desi en la cervele
6116   En est coulee l'alemele.
         Son cop estort de grant aïr.
         A la terre le fist venir
         As deus genous molt vistement;
6120   Mais il relieve isnelement,
         Si est Gavain alés requerre.
         Onques encor en nule terre
         Dui homes tant ne se greverent.
6124   Et li troi chevalier qui erent
         Iloec pres d'els, quis esgardoient,
         Dient que mervailles faisoient
         Qui se conbatent a cele ore.
6128   Li noirs chevaliers sans demore
         A dit a monseignor Gavain:
         "Vassal, ne soiés pas vilain,
         Mais soions huimais a repos;
6132   Quant li jors ert demain esclos,
         Si resoions ci pié a pié:

That you may proceed on your way—
Completely safe and sound with these three—
6096   As long as you leave the four
Good horses to me of your own free will,
As well as this young woman
Who is waiting for you under this elm tree.
6100   You will be the better off,
For you will have saved your life."
Gawain replied, "This is a great folly
That you suggest, so help me God!
6104   So long as this sword does not fail me,
I will offer you such a battle that,
Before you and I part,
I will have the woman and the horses."
6108   Then the two knights clashed
So ferociously, with such violence,
That before either of them knew it,
They were both badly wounded.
6112   Gawain gave him such a blow
On top of his engraved helmet
That the sword broke it
In two; the blade sliced down
6116   Almost to the brain.
The blow was very powerful;
He caused the black knight
To drop quickly to his knees.
6120   But he got back up on his feet quickly
And returned to battle with Gawain.
Never before on earth had two men
Done so much harm to one another.
6124   And the three knights who were
Nearby and who observed the battle
Said that it was unusual to fight
At such a late hour.
6128   Without delay, the black knight
Said to Sir Gawain,
"Vassal, don't be a villain;
Let us take a rest tonight;
6132   At daybreak tomorrow,
We can meet again together;

Veés com il est anuitié.   [41va]
Si avrois ces chevaus o vos,
6136   Par un covent que entre nous
Les ramenrons demain ichi,
Et la damoisele autresi,
De ce vol jou estre certains."
6140   "Par foi," ce li a dit Gavains,
"Je n'en voel ja nesun mener,
Se vers vos nes puis conquester;
Que trop vos voi fel et gaingnart."
6144   "Dans chevaliers, il est trop tart,"
Fait li noirs chevaliers oscur;
Mais soiés trestout aseür
Que je vendrai le matin ça."
6148   Dist Gavains: "Ce n'avendra ja,
Se Dieu plaist, que nos departons
Desi que je savrai ou non
Se je en merrai les cevals
6152   Et la pucele et les vassaus,
Sans calonge et sans contredit."
"Et vos me prisiés molt petit,
Dans chevaliers, ce m'est avis,
6156   Pour ce que je vos ai requis
De la trive premierement.
Ja mais ne me troverés lent,
Ains vos troverai molt bataille:
6160   Ja del mien qui un denier vaille
N'en avrois en tout mon aage,
Se par force ou par vasselage
Nel poés conquerre vers moi.
6164   Et si sai molt bien et si croi
Q'os estes cortois et vaillans;
Pour ce vos requier et demant
Que me desissiés vostre non:
6168   Que ce est bien drois et raison
Que je le sace et vos le mien.
Et puis vos pri sor toute rien
De faire tout vostre pooir.   [41vb]
6172   Mais je voel vostre non savoir
Et itant savoir de vostre estre,

You see how night is falling.
You may take the horses with you,

6136 On the condition that we meet
Again here tomorrow with them
And with the young woman also;
Of this I want to be certain."

6140 "In faith," Gawain said to him,
"I do not want to lead anyone away
Until I have won them by defeating you;
I see just how criminal and cruel you are."

6144 "Lord Knight, it is too late to fight,"
Said the somber, black knight,
"But be fully assured
That I will return here in the morning."

6148 Gawain said, "I will not agree,
So help me God, that we part
Until I know, yes or no,
If I can take the horses,

6152 The maiden, and the vassals
Without dispute or conflict."
"You hold me in very little esteem,
Lord Knight, it seems to me,

6156 For I have asked you
For the truce first.
You will never find me hesitant
To fight you whenever you want.

6160 While I am alive you will have
Nothing that belongs to me,
Unless by force or feudal rights
You are able to defeat me.

6164 I think—in fact I am quite sure—
That you are courteous and valiant;
For this reason I ask and require
You to tell me your name,

6168 For it is right and reasonable
That I know it and you know mine.
And then I ask you to spare nothing
And do all of which you are capable.

6172 But I would like to know your name
And thus know who you are,

Car ice m'ensegna mon mestre
C'a home ne me conbatisse
6176   Que son non ne li enqueïsse,
Si n'iere pas faus ne vilain."
"Par foi," fait il, "j'ai non Gavain."
"Gavain, voire, neveu le roi?"
6180   "Issi ai je non, par ma foi,
Fait Gavains; "vos avés bien dit.
Ja mais mon non, se Diex m'aït,
Ne celerai a chevalier."
6184   Et cil se volt agenoillier
Devant lui pour merci crier:
"Bien porroie," fait il, "jurer
Que ja mais home ne creïsse,
6188   Se a mes eus ne vos veïsse;
Qu'en dit que l'Orguellex Faé
Vous avoit mort et decaupé
Par orguel et par estoutie.
6192   Nel tenés pas a vilenie.
Frans chevaliers prex et cortois,
Foi que je doi Artus li rois,
Qui est me sire et mes amis,
6196   Vous m'avés vencu et conquis.
Ves m'espee, je la vos rent.
Molt sui courechiés et dolent
De ce que je ne vous counui.
6200   Bien sai que vos ai fait anui,
Si m'en repent, se Diex me saut.
Ce vos di bien, de cest assaut
Sui je tout matés et conquis,
6204   Si vous di bien ce m'est avis
Que por cent mars ou encor plus
N'en porroie je souffrir plus.
Et pour ce que je sui matés,
6208   Je me renc a vos; recevés   [42ra]
M'espee, que je la vous rent."
Et Gavains li dist erranment:
"Biaus amis, or gardés l'espee,
6212   Qu'ele est en vos bien aloee,
Que hardis estes et osés.

For my mentor taught me this—
That I should not fight any man
6176   Without first asking his name,
So as not to be false or vile."
"In faith," he replied, "my name is Gawain."
"Gawain? Truly? The nephew of the king?"
6180   "That's my name, I swear it,"
Said Gawain, "you said it correctly.
So help me God, I will never hide
My name from any knight."
6184   At that the black knight wanted to fall down
On his knees and cry for mercy.
"I can surely swear," he said,
"That I would never have believed this
6188   If I had not seen you with my own eyes;
For I was told that the Proud Magician—
Out of pride and folly—
Had killed and dismembered you.
6192   Don't take me for a villain.
Generous knight, valiant and courteous,
For the allegiance I owe to King Arthur,
Who is my lord and friend,
6196   You have completely conquered and defeated me.
Lo here, my sword, I surrender it to you.
I am angry with myself and chagrinned
That I didn't recognize you.
6200   I know that I have made trouble for you,
And I am sorry about this, so help me God.
I tell you truly that in this assault
I am completely conquered and defeated.
6204   I say further that, in my opinion,
I could not suffer more even if
Offered a hundred marks or more.
And because I am defeated,
6208   I surrender to you; take my
Sword that I hand over here to you."
And Gawain quickly said:
"Dear friend, keep your sword
6212   That is well-suited to you
Who are so brave and daring.

Et quel non estes apelés?"
"Sire, j'ai non li Lais Hardis;
6216   Del lait ne sui je pas fardis.
L'autre soir m'esmui de ma terre
Por aler cerquier et enquerre
Se de vos noveles oïsse.
6220   Sachiés bien que tant vos queïsse
Que bien en oïsse parler
Ains que volsisse retorner.
Or m'en sui a vos combatus,
6224   Si m'en est molt bien avenu;
Que s'eüst plus duré l'estour
G'eüsse de ma mort paour."
    Quant Gavains a ce entendu
6228   Que c'ert son ami et son dru,
Gete l'escu, l'iaume deslace;
L'un d'els l'autre acole et enbrace,
Si s'entrefirent molt grant joie.
6232   Je ne quit mais que nus hom voie
Deus chevaliers si bien apris;
Cascuns d'els ert de molt grant pris.
Or ert molt l'un vers l'autre estous;
6236   Or sont molt paisibles et dous.
Si vindrent andui erranment
A cele qui encor l'atent,
Si l'ont delivrement montee.
6240   Puis si ont lor voie aroutee.
Entre Gavain et le Faé
Et Espinogre, ont amené
Gomeret a sa damoisele.
6244   A Gavain conte la nouvele
Comment il s'estoit combatu,   [42rb]
Et com cil s'ert a lui rendu,
Com doit venir en sa merchi.
6248   Et Gavains li a dit: "Amis,
Molt m'avés grant servise fait.
Ensi grant bone aventure ait
Vostre cors, comme je vaudroie."
6252   Ensi chevauchent tote voie,
Car il estoit molt pres de vespre.

And what is your name?"
"Sir, my name is Lais Hardis;

6216 For the ugliness I'm not responsible.
The other night I left my country
To go seek and find out
Whatever news I could about you.

6220 Be assured that I would have searched
Until I had heard some news of you
Before I would think about returning.
Now I have fought with you,

6224 And things have turned out well.
If the battle had lasted any longer
I would have had to fear for my life."
When Gawain had understood

6228 That this was a friend and companion,
He threw down his shield, unlaced his helmet,
And they embraced one another,
Mutually expressing great joy.

6232 I do not believe that anyone has ever seen
Two knights behave so well;
Each of them was worthy of great praise.
One minute they are enraged with one another;

6236 The next minute they are gentle and peaceful.
And they both went quickly
To the young woman who was waiting for them,
And they quickly got her up on her horse.

6240 Then they set out on their way.
The three of them—Gawain, the Magician,
And Espinogre—led away
Gomeret and his young woman.

6244 Espinogre told Gawain the story
Of his fight with Gomeret and
How his enemy surrendered to him,
How he was forced to beg mercy.

6248 And Gawain said to him, "Friend,
You have performed a great service for me.
You had very good luck,
Just as I had hoped."

6252 They quickly followed the road,
For it was near the end of the day.

L'un d'els conte a Gavain son estre,
Tant que chascun li a conté
6256 Com il l'ont fait, com ont erré.
Tant ont lor parlement tenu
Qu'il sont tuit ensamble venu
A l'ostel Tristran qui ne rit,
6260 Qui a Gavain grant honor fist,
Et Espinogres ensement.
Tristran saut sus isnelement
Maintenant qu'il les ot veüs:
6264 "Segnors, bien soiés vos venus,"
Fait soi Tristran qui molt fu sage,
Et n'ert pas de trop grant aage,
Ains ert chevalier bel et gent.
6268 A l'estriu sailli erranment
A Gavain, si le fist descendre;
Vaslet corent son ceval prendre,
Dont molt i avoit de cortois.
6272 Les autres chevaliers tous trois
Firent descendre isnelement.
Assés ot iloec quis descent,
Les damoiseles ambedeus.
6276 Et sachiés bien que avoec eus
Estoit a pié li Lais Hardis,
Qui n'ert couars ne alentis
De servir monsegnor Gavain.
6280 Et Tristrans le prent par la main,
Si le maine el palais amont,
Si com franchise le semont,   [42va]
Si s'est del servir molt penés.
6284 La nuit orent a grant plenté
Pain et vin et oisiaus rostis,
Ploviers et faisans et pertris
Et grans cisnes, a lor mengier,
6288 Car molt en avoit el vergier.
Tristran, qui bien garni estoit
De quainque prodom covenoit,
Lor a la nuit tele onor faite,
6292 Ne l'aroie en piece retraite,
L'onor qu'il a fait a chascun.

Each of them, as they rode along,
Told Gawain about himself, until each one
6256 Had told a story about how he had fared.
Thus their conversation continued
Until they all arrived together
At the castle of Tristan Who Never Smiles,
6260 He who had shown such great honor
To Gawain and Espinogre.
Tristan jumped up quickly
As soon as he saw them.
6264 "My lords, you are most welcome,"
Said Tristan himself, he who was very wise
And who was not of a very advanced age,
But who was a noble and handsome knight.
6268 He quickly moved toward Gawain's
Horse and helped him to dismount.
Servants ran to take his horse away,
And there was much display of courtesy.
6272 The other three knights were also
Quickly helped down from their horses.
Plenty of help came forth
For both of the young women.
6276 And you can be sure that Lais Hardis
Was already on his feet,
For he was not lax or slow
To serve Sir Gawain.
6280 And Tristan took him by the hand
And led him up into the hall
And invited him there courteously.
He took great pains to serve them well.
6284 There was a great plenitude of food
To eat that night: bread and wine,
Roasted birds, plovers, pheasant hens,
Partridges, and large swans.
6288 The grounds were full of them.
Tristan, who was well-supplied
With whatever suited a nobleman,
Received them with such honor that night
6292 That I cannot tell in a few words
The honor that he gave to each one.

Bien les coucha par un et un
Pour dormir et pour reposer,
6296 Qu'il estoient las de l'errer,
Et traveilliés et confondus:
Il paroit bien a lor escus
Qu'il orent sosfert grant estour.
6300 Grant joie ot Tristran de l'onor,
Qui la destre Gavain acointe,
Et saciés que molt se fait cointe
Qu'il a deus fois esté son oste.
6304 Vers le Lai Hardi se racoste,
Qui molt estoit gentils et frans:
"Sire," fait il, "je croi et pans
Que vos estes molt travelliés;
6308 Bien sai que vos estes plaiés
Et navrés sos la coiffe blance.
Et j'ai une fille molt franche
Qui tel entrait vos i metra
6312 Que la dolor vous en traira:
Ja puis angoisse n'i avrois
Que il i ert mis une fois;
Sempres ert la plaie garie."
6316 Li noirs chevaliers l'en mercie,
Qui de la pramesse a grant joie;
Et mesire Gavains li proie
Qu'il li aït, s'il onkes puet.   [42vb]
6320 Et Tristran maintenant s'esmuet
En la chambre ou sa fille estoit,
Si li prie, s'ele savoit
Aidier a itel chevalier,
6324 Que li aït sans demorier.
Et cele qui n'ert pas vilaine
Li dit: "La plaie n'ert pas saine,
Se Diex m'aït, hui en cest jour."
6328 Une herbe de molt grant valor,
Qui estoit toscane apelee,
Sour la plaie li a bendee;
Puis se dormi a grant loisir,
6332 Tant que fist Diex le jor venir,
Qu'il se lievent et atornerent.

He arranged a good bed for each
To lie down and sleep in,
6296 For they were tired from travelling:
They were completely worn out!
It was apparent from their shields
That they had endured a great battle.
6300 Tristan took great joy in the honor
Of taking Gawain by the right hand,
And you may be sure that he was proud
To have been his host for a second time.
6304 He turned toward Lais Hardis,
Who was very polite and noble:
"Sir," he said, "I think
That you are quite exhausted;
6308 I know perfectly well that you are wounded
And hurt under your white cap.
I have a very noble daughter
Who can provide such medicine
6312 That she will draw all suffering from you.
With one application, you will
Have no more pain.
The wounds are always cured!"
6316 The black knight thanked him;
He was very happy about this promise.
And Sir Gawain begged Tristan
To aid him, if he was able to.
6320 And Tristan went right away
To the room where his daughter was
And asked her, if she knew how
To aid such a knight,
6324 That she would do it without delay.
And she, who was gracious,
Said to him, "The wound will not be cured,
Even if God helps me, in just one day."
6328 She bound up the wound
With a very powerful herb
That was called tuscany.
Then he was free to sleep
6332 Until God caused day to break
And the knights got up and dressed.

El chastel andui sejornerent
Trestout le jor jusqu'au demain;
6336   Puis parla monsegnor Gavain
Comme par courous et par ire.
A l'oste commencha a dire:
"Biax dous ostes, frans, debonaire,
6340   Vous savés bien tout nostre afaire,
Ensi com nos avons erré.
Or voil que il nos soit mostré
Et l'escrin et le bras ensamble
6344   Que me moustrastes, ce me samble,
La nuit que primes chaiens jui."
Et Tristran regarda celui
Qui Orguelleus Faé a non.
6348   "Sire, il vos dit droit et raison,"
Ce respont l'Orguelleus Faé.
"Tant m'a a armes demené
Qu'il m'estuet en sa segnorie
6352   Contenir et moi et m'amie.
Mais il i a tel covenant,
Se je pooie vivre tant
Que le cors que je vos baillai
6356   Tout sain et sauf le vos rendrai,   [43ra]
Tel covenant ai a Gavain
Que sel vos rent et fort et sain,
Que je avrai sa druerie,
6360   Et me rendra quite m'amie,
Mais que je li ferai itant:
Le vaslet trestout cler veant
Li rendrai et tout sain sans faille;
6364   Covenant l'oi en la bataille,
Et Gavains le m'a creanté."
"Certes," fait il, "c'est verités
Que issi le vous creantai.
6368   N'en soiés ja point en esmai."
"Sire," dist l'Orguelleus Faé,
"Isnelement soit aporté
Le bras et le cors et l'escrin."
6372   Et Tristran se mist al cemin,
Si li aporte maintenant;

They enjoyed themselves in the castle
All day long until the next day.
6336 Then Sir Gawain spoke,
In a grave and troubled manner.
He addressed his host thus:
"Dear sweet host, generous and debonair,
6340 You know all about our affair,
How we have been travelling about.
Now I would like you to show us
The arm that you once showed to me,
6344 Together with its case,
The first night that I stayed here."
And Tristan looked at him
Who was called the Proud Magician.
6348 "Sir, he has spoken properly and reasonably,"
Replied the Proud One.
"He pressed me so hard in battle
That he forced my friend and me
6352 To be placed under his command.
We have made an agreement—
That I could live so that
I could restore completely safe and sound
6356 The body that I entrusted to you.
The agreement with Gawain is that,
If I make it whole again,
I will have his friendship
6360 And he will give my friend to me,
If I also do the following:
If I hand over to him without fail
The young man, completely cured of his blindness.
6364 I have made this pledge in battle,
And Gawain accepted it."
"Certainly," Gawain replied, "this is the truth;
Just so I granted you this.
6368 Don't be at all worried about it."
"Sir," said the Proud Magician,
"Have the arm and body in their cases
Brought here right away."
6372 And Tristan set out on his way
And brought them to him right away.

L'escrin li avoit mis devant,
Et le Faé l'a descosu.
6376   Et l'escrin estoit ja venu
Ou le bras ert au chevalier;
Et le Faé sans delaier
A le bras de l'escrin osté
6380   Et el cors ariere posé.
Puis fu plus sains que nul poisson,
Et cels en orent fait le don
A l'Orgelleus qui ert Faé.
6384   Le chevalier lor a conté
Comme cil el bois le trova,
Et comment a lui se mesla,
Et comment il se combati,
6388   Com il morut, ainc nel senti,
Com il a esté en repos
Dedens le cuir de cerf enclos.
Molt s'en est Gavains merveillié;
6392   De la merveille s'est sengnié,
Et le Lai Hardi ensement.   [43rb]
Et Tristran et toute sa gent
Qui ont la merveille veüe
6396   De demander forment s'argue
Qui li dona tel destinee.
Et cil dit: "El me fu donee
En cele nuit que je fui né."
6400   Et Gavains a lors demandé
Le non del chevalier ocis.
"Sire," fait il, "je vos plevis
Que le Cortois de Huberlant
6404   M'apeloient mi conoissant."
Grant joie firent tuit ensamble;
Toute la cort de joie tramble,
Et demainent molt grant deduit,
6408   Tout le jor desi a la nuit.
A la nuit se sont tuit cochié.
Au matin, quant fu esclairié,
Il metent les frains et les seles
6412   Et montent les deus damoiseles—
L'une ert amie Gomeré

He placed the one case before him,
And the Magician opened it up;
6376 The other case had already been brought,
The one with the arm of the knight.
Without delay, the Magician
Removed the arm from the case
6380 And placed it beside the body.
Suddenly it was livelier than a fresh fish.
And thus they were given this gift
By the proud one who was a magician.
6384 The revived knight told them how the Magician
Found him in the woods,
How he had quarrelled with him,
How they had battled one another,
6388 How he had died, thus feeling nothing,
How he had been laid to rest
In the skin of a deer.
Gawain marvelled greatly at this;
6392 He crossed himself in amazement,
As did Lais Hardis as well.
And Tristan and all his people
Who had seen the miracle
6396 Hastened to ask who had given
The Magician such magic power.
And he replied, "It was given to me
On the night that I was born."
6400 And Gawain asked the name
Of the knight who had been killed.
"Sir," he said, "may it please you,
Those who know me call me the
6404 Courteous One from Huberland."
Then they were all very joyous;
The whole court shook with joy
And celebrated in delight
6408 All day long until nightfall.
At night, they all went to sleep.
In the morning, when day had broken,
They sent for saddles and harnesses
6412 And helped the two young women to mount.
(The one was the friend of Gomeret

Et l'autre a l'Orguelleus Faé—
Puis se mistrent tuit a la voie.

6416 Tristran lor oste les convoie
Desi ke outre le vaucel
Et dit: "Sire, s'il vos ert bel,
G'iroie a cort ensamble o vos,

6420 Et si merroie avoques nos
Ma fille, qui est bele et gente,
Ou Nature a mise s'entente;
Et je l'ai ja bien atornee:

6424 Ves la sor la mule montee."
Gavains l'entent, sin a grant joie:
"Sire," fait il, "se Diex me voie,
Molt avés or dit que cortois."

6428 Or sont les damoiseles trois
Et li chevalier set par conte,
Si com l'estoire le reconte.   [43va]
Tant ont erré et chevauchié

6432 Qu'endroit midi ont aprocié
Le chastel Cadroain le Rous,
Qui molt est fiers et corajous.
Iloec estoient a sejour

6436 Icil qui furent en l'estour
O Cadrés quant rescoust s'amie
Qui ot secours et bone aïe,
S'i fu Raguidel de l'Angarde.

6440 Celui pucele le regarde,
Cele qui vea a Gavain
Le vin et le char et le pain,
Et tuit cil l'orent couneü

6444 Tantost com Gavains fu venu
Qui l'atendoient au chastel.
Savoir poés molt li fu bel.
Tout son conte lor a conté,

6448 Si com je vos ai chi conté,
Comment il a puis esploitié,
Et comment il se combatié
Encontre l'Orguelleus Faé

6452 Et Espinogre a Gomeré,
Comment lor acorde fu faite.

And the other the friend of the Proud Magician.)
Then they all set out on the road.

6416 Tristan, their host, accompanied them
Until they were outside the valley
And then said, "Sir, if you please,
I would go to the court together with you,

6420 And I would take my daughter with us,
She who is beautiful and gracious,
With whom Nature has taken great care.
I have clothed her beautifully:

6424 You see her there on her mule."
Gawain was very happy to hear this.
"Sir," he said, "so help me God,
You have now spoken very courteously."

6428 Now there are three young women,
And you may count seven knights,
So the story says.
They travelled along this way

6432 Until they approached, about noon,
The castle of Codrovain the Red,
Who was very strong and courageous.
They were resting there,

6436 Those who had been in the battle
With Cadrés, when he rescued his friend
And experienced help and succor.
Ragidel of Angarde was there also.

6440 They saw the young woman there,
She who had refused Gawain
The wine, the meat, and the bread.
As soon as Gawain arrived,

6444 All the others who awaited him
At the castle recognized him.
You can imagine their happiness.
He told them his story,

6448 Just as I have told it to you,
What he accomplished since leaving them,
How he had battled
With the Proud Magician,

6452 And Espinogre with Gomeret,
How they had reached an accord.

Cascun d'els forment s'en rehaite,
Et molt li firent grant hounor,
6456   Et dit que por la soie amor
Sejorneront un jor tot plain.
"Segnor," ce lor a dit Gavain,
"Vous dites bien, vostre merchi,
6460   Mais ains que soit demain midi
Vaudroie estre a Carlion,
Entre moi et mi compaignon;
Si merrai avoec mes puceles,
6464   Qui molt sont courtoises et beles."
"Sire, sire," ce dist Cadrés,
Je vos herbergerai hui mes   [43vb]
En cest chastel a Cadroain.
6468   Quant vos verrois le jor demain
S'irons en vostre compaignie."
Dist Gavains: "Je nel refus mie
Tel compaignie ne tel rout."
6472   Ne vos aconterai ja toute
La joie qu'il ont demenee,
Quels lus i ot et quel povree,
Quel pain ne quel poisson de mer,
6476   Quels vins il burent au souper.
La nuit furent a grant deduit.
Au matin sont monté trestuit
Sor lor chevaus delivrement;
6480   Cadeain fait monter sa gent,
Soissante et quatre chevalier
Trestous armés sor lor destriers,
Por l'amor monsegnor Gavain.
6484   Li chevalier oirrent a plain;
Au chevauchier ont entendu
Tant qu'en la forest sont venu
Iloec ou l'Orguelleus Faé
6488   Ot le vaslet les eus crevé.
Tant enquist Gavains des noveles
Qu'il a trovees les puceles
Qui li conterent del Faé,
6492   Si com li contes a conté.
En la forest ert lor manoir.

Each one of them rejoiced in this
And showed him very great honor,
6456 And said that, for love of him,
They should stay for a full day.
"Lords," said Gawain to them,
"You speak well and I thank you,
6460 But before tomorrow noon
I would like to be at Carlisle,
Both I and my companions;
I will take my young women along,
6464 Who are courteous and beautiful."
"My dear sir," said Cadrés,
"I will provide hospitality tonight
In this castle of Codrovain.
6468 When you leave tomorrow,
We will accompany you."
Gawain replied, "I would never refuse
Such company nor escort."
6472 I will not recall for you
All the joy they exhibited,
What pike fish was there and what pepper stew,
What bread and what other fish from the sea,
6476 What wines they drank with dinner.
They passed the night in great delight.
In the morning they were all
Quickly mounted on their horses.
6480 Codrovain had his men mount—
Sixty-four knights
Fully armed on their war horses—
Out of love of Sir Gawain.
6484 The knights galloped away.
After they had ridden for a while,
They came to the forest
Where the Proud Magician
6488 Had pierced the eyes of the young man.
Gawain inquired after news
Until he found the young women
Who had told him about the Magician,
6492 Just as the story has recounted.
Their house was in the forest.

Cascuns a le cuer tristre et noir
Del doel de monsegnor Gavain.
6496 Tuit quidoient estre certain
Que il fust mors et decoupé.
Et Gavains lor a demandé
Del vaslet, comment li estait:
6500 "Sire," fait ele, "issi li vait
Com cil qui ne voit ciel ne terre."
"Alés le moi," dist Gavains, "querre,
Sel m'amenés delivrement."   [44ra]
6504 Et cele i ala erramment;
Ele a le vaslet amené,
Qui molt estoit bien atorné.
Il estoit sages et cortois:
6508 S'il fust fils de conte ou de rois,
Si fust il bel et avenant.
Et l'Orguelleus Faé a tant
Li trait sa main aval sa chiere,
6512 Si li a rendu sa lumiere,
Si vit plus cler que cerf ne dain.
Si connut erranment Gavain
Tout maintenant qu'i l'ot veü.
6516 "Sire, bien soiés vous venu,"
Fait li vaslés molt doucement.
"Je quidoie, se Diex m'ament,
Que vos fussiés tout detrenchié,
6520 Mais bien sai q'os fustes cangié
A cel chevalier la devant:
C'est le Cortois de Huberlant,
Qui onques de cort ne volt estre."
6524 Li vaslés conte tout son estre,
Si com li livres l'a conté.
Mais Damlediex l'a regardé,
Qui li a rendu sa veüe.
6528 Ne fist iloec plus atendue,
Anchois monterent enislore.
Mesire Gavains sans demore
Fist les trois puceles monter,
6532 Et si n'i volt pas oublier
Le vaslet, qui ot non Martin,

Their hearts were sad and melancholy,
Because of their grief over Sir Gawain.
6496 They were all convinced
That he was dead and dismembered.
And Gawain asked them about
The young man, and how he fared:
6500 "Sir," said one of them, "he fares like those
Who can see neither heaven nor earth."
"Go seek him for me," said Gawain,
"And bring him here quickly."
6504 And she went to do this right away;
She brought the young man back,
Who was very well-dressed.
He was wise and courteous;
6508 He might be the son of a count or a king,
He was so attractive and handsome.
And the Proud Magician had only
To move his hand before his face
6512 To bring sight to him again
So that he saw more clearly than doe or stag.
The young man immediately recognized Gawain
As soon as he had seen him.
6516 "Sir, you are very welcome here,"
Said the young man graciously.
"I believed, so help me God,
That you were completely dismembered,
6520 But now I know that I mistook you
For this knight standing before you:
This is Huberland the Courteous,
Who never wanted to belong to a court."
6524 The young man told all about himself,
Just as the book has told it.
But the Lord God who gave him
Back his sight looked over him.
6528 They didn't linger there any longer;
That very day they remounted.
Without waiting longer, Sir Gawain had
The three young women placed on their horses,
6532 And he certainly didn't want to forget
The young man, who was called Martin:

Sel fait monter sor un roncin.
Puis chevaucent a grant esploit;
6536 A Carlion vindrent tot droit,
A l'ore que on doit souper.
L'en ot ja fait l'eve corner,
Et si asistrent au mengier.
6540 A tant es vous un chevalier   [44rb]
Qui lor avoit dit ces noveles;
Au roi furent bones et beles
Et a trestous chels de la court.
6544 Tous li pueples contre lui cort,
Li rois i cort et la roïne;
N'i a pucele ne meschine
Qui de lui n'ait joie molt grant.
6548 Et li rois le baise en riant,
Qui de sa uenue ot grant joie;
Et cil li conte toute voie
Comment il avoit puis erré.
6552 Tout li a le conte conté,
Comment il li ert avenu.
Il sont tuit a pié descendu.
Il n'i ot conte ne baron,
6556 Ne roi ne prince, en la maison,
Qui ne se paint molt de servir
Cels q'o Gavain virent venir.
Le roi a forment onourés
6560 Les chevaliers, et apelés;
Et la roïne, d'autre part
Et le damoisele s'em part,
Si les en a toutes menees
6564 En ses chambres encortinees,
Si lor a fait molt grant honor,
Por la franchise et por l'amor
Que ele a de monsegnor Gavain.
6568 Cele nuit jusqu'a l'endemain
Furent trestuit paisible et qoi.
Au matin se leva le roi,
Si est venus devant la sale;
6572 Et Gavains les degrés avale,
Si s'est jouste lui acosté,

He too was mounted on a horse.
Then they galloped at great speed.
6536   They soon arrived at Carlisle
At the usual hour for dinner:
The horns had announced the arrival of water,
And everyone had just sat down to eat.
6540   At this moment a knight appeared
Who told them the news:
The king and all those in the court
Were greatly pleased.
6544   All the people ran up to Gawain,
Including the king and the queen.
There wasn't a young woman or girl there
Who didn't express great joy;
6548   The king, smiling, kissed him,
He who was so happy about his arrival.
And Gawain told him his whole story,
How he had travelled since leaving;
6552   He retold everything
Just as it had happened.
They were all helped to dismount;
There wasn't a count or baron,
6556   Not a king nor a prince in the hall,
Who didn't take pains to serve
Those who had arrived with Gawain.
The king gave great honor
6560   To the knights and spoke with them.
And the queen, for her part,
Went off with the young women;
And she led them all
6564   Into their tapestried chambers.
She showed them very great honor,
Out of generosity and the love
That she had for Sir Gawain.
6568   All that evening until the next morning
They were made comfortable and calm.
The next morning the king rose
And came into the great hall.
6572   And Gawain came down the steps
And approached him

Si li a dit et reconté
Com il a de grant paine traite
6576   Icele que il prist en l'etre;
Puis li dist com il conquesta   [44va]
Cele qu'Escanor amena.
Toutes conte les aventures
6580   Qu'il a trovés pesmes et dures.
Puis si lor rent a aconter
Qu'il li estuet guerredoner
L'onor que trestuit li ont faite,
6584   Qu'il li a conté et retraite.
        Li rois en est liés a merveille;
As bontés rendre ne somelle,
Ains li plaist molt et vient a gré
6588   Quant il fait honor et bonté.
Et li dist: "A vostre plaisir
Me voil je de ce contenir.
Mais je voel ains estre vengié
6592   De cil qui tant m'a coroucié,
Qui as gens se vantoit a tort
Qu'il vous avoit ocis et mort.
De ce voil jou venjance avoir."
6596   Gavains respont: "Por nul avoir,
"Sire, nel voldroie je mie;
Qu'il vendrent en ma compaingnie,
Si oi o els tel covenant,
6600   Dont il ont fait tot mon creant,
Por quoi il sont tuit aseür."
"Par foi," ce dist li rois Artur,"
"Il ert issi com vos vaudrois."
6604   "Sire," fait Gavains, "vos dorrois
As deus chevaliers lor amies:
Onques puis le tans Jeremies
Ne veïstes deus plus cortois.
6608   La soe Espinogre dorrois,
S'espousera Cadrés s'amie,
Et Raguidel n'i faudra mie
A la soe, qu'il m'ot mestier,
6612   Qu'il me douna un bon destrier."
        Li rois li a dit et conté   [44vb]

And spoke to him and told him
How he had saved with great difficulty
6576　The woman he found in the cemetery;
Then he told how he had conquered
The woman whom Escanor led;
He told about all the adventures
6580　That he had found difficult and challenging.
Finally he told about how
He needed to repay
The honor that all had offered him,
6584　Just as he had recounted to him.
　　　The king was quite happy about this.
He was not slow to give gifts;
Thus it pleased him very much
6588　To be honorable and generous.
And so he said, "Your wishes
Are my desire in this affair.
But I also want to be avenged
6592　Against him who angered me
By wrongly bragging in public
That he had struck and killed you.
For this I want to have revenge."
6596　Gawain replied, "Not at all, sir,
Do I want this to happen;
For they came here in my company,
And I have an agreement with them;
6600　Because they have fulfilled all promises,
They should be granted surety."
"By my faith," King Arthur then replied,
"Everything shall be just as you wish."
6604　"Sir," said Gawain, "you should grant
The two knights their loved ones.
You've never seen two more courteous people
Since the time of Jeremiah.
6608　You should give Espinogre his,
And Cadrés will marry his friend,
And Ragidel will not fail
To have his, for he helped me
6612　By giving me a good war horse."
　　　The king spoke and told Gawain

Del roi de la Rouge Chité,
Com il s'estoit a lui rendus,
6616   Com il fu de cort revenus,
Qu'il onques mais n'i ot esté,
Et comment il li a juré
Que il tendra chiere s'amie.
6620   Et monsegnour Gavain li prie
Des deus vaslés q'ot amenés
Q'erranment soient adoubés,
Et chevaliers face noviaus,
6624   Et lor donst terres et chastiaus.
Trestout ont lor orre apresté
Si com il dui l'ont devisé,
Si ont les mariages fais
6628   Sans contredit et sans grans plais.
Au moustier les mainent errant;
La procession fu molt grant
Si com a tel chose dut estre.
6632   Li evesque Reniés de Cestre
Les a maintenant espousees
As chevaliers qui creantees
Erent par le conseil le roi.
6636   Le mostier ne fu mie quoi,
Anchois i ot joie molt grant
Qui font li petit et li grant.
Cil jougleour de pluisors terres
6640   Cantent et sonent lor vieles,
Muses, harpes et orcanons,
Timpanes et salterions,
Gigues, estives et frestiaus
6644   Et buisines et calemiaus.
Cascuns d'els grant joie demainne.
De joie est toute la cors plaine,
Car molt ert li rois Artus rices;
6648   Onques ne fu malvais ne chices.
Molt lor fist bien a tous aidier
De quainques il lor fu mestier.   [45ra]
Et jut cascuns o s'espousee,
6652   Si comme li plest et agree.
         Au matin, quant il fu grant jour,

About the King of the Red City,
How he turned himself in,
6616 How he appeared at court—
He who had never been there before—
And how he swore to him
That he would henceforth hold his friend dear.
6620 And Sir Gawain requested, on behalf of
The two young men he had led there,
That they be dubbed right away
And made new knights
6624 And be given land and castles.
Now one and all got things ready,
Just as the two had planned,
And the marriages were accomplished
6628 Without great trouble or difficulty.
They quickly led the couples to the church;
The procession was very grand,
As it should be in such a case.
6632 Bishop Raignier of Chester
Married the young women immediately
To the knights they had been given to
By the commandment of the king.
6636 The church was certainly not tranquil:
Each one was very joyous,
Both those of high rank and low.
Musicians from many lands
6640 Sang and played their fiddles,
Bagpipes, harps, and organs,
Drums and psalteries,
Rebecs, hornpipes, and panpipes,
6644 Trumpets and shawms.
Everyone expressed great joy.
Joy was to be found everywhere in the court,
For King Arthur was very generous;
6648 He never was evil or miserly.
He saw that all were provided
With whatever they needed.
And each one lay with his spouse,
6652 As he pleased and desired.
In the morning, when it was daylight,

Furent paié li jougleor.
Li un orent biax palefrois,
6656   Beles robes et biaus agrois,
Li autre lonc ce qu'il estoient;
Tuit robes et deniers avoient,
Tuit furent paié a lor gré.
6660   Li plus povre orent a plenté.
Quant li jougleour sont paié,
En lor païs sont repairié,
Et la cours estoit departie.
6664   Cascuns chevaliers o s'amie
S'en vait a joie et a baudor;
Trestuit li grant et li menor
S'en repairent en lor contrees
6668   Quant les noces furent finees.
Si sacent tuit bas et haut
Car li Aitres Perilleus faut
Des que Gavains a tant erré
6672   Qu'il est a cort a sauveté,
Si fine ichi nostre romans.
Que Diex nos donst vivre cent ans
En grant joie et en grant honor,
6676   Et il nos donst joie et baudor.
EXPLICIT DE L'ATRE PERELLEUS.

The musicians were paid.
To some were given handsome palfreys,
6656 Beautiful robes, and elegant harnesses;
To others was given what they needed;
All received clothes and money,
All were paid as they wished.
6660 The poorest was satisfied.
When the musicians had been paid,
They left for their own lands,
And the court dispersed.
6664 Each knight left with his *amie*,
Full of joy and gladness.
All the other guests, great and small,
Returned to their lands
6668 When the marriages were accomplished.
Let it be known by all, high and low,
That the story, *The Perilous Cemetery*—
Now that Gawain, after so much wandering,
6672 Has returned to court—
Has come to an end.
May God grant us a hundred years
Of much happiness and great honor;
6676 May He grant us joy and gladness.
HERE ENDS THE TALE OF THE PERILOUS CEMETARY.

LIST OF EMENDATIONS

The numbers before each note below indicate the line of verse in the Garland edition. The reading to the left of the bracket is the portion of the text under consideration and represents an accepted reading that differs from copytext. The source of the reading is identified after the bracket according to the following symbols:

N¹	B.N.fr. 2168
N²	B.N.fr. 1433
A	Chantilly 472
W	Woledge edition
G	Garland edition

The reading after the semicolon is the rejected reading of the copytext and any other text in which that reading appears. Abbreviations are expanded, and the letters *i, j, u,* and *v* are treated as in the Garland text. An asterisk is placed before an entry when the reading is discussed in the Textual Notes.

51	vostre] W N² A; ure N¹
*65	De çaiens ne de] W; De çaiens de N¹; De ma court et de N²; E ma court et de A
109	porterent] W; porteret N¹; portoit N²; reportoit A
169	est] W N² A; missing in N¹
223	ses] W N² A; son N¹
256	damoisele] W N² A; damoise N¹
293	remonte] W; remote N¹; montee N²; monte[?] A
310	qu'il ont] W N²; qui ont N¹; qu'il l'ont A
312	il] W N²; missing in N¹ A
335	et] W N²; missing in N¹ A
389	qui si vous] W N² A; qui vous N¹
395	qu'il amoit tant] W N²; qu'il tant N¹; line missing in A
404	lever a quel que] W; lever que quel que] N¹; lever a mout grant N²; lever a que que[?] A
472	fait l'une] G N² A; fait cascune N¹; fait li une W
473	Fussiens] W A; Fussies N¹; Fussons N²

481 gesir] W N²; missing in N¹; jesire A
504 pasmee] W N² A; pasme N¹
531 de cui] W A; du cui N¹; de çoi N²
532 il] W N² A; missing in N¹
535 niés] W A; rois N¹; mes[?] N²
*556 eslaiscié] W; eslaisié N¹; line missing N²; eslaissié A
569 il estoit tous] W N²; cascuns estoit N¹; tos i estoit A
593 Qui] G N²; Qi N¹ W; Que A
612 certainement] W; certainemet N¹; a ensient N²; certain-
     nement A
616 fait il] W; fait N¹; dist il N² A
629 grant] W N² A; gnt N¹
659 reperiés] W; reperiiés N¹; repairiés N² A
672 et de quarrel] W N²; et quarrel N¹; et de quarriel A
705 un mantel gris] W N²; un gris N¹; un mantiel gris A
723 noient] W N² A; noiet N¹
727 sera] W N²; se N¹
788 eüstes vous de] W N² A; eüstes de N¹
*789 Paor] W A; Pauor N¹; Paour N² W
790 Sire] W N² A; Si N¹
805 herbegerai] W N²; herberai N¹; herbergerai A
821 Diu] W A; du N¹; Dieu N²
841 vers] W N² A; vous N¹
910 grant] W N² A; grat N¹
954 i ara] W A; a ara N¹; auenra N²
978 orains] W N²; orais N¹; jehui A
996 vaut] W N² A; vait N¹
1000 truisce] W; tuisce N¹; truise N²; truisse A
1059 par] W N² A; per N¹
1079 se] W N² A; s'en N¹
1106 la rarai] W; rarai N¹; l'arai N²; line missing A
1110 Entre] W N² A; Autre N¹
*1141 Contremont] W N² A; Contre[?] N¹
1142 Mervelliés fu] W; illegible N¹; merveille ot N²; Mervilla
      soi A
1143 Qui] W N² A; illegible N¹
1144 Et] W N² A; illegible N¹
1145 Que les piéz li ostent de tere] G N²; illegible N¹; Que li
      piet li sordent de terre A; Que les piés li sordent de terre
      W

1146   Il va un autre siege querre] W N²; illegible N¹; Il vait un autre siege querre A

1147   Car cheli ne li gree pas] G N²; illegible N¹; Car celui ne li graoit pas A; Que cil ne lui agree pas W

*1170   cevalier] W; cevlier N¹; chevalier N² A

1186   meïsmes] G N² A; meimes N¹ W

*1197   Que j'en isci] W; Que j[?] N¹ has tear in parchment; Que j'en issi N²; Que je issi A

1198   un lonc tans] W N²; un [?] [?] N¹; molt lonc tens A

1203   mist] W N² A; mest N¹

1232   c'est ci] W A; cest N¹; che est N²

1232   l'Atres] W A; l'Atre N¹ N²

*1263   De armer] W; [?] armer N¹; Del armer N²; Datorner A

1264   Son escu] W A; illegible in N¹, due to tear; Sen escu N²

1265   Estes vous le diable] W; [?] [?] [?] ble N¹; Estes vos le diable A; Estes vous le diale N²

1266   Or soiés, fait ele] W N² A; illegible in N¹

1267   Ens est entrés par mi la porte] W; only last four letters of line are visible in N¹; Ens est entrés par mi le porte N2; Ens est entrels parmi la porte A

1268   Pute, fait il, vous estes morte] W; only last three letters of line are visible in N¹; Putain, fait il, vous estes morte N²; Pute, fait il, vos estes mortes A

1269   Et vostre lechierres honnis] W; illegible in N¹; Et vostres lechierres honnis N²; Et vostre leceors honnis A

1270   Vilainement ert departis] W; only first two letters of line are visible in N¹; Vilainement iert departis N²; Vilainnement iert departis A

1271   cest parlement] W; illegible N¹; chest parlement N²; cis parlement A

*1274   Certes] W A; C[?]tes N¹; Chertes N²

1284   vers] W A; ver N¹

*1308   Cent caus li done] W; illegible in N¹; Cent cols li done A

1344   a l'ains] W; alais N¹; si tost N²

1354   Gavains tint] W N² A; Gavains qui tint N¹

*1363–64 "Li diables...s'esforça] W N² A; order of lines reversed in N¹

1364   s'esforça] W; s'erforça N¹; s'efforcha N²; s'enforça A

1482   ce] W A; cel N¹; che N²

1520	Qu'il] W N² A; Qil N¹
1538	loer] W N² A; conter N¹
1563	nul liu] W A; nuliu N¹; nul lieu N²
1575	cose] W N² A; cosi N¹
1588	gardisciés] W; gardés N¹; gardissiés N²; gardisiés A
*1663–64	Dounai trestout en mariage/ A un chevalier preu et sage] W; A un chevalier preu et sage/ Dounai trestout en mariage N¹; Donnai trestout a mariage/ A un chevalier preu et sage N²; Donnai trestout en mariage/ a un chevalier preu et sage A
1676	vostre] W N² A; vre N¹
1679	truisons] W N²; ruisons N¹; truissons A
1694	quier] W N² A; quie N¹
1708	loisir] W N²; loisgir N¹; loissir A
1718	dusqu'en] W A; dusque en N¹; iusqu'en N²
1737	Ens] W; En N¹
1746	vous soufrés] W; soufrés N¹; vous souffrés N²; vos soufrés A
1790	de cel forfait] W; a il for forfait N¹; de chel forfait N²; le forfait A
1794	encor] W; encore N¹
1801	l'a] W N²; le N¹ A
1810	fait il] W A; fait N¹
*1812	Non ferai] W N²; illegible N¹; Non feraie A
1813	De rien que] W; illegible N¹; De riens que N²; De rien dont A
1852	reprovier] W A; reproviier N¹; reprouvier N²
1857	Ne li] W N² A; N'i N¹
1868	ains] W N²; ais N¹; line missing A
1878	vostre] W N² A; vre N¹
1913	ciés] W A; cief N¹; chiés N²
1919	toute] W; toutoute N¹
1971	sa] W A; son N¹; se N²
*2012	çanbel] W; çanbeli N¹
2014	ne veïstes si rices] W A; si rices ne veïstes N¹; ne veïstes plus riches N²
2083	des ier] W N² A; dessier N¹
*2115	Escanors] W; scanors N¹; Escanor N²; .E. A
2119	grant] W N² A; grat N¹
2158	car] W N² A; cor N¹

2162   que il veut] W A; qu'il veut que N^1
2179   quarree] W N^2 A; quarre N^1
2180   si prou] W; prou N^1; si boin N^2; cel A
2184   par] W; pas N^1 N^2; au A
2218   en ai grant] W N^2 A; en grant N^1
2236   pensis] W N^2 A; pensus N^1
2265   volee] W N^2 A; vole N^1
*2279   mervella] G; mevella N^1 W; merveilla N^2; s'esmervilla A
2316   grant] G N^2 A; gnt N^1
2324   u a] W; u a a N^1; ou a N^2; ne a A
2333   A l'encontrer] W A; a encontrer N^1; a encontre N^2
2354   Car] W N^2 A; Ca N^1
2372   saciés] W A; cascuns N^1; sachiés N^2
2373   l'uns l'autre] G A; li uns d'ex N^1; l'un l'autre N^2; li uns l'autre W
2385   maleüree] W N^2 A; maleüre N^1
2405   Chevalier] W N^2 A; [?]hevalier N^1
2493   Lors] W N^2 A; Tant N^1
2525   bruel] W A; breul N^1
2559   moi] W N^2 A; moi que N^1
2562   moie amor] W A; moi amor N^1; l'amor de moi N^2
2564   Tant que] W N^2 A; Et quant je N^1
2567   bien porras] W N^2; bien li porras N^1; bien poras A
2630   paissoie] G N^2 A; paisoi?ee N^1; paisçoie W
*2637   Jel] W N^2; Iel N^1; not in A
2660   Il] W N^2 A; Ains N^1
2710   por] W A; par N^1; pour N^2
2713   porpens] W A; porpes N^1; pourpens N^2
2728   conment cil ment] W A; a escient N^1; conment chil ment N^2
2729   Qui de] G N^2 A; Que N^1; Que de W
2730   s'eslongne] W A; s'elongne N^1; s'enlonge N^2
2780   truiscent] W; truiscet N^1; truisent N^2; truisse A
2790   bien garir] W N^2; garir N^1; Bien...garir A
2806   di que] W; di jou que N^1
2826   niés] W N^2 A; rois N^1
2870   anbedui] W A; ambedui N^1 N^2
2875   conment] W N^2; conmet N^1
2895   je demanderai] W; jed demanderai N^1; jou demanderai N^2; demanderai A

2897   vostre] W N² A; vostr N¹
3004   sire] W N² A; fire N¹
3021   avenu] W N²; avene N¹; line missing A
3024   fu] W N² A; fas N¹
3044   moult] W; mlt N¹; mout N²; molt A
3045   ostel] W N² A; ostes N¹
3099   seulement] W N²; selement N¹; solement A
3104   seürement] W N² A; seüremet N¹
3108   Ke je] W; Ke N¹; Que je N² A
3117   Que] W A; Quant N¹ N²
3131   de tout sorfait] W; de sor fait N¹; de tout malfait N²
3133   Quant] W; Qua N¹; Puis qu'ele N²
3152   Si li] W N²; Si N¹
3153   me fist] W N²; fist N¹
3166   ma proiire] W; la proiire N¹; ma priere N²
3215   Que] W; Qui N¹
3220   itel] W N² A; nule N¹
*3227   Ja] W; Ia N¹; Que N² A
3249   le vous demant] W N²; le demant N¹; je vos demant A
3276   repondre] W; rrenpondre N¹; respondre N² A
3282   bien] W N² A; tant N¹
3305   fax] G; fox N¹ W; faus N²; fols A
3306   sax] W; sox N¹; saus N²; sals A
3310   c'est] G A; ses N¹; chest N²; s'est W
3322   fax] W; fox N¹; faus N² A
*3347   en painne] W; lan painne N¹; en paine N²
3361   le] W; la N¹ N²
3377   por] W A; par N¹; pour N²
3385   Ki] W; K N¹; Qui N² A
3392   frousce] W; fusce? N¹; froisse N² A
3407   ses caus] W; ses g caus N¹; ses cous N²; ses cols A
3432   vostre] W N² A; vostr N¹
3466   doutés] W N² A; doutas N¹
3480   Lors] W N²; S Lors N¹
3486   s'entrencontrerent] W N²; s'entrencontreent N¹; eser-
        recontrerent A
3493   fist sans] W N² A; tant fist N¹
*3510   amis ne joï] W N² A; joï amis N¹
3523   La] W A; Qa N¹
3526   Puis] W N²; Puist N¹

3543   venisons] W; venisgons N¹; venison N² A
3551   preïscent] W; preïstent N¹
3582   conbatront] W N² A; conbatra N¹
3592   mer dusques] W; merelier N¹; Espagne jusqu'en N²
3624   Sor] W N²; Sox N¹; Sot A
3635   Qui a bien] W N² A; Qui a a bien N¹;
3637   sox] W N¹; sor N¹; sous N² A
*3641   cointe] W; coite N¹; riche N² A
3664   l'esgardent] W; l'esgarde N¹ N²
*3671   Moult] W A; Mlt N¹; Mout N²
3701   Que il li die] W N² A; Et qu'il li die N¹
3729   vostre] W N² A; vre N¹
3730   que je l'oie] W A; que le l'oie N¹; que jou l'oie N²
3738   nous] W N²; nou N¹; nos A
3738   ciere] W A; here N¹; chiere N²
3742   se je de] W N² A; se de N¹
3747   fist] W N² A; fust N¹
3752   moult] W A; mlt N¹
3764   Durast] W N² A; Dura N¹
3765   n'ameroit] W A; n'ama N¹; n'amoit N²
3772   tant] W N² A; tat N¹
3775   sortit] W; sort N¹
*3790   el en] W; el len N¹; chele en N²; ele en A
*3792   el ne l'ose] W; el elole N¹; ele n'ose N²; ele n'osa A
3834   mais] W N²; mes N¹ A
*3861   Car tantost] W N²; Car ta tantost N¹; Car ançois A
3864   que] W N² A; qui N¹
3874   enpris] W N² A; pris N¹
3887   vaurés] W A; vau N¹; vaurrés N²
3889   serai] W N²; seru? N¹; serrai A
3898   mon grant outrage quier] W N² A; mon outrage requier N¹
3919   fait il] W; fait N¹ N²
3934   Se je n'ai] W N² A; Se n'ai N¹
*3965   Je] W N² A; Ie N¹
3990   vostre] W N² A; vre N¹
*3999   quanques ele i vit] W A; quant ele le vit N¹ N²
4001   siet] W N² A; sient N¹
4025   A autre] W A; A a autre N¹; Autre N²
4026   matire] W; matir N¹; matere N² A

*4029 Qu'il en i ait] W A; Qui i en i ait N¹; Qu'il en i a N²
4071 Flans] W N²; Blans N¹
4081 orgelloxe] W; orgellox N¹; orguelleuse N²; orguillous A
4088 qui a orguel] W A; qui orguel N¹; qui a orgueul N²
4089 liu] W A; lie N¹
4093 fait il] W N² A; fait N¹
4111 seul] W N²; seu N¹; sol A
4132 Erent] W; Serent N¹; Seroit N²; Serra A
4150 l'en mainne] W A; se maine N¹; l'en maine N²
4154 loiscirs] W; loisens? N¹
4160 cele] W A; ce N¹; chele N²
4179 estut] W; estue N¹
4190 ens en la] W; en en la N¹; en cheste N²; en ceste A
4202 l'atent] W; l'en atent N¹; est N²; siet A
*4221 Je] W A; Ie N¹
4236 sor son] W A; son N¹; seur son N²
4252 vous] W; nous N¹ N²; vos A
4253 chevaliers] W; chevalier N¹ N² A;
*4256 une] G N²; uene N¹ W; .j. A
4287 grant] W N² A; gnt N¹
4325 moult] W A; mlt N¹; mout N²
4341 vous tient] W N²; je tient N¹
4368 K'il] W; Ki N¹; Qui N² A
4374 chevaliers] W N² A; crhevaliers N¹
4378 desconfist] W N²; deconfist N¹; dessconfit A
4386 n'ot] W; n'en ot N¹; n'oit N² A
*4400 estendu] W N² A; estu N¹
4458 Ançois] W; Ancors N¹; Anchois N²
4461 avinrent] W N²; avinret N¹
4474 porficent] W; porficet N¹; pourfichent N²
4478 Codrovains] W; Codrovain N¹; Cadrovains N²;
        Cardoiains A
4485 Por ex çou] W; Por çou N¹; Pour eux che N²; Por els ce
        A
4492 ça est tant] W A; ça en tant N¹; cha est tant N²
4504 avoit] W N² A; ot N¹
4543 Et se] W N² A; Et N¹
4545 o nous] W; la N¹; o moi N²; o nos A
4559 en si] W A; a si N¹
4569 K'il] W; Ki N¹; qu'il N²; Qu'il A

*4579	oirrent] W; orrenet N¹; crient N²; oirent A
4588	itel maniere] W N² A; etel manier N¹
4655	cor] W N² A; cors N¹
4657	sivent l'ont] W; souvent l'ot N¹ N²; sivent les ont A
*4687	jetee] W A; jetee (with dot below t to cancel) N¹; getee N²
4705	passerent] W N² A; tasserent N¹
4755	son frain] W N²; fen le N¹; forment le A
4776	que] W A; qui N¹ N²
4801	vienent] W N²; vinent N¹; venent A
4803	el camp] W N²; es camp N¹; en camp A
4815	du chevalier] W N²; des chevaliers N¹; del chevalier A
4816	Ki avoit] W; Ki orent N¹; Qui avoit N²; Qui so? A
4835	se movra] W; movra N¹; se mouvra N² A
4881	plaiscir] W; pooir N¹; plaisir N²; plaissir A
4938	par viles] W N² A; par l viles N¹
4939	trovee] W; troovee N¹; truvee N²; trovees A
4988	K'el] W; K'i N¹; Qu'el N²; Qu'il A
*5017	Je] W N² A; Ie N¹
5022	poignant] W N² A; arms N¹
5054	Je] W A; J N¹; je N²
5058	J'avoie] W N² A; J'avoi N¹
5081	esploitierent] W A; esploitieret N¹; esploiterent N²
5120	dounee] W; doune N¹; donnee N²; donrai A
5146	nel] W N² A; les N¹
5167	ja mais] W A; james N¹; jam mais N²
5167	me viegne] W; ma viegne N¹; m'en souveigne N²; moi souviegne A
5180	cors] W N² A; cor N¹
5187	cascuns] W; casca?ns N¹; aucun N²
5195	coffre] W N²; coffra? N¹; cofre A
5207	moult] W A; mlt N¹; mout N²
5214	vous veul] W N² A; vous N¹
5222	K'ont] W; Ke il N¹
5223	que il] W N² A; qu'il a N¹
*5224a–d	Text taken from A
5225	Moult laidement quant il l'ocissent] W A; Et que moult laidement l'ocissent N¹; Et mout laidement il l'ochirent N²
5228	n'esgart] W A; esgart N¹; l'esgart N²

*5242   plaisans] W N²; plainsan N¹; plaissans A
5273   tiers] W N² A; ters N¹
5273   ne] W N² A; ni N¹
5314   El doutent] W; Eles dout N¹; Eles doutent N²; Qu'eles doutent A
5320   n'avroient] W; n'avoroient N¹; n'aroient N²; n'avoient A
5321   Oste] W; Este N¹; Ostes N² A
5327   tans] W; tas N¹; cheus N²; atant A
5329   forfait] W A; sorfait N¹; fourfait N²
5371   querant] W N²; querent N¹; quirant A
5383   que] W N² A; qui? N¹
5391   tous] W N²; nous N¹; nos A
5399   çou] W; ce N¹; che N²; ço A
5409   avenir] W N²; auuenir N¹; avrenir? A
5468   nostre] W N²; nre N¹; no A
5477   me menra] W N² A; menra N¹
5590   les] G N² A; le N¹; lé W
5592   Ke ele] W; K'ele N¹; Si qu'ele N²; Si qu'en A
5613   en] W N² A; e N¹
5633   chevaliers] W A; chevariels N¹; chevalier N²
5655   Quant] W N² A; Quauant N¹
5659   menue] W N² A; entor N¹
5660   tenue] W N² A; netor N¹
5694   otrie] W N² A; trie N¹;
*5698   chevaliers] W N² A; chevalierls N¹
5711   je] W N²; e N¹; rien A
5711   tant] W N² A; tat N¹
5716   Chevalier] W N²; Chevalierl N¹; Chevaliers A
5720   atorne] W A; e?torne N¹; atourne N²
5752   seus] W A; veus N¹; seuz N²
5771   por] W A; par N¹; pour N²
*5773–74   Le grant doel qu'eles demenoient/ Demandai por quoi le faissoient] W; Le damage por quoi faisoient/ Le grant doel qu'eles demenoient N¹; Le damage pour quoi faisoient/ Le grant duel qu'eles demenoient N²; Et le grant dol qu'eles menoient/ Demandai por çoi le faissoient A
*5792   Lors laissent corre] W; Cil torna vers els N¹; Chil tourna vers eux chele part N²; Lors laissent A
5803   Ont] W A; Dont N¹; C'ont N²

5812   Uns chevaliers] G N² A; Un chevalier N¹ W
*5813   l'arbroie] W; uanque N¹
5825   feïstes] W N² A; seüstes N¹
5833   renderai cel] W A; rendee nel N¹; renderai chel N²
5839   Fera] W N²; Sera N¹; Ferai A
*5843   li dist] W; dist il N¹ N² A
5924   sont] G N²; soit N¹; erent A; sent W
5926   ot] W; ont N¹; a N²; et A
[22]   servi] W; servir A
[36]   widie] W; wiidie[?] A
[53]   Les Espinogre et Gomerés] W; Les .e. et le .Go. A
5941   remaindrois] W; revendrois N¹; remaurres N²; m'aten-
        dres A
5971   hidous] W; li dous N¹; hydex A
5972   ennuious] G; ennuions N¹; enviex A
5976   Ja] W N²; Je N¹
5981   S'ert li vostre en la] W; Si ert la vostre en sa N¹; Si iert la
        vostre en la N²; S'ert li vostre en A
6067   dire] W; lire N¹
6077   je] W N²; jie N¹
6121   alés] W N² A; aler N¹
6145   oscur] W; ocscur N¹; obscur N²; oscurs A
6172   Mais] W A; Que N¹ N²
6182   mon non] W N²; mon N¹; mes nons A
6196   conquis] W N² A; pramis N¹
6206   porroie] W N²; porroi N¹; poroie A
*6216   ne sui je pas fardis] W N²; ne sune pas fardis N¹; ne sui
        je par sordis A
*6272   autres chevaliers tous] W; damoiseles toutes N¹ N²;
        autres chevaliers tos A
6280   Tristrans] W A; Gavains N¹ N²
6309   sos] W; sor N¹; sous N² A
*6313   n'i] W N² A; i N¹
6324   Que li aït] W A; Qu'il li aït N¹ N²
6331   dormi] W N² A; dormir N¹
6342   nos] W; vos[?] N¹ A; nous N²
6350   Tant m'a a armes] W A; Tant m'a ore mes N¹; Tant m'a
        par armes N²
6355   cors] W N² A; ces N¹
6358   Que sel vos rent] W; Que jel vos rent N¹; Si li rendrai

N²; Se le vos renc A
6359 druerie] W N² A; deverie N¹
6373 li aporte] W N² A; li a aporté N¹
6439 fu] W N² A; fui N¹
6443 l'orent] W N² A; orent N¹
6449 puis] W N² A; plus N¹
6450 Et comment il se combatié] W N² A; missing in N¹
6472 Ne] W; Je N¹ N²
6513 que] W N² A; ne N¹
6523 Qui onques] W N² A; C'onques N¹
6566 l'amor] W A; l'onour N¹; l'onnor N²
6579 conte] W N² A; contes N¹
6594 vous] W N²; vois N¹
6650 quainques] W; quainque N¹; quant que N²; quaquis A
6669 sacent] W A; sasient N¹; sasieent N²

Appendix:
29   maine] W; missing N²
51   l'en] W; s'en N²
187 ochire] W; ochis N²
351 Il] W; I N²
380 qui] W; quil N²
502 envaïe] G; envaÿe W; envayne N²

TEXTUAL NOTES

Title.   *Atre* refers to the parvis in front of a church and by extension to a cemetery located nearby. Godefroy gives the example of the Aître Notre-Dame at Rouen, which refers to the paved area in front of the church; he also gives examples of two cemeteries referred to as *aitre*: that at Saint Maclou and Saint Cande. He also notes that there is a street named *Petit-Atre* in Arras, so called because it lies near a cemetery. According to the *Dictionnaire historique*, the word stems from the Latin *atrium*.

1.   Walters (22, n. 18) remarks upon the similarity between this opening and that of Chrétien de Troyes's *Lancelot*, and Busby points to a similar reference to the *bon chevalier* at the opening of *Le Chevalier à l'épée* ("Diverging" 102).

3.   I have retained the Old French expression *bon chevalier* for "the good knight" in my translation here and at 577, 590, 1411, 2412, etc. See Busby, "Li Buens," for a discussion of the use of the term in *Perlesvaus*.

8.   Pentecost is a Christian holiday which falls on the seventh Sunday after Easter and which celebrates the descent of the Holy Ghost on the disciples (*Acts* 2: 1–41). Arthurian romances often begin with a gathering of the knights for Pentecost, as for example in Chrétien de Troyes's *Yvain* or *La Queste del Saint Graal*.

11.   Copytext provides two other examples of the *que en* construction; Woledge's emendation to *qu'en* seems unnecessary.

18.   According to the church calendar, "nones" is one of the hours of the day reserved for prayer, the ninth hour after sunrise, or about 3 o'clock in the afternoon.

19–21.   The letters at the start of these lines are badly rubbed, but legible with the help of Woledge's reading, accomplished at a time when the manuscript was presumably in a better state. The same is true of the first letter at lines 24 and 26.

24.   *Samit* is a heavy silk fabric, often embellished with gold or silver threads.

26.   There is a parallel line at 2578 and a similar one at 2969.

28–37.   The first letters of these lines are badly rubbed; the readings can be reconstructed by reference to Woledge's edition and the readings of the other two manuscripts.

30.   *Metre* is written by the scribe on the line below.

38.   I have read the scribe's abbreviation following the "q" to mean either "ue" or "uer." *Quere* never appears in copytext, but *querre* is written out fully in four places.

39.   A "rash boon," the granting of a request before its terms are announced, is a medieval romance convention, often accompanied by assurances that the request will not be outrageous or impossible to fulfill.

42.   Woledge notes that this line appears twice in *Mantel mal taillé* (Wulff 186 and 862).

49.   Godefroy defines the Old French *boutelliere* as "dispensatrice" and gives as an example Gautier de Coinci's "Dame, de grace boutilliere" in the *Miracles de Nostre Dame* (I, 3, 786). Robert's *Dictionnaire historique de la langue française* derives the word from the medieval Latin *buticularius*, "l'un des grands officiers de Cour chargé de l'intendance du vin."

61.   The conventional romance address to a woman as *Bele* is translated variously here as "Fair one," "Beautiful one," or "My pretty one," depending upon the degree of sexual innuendo called for by the context.

65.   The *ne* is needed in this line to convey the sense of "either...or," which is also conveyed by the N^2 and A readings.

74.   *Drois* is badly rubbed.

90.   *Pucele* is variously translated as "maiden" or "young woman."

112.   The scribe wrote *joie leva* but added marks to indicate the two words should be transposed.

120.   Woledge notes a parallel line in *Mantel mal taillé* (Wulff 79).

138.   A punctuation mark that looks like a period follows *Carados* in copytext.

148.   Woledge notes a parallel passage in *Erec* (Roques 5851–53).

155.   The noun "vassal" may be translated as "knight" or "vassal." The term emphasizes the subordinate rank of the knight referred to and is often used in a derogatory sense, especially in the context of a defiance (for example, see 2076, 5994, 6093, and 6130). The sudden appearance of a knight interrupting a meal is a common episode in Arthurian romances.

164.   The text says he "grabbed her by the shoulders," but the illustration in B.N.fr. 1433 clearly shows him grabbing her by the wrist, visual shorthand for rape. See Wolfthal 41 and cf. l. 4271 below.

167.   A *destrier* is a valuable war horse. Other terms used for horses in this romance are *ceval, bai, roncin, palefroi,* and *bauçant.*

169.   Where the meaning of *amie* ("friend" or "lover") is particularly ambigious, as in this passage, I have chosen to retain the Old French word.

217.   Chênerie (254) notes the repetition of lines parallel to *que ne beü ne ne menga* in *Erec* (Roques 3128), *Hunbaut* (Winters 903), *Continuation de Manessier* (37689), and *Fergus* (84, 22; 88, 20; 99, 21), but she does not mention this line in *L'Atre Périlleux.*

236.   The line is written in at the bottom of the column. Woledge reports seeing two "*a*'s" written in the left margin by the scribe to indicate that the line should be inserted here. The marginal notations are no longer visible.

254.   The first letter of this line is badly rubbed.

269.   A seneschal, in a medieval court, is an official in charge of servants, financial accounts, and domestic affairs. For a good study of the etymology and use of the term in Old French texts, see Woledge, "Bons vavasseurs et mauvais sénéchaux," pp. 1272–77.

277.   The boss (*boucle*) is a raised metal piece attached to the outside of the shield (*escu*). Kay is also protected by a hauberk (*haubers*), a knee-length tunic of chain mail (*maille*).

286.   Kay's right arm is also broken in Chrétien's *Perceval* (Roach 4311–13).

288.   The scribe wrote *s'aroute* but corrected it by writing a "t" above the "r."

328.   As Woledge notes, a similar line is found in *Mantel mal taillé* (Wulff 424).

368.   The Old French *vallet* or *vallés* is translated variously as "servant," "young man," "squire," or "retainer," depending upon the context and social rank of the individual referred to.

375.   The word *vers* has been inserted by the scribe above the line.

378–87.   Woledge notes a similar passage in *Lancelot* (Kibler 259–67), in which Gawain sees Kay's riderless horse approaching.

412.   *Malvais* is followed by a punctuation mark (.'), which appears to represent an exclamation point.

437.   *Qu'il* has been corrected by the scribe.

450.   Woledge reads *le* for *se*, but he indicates that the "l" in *le* has been corrected by the scribe. I was unable to see evidence of a correction.

481.   *Damoisel* is translated here as "young man." More usually, the wounded man is referred to as *vaslés* or *vallet*; thus, in most later instances the English translation refers to him as a "squire," which

stresses both his youth and his inferior status to Gawain.

515.   There is a mark, possibly the abbreviation for "n," above the second "o" in *l'ocoison.*

524.   Woledge notes a parallel line at 4981.

530.   The scribe originally wrote *savoit* but corrected the "t" by writing an "r" above the line.

538.   Proper chivalric behavior dictates that a fully armed knight not attack an unarmed knight (see also l. 554).

540.   Woledge notes that the same line appears in *Lancelot* (Kibler 4568).

554.   Proper chivalric behavior demands that the attending knights refrain from joining the battle; hence, this is the second transgression committed by the three knights.

556.   Woledge silently emends the copytext reading. Although I have not attempted to regularize variant spellings, there are no other examples of *eslaisié* in the text, and hence the missing "c" seems to be an oversight on the part of the scribe.

581.   The scribe wrote a punctuation mark (.'), indicating an exclamation after *Ahi* and *mors.*

598.   Woledge's *messire* appears to be an error. The copytext reading of *mesire* is clear and constitutes the normal spelling of the word in N[1]. There is only one other example of *messire* in copytext.

599.   Woledge's edition does not have a capital "B" to indicate the start of a new stanza in copytext.

603.   Woledge's spelling is an apparent error; both scribes regularly spell the word *monsegnor*, when used as a title. *Monseignor* does not occur in copytext.

656.   The author has thus introduced the theme of the *incognito*

knight. However, Gawain will continue to use his name until he defeats Escanor at the end of the first conflict. Thereafter, he will be known as *cil sans non* until the end of the romance.

671.   There is a scribal "L" visible to the left of the prickings to indicate to the rubricator that an initial "L" is to be placed here. Similar scribal directions are visible from time to time, but not noted here.

674.   Woledge notes a similar line in *Yvain* (Roques 3770).

681.   I follow Woledge in not emending to the more usual spelling; *cevalier* is also found in N^1 at l. 1170.

698.   *Biax* has been corrected from *bix* by the scribe.

707.   *Moult* has been corrected from *mout* by the scribe.

718.   *A le* at the start of the line has been cancelled by the scribe.

758.   There is a scribal mark (|) between *capela* and *va*.

789. N^1 spells the word *paor* in three other places; hence, the A reading is preferable to N^2, which was adopted silently by W.

790–91.   I have kept the N^1 reading here, although obviously an error has been clumsily corrected. Woledge notes that none of the manuscripts provides a satisfactory reading, and he suggests that perhaps a line to rhyme with 792 was missing. It is more likely that the confusion arose because of the need to leave space for the initial "S," which is not present at this line in the other two manuscripts. The passage would make better sense if line 790 were omitted, but that would leave no rhyme for the previous line. N^2 has *Paor quant je vos apielai/ Sire, dist il, je vos dirai.* A's reading is similar: *Paour quant je vous apelai/ Sire, dist il, je vous dirai.* Neither N^2 nor A has line 791; both include a line after 792 to rhyme with *perellox*.

802.   Woledge (236) notes that the metaphor *ariver a mal (bon) port* was current in Old French and cites five other instances of this phrase in medieval texts.

846.   Gawain is noted for his attachment to his horse, Gringalet.

882.   The contrast between excessive height and handsome appearance is also found in the English romance, *Sir Gawain and the Green Knight*.

914.   The "g" in *guerpi* is badly rubbed.

918.   The scribe has placed this line at the bottom of column a; Woledge saw a scribal "a" in the margin to indicate placement here. The "a" is no longer visible.

925–26.   Woledge notes similar lines in *Yvain* (Roques 4251–2).

939.   Woledge notes a similar line in *Eliduc* (Rychner 142).

959.   There is a scribal correction of *Nestoit* either from or to *Nastoit*.

968.   Woledge has *grans* but copytext clearly has *grant*, the reading also found in N^2 and A.

984.   *Garderoit* appears to have been corrected from *serviroit*.

1008.   Woledge notes that this line is identical to 1894.

1012.   Woledge notes parallel lines in *Hunbaut* (Winters 2204 and 2526).

1040.   Woledge notes that *Que* here means *Que que*, introducing the second term of the comparison.

1050.   The "i" has been corrected from "a."

1058.   The last three words in this line are badly rubbed.

1068.   The first letter of this line is badly rubbed.

1086.   The use of the words *sa drue* is highly ambiguous here. Does this imply that Gawain has had a sexual relationship with the kidnapped woman? Or does it refer only to his commitment to King

Arthur to "protect" her?

1115.   Woledge has *soulement*, but the "e" in N^1 *seulement* is very clear.

1135–36.   Woledge notes similar lines in Chrétien's *Cligés* (Foerster 773–75).

1138.   The second word in this line is badly rubbed.

1141–47.   The manuscript is in poor condition here. Consult the list of emendations for legible words. Woledge relies upon Schirmer's edition (published in 1868), arguing that the manuscript would have been in better condition then. However, Schirmer's readings of N^1 are unreliable; for example, he records fewer words in lines 1141–42 than are visible today. Therefore, I have adopted the N^2 reading, since that manuscript is closely related to N^1.

1163.   Chênerie believes the two-colored dress has symbolic meaning: "Elle est habillée de vert comme li démon de la mort et de rouge comme l'amour divin" (671).

1170.   See note at 681.

1197–98.   A tear in the parchment accounts for the illegible words in these two lines.

1206.   The first letter of this line is badly rubbed.

1220.   There is a period after *nuit* to indicate enjambment.

1223.   The abbreviation for *Et* has been corrected to *A* by the scribe.

1225–37.   The manuscript has been repaired: writing in a more modern hand is found on a new piece of parchment spliced into the old. Unless noted in the List of Emendations, I have adopted the readings in the modern hand and indicated these by square brackets in the Garland edition.

1263–71.   This section constitutes the other side of the repaired folio. The gaps in the text have not been filled in as on the reverse side. See the List of Emendations for a record of the legible sections and readings adopted.

1274. A fold in the parchment obscures the reading of the first word of this line.

1287–88. Woledge notes that these lines are repeated at 2247–48.

1306. Woledge notes similar phrases in *Erec* (Roques 948).

1307–08. Woledge notes similar lines in *Erec* (Roques 971–72), but the similarity may be only such as is common to many battle scenes.

1308. A fold in the parchment makes the first four words illegible.

1362. The scribe has written the last word of this line above *nel*.

1363–64. Woledge describes letters written by the scribe in the margin to indicate that the order of these lines should be reversed. These letters are no longer visible.

1374. There is a scribal exclamation mark after *A*.

1398. The scribe crossed out *fiert* and wrote *voit* above it; *en* is crossed out after *nue*.

1400. Woledge notes that this line is repeated at 2458.

1425–33. This transitional passage ignores the fact that some people in the town had already gone to the castle wall to observe the battle (cf. ll. 1118–30).

1478. The scribe has used slashes to indicate the reversal of word order.

1560. This characteristic—that a knight's strength increases until a certain hour of the afternoon—is most often attributed to Gawain himself.

1568. "Compline" is the last canonical hour of the day.

1573.   There is an abbreviation sign (7) above the "r" of "chevalier."

1577.   Gawain's mother is identified in Chrétien's *Perceval* (Roach 8748–53) but with no mention of her divining powers.

1588.   The scribe crossed out *cest* of *cestui* and wrote an "l" above it.

1598.   There is a period before and after the name "Escanors" in copytext. Escanor is the hero of a romance (ca. 1280) by Girart d'Amiens (*Arthurian Encyclopedia* 236).

1609–10.   For the proverbial nature of these lines, see Morawski and Schulze–Busacker, number 578 (*Diaus trespasse, més honte dure*) and number 1272 (*Mius vaut morir a joe que vivre a onte*).

1663–64.   Both N² and A agree on the order of these two lines, and Woledge's emendation makes the lines comprehensible.

1749.   Woledge notes a similar line in *Erec* (Roques 2661).

1770.   *Lies* has been corrected by the scribe.

1781.   The literal translation of the Old French would be: "God made incarnate through the son of Mary."

1805.   The scribe has written a mark that looks like an exclamation point (.') at the end of this line, although the sense of the passage does not demand it.

1812–13.   The beginnings of these two lines are badly rubbed.

1819.   *De cele da* has been crossed out by the scribe at the start of the line.

1870.   Woledge emends *tox* silently to *tous*.

1876.   The scribe corrected *ce* to *je*.

1888.   Woledge describes the repetition of *coustox* as unauthentic; he suggests that A has the better reading, but he does not emend the line.

1891.   The scribe has placed an "i" above the line to correct the second "e" in *velenie*.

1915.   There is a period after *armes* to indicate enjambment.

1936.   The scribe has written the "stel" of *lostel* above the line.

1965.   It was the custom for the meal to begin with the washing of hands. See also ll. 4968 and 6538.

1991.   Woledge notes that *grant jor* does not fit the line following and suggests that N² and A provide better readings: *Au matin quant il vit le jour* N²; *Au matinet quant il fu jors* A.

1992.   Woledge emends *desplaist* silently to *desplest*.

2012.   I read *cambeli* in N¹, but Woledge notes a vertical stroke after the "l" in "cambel."

2082.   Saint Lazarus most likely refers to the St. Lazarus of the parable (Luke 16: 19–31), patron saint of lepers, not Lazarus, the brother of Mary and Martha. However, there was frequent confusion between the two figures. Some time after 1050, Avallon had a relic with the head of Lazarus (Grivot and Zarnecki 17). *Lasre, lasdre* means "leper" in Old French (Greimas 358).

2102.   Woledge's *vaslet* appears to be an error; cf. *vallés* (N²) and *vallet* (A). *Vaslés* occurs frequently in N¹.

2115.   Space has been left for the initial "E," but it was never executed.

2186.   Woledge notes a similar line in *Milun* (Rychner 305).

2207.   There is a horizontal line (—) after *lances*, probably to indicate enjambment.

2209.   The initial "A" here has a more elaborate tail than is usual in this manuscript.

2218.   Woledge emends to *meïsmes*. However, since both forms are found in copytext, an emendation is unnecessary.

2233.   Woledge notes the proverbial nature of this line; see Morawski and Schulze-Busacker, number 761 (*Forte chose a en "faire l'estuet"*) and number 814 (*Grant chose a en "faire l'estuet"*).

2245.   The first two words of this line are very faint.

2258.   *Escanors* is abbreviated in N[1] as *Escan.* and the customary slash above an "i" is to be found above the period.

2279.   Although Woledge does not emend here, there is no other example of this word in N[1]; however, see the infinitive *mervellier* at l. 2303.

2309.   Antioch, a city in southern Turkey, was a legendary place of wealth and the site of a famous battle during the First Crusade.

2317.   The scribe has cancelled *u que des* at the end of the line.

2362.   An *arpent* is a measure of land, translated here as "acre."

2390–91.   For the proverbial nature of these lines, see Morawski and Schulze-Busacker, number 2274 (*Sorfait noyst, ço dit li vilains*).

2407–08.   Woledge doubts the authenticity of these lines, which are missing in N[2] and A.

2437–38.   Woledge notes similar lines in *Erec* (Roques 969–70). It is not clear here who strikes whose helmet. The passage would make better sense if Gawain continued to hit Escanor, but Escanor's helmet has already flown off his head onto the ground.

2440.   After *durement* the scribe has cancelled *que tout lesto*.

2443.   As Woledge notes, A adds two lines here, which state that Escanor has broken his sword.

2502.   Line 2518 repeats this line, as Woledge notes.

2509.   There is a period after *Gavain* in copytext.

2524.   The scribe has cancelled *jornee* and written *contree* above.

2531.   Woledge notes an identical line in *Erec* (Roques 4284).

2607.   Copytext has a period after *conterai* to indicate enjambment.

2614.   A Gascon bay is a horse of reddish-brown color from the region of Gascony. This is the only reference to this type of horse in the romance.

2619.   The sparrow hawk is a motif that occurs in a number of romance adventures, beginning with Chrétien de Troyes's *Erec et Enide*.

2632–33.   Woledge notes that the better reading is probably that of A at l. 2632 (*Li espreviers qui ert sorsis*) and that of N² A at l. 2633 (*S'esbati si m'est escapés*).

2637.   The initial is actually an "I," modernized here to "J" in accordance with modern editorial practice.

2690–91.   For the proverbial nature of these lines, see Morawski and Schulze-Busacker, number 1570 (*Ou pou ou envis set famme voir dire*) and 1791 (*Qui a fame s'acompagne si a assez tançon*).

2707.   There is a horizontal stroke above the *seut*.

2718.   The scribe has corrected *juerai*.

2765.   Woledge's *tere* is an error in transcription; the scribe has clearly written *terre*.

2786.   The scribe appears to have corrected *jewi*. Woledge's *jeui* is not justified; there is no other example of *jeui* in N¹.

2820–21.   The translation of these lines is made difficult by the uncertain meaning of *destois*. Ollier believes it means "une sorte de niche." The verb *caver* carries the sense of being in a hollow or cave. In N² the line is replaced by *Qui estoit mout biax et moult drois*. Line 2820 is missing in A.

2828.   Woledge notes a similar line in *Eliduc* (Rychner 319).

2850.   Woledge mistakenly indicates that column b begins two lines later.

2857.   Woledge drops the "s" from *Gavains*.

2876.   Woledge notes that l. 3007 is identical.

2882.   Woledge's *respint* appears to be an error; the "o" in *respont* is clear.

2884.   The scribe wrote *issici* and cancelled the first three letters.

2912.   The scribe has corrected *plaist*.

2945.   Woledge does not indicate the start of a new stanza and the initial "P" here.

2958.   The scribe has cancelled *la que pi* after *Desi*.

2960.   The scribe wrote *fust*, then cancelled the "u" and wrote "i" above it.

2963.   Lines 2854–55 indicate that the knight and squire are each riding a horse and that the squire leads an extra horse (*ceval*). The knight gets down from his horse (*palefroi*) and gives it to the sparrow-hawk woman (ll. 2913–17). The knight gives Gawain the horse (*ceval*) that the squire was leading (l. 2909). Then the knight has the squire get down from his horse (*roncin*), which he mounts and rides away. Ollier (*La Légende* 651, n. 1) points out that the text is unclear about how the squire departs from the scene.

2992–3479.   Nitze (295) notes other instances of marriage promises enforced in *Hunbaut* (1890–2165) and *Perlesvaus* (3763–3829).

3002.   N² reverses the order of ll. 3001–02 and adds a 666-line interpolation after l. 3002; see Appendix.

3068.   There is no basis for Woledge's *elle* here.

3075. Woledge notes that *respondist* depends on *priai* (3072) and that a *que* is needed for the sense.

3123. Copytext clearly has *sacai* here, not Woledge's *saca*.

3126. Woledge notes that this line is also found at 3154, 3168, and 3200.

3155. The scribe has cancelled *nestoie* after *entrepris*.

3175. The scribe has corrected *contree*.

3188. Woledge notes that one should probably understand a *que* before *encore*.

3189–90. For the proverbial nature of these lines, see Morawski and Schulze-Busacker, number 2128 (*Ki se loe si s'en boe*).

3227. The initial is actually an "I," modernized here to "J" in accordance with modern editorial practice.

3233. Woledge emends *l'ensegnié* silently to *l'enseignié*.

3248. Woledge does not note the start of a new stanza and the initial "N" here. The scribe appears to have corrected an "i" in *il* to an "e."

3264. W has *vos* here and at l. 3364, but the first scribe regularly used the "u⁹" abbreviation for *vous*.

3283. The scribe wrote *devant* but cancelled the "de" and wrote "a" above it.

3290. As Woledge notes, the line is identical to 3553; see also *Cligés* (Foerster 3241) and *Mantel mal taillé* (Wulff 19 and 678).

3301. Tours is a city in France situated on the Loire River.

3302. There is a scribal mark (') above the "a" in *tans*.

3308. Woledge mistakenly lists the N¹ reading in the textual notes (238) as *nouvelement,* when in fact it is *novelement,* the reading retained in G. There is no basis for Woledge's emendation to *nouvelment*.

3316.   Woledge's *un'autre* is an error.

3347.   The scribe wrote *ai lan* but cancelled the "l" and corrected the "a" to an "e."

3349.   The scribe corrected the "r" in *corox* from "x."

3353.   Woledge does not note the start of a new stanza here and the initial "G."

3354   Woledge notes a parallel line in *Charete* (Kibler 2480).

3384.   Woledge notes a similar line in *Hunbaut* (Winters 2000).

3387.   The initial "Q" has an especially long tail that extends horizontally across the column and down the far-right margin. It is cut off at the bottom of the page, a clear indication that the folio sheets have been cut down from an earlier, larger size.

3391–92.   Woledge notes that these lines occur in N^2 and A at 6003–04; they may also be found in *Erec* (Roques 5905–06).

3393–95.   Woledge notes that none of the manuscripts has a satisfactory reading: *Mais quant l'uns dut l'autre encontrer/ Si s'entrehurtent au hurter/ Car il vinrent si radement* N^2; *Mais l'uns dut l'autre eskiver/ Si se hurtent a l'encontrer/ Car il vinrent si roidiment* A

3400.   The customary slash for an "i" is written above the "u."

3411.   The second "s" in *s'esmaiast* is written above the line.

3421.   The "a" in *painne* appears to have been corrected.

3510.   The scribe wrote *mes joi amis* but put in marks for reversal of word order.

3547.   There is a mark that looks like an "i" or an abbreviation mark above the "v" in *diverse*.

3591.   There is a period after *chevalier*.

3631.   There is a mark, possibly the abbreviation for "n," above the "e" in *puet*.

3641.   The scribe corrected "i" to "c" in *cointe*.

3660.   Woledge remarks that this line is identical to l. 3630 and seems out of place here.

3671.   There is a stain here on the parchment that probably covers the abbreviation mark in *mlt*.

3739.   The scribe wrote *nous* after *moult* and then cancelled it.

3748.   The scribe corrected *feste*.

3768.   The scribe corrected *porroie*.

3790.   The *l'en* in the N^1 reading has been corrected.

3792.   A letter has been rubbed out between *el* and *elole* in the N^1 reading.

3803.   W emends *tele* silently to *tel*.

3816–17.   For the proverbial nature of these lines, see Morawski and Schulze-Busacker, number 2128 (*Ki se loe si s'en boe*).

3818.   W emends *Ke* silently to *Que*.

3838.   A letter before *Ce* has been rubbed out.

3840.   The scribe wrote *dist et reconta* and cancelled *et re* and wrote *qu'il les* above.

3861.   Woledge does not note the start of a new stanza here and the initial "C."

3878.   There is a period after *chevalier*.

3909.   The scribe wrote *et re s escuse* and cancelled *re s.*

3922–24.   For the proverbial nature of these lines, cf. Morawski and Schulze-Busacker, number 1959 (*Qui honor chace honor ataint*).

3953.   Woledge's emendation of N¹s *convenencié* to *convenancié* is unnecessary.

3965.   The actual initial is an "I," modernized in W and G to "J."

3982.   According to Woledge, the scribe corrected *je* to *ce,* but I can't see this.

4000.   The scribe wrote *si a condli a* and cancelled *a cond.*

4004.   Woledge notes the proverbial character of this line: see Morawski and Schulze-Busacker, number 1037 (*La sorsome abat l'arne*).

4006.   The *re* on *fare* in written below the line.

4007.   There is a period at the end of the line.

4010–11.   See Morawski and Schulze-Busacker, number 1791 (*Qui a fame s'acompagne si a assez tançon*).

4029.   The *Qui* has been corrected.

4032.   Literally, the line means "It is good that you have two bodies."

4044.   The scribe wrote *senestres* and cancelled the last "s."

4046.   The scribe wrote *L si* and cancelled the "L."

4086–87.   For the proverbial nature of these lines, see Morawski and Schulze-Busacker, number 2387 (*Tout destruit orgueus ou il se me[s]t*).

4093–94.   There appears to be a contrast between *pucele* and *damoisele*, which I have emphasized in my translation.

4102.   Woledge notes a similar line in *Erec* (Roques 606).

4126–27. Woledge notes a similar line in *Hunbaut* (Winters 854–55). He also notes the proverbial nature of these lines; see Morawski and Schulze-Busacker, number 1319 (*Mult waste paroles ki a chiens va*).

4144. The scribe corrected the second "d" in *dides* to "t."

4200. *Ens* seems to have been corrected.

4205. The Old French contrasts *sire chevalier* in the dwarf's address to Gawain (l. 4197) to the girl's *sire vassal* here.

4217. Woledge notes that this line is identical to 4286.

4221. The actual initial is an "I," modernized to "J" in W and G.

4222. *Drois* has been corrected and is difficult to read.

4235. The *song* in *besong* is written above the line.

4241. The scribe has corrected *li*.

4256. The *uene* of N¹ and W seems an error and hence is emended here to the N² *une*.

4271. In visual art, the gesture of a man grabbing a woman by the arm is a sign of rape (see note to l. 164); the scene is thus an ironic inversion of the opening scene in *L'Atre Périlleux*.

4284. The scribe has corrected the last letter of *Aimmi*.

4301. For a discussion of other uses of the verb *tresoïr*, see Holden.

4321. The scribe has corrected the "t" in *Dont* from "d."

4373. Woledge silently emends to the A reading of *del*, but there are numerous other examples of *du castel* in N¹.

4397. Woledge notes a similar line in *Richars li Biaus* (Holden 2716). Woledge's *chil* in this line is an error for *cil*.

4399–4400.   Woledge notes a similar line in *Charete* (Kibler 5943–44).

4440.   Folio 30ra begins at l. 4441, not 4440 as noted by W.

4449.   The scribe has corrected *que* from *qui*.

4451.   Woledge's *le noise* is an error; the noun is feminine.

4464.   The scribe has corrected *el*.

4475–76.   The rhyming words were written in reverse order, but the scribe used slashes to indicate that they should be reversed.

4548.   Woledge's *loiaumant* is an error.

4555.   Since the scribe has often substituted *Ke* for *Que*, there seems no reason to emend N^1 to *Que* as W does.

4561.   Although he does not emend, Woledge notes that he prefers the N^2 and A readings: *Jamais nul jor liez ne seroit* N^2; *Jamais nul jour lies ne serroit* A.

4575.   The scribe wrote *tes* but corrected the "t" to "l."

4579.   There is a slash like those used above "i" over the first "r" in *orrenet*.

4585.   The scribe wrote *sascies* but cancelled the second "s."

4655.   There are numerous parallels to the great battle of Roland and Oliver in *The Song of Roland* in this section: two knights fighting an army; the defense of a narrow place; the sounding of the horn.

4659.   The *au* is written by the scribe above the first three letters of *acorner*.

4672.   There is a scribal mark, possibly an "s," after the abbreviation for *Espinogre*.

4679–80.   Woledge notes that these lines are identical to 4697–98 and that parallel lines to 4680 may be found in *Cligés* (Foerster 3592) and *Erec* (Roques 2858).

4687. The scribe has mistakenly placed a dot below the "t" in *jetee* to cancel the letter.

4764 and 4782. W has *tere*, but N¹ clearly has *terre*.

4870. There is a scribal mark above the "a" in *castel*.

4901. The "s" in *boscage* has been corrected.

4932. The "s" in *s'il* has been corrected.

4983. The scribe wrote *meen* with a stroke above the first "e" as usually written above an "i."

4990. There is an exclamation mark after *Ahi*.

5017. The actual initial is "I," modernized to "J" in W and G.

5094. The scribe wrote *sons* but cancelled the second "s."

5124. The "Red Knight" refers to Perceval in Chrétien de Troyes's romance *Le Conte du Graal.*

5202. The scribe wrote *Kui* but corrected it to *Ki li.*

5205. There is a period after *soit* to indicate enjambment.

5224a–d. This section from A is necessary to complete the sense of the passage; I have retained Woledge's line numbering.

5228. Woledge notes that *esgarder* has the sense of "to judge" or "to conclude."

5231. There is a scribal mark at the end of this line that Woledge believes is a question mark.

5232. There is a horizontal stroke at the end of the line.

5237.   There is a horizontal stroke after *non* to indicate enjambment.

5240.   There is a red mark between the "A" and *mervelle*.

5242.   The scribe has corrected the last letter of *plaisans*.

5253–54.   Woledge notes that the A reading is better: *Des cheva-liers que il va querre/ Et de lor nons et de lor terre.*

5256.   The Old French name means literally "Proud Fairy."

5267–72.   There is verbal play on the meanings of *assez* and *trop*, which I have translated as "enough" and "too much."

5336–38.   Woledge notes the similarity of these lines to 5416–18.

5346.   The scribe wrote *enquirrt* but corrected the first "r" to "e."

5390.   Because the scribe's "n" and "u" (for "v") are very hard to distinguish, one could also read *vous…nostre* here.

5400.   It is not clear whether Gawain or Espinogre replies.

5426 and 5433.   A vavasor is a member of the lower nobility, a vassal belonging to a nobleman rather than to the king, who usually resided in a manor house away from court. See Woledge, "Bons vavasseurs" 1263–72.

5449.   Woledge believes that this line was influenced by 5451 and that the other two manuscripts preserve better readings: *Que Tristan enseignié lor ot* N²; *Que Tristrans ensignié lor oit* A

5476.   *Je* has been corrected.

5478.   Woledge's *cest'* is an error for *ceste*.

5487.   The scribe wrote *aune*, then cancelled it, and wrote *oirre* above it.

5506 and 5510.   There is a contrast made in the form of address:

Espinogre addresses Gomeret politely as *Dans chevaliers,* and Gomeret replies with *Sire vassal.*

5529.   There is a horizontal stroke after *armes* to indicate enjambment.

5550.   The scribe wrote *assiscent* but corrected the "c" to "s."

5562.   The last word of this line has been corrected.

5589.   The scribe wrote *Au* but cancelled the "u."

5602 and 5606.   These lines were written out of order; the correct order was reestablished by the scribe who wrote "a" in the margin before 5601, "b" before 5602, "c" before 5606, and "d" before 5607.

5602.   The scribe wrote *eppinogre* but corrected the first "p" to "s."

5613.   At the bottom margin of folio 37v, in another hand, is the following: *on ne pueit fraide[?] bien faire se dit on;* W reads *on ne puet...de bien faire se dit on.*

5681.   There is a period after *blechies* to mark enjambment.

5698.   The last letter of this line is badly rubbed.

5705.   There is an exclamation point after "A."

5711.   The "s" in *siecle* has been corrected.

5737.   Woledge's *suis* for *sui* appears to be an error.

5741.   A new hand begins here.

5743.   The second scribe often places periods at the end of the line, which have no apparent value and are not noted here.

5773–74.   The lines make better sense reversed as in W and A, although there is no scribal indication in N^1 of this.

5776.   There is a horizontal stroke after *Sire.* Earlier the text speaks

of the young man's eyes as pierced or punctured, but here they have
been gouged out.

5792–96.   See Woledge's discussion of this emendation in *Etudes* 33–34.

5813.   There is a horizontal stroke above the "q" in *uauque*.

5842.   The last letter in *gari* is badly rubbed.

5843.   It is clearly Gawain who is speaking here; see Woledge,
Etudes 27.

5851.   Woledge does not note the start of a new stanza and an initial "S" here; his *l'Orguelleus* is a misreading of N¹.

5864.   Compare *noire…plus que meure* here to *noir que moure* at l. 5538.

5886.   The scribe wrote *que il* but cancelled the "i."

5894.   The scribe wrote *soir* but cancelled the "i."

5911.   Woledge notes a similar line in *Erec* (Roques 869).

[A 1–58]   Although these lines are found only in A, ll. 5936–37 in
N¹ make little sense without them.

[12]   The repetition of *estoit* in W is a modern error, not present in A.

[45]   W expands the abbreviation *m'lt* as *molt*, but the scribe of A
uses the spelling *moult*.

5951–55.   A tear in the parchment was stitched before the scribe
wrote; half lines are arranged around the repaired tear.

5982 and 5991.   These lines are arranged around the stitching, the
reverse of the repaired tear.

5989.   The second scribe of N¹ expands *m'lt* as *molt*, a practice followed in G; thus, this line contains *molt…m'lt*.

6022–24.   These lines are spread out over six folio lines to accommodate the repaired tear.

6026.   There appears to be an erasure between *coup* and *vengier*.

6035.   Woledge is puzzled by the meaning of this line.

6037–42.   It is not clear how the blow to the helmet could come after splitting the shield and breaking the chain mail. Ollier does not translate lines 6041–42, because of the problems in establishing the text. N^2 follows N^1 closely; A omits ll. 6039–40, suggesting that Gawain covered his head with his shield.

6050.   Woledge's reading of *moult* in N^1 is in error. The scribe has written out *molt*.

6056–59.   These lines are spread out over six folio lines to accommodate the repaired tear.

6079.   There is a horizontal stroke after *dist*.

6096.   I have translated *norois* very freely as "good," in the interest of producing a smooth translation. Godefroy gives "norvégien" as the meaning when applied to horses; Tobler-Lommatzsch says "von nordischer (norwegischer) Rasse." *Norois* in modern French means "a North-West wind."

6100 and 6106.   Woledge's *vous* is in error; the N^1 scribe has written out *vos* both times.

6188.   W notes a more "authentic" reading in A, which adds two lines to a variant of this one: *Se a mes jeols ne le veïsse/ Que vos fuissies ne sains ne vis/ C'on disoit par tot le pais.*

6124.   There is a period after *troi*.

6128.   There is a period after *noirs*.

6209.   There is a period after *espee* to mark enjambment.

6210.   Woledge's *erramment* is a misreading of N¹'s *erranment*.

6215.   *Lais Hardis* means "the brave but ugly one."

6216.   Woledge notes the obscurity of this line; although he suggests that the A reading *sordis* may be better, I follow him in not emending.

6230.   Woledge's *embrace* is either a misreading of N¹s *enbrace* or a silent emendation.

6235.   It appears that the scribe wrote *estout* and corrected the second "t" by writing an "s" below the line.

6272.   The N¹ and N² readings do not make sense; see Woledge, *L'Atre* v.

6313.   The scribe wrote *n'i* but cancelled the "n."

6345.   Woledge notes that Gawain has not stayed overnight with Tristan; cf. 5363–65.

6356 and 6370–80.   The narrative here assumes that Tristan has not only the arm but also the body of the mutilated knight. The earlier passage (ll. 5172–73) speaks of Tristan having only the arm.

6381.   Woledge notes a similar comparison in *Anseïs* (5391).

6382.   As Woledge notes, the meaning of this line is unclear.

6391.   Woledge's *mervellié* is a misreading of N¹ *merveillié*.

6418.   The line has been spread out on either side of a hole in the parchment, as are also ll. 6420–23 and 6428–29.

6420.   Woledge's *avocques* is a misreading of N¹ *avoques*.

6422.   Woledge notes a similar line in *Erec* (Roques 412–13).

6463–67.   These lines are arranged around a stitched tear over seven lines.

6474.   The left justification of this and the succeeding nine lines moves to the right to accommodate a tear.

6504.   The confusion in spelling of *erramment* may occur because the "n" (or "m") is frequently abbreviated. When the scribe writes out the word, both forms are found, an inconsistency that in preserved in G. Hence, N¹ has *erranment* at 6210 and 6514 but *erramment* here. When the abbreviation is used, G consistently expands it as "n."

6540.   There is a period after *un*.

6565.   *Honte* has been corrected to *honor*.

6594.   The *oi* in *avoit* is badly rubbed.

6595.   The *ven* in *venjance* is nearly rubbed out.

6612.   This line is spread out over two lines to accommodate a repaired tear.

6614.   The King of the Red City appears only in the 666-line interpolation in N², reprinted here in the Appendix. The appearance of this reference is evidence that N¹ and N² stem from a common archetype (Woledge, *Etudes* 28).

6621.   Presumably these two men are: (1) the young man whom Gawain met in the Perilous Cemetery and (2) Martin, the young man whose sight was restored.

6650-51.   There are similar lines in *Erec* (Roques 2055-56).

Appendix. 1.   It is not clear if *carbonnier* refers to a charcoal (*charbon de bois*) or coal (*charbon de terre*) seller. Coal was mined in France at least as early as 1095 (Gimpel 81).

35-36.   The two lines do not rhyme.

56.   There are no other examples of the number fifty written out in any of the manuscripts; I have taken the form used by Chrétien (Foerster, *Wörterbuch* 60).

137.   Woledge notes a similar line at 1187.

141.   Woledge notes that the same line appears at 2601.

147.   Woledge emends to *Avoecques* here.

177–78.   Woledge notes similar lines in *Mantel mal taillé* (Wulff 517–18).

224.   There is a slash in N² between *savés* and *par*.

261.   Woledge notes a similar line at 1659.

266.   Woledge thinks this line echoes ll. 1271–72.

276.   Woledge notes many similarities in this section to Erec's fight with Yder (Roques 863 ff. and 968–1003).

323–24.   Woledge notes similar lines at 2351–52.

492–93.   Woledge notes nearly identical lines at 2364–65.

500.   Woledge notes a similar line at 2457.

514.   Woledge notes a nearly identical line at 4402.

527.   *Prison* has been corrected from *prion*.

550.   There is a slash between *plus* and *dit* in N².

553–54.   Woledge notes similar lines at 2563–64.

617.   Woledge notes a similar line at 3001.

633.   Woledge emends to *s'entredeffient*.

665–66.   Woledge notes similar lines at 2991–92.

INDEX OF PROPER NOUNS

Alemaingne Germany 1718; Alemaigne Appendix A 23

Angarde title of Ragidel 4309, 6439; see Ragidel

Antioce Antioch, a city in southern Turkey 2309

Arés the son of Pellinor and father of Tor 136

Artu Arthur, King of Britain 535, 3232, 3814; Artur 269, 1171, 1856, 2182, 2826, 5128, 6602, Appendix A 537; Artus 9, 128, 962, 5133, 5869, 6194, 6647

Atre Perillous (l') the Perilous Cemetery, title of the romance and cemetery in which Gawain's battle with the devil takes place incipit; Atres Perellox 792; Atre Perellox 937, 952, 960, 990, 1182; Atre Perelox 1121; Atres Perilleus 1232; Atre Perelleus 6677

Avalon modern Avallon, a town in the department of Yonne in Burgundy 2082, see Saint Lasdre

Bon chevalier see Gavain

Bretaigne Great Britain, kingdom of Arthur 1531, 1597, 1717

Brun sans Pité Brun Without Pity, King of the Red City Appendix A 558

Cadrés a knight encountered by Gawain 4580, 4585, 4594, 4618, 4675, 4738, 4760, 4765, 4775, 4810, 4811, 4869, 6437, 6465, 6609

Cadroain see Codrovain

Carados Briesbras knight of the Round Table 138

Carduel town of Carlisle in Great Britain, residence of King Arthur 988, 2526, 2558, 3434, 5212

Carlion Caerleon-on-Usk in Monmouthshire 3057, 6461, 6536

Cestre Chester, a city in England 6632

Chevalier Vermel Perceval, knight of the Round Table 5124

Cil sans non see Gavain

Codrovain a knight, the eldest of seven brothers 4285, 4305, 4500, 4851; Codrovains 4871; Codrovain le Rox 4411; Codrovains li Rous 4478; Codrovains a la Teste Roxe 4540; Cadrovain le Rox 4777; Cadrovain 4788; Cadroain le Rous 6433; Cadroain 6467; Cadeain 6480

Constentinoble Constantinople 3613

Cornuaille Cornwall in England 11

Cortois de Huberlant (le) knight who is killed in mistaken belief that he is Gawain, but who is restored to life by the Orgellox Faé 6403, 6522

Creator synonym for God 2791, 2824

Damedix synonym for God 5326

Damlediex synonym for God 6526

Dix God 80, 347, 362, 388, 392, 458, 544, 775, 780, 968, 1176, 1606, 1686, 1689, 1781, 2026, 2028, 2202, 2594, 2648, 2746, 2948, 2982, 2996, 2998, 3304, 3919, 3923, 3927, 3930, 4161, 4277, 4283, 4924, 4990, 4995, 5060, 5154, 5193, 5209, 5243, 5435, 5465, 6103; Appendix A 222, 337, 504, 629; Dieu 6149, Appendix A 84; Dé Appendix A 589; Diex 5947, 6182, 6201, 6327, 6332, 6426, 6518, 6674

Engletere England 3093; Engleterre 3992

Erec knight of the Round Table 137

Escanor knight who abducts Arthur's cup-bearer and whom Gawain kills in battle 2305, 2307, 2336, 2359, 2550, 6578; Escanors 1766, 1824, 1883, 1922, 1990, 2001, 2091, 2080, 2115, 2127, 2208, 2209, 2249, 2258, 2361, 2379, 2427, 2442, 2467; Escanors de la Montaigne 1598

Espaigne Spain 4215; Espaingne 5789

Espinogre knight whom Gawain forces to be loyal to his *amie* 3435, 3650, 3877, 4580, 4652, 4672, 4827, 5860, 5906, [53], 6242, 6452, 6608; Espinogres 4031, 4589, 4600, 4632, 5374, 5472, 5484, 5504, 5523, 5566, 5602, 5610, 5898, 5915, 6261

Faé Orgellox (le) a knight who possesses magic powers and is lord of a town known as Roce Faee 5256; Feés Orgellox 5253; Faé (le) 6241, 6375, 6378, 6491; Orgellox (li) 5454; Orgellox Faé (l') 5627; Orguelleus Faé 5827, 6347, 6349, 6369, 6414, 6451, 6487, 6510; Orgelleus qui ert Faé (l') 6383; see Roce Faee

Gales Wales 3093, 3992; see Wales

Gascogne Gascony 2614

Gavain Gawain, knight of the Round Table, Arthur's nephew 93, 97, 112, 266, 315, 558, 564, 571, 603, 610, 712, 736, 1033, 1153, 1276, 1332, 1376, 1419, 1431, 1480, 1740, 1793, 1881, 1907, 1914, 1947, 1967, 2000, 2197, 2229, 2237, 2254, 2261, 2287, 2297, 2300, 2401, 2403, 2509, 2797, 2857, 3233, 3371, 3413, 3507, 3575, 3585, 3650, 3815, 3877, 3905, 3931, 3940, 4045,

4217, 4286, 4369, 5099, 5113, 5157, 5191, 5206, 5211, 5222, 5233, 5285, 5294, 5359, 5455, 5507, 5619, 5798, 5803, 5807, 5877, 5887, [56], 6013, 6053, 6121, 6129, 6178, 6179, 6241, 6244, 6254, 6260, 6269, 6279, 6301, 6336, 6357, 6441, 6458, 6483, 6495, 6514, 6558, 6567, 6620; Appendix A 209, 230, 289, 337, 379, 417, 430, 494, 503, 646; Gavains 102, 118, 136, 208, 319, 324, 340, 375, 380, 388, 426, 438, 448, 465, 487, 505, 534, 553, 598, 626, 669, 746, 753, 778, 787, 826, 846, 852, 871, 945, 984, 989, 1010, 1119, 1131, 1164, 1260, 1281, 1294, 1305, 1316, 1334, 1338, 1354, 1364, 1398, 1450, 1484, 1506, 1523, 1547, 1633, 1732, 1801, 1817, 1883, 1920, 1928, 1938, 2005, 2020, 2026, 2058, 2070, 2074, 2098, 2117, 2129, 2135, 2138, 2185, 2209, 2238, 2255, 2263, 2268, 2275, 2279, 2301, 2332, 2344, 2350, 2409, 2424, 2429, 2445, 2465, 2468, 2495, 2497, 2519, 2522, 2538, 2570, 2590, 2642, 2699, 2708, 2732, 2761, 2810, 2868, 2873, 2882, 2896, 2904, 2922, 2946, 2954, 2967, 2999, 3020, 3035, 3245, 3294, 3305, 3353, 3370, 3401, 3417, 3433, 3451, 3462, 3474, 3476, 3493, 3520, 3529, 3675, 3690, 3698, 3724, 4005, 4031, 4867, 5239, 5319, 5349, 5734, 5781, 5843, 5927, 5956, 5988, 6021, 6026, 6045, 6064, 6079, 6089, 6102, 6112, 6140, 6148, 6181, 6210, 6227, 6248, 6318, 6365, 6391, 6400, 6425, 6444, 6470, 6489, 6498, 6502, 6530, 6572, 6596, 6604, 6671; Appendix A 16, 82, 118, 121, 256, 257, 268, 294, 328, 343, 395, 398, 425, 430, 449, 464, 469, 495, 498, 507, 519, 526, 561, 575, 594, 632, 641, 652; bon chevalier 3, 241, 536, 577, 590, 1374, 1411, 2412, 3315, 5009; cil sans non 4064, 4143, 4178, 4382, 4395, 4446, 4567, 4658, 4689, 4744, 4806, 5013, 5069, 5208, 5265, 5279, 5459, 5479, 5626, 5667, 5686, 5700, 5717; celui sans non 4676; cis sans non 5189

Gomeret Mor knight who, together with the Orgellox Faé, killed Cortois de Huberland in the belief he was Gawain 5896; Gomeret 5918, 6243; Gomeré 6413, 6452; Gomerés [53]; Goumerés 5452, 5490, 5511, 5517, 5528, 5590, 5604, 5623; Goumerés sans Mesure 5263, 5342; Goumeret 5477

Gringalet (le) Gawain's horse, stolen by Codrovain 2355, 2571, 3570, 4360, 4445, [58]

Huberlant see Cortois de Huberlant

Iders Yder, knight of the Round Table 328

Islande Iceland 3592

Jeremies the prophet Jeremiah 6606
Keu Kay, knight of the Round Table, Arthur's seneshal 290, 336, 379, 404; Kés 268; Kex 276, 281, 284, 295, 412, 434, 442; Qex 222
Lais Hardis (le) knight of the Round Table, also called the noir chevalier 6215, 6277; Lai Hardi 6304, 6393; noirs chevaliers 5900, 5950, 6092, 6128, 6145, 6315; noir chevalier 5932, [29], 5995; chevalier noir [25]; cil qui ert noir 6012
Logre a kingdom in England 3436, 3649, 4828
Lombardie Lombardy, region of Northern Italy 3628
Marie 1781; see Sainte Marie
Martin young man who is blinded while protecting Cortois de Huberlant, but whose sight is restored by the Orgellox Faé 6533
Mors Death 581, 584, 4211
Nature 4079, 6422
Noir Chevalier see Lais Hardis
Normendie Normandy 2149
Nu Nuc, father of Yder 328
Olivier companion of Roland in the *Song of Roland* 3870; see Rollant
Orgellox see Faé Orgellox
Paris 2585
Pavie Pavia in Italy, famous for its armor 1346
Qex see Keu
Ragidel knight entitled *de l'Angarde* who begs a boon of Gawain in exchange for a horse 4309, 4869, 4891; Ragidiax 4543; Raguidel 6439, 6610; see Angarde
Reniés Bishop of Chester 6632
Reonde Table (la) Round Table 3256; Taule roonde Appendix A 155
Roce Faee (la) town belonging to Orgellox Faé 5259
Rollant hero of the *Song of Roland* and nephew of Charlemagne 3870; see Olivier
Rome city in Italy 348, 3027, 3354, 4214, 4438, 5068, 5970
Rouge Chité the Red City, home of Brun sans Pité 6614; Appendix A 11, 143, 285, 378, 559; see Brun sans Pité
Saint Amant possibly Saint Amandus, bishop of Maastricht Appendix A 309
Saint Lasdre d'Avalon Saint Lazarus, patron saint of lepers, associated with the church at Avallon 2082
Saint Pol the apostle Saint Paul 5954

Saint Thumas the disciple Saint Thomas Appendix A 225, 520
Sainte Marie mother of Jesus 773; see Marie
Salemons King Solomon 4009
Sanson the Biblical Samson Appendix A 170
Senlis French city in Picardy, the department of Oise 2011, 5534
Taule Roonde see Reonde Table
Tors knight of the Round Table 136
Tors Tours, French city in the department of Indre-et-Loire 3301
Tristrans qui ne rit Gawain's host who provides information leading
          to the recovery of Gawain's name 5392; Tristran qui ne rit
          6259; Tristrans 5449, 5451, 6280; Tristran 5468, 5632, 6262,
          6265, 6289, 6300, 6320, 6346, 6372, 6394, 6416
Wales 135; see Gales
Wi kingdom of Espinogre 3439

Appendix

Interpolation in Bibliothèque Nationale, fonds français 1433

1   Lors a un carbonnier ueü,
     Que il n'a gaires conneü,
     Venir uers eux le grant chemin.
4   Deus asnes maine et un ronchin
     Si uenoit mout grant aleüre.
     Gavains li demande a droiture
     Nouveles, se il les sauoit,
8   De quele part il trouveroit
     Plus pres hostel a herbegier.
     "Sire," che dist le charbonnier,
     "Chi pres est la Rouge Chité,
12   Mais ne vous viengne a pensé,
     Ne pour besoing ne por destroit,
     Que vous ailliés ja la endroit;
     Qu'il y a un malvais trespas."
16   Gavains li dit isnel le pas:
     "Biaus amis," dist il, "dites moi
     Quel li trespas est, et de quoi
     Vous m'aves ainsi devisé."
20   "Sire, le roi de la chité
     Est mout outrequidiés et fier;
     Si n'a nul si boin chevalier
     Des les pors dusqu'en Alemaigne.
24   Chi devant a une fontaine
     Le trouverés ja tout armé,
     Car ainsi l'a acoustumé:
     Les quatre jours de la semaine,
28   Vient tout jours a chele fontaine;
     Avoec li maine une puchele,
     Onques homme ne vit si bele.
     De li ne vous sai plus conter,
32   Mais qui bien seüst deviser
     Tout son atour et sa biauté,
     Dire peüst en verité
     C'onques ne fu si bele femme,
36   Car ele est tant et bele et gente,
     N'ot pas le quart de sa biauté.
     Et sachiés bien de verité
     Que le puchele iert en grant paine,

1   Just then he saw a coal seller,
    Whom he scarcely knew,
    Coming toward him along the road.
4   He led two donkeys and a horse,
    And he was approaching very quickly.
    Gawain straight away asked him
    For information—did he know
8   Where nearby he could find
    A place to lodge?
    "Sir," the coal seller replied,
    "Near here is the Red City,
12 But don't even think of going
    To that place—no matter
    How needy or pressed you might be—
    For there a terrible crime is committed."
16 Gawain quickly replied:
    "Dear friend," he said, "tell me
    What the crime is and more about
    What you have just referred to."
20 "Sir, the king of the city
    Is most outrageous and cruel;
    In fact, there is no knight so hardy
    Between here and Germany.
24 There in front, near a spring,
    You will find him already well-armed,
    For this has been his practice:
    Four days out of the week
28 He comes each day to this spring;
    With him he brings a girl,
    None more beautiful is to be seen.
    I cannot tell you more about her,
32 But if someone were able to describe
    All her clothing and her beauty,
    He could certainly verify
    That no woman was ever so beautiful,
36 For she is so pretty and noble
    That others haven't a quarter of her beauty.
    And you can be certain of this,
    That the girl will be in great pain,

40   Car toute nue en le fontaine,
       Qui mout estoit froide et obscure,
       Veulle ou non, jusc'a la chainture
       La fait entrer ens encor plus,
44   Si qu'il em pert tout par desus
       Le teste et toute le poitrine,
       Plus blanche que n'est flor d'espine.
       Ainsi est ilec toute jour
48   En le fontaine a le froidour,
       Ne ja hors de l'iaue n'istra
       Devant chou qu'il avesperra;
       Dont l'en retrait et si remonte.
52   Il n'est nul si haut roi ne conte
       Se il parloit ne poi ne grant
       Qu'il ne morust des maintenant,
       C'a lui le couvenroit combatre;
56   Et sachiés que cinquante et quatre
       Se sont a li ja combatu,
       Qu'il a tous ochis et vaincu,
       Tout decopés et detrenchiés,
60   De chiaus du pais plus prisiés
       Qui fussent en tout le regné.
       Or sont si tuit espoenté,
       Et tant en ont veü morir,
64   Qu'il n'en osent mais plait tenir.
       Quant matés les a et vaincus,
       Si fait fichier en peus agus,
       Qu'il a fait fichier en estant
68   Le chief et le hiaume luisant.
       Il ne puet estre si prodom
       Qu'il ait ja autre raenchon,
       Que li rois l'a juré ainsi,
72   Et vous le verres ja ichi;
       Se vous alés en la chité
       Il ne puet estre trestourné
       Que n'aillés par devant le roy.
76   Biau sire, prenés bien conroy
       De vostre vie garandir;
       Se par yloec volés venir,
       Vous morrés ja en fin sans faille.

40 For there, completely nude in the spring,
Which is very dark and frigid,
Whether she wants to or not, he forces
Her in up to her waist and more,
44 So that one is able to see only
The head and all of her bosom,
Whiter than a hawthorn flower.
Thus she stays there all day long
48 In the spring, in the freezing water,
Nor is she able to leave the water
Before the sun has set;
Only then does he take her out.
52 There is no king nor count so noble,
No matter how slightly or grandly he speaks,
Who would not die immediately,
For he would have to battle him.
56 You should know that fifty-four
Have already fought with him,
That all have been conquered and killed,
All chopped up and dismembered,
60 All those the most prized
In all the royal lands.
Now they are so completely frightened
And have seen so many die,
64 That they don't dare complain.
After he has beaten and conquered them,
He has the head and gleaming helmet
Placed on pointed stakes,
68 Planted upright in the ground.
No one, no matter how good a man,
Can have any other ransom,
For the king has declared it thus,
72 And you will see so for yourself;
If you go into the city,
There is no way to avoid
Passing by the king.
76 Dear sir, take care
To protect your life.
If you want to go that way,
You will certainly end up dead.

80   Ja n'en passerés sans bataille,
        Se en parlés ne tant ne quant."
        Et Gavains li dist maintenant:
        "Amis, trop m'en aves conté.
84   A Dieu soiés vous commandé;
        Mais itant sachiés bien de voir
        Que je irai la pour veoir
        Le puchele et le chevalier,
88   Chil qui a fait les peus drechier
        Seur le chemin par son orguel,
        Si li dirai que savoir vel,
        Si li plaist et vient a talent,
92   Son estre et son contenement,
        Car mout volentiers le saroie."
        A chest mot se met a la voie,
        Si se parti du carbonier.
96   Tant esperonne le destrier
        Qu'il ot passee le montagne;
        Lors a veüe la fontaine,
        Qui sist mout pres de le chité,
100   Et vit le chevalier armé
        Sor un destrier fort et hardis.
        Onques en trestout le païs
        N'en ot un si tres bel veü.
104   Et sachies bien que son escu
        Sanloit estre de cuir tané,
        Mais tant fu fort et bien ouvré
        Que mout vous seroit fort a dire;
108   Car n'est pas legier a descrire
        S'armeüre qui tant est riche,
        Si com li contes nous afiche.
        Il n'i ot seur li point de blanc,
112   Ains iert plus rouge que nul sanc
        Lanche roide grosse et quarree,
        El fer devant bien acheree,
        Espee fourbie et trenchant,
116   De coulor rouge flamboiant,
        Et fu es estriers affichiés.
        Es vous Gavains tout eslaissiés,
        Si salue le damoisele,

80	You will never get away without a battle,
	If you make the least little objection."
	And Gawain now told him:
	"Friend, you have said too much;
84	I commend you to God.
	But you can be certain of this,
	That I will go there to see
	The girl and the knight,
88	This one who, in all his arrogance,
	Has had stakes put up along the road.
	I will say to him that I want to know—
	If it pleases him and he wants to tell me—
92	Who he is and what he's about,
	For I would certainly like to know it."
	With these words, he set out on his way
	And parted from the coal seller.
96	He spurred his horse on, so
	That he had soon crossed the mountain.
	There he saw the spring
	That was located very near the city,
100	And he saw the armed knight
	On a mighty, strong horse.
	Never in all the countryside
	Had he seen one so beautiful.
104	And this you should know, that his shield
	Appeared to be made of tanned hide,
	But so strong and beautifully tooled,
	That it would be hard to describe it;
108	For it is not easy to describe
	His armor, which was so very elegant,
	Just as the story affirms it was.
	There wasn't a bit of white:
112	His mighty lance, large and well-shaped,
	Was brighter red than any blood,
	With very sharp iron at its tip;
	The sword, polished and sharp,
116	Was of a blazing red color;
	He was firmly fixed in his stirrups.
	Behold, Gawain galloping up!
	He greets the demoiselle,

120   Qui estoit a mervelle bele,
       Puis li dist monseigneur Gavains,
       Qui de grant franchise fu plain:
       "Sire," fait il, "pour quel meffait
124   Faites a ma dame si lait,
       Et si vielment le deménes?"
       "Vassal, se savoir le volés,
       Dites li qu'ele le vous die,
128   Et vous ferés grant courtoisie
       Se vous l'en poés geter hors;
       Mais vostre vie et vostre cors
       Y couvient remanoir en gages."
132   Dist Gauvains, "Vous dites outrage,
       Si vous convenroit adrechier.
       Aler le veul ore prier,
       Se il li plaist, qu'ele me die,
136   Par amor et par courtoisie,
       Pour quoi et des cant et comment
       Il vous fait souffrir chest torment,
       Chest grant anui et cheste paine."
140   Chele qui iert en la fontaine
       Li respont: "Sire, volentiers.
       Sachiés bien que chis chevaliers
       Est rois de la Rouge Chité;
144   Mais tant est fel et sorquidié
       Qu'il ne crient nul homme vivant.
       L'autre an m'aloie deduiant
       Avoec li en un vergier;
148   Il dist qu'il n'auoit chevalier
       El roiaume le roi Artur,
       De chou iert il bien asseür,
       Qu'il ne conquisist par bataille.
152   Et je li dis sans nule faille,
       Comme chetive et mal senee,
       Que on disoit en ma contree
       Que chil de le Taule Roonde
156   Erent tuit li mellor du monde.
       Et mes sires me respondi:
       'Damoisele, si com je qui
       Il n'i a nul meillor de moi.'

120   Who was marvelously beautiful,
And then milord Gawain spoke,
He who was so full of courtesy:
"Sir," he said, "for what crime
124   Do you make this lady suffer?
Why do you treat her so cruelly?"
"Vassal, if you want to know this,
Ask her to tell you herself;
128   You will be doing her a great courtesy,
If you can pull her out of there,
But your body and soul
Will have to be pledged in return."
132   Gawain replied, "You are outrageous!
You ought to change your ways!
I'm going there right now to ask her,
If she please, that she tell me,
136   Out of politeness and affection,
Why, since when, and how
She has had to suffer this torment,
This great sorrow and such pain."
140   She who was immersed in the spring
Replied: "Sir, gladly.
Understand that this knight
Is the King of the Red City,
144   But he is so cruel and swollen with pride
That he fears no man alive.
Last year I went out for pleasure
With him into an orchard.
148   He claimed that there was no knight
In all of Arthur's kingdom
Whom he—and he was sure of this—
Could not conquer in battle.
152   And I said without hesitating—
Miserable and stupid as I am—
That in my country it was said
That the Knights of the Round Table
156   Were by far the best in the world.
And my lord replied to me:
'Young lady, it's my belief
That there is no one better than I.'

160   Je di, 'Sire, je quit et croi
      De mellors en y a assés:
      Mout est chil fol et sourquidiés
      Qui quide estre tout le mellor
164   Et d'un roiaume et d'une honnor.'
      Il me respondi par afit:
      'Damoisele, a mout grant despit
      Me tenés, ore bien le sai,
168   Et de che mie ne m'esmai,
      Car chou avons assés veü.
      Sanson fortin qui tant preu fu
      Fu decheüs par sa moullier;
172   Femme veut tous jours mix prisier
      Autrui que le sien par nature.
      Vis li est qu'ele a la resture
      De trestous chiaus de la contree,
176   Si s'en tient mout a enganee,
      Et s'il iert le melleur d'un ost
      Tant le honniroit ele plus tost.
      Or sachiés bien de verité
180   Trop avés le cuer escaufé
      Quant vous m'avés si despisié,
      Si veul qui vous soit refroidié.
      Pour che que vous m'avés blasmé,
184   Jusqu'a tant que aiés trouvé
      Qui me puisse d'armes oster
      Et par forche vaintre et mater,
      Ou tout mors ochire en bataille,
188   Iert seur vous prise si grant taille.
            "De le semaine quatre jours
      Vous ferai entrer voiant tous
      En le noire fontaine obscure;
192   Sans point de nule vesteüre
      Serés ileuc tout en estant,
      Dusques a soleil esconsant,
      Loiaument le jur et plevis.
196   Et si mandés a vos amis,
      Se vous vous i fiés de riens,
      Car je quit et croi et sai bien
      S'aucun venoit par son desroi

160   I said, 'Sir, I believe there are
       Plenty of others who are better:
       He who believes he is the best
       In a realm or fiefdom
164   Is foolish and swollen with pride.'
       He replied defiantly:
       'Young lady, you must hold me
       In great disdain; now I understand,
168   And I'm not surprised,
       For we've seen plenty of it.
       The mighty Samson, who was so brave,
       Was ruined by his wife;
172   A woman, by nature, always values
       What she doesn't have more than what she has.
       She thinks she has the worst man
       Of all those in the country
176   And considers herself much wronged;
       And if he were the best of a whole troop,
       She would quickly cover him in shame.
       Now you can be sure of this truth:
180   You have heated up my heart too much
       By despising me like this,
       And so I want it to be cooled again.
       Because you have scorned me so,
184   Until you have found someone
       Who can take away my armor
       And defeat and conquer me by force
       Or strike me dead in battle,
188   The following judgement applies:
       '"For four days in every week
       I will force you in front of everyone
       To enter the deep, black spring.
192   Without a single piece of clothing,
       You will stay there standing upright
       Until the sun sets;
       This I solemnly swear and promise.
196   And so summon your friends,
       If you have any confidence in them,
       For this I believe and know perfectly well:
       Should anyone be so foolish as to arrive

200 Qui vausist desraignier vers moi
C'a tort vous faiche chest anui,
Se je vieng au dessus de lui,
Chest jugement est tous seüs,
204 Que pres de vous en peus agus
En ferai les testes fichier,
S'il en y venoit un millier.'"
Entre tant que la creature
208 Qui iert en l'iaue a le froidure
Parloit a monseigneur Gavain,
Li rois, qui n'estoit pas vilain,
A le damoisele apelee
212 Que Gauvains avoit amenee,
Si li prie qu'ele li die
Par amour et par courtoisie,
"Qui est chest chevalier armé
216 Qui tant est fol et sourquidié
Qui est venus par estoutie
Voiant moi parler a m'amie?
Mout grant talent ai de savoir
220 De son estre trestout le voir."
Chele respont mout franchement:
"Sire," fait ele, "se Dix m'ament,
Je ne vous sai dire son non."
224 "Ne le savés?" "Par mon chief, non."
"Comment va dont, pour Saint Thumas?"
Chele li conte isnel le pas
Com il l'avoit u bois trouvee;
228 L'aventure li a contee,
Onques ne l'en deigna mentir.
A Gavain m'estuet revenir,
A qui chele de le fontaine
232 Conte son anui et sa paine
Qu'ele a plus de trois ans soufferte.
Mais plus l'empoise de le perte
Des nobles chevaliers de pris
236 Qu'il a par bataille conquis.
Et quant il les avoit vaincus,
Si fait fichier des peus agus;
Le teste y met o l'iaume cler.

200   And dare to assert that
       I am wrong to impose this torture,
       And I succeed in conquering him,
       This penalty will be known by all;

204   For near you on sharp stakes,
       I will attach their heads,
       Even if a thousand come here.'"
       During the time that this creature,

208   Who was plunged in the freezing water,
       Spoke with milord Gawain,
       The king, who was no boor,
       Addressed the young woman

212   Whom Gawain had brought with him
       And asked her to tell him,
       Out of friendship and politeness,
       "Who is this armed knight,

216   So foolish and presumptuous,
       Who has so audaciously dared
       To talk to my *amie* right in front of me?
       I certainly would like to know

220   Everything there is to know about him."
       And so she replied frankly:
       "Sir," she said, "so help me God,
       I cannot tell you his name."

224   "You don't know it?" "I assure you, no."
       "In the name of St. Thomas, how is that possible?"
       She immediately told him
       How he had found her in the forest;

228   She told him all about the adventure,
       Without lying about anything.
       Now I must return to Gawain
       Whom the lady in the spring

232   Was telling about the pain and torture
       She had suffered for more than three years.
       But what weighed on her more was the loss
       Of the many noble and valorous knights

236   Whom he had overcome in battle.
       After he had defeated them,
       He had them attached to sharp stakes,
       The head, that is, with the bright helmet.

240   "Chi devant en voi un ester
       Ou il n'a encor riens fichié,
       Ne mais qu'il y a apoié,
       Che veés vous bien, un escu:
244   Il fu au derrain vaincu.
       Che sachiés bien chertainement
       Que li peus vostre teste atent.
       Il atent qu'ele y soit fichie,
248   Si com le chose est prononchie.
       Des qu'il iert yleuc ferus,
       Uns autre pel iert embatus
       Delés cheli, qui atendra
252   Tant que uns autre revenra.
            "Sire, or sachies de verité
       Que mon estre vous ai conté,
       Se vous l'avés bien entendu."
256   Et Gavains li a respondu.
       Gavains dist, "Damoisele, lors
       Issiés de le fontaine hors,
       Par un couvenant que orrés:
260   Que vous jammais n'i enterrés
       Tant com je soie sains ne vis."
       Ele a erraument ses dras pris,
       Qui ierent pres de le fontaine.
264   Le chevalier a longue alaine,
       Si escrie mout fierement:
       "Mar veïstes chest parlement,
       De che soiés trestout chertain."
268   "Vassal," chou li a dit Gavains,
       "Manechiés tant com vous plaira.
       Je sui chil qui ja ne fuira
       Pour vous ne pour vostre manache,
272   Ains serai trouvés en le plache
       Tous appareilliés de deffendre,
       S'est qui estour me veulle rendre;
       Veés me chi tout apresté."
276   L'un d'eus a l'autre deffié
       Si s'alerent entre ferir
       Tant com cheval les puet ramir,
       Et fierent par mi les escus

240   "Over there in front I see one
       That has not yet been placed in position,
       Except that it has been propped up,
       This you can clearly see, against a shield:
244   He was the last to be conquered.
       Of this you can be certain,
       That the sharp stake awaits your head.
       It is only waiting for him to attach it,
248   Just as he has vowed to do.
       As soon as this has happened,
       Another stake will be set
       Next to this one to wait
252   Until another has arrived.
          "Sir, now you know the truth—
       I have told you everything—
       If you have been listening carefully."
256   And Gawain answered her.
       He said, "Young lady, now
       Climb out of the spring,
       And listen to the following terms:
260   You will never again enter it
       So long as I am alive and well."
       She quickly grabbed her clothes,
       That were lying near the spring.
264   The knight at the top of his voice
       Cried out furiously:
       "This conversation will cost you dearly;
       Of this you can be quite certain!"
268   "Vassal," Gawain replied to him,
       "Threaten me as much as you want,
       But I am one who will not flee,
       Not for you or your threat.
272   I can be found in place
       All ready to defend myself,
       If there is anyone who wants a fight:
       You can see that I am all set!"
276   They challenged one another
       And set their horses galloping
       Toward each other as fast as they could go;
       They struck in the middle of their shields

280 Grans cops des fers trenchans agus,
    Que les escus perchent et croissent.
    Les lanches esclichent et froissent
    Et si volerent en asteles
284 Ains l'un d'aus ne se mut des seles.
    Le roi de la Rouge Chité
    Fu mout dolent et abosmé
    Quant voit qu'il ne l'ot abatu.
288 Il trait le boin brant esmolu,
    Si fiert Gavain ireement
    Amont en l'iaume qui resplent,
    Qu'il li fent jusqu'a capeler.
292 A poi qu'il ne le fist verser,
    Mais bien se tint qu'il ne chaï,
    Et Gavains ra lui envaï,
    Si l'a si radement feru
296 Amont u plus haut de l'escu
    Que par le boucle l'a copé,
    Et que du boin auberc saffré
    En a mil mailes abatues.
300 Le branc descent du cop qui rue
    Par entre l'archon et le roi:
    Le feutre et trestout l'aroi
    Li trencha tout rouondement,
304 Et le boin destrier ensement,
    Si que li rois est trebuchié
    Entre les deus tronchons a pié.
    Mais mout fu tost em piés saliz;
308 N'estoit pas des armes falis.
    Puis dist: "Vassal, par Saint Amant,
    Chest cop ne fu mie d'enfant.
    Ains ne m'ama ne ne tint chier
312 Qui seur moi vint tel cop lanchier;
    Mais quant de moi departirés
    Ja mar vostre coupe en batrés
         "Or soiés franc et afaitié
316 Si descendés o moi a pié.
    Se ne faites, tant vous veul dire
    Vostre cheval ferés ochirre,
    Si ferés moult plus que vilain."

280   With great blows from their sharp, cutting blades,
So that the shields were pierced and broken.
Their lances splintered and broke,
And they flew into pieces,
284   But neither could displace the other.
The King of the Red City
Was quite annoyed and fed up
When he saw that he had not struck him down.
288   He pulled out his trusty blade
And quickly attacked Gawain,
Striking his gleaming helmet,
So that he ripped through to the cap below.
292   Just a little more and he would have thrown him,
But Gawain sat firm so that he didn't fall.
He in turn rushed to attack the king,
And he struck him violently
296   High up on the shield
So that the boss was split
And the beautifully ornate mail
Was broken into a thousand pieces.
300   The blade came down with mighty force
Between the saddlebow and the king:
The padding and all the trappings
He cut off cleanly
304   And the good horse likewise,
So that the king was thrown
Down between the two pieces.
However, he jumped quickly to his feet;
308   He was not lacking weapons.
Then he said, "Vassal, by St. Amant,
This was no child's blow.
He who came to deliver this blow to me
312   Did not come in love and friendship.
However, before you leave me
You will be sorry for it.
     "Now be the noble and generous knight you are
316   And come down on foot with me.
If you do not do this, I tell you,
Your horse will be killed,
And you would be behaving badly."

320 Adont se pourpense Gauvains
     Que de che li dist il bien voir,
     Qu'il puet a enscient savoir
     A che qu'il est trop fort et fier
324 Ja li ara mort son destrier.
     Par tant descendi a le tere,
     Si va son anemi requerre.
     Mais chil si bien se deffendi
328 Que Gavains tout s'en esbahi;
     Qu'il li avoit tel cop donné
     Amont seur le hiaume gemé
     Qu'il en embati contreval
332 Fleurs et bericle et esmal.
     Desseur l'escu le cop descent;
     L'escu jusqu'a le boucle fent,
     Et le hauberc les le costé
336 Est tout trenchié et decopé.
     Dix fu bien a Gavain garant
     Quel poing tourna arrier le branc;
     Si ne li fust el poing tourné
340 Jusqu'el foye l'eüst copé.
     Chil l'a empaint de tel vertu
     C'a poi qu'il ne l'a abatu,
     Mais Gavains pas ne s'en esmaie,
344 Quanqu'il li doit mout bien li paie.
     Une envaye li a faite;
     Seure li keurt l'espee traite,
     Et chil l'a mout bien requelliz.
348 Mout par fu grans li fereïs
     Qu'il font seur les hiaumes gemes.
     Toute le gent de le chitez
     Il sont a grant eslais venu:
352 N'i remest jone ne chanu,
     Homme ne femme, droit ne tort,
     Grant ne petit, feble ne fort,
     Qui aler puisse, qu'il n'i voise.
356 En le chité ot mout grant noise
     Et grant bruit par toutes les rues;
     Car les grans gens et les menues,
     Clers et bourgois et chevaliers,

320   Thus Gawain realized
        That what he said was true;
        He could have no doubt that,
        Strong and fierce as he was,
324   He would kill his horse.
        Thus he got down on the ground
        And ran to challenge his enemy.
        But he defended himself so well
328   That Gawain was astonished:
        He had given him such a blow
        On top of his jeweled helmet
        That he knocked off
332   Flowers, beryl gems, and enamel.
        The blow fell onto the shield,
        Splitting it from the boss,
        And the mail on the side
336   Was completely split into pieces.
        God certainly defended Gawain
        When his hand turned back the blade;
        If he had not turned it aside,
340   It would have cut him to the quick.
        The blow threw him with such force
        That he was almost defeated,
        But Gawain did not give up;
344   He paid him back as best he could.
        He started a new attack;
        He ran toward him with drawn sword,
        But the other put up a good fight.
348   The blows that struck the jeweled
        Helmet were terrible.
        All the people in the city
        Had run up to watch the fight:
352   No one remained, neither young nor old,
        Man nor woman, straight or bent,
        Tall nor short, feeble or strong;
        Anyone who could walk made his way there.
356   In the city there was much commotion
        And lots of noise in every street,
        For everyone, the greatest and the least,
        Clerks and bourgeois and knights,

360   Dames, pucheles, esquiers,
       Y keurent tous communaument
       Pour veïr lor contenement.
       Le campagne ont avironné,
364   Et li rois lor a quemandé
       Si chier com cascuns a sa vie
       Qu'il n'i ait un seul qui mot die
       Pour riens qu'il oye ne qu'il voie.
368   "Car a mes deus mains l'ochirroie,
       Ja ne seroit de tel renon.
       Ne vaurroie que traïson
       Fust a li faite plus qu'a moi,
372   Et je li jur bien et otroi
       Se il se puet de moi deffendre,
       Ja ne li estuet garde prendre
       D'autrui; ne soit ja en freour."
376   Grant paour ont de lor seignour
       Trestuit li baron du rengné;
       Le roy de la Rouge Chité
       Si dist a monseignor Gavain,
380   Com chil qui n'estoit pas vilain:
       "Vassal," fait il, "que vous est vis?
       Contre le gent de mon païs
       Qui vienent ver le bataille
384   Je vous afi et jur sans faille
       Ne soiés ja en nul effroi,
       Que n'avés garde fors de moi
       Ychi pour nul meschaement.
388   Tous sui el dessus de ma gent,
       Qu'il n'i a conte ne baron
       Qui pour le barbe du menton,
       Ne pour le nes ne por le dent,
392   Trespassast mon commandement;
       Et je vous ai asseüré,
       Loiaument plevi et juré."
          Gavains respont, "Vostre merchi.
396   Couvrés vous dont, je vous deffi."
       "Et je vous," dist le chevalier.
       Mais Gavains le feri premier
       Amont seur l'iaume rougoiant;

360   Ladies, girls, and squires,
       All ran there together
       To see how they would behave.
       The whole field was filled,
364   And the king made a pronouncement:
       That as dear as each held his life,
       Not a single person should say a word
       No matter what he heard or saw.
368   "For I promise to kill him with my own two hands,
       No matter how esteemed he might be.
       I do not want treason committed
       Against him any more than against me,
372   And I solemnly vow and promise,
       If he can defend himself against me,
       He will not have to defend himself
       Against anyone else; he should have no fear."
376   All the barons of the kingdom
       Were frightened of their lord;
       The King of the Red City
       Thus said to milord Gawain,
380   As one who is no boor should:
       "Vassal," he said, "what do you think?
       To all the people of my country
       Who have come to this battle
384   I have promised and vowed solemnly—
       You need have no worry—
       You don't have to defend yourself against anyone but me,
       Whatever misfortune might arise.
388   I am completely in charge of my people;
       There is neither count nor baron
       Who, for the sake of the beard on his chin,
       For his nose or even a tooth,
392   Would challenge my commandment;
       And this I have affirmed,
       Promised, and solemnly sworn."
          Gawain replied, "Thank you.
396   Now get ready, for I challenge you."
       "And I you," said the knight.
       But Gawain struck the first blow
       On top of the gleaming helmet;

400 L'escu li trenche par devant,
 Si qu'il li trencha les enarmes
 Et chil qui mout savoit des armes
 En paint son cop de tel vertu
404 Que l'auberc a tout derompu
 Et trenchié par dessus l'aissiele,
 Que res a res de la mamele
 Li trencha le char du costé.
408 Laidement fu le roi navré;
 Le sanc l'en keurt a grant randon
 Aval dessi qu'a l'esperon.
 Quant li rois se senti blechié,
412 A grant merveille fu irié;
 Mais ne fu pas espouenté.
 Il tint le boin branc acheré
 Ou il se fie durement;
416 En li a pris son hardement.
 Gavain feri de tel aïr
 Que tout en fait l'escu croissir,
 Et le branc en fist enbraier
420 En l'iaume jusqu'au chapeler:
 Jusc'au tes li achiers n'areste.
 De l'os li trenche de la teste,
 Que mout iert trenchans l'alemele,
424 Mais ne toucha en la chervele.
 Gavains a sentue le plaie
 Qui de riens nule ne s'esmaie,
 Ains le requiert moult vassaument,
428 Et chil mout tres bien se deffent.
 Bien escremissent ambedui,
 Chil fiert Gavain et Gavains lui;
 Et nepourquant tel cop li donne
432 Seur le hiaume que tout l'estonne.
 Et chelui a li referu,
 Que le moitié de son escu
 Li trencha tout roondement,
436 Et del auberc cent mailles prent,
 Si que le branc est descendu
 Deseur le brach tout nu a nu,
 Si l'a navré jusques a l'os,

400	He cut through the shield
	So that he broke the straps,
	And he who knew so much about fighting
	Struck a blow with such force
404	That it completely ripped through the mail
	And broke it up to the armpit,
	So that, striking flush with the breast,
	It ripped away the flesh on the side.
408	The king was badly hurt;
	The blood ran freely
	Down to his spurs.
	When the king perceived his wounds,
412	He was furious beyond belief;
	But he was not discouraged.
	He held his good, sharp blade
	On which he relied completely;
416	In it he placed his strength.
	He struck Gawain with such force
	That he broke the shield,
	And he forced the blade
420	Into the helmet down to the cap below;
	The steel continued to the skull.
	He cut some bone from the head,
	So effective was the sharp blade,
424	But it did not reach the brain.
	Gawain felt the wound,
	But he was not otherwise affected;
	He attacked the king valiantly,
428	And he in turn defended himself well.
	He stuck Gawain and Gawain struck him:
	They put on quite a fencing match.
	Nevertheless, he gave him such a blow
432	On the head that he was completely stunned.
	And he in turn struck back
	So that he completely cut off
	Half of his shield
436	And took off a hundred pieces of mail;
	The blade descended
	Under the arm, leaving it exposed,
	So that he wounded him up to the bone;

440   Que le sanc en defile hors,
      Que tout contreval le braihier
      L'en fait le sanc vermeil raier.
      Mout sont fier andui li vassal,
444   Si se combatent par ingal
      Que nus qui le voir en veut dire
      N'en seüst le meilleur eslire,
      Li plus preuz ne li plus hardiz,
448   Plus enprenant ne alentis,
      Fors tant que monseignor Gavains
      L'assaloit tous jours premerain.
      Mout sont lor auberc derompu,
452   Et detrenchié sont lor escu,
      Si que d'entier n'i avoit tant
      Qui lor peüst estre garant.
      A descouvert souvent se fierent;
456   Mout s'entre blechent et en pirent.
      Ainsi dura cheste bataille
      De l'eure de tierche sans faille
      Dessi a soleil resconsant.
460   Ambedui ierent si vaillant
      Que nus ne puet l'autre grever
      Ne conquerre en camp ne mater;
      Nepourquant mout tres bien l'assaut
464   Gavains com chil a qui ne faut
      Proeche, forche ne hardement,
      Et chelui mout bien se deffent,
      Qu'il ne doute pas par samblant
468   Une seule frese vaillant.
          Gavains fu durement irié
      Que la bataille a tant duré.
      Seure li keurt par mout grant ire,
472   Laidement le bleche et empire.
      Si l'a de tel aïr feru
      Seur le penne de son escu,
      Si que le cop en vint glachant:
476   Seur le poing ou il tint le branc
      Est descendus li achiers frois.
      Le pauch et dui des autres dois
      Li eüst copé tout a net,

440 And the blood ran out
   So that it flowed down to the waist
   And was shining bright red.
   Both of them were ferocious,
444 Fighting one another so equally
   That no one who watched could choose sides
   Or say who was the best,
   The most brave or the most hardy,
448 The most enterprising or the most timid,
   Except that milord Gawain
   Was always attacking first.
   Their mail was quite ripped apart,
452 And their shields were broken,
   So that there was nothing left
   That could guarantee them protection.
   Thus exposed, they struck many blows;
456 They pressed hard and inflicted many wounds.
   Then this battle continued
   Uninterrupted until the hour of terce
   When the sun began to set.
460 Both of them were so valiant
   That neither could wound the other,
   Nor claim victory or checkmate;
   Nevertheless, Gawain attacked him
464 Forcefully like one who didn't lack
   Prowess, strength, or hardiness,
   And he in turn defended himself well,
   So that he did not seem to dread
468 Any valorous man alive.
     Gawain was enraged because
   The battle had lasted so long.
   In his anger he made a direct attack,
472 Wounding and weakening him badly.
   He struck with such force
   On the edge of his shield
   That the blow slid all the way down:
476 The icy blade descended down
   To the fist with which he held the blade.
   The thumb and two other fingers
   Were cut through cleanly,

480   Mais tant vint l'espee a souhet
        Qu'il tenoient encore ad ners.
        Du poing li vole en trauers
        Le boine espee loing de lui.
484   Mout ot grant ire et grant anui
        Quant il se vit ainsi blechiés;
        Par grant ire s'est efforchiés
        Et avoit saisie s'espee,
488   Et a sa guiche retournee,
        Et prent l'espee a l'autre poing
        Si com li ensengne besoig,
        Et keurt vers li plus que les saus.
492   La veïssiez mout durs assaus
        Menuement recommenchier.
        Chil fiert Gavain du branc d'achier,
        Et Gavains a lui referu
496   C'a poi qu'il ne l'a abatu.
        Le roy de son escu se keuvre,
        Et chil Gavains son cop rekeuvre
        Et quida ferir de rekief
500   A descouvert par mi le kief.
        Mais chelui tint l'espee traite;
        Une envaïe li a faite,
        Dont Gavain deut estre grevé
504   Se Dix ne l'en eüst gardé,
        Amont seur le hiaume d'achier,
        Qu'il le couvint agenoullier.
                Puis va Gavains par tel angousse
508   Fiert son escu qu'il li deffroisse,
        Fiert et refiert tout a bandon,
        Vint cops li donne d'un randon.
        Le hiaume esquartele touz,
512   Et le ventaille de dessous
        Li avoit hors du chief tiree.
        Le teste li eüst copee,
        Mais chil qui se senti matés
516   Li dist, "Merchi, vaincu m'avés.
        Puis qu'il ne puet estre autrement,
        Tenés m'espee, je le vous rent."
        Mais Gavains ne la rechut pas,

480 But the sword stopped in time
So that they were held on by a thread.
The trusty sword of the king
Flew out of his hand far from him.

484 He was very angry and upset
When he saw how he was wounded;
In his anger he made one more effort
And ran toward his sword,

488 Turned the strap around,
And picked it up in the other hand,
Just as necessity dictated,
And launched a fierce attack.

492 There you could see, step by step,
A terrible battle start up again.
He struck Gawain with his steel blade,
And Gawain struck him back again

496 So that he almost defeated him.
The king covered himself with his shield,
And Gawain regained the upper hand;
He wanted to strike him anew

500 On top of his exposed head.
But the king held out his sword;
He struck him so hard
On top of his steel helmet

504 That Gawain would have been wounded
If God had not protected him;
He forced him onto his knees.
Then Gawain ran up to attack his shield

508 With such violence that he broke it;
Then he struck again and again,
Giving twenty blows at once.
He broke apart the helmet,

512 And he tore off from the head
The visor that was underneath.
His head would have been cut off,
But, realizing he was defeated,

516 He said, "Have mercy, you have won.
Since it can be no other way,
Take my sword; I give it up."
But Gawain would not take it

520   Ains en a juré Saint Thumas:
       "A bien poi que ne vous ochi."
       "Ha! gentiex chevalier, merchi;
       Trop grant mesproison feriés,
524   Se vous hui mais m'ochiés
       Quant en vostre merchi me rent."
       Gavains li a dit esraument:
       "Prison vous couvient afier,
528   Et le matin sans demourer
       Entre vous et vostre puchele,
       Qui est franche, courtoise et bele,
       Vous rendrés a le court le roi,
532   Et si li dites de par moi
       Que de vous li fais un present
       Et a la roïne ensement.
       Conterés toute le melee
536   Ainsi comme ele est alee,
       A li et au boin roy Artur."
       Et chil respont, "A beneür,
       Vostre plaisir en ferai tout,
540   Ja mar en serés en redout
       Que je mout volentiers n'i aille.
       Le verité de le bataille
       Si com faite l'avés vers moi
544   Conterai je mout bien au roi,
       Mais vostre non savoir vaurroie.
       Que dirai je qui m'i envoie,
       Quant a le court serai venu?"
548   "Biaus amis, j'ai mon non perdu,
       Je sui le chevalier sans non."
       "N'en sarai plus?" Dit, "Par foi, non.
       Ytant dites en cheste voie:
552   Que chil sans non vous y envoie,
       Si vous apelent et honourt
       Tant que je reviengne a le court.
       Dites bien que je revenrai
556   Quant je men non trouvé arai.
       Or me dites le vostre non."
       "Brun sans pité m'apele on.
       Rois sui de le Rouge Chité."

520 And swore instead by St. Thomas:
  "I'll be damned if I don't kill you."
  "Ah! noble knight, have mercy;
  You would commit a great misdeed

524 If you killed me now
  That I have placed myself in your hands."
  Gawain addressed him at once:
  "You must become my prisoner,

528 And tomorrow without delay
  You and your young woman,
  Who is noble, courteous, and beautiful,
  Shall present yourselves at the royal court.

532 Indeed, you should say on my behalf
  That I give you over to the king—
  And likewise to the queen.
  You should tell the whole story

536 Of the battle, exactly as it happened,
  Both to the queen and to the good King Arthur."
  And the king replied, "Certainly,
  I will do all that you ask,

540 You need have no fear
  That I will not gladly go there.
  The truth about the battle,
  Just what you did to me,

544 I will report truthfully to the king,
  But your name I need to know.
  Who should I say has sent me
  When I arrive at the court?"

548 "Dear friend, I have lost my name;
  I am the knight without a name."
  "You no longer know it?" "I swear it, no.
  And so say the following:

552 That the knight without a name has sent you,
  So that they will welcome and honor you
  Until I return to the court.
  Assure them that I will return

556 As soon as I have found my name.
  Now tell me your name."
  "Brun Without Pity is how I am called.
  I am King of the Red City."

560 "Vous n'estes de riens sournommé,"
Fait Gavains, "che sachiés de voir.
Mais une cose poés savoir:
Anuit mais serés en repos,
564 Et quant li jours sera esclos
Si ferés metre vostre sele
Entre vous et vostre puchele
Si com vous m'avés couvenant."
568 Et chil li affia errant
Qu'il se rendra en sa prison.
Les gens qui furent environ,
Chevaliers, bourgois, vavassor,
572 Mout font grant deul de le seignor,
Qui mout laidement iert navré,
Et vont tout droit a le chité.
        Et Gavains dist qu'il s'en ira
576 Et que plus ne sejornera.
A le damoisele quemande
Qu'il trouua el bois en le lande
Qu'ele mont sor son paleffroi.
580 "Par foi," chou li a dit le roi,
"Je vous pri requier par franchise,
Se il puet estre en nule guise,
Que vegniés o moi herbegier."
584 Tuit l'emprient li chevalier
Et le courtoise damoisele,
Qui mout iert avenans et bele.
Mais il lor dit que riens ne monte,
588 Il ne remaurroit pour nul conte;
Si les commande tous a Dé,
Et eux y ont lui quemandé.
Mais li rois li jure et otroie
592 Demain se metra a la voie
Sans faire plus de demourer.
Gavains ne se veut plus targer;
A son droit chemin s'en retrait
596 Et ot mout grant mestier d'entrait
Pour ses plaies medeciner.
Chele ne finoit de plourer
Qui aloit en se compagnie.

560   "It's not for nothing you are named this,"
Said Gawain, "this is surely true.
But one thing you ought to know:
You only have one night to rest;
564   At the first break of day,
Have your horse saddled,
Both for you and your woman,
And do as you have promised me."
568   And so the king quickly swore
That he would be his prisoner.
Meanwhile the people who were watching,
The knights, merchants, and vavasors,
572   Had great sorrow on account of their lord,
Who was very badly wounded;
They all went straight back to the city.
    And Gawain said that he would be on his way
576   And not stay there any longer.
And he told the young woman,
Whom he had found in the woods,
That she should mount her horse.
580   "By my faith," the king said to him,
"I pray you, please accept my invitation,
If it is at all possible,
That you come spend the night with me."
584   All the knights implored him
And the courteous young lady,
Who was very attractive and beautiful.
But he told them that nothing could change him,
588   He would not stay there for anything;
He commended them to God,
And they did the same to him.
But the king swore and promised him
592   He would set out on the road tomorrow
Without any further delay.
Gawain did not want to wait any longer;
He returned to the correct road,
596   And he had great need of medicine
To cure his wounds.
She whom he had in his company
Did not cease to cry.

600 Il li dist, "Bele douche amie,
　　　Ne plourés pas, je garrai bien.
　　　Une chose sachiés vous bien:
　　　Onques mais en tout mon aage
604 Ne vi hom de tel vasselage
　　　Comme est chestui chevalier.
　　　Je ne veul o lui herbegier,
　　　Car chou n'iert pas drois ne raison.
608 Trop fesisse grant mesprison
　　　Se je me herbegaisse o lui,
　　　Car trop li ai fait grant anui.
　　　Mais de tant sui je moult irié
612 Que n'avés beu ne mengié."
　　　"Ha! biau sire, je n'ai pas fain:
　　　Il n'a el monde si boin pain
　　　Dont je mengaisse orendroit pas."
616 Ainsi s'en vont plus que le pas,
　　　Ne sai quel part, querre aventure.
　　　Mais les a coisi a droiture
　　　Uns chevalier armé et fort
620 Qui un chevalier avoit mort
　　　Yleuc trestout nouvelement.
　　　Encore en iert trestouz sanglent
　　　Son branc d'achier cler et fourbi,
624 Qui mout iert fort si com je qui.
　　　Si le salue franchement,
　　　Mais chelui mie ne li rent
　　　De son salu, mais li escrie:
628 "Vassal," fait il, "n'en menrés mie
　　　La dame ainsi, se Dix me saut.
　　　Je vous ferai ja un assaut
　　　Que vous comperrés moult tres chier."
632 Dont estuet Gavains courouchier.
　　　　　　Puis s'entres deffient et fierent.
　　　As fers des lanches se requierent
　　　Andui de toutes lors vertus,
636 Qu'il depiechent tous lor escus,
　　　Si sentrefierent vassaument.
　　　Chelui le fiert premierement
　　　Sus en l'iaume par tel aïr

600 He said to her, "Dear, sweet friend,
     Don't cry, I will certainly heal.
     One thing you ought to know:
     Never in all my life
604 Have I seen a man of such valor
     As this knight we just left.
     I did not want to stay with him,
     For that would not have been right or reasonable.
608 I would have made a big mistake
     To lodge with him
     After he caused such great distress.
     But I am quite annoyed about one thing—
612 That you have not eaten or had anything to drink."
     "Ah! dear sir, I am not hungry:
     There isn't in all the world bread so good
     That I would eat any now."
616 They rode on a little way,
     I don't know where, seeking adventure.
     But nearby on the right he saw
     A knight well-armed and strong
620 Who had just killed another knight
     Very recently.
     His steel blade, bright and polished,
     Which was, I gather, very strong,
624 Was still covered with blood.
     Gawain greeted him courteously,
     But he did not respond
     To this greeting, crying out instead:
628 "Vassal," he said, "you will not take
     That woman any further, if God is with me.
     I will show you a battle
     That you will pay for dearly!"
632 At this Gawain grew very angry.
          Thus they challenged each other and fought.
     They attacked with iron-tipped lances,
     Each of them with all the force they could muster,
636 So that they broke their shields:
     Thus they fought vigorously.
     The knight struck first
     With such force on the helmet

640   Que il en fait le fu salir;
      Et Gavains a lui referu
      A descouvert seur son escu
      Qu'il la fendu dusques au foie.
644   Le destrier saut et va se voie,
      Au travers par mi le forest.
      A Gavain merveille desplest,
      Car ne se sot pas conseillier;
648   Qu'il ne veut pas seule laissier
      Pour nul besoing le damoisele.
      Le destrier traïne la sele,
      Fuiant s'en va mout effraés;
652   Et Gavains s'en est retournés
      Que le puchele n'ait paour.
      Chele nuit dessi qu'a grant jour
      Ont trestous deuz el bos geü,
656   Et quant il ont le jour veü,
      S'en sont d'ilec andui tourné.
      Pour son escu qui fu usé,
      Qui ne li puet avoit mestier,
660   A pris l'escu au chevalier;
      Puis montent andui si s'en vont.
      Trestoute jour chevauchié ont
      Dusques bien pres de mïedi,
664   Et sachiés que il iert tierz di
      Qu'il n'orent mengié ne beü,
      Lors ont un chevalier veü…

640	That he made it fly into the air,
	And Gawain struck back
	In the exposed area of the shield
	So that he bored through to the quick.
644	The horse jumped and ran away
	Out through the woods.
	Gawain was greatly annoyed,
	For he did not know what was best:
648	On no account did he want to leave
	The young woman all alone.
	The horse was trailing the saddle
	And had taken off in great fright;
652	And Gawain turned back
	So that the young woman would not be afraid.
	All that night until the break of day
	The two of them lay in the forest,
656	And when they saw the sun rise,
	They got up and went away from there.
	In place of his shield that was worn out,
	Which could not be of any use to him,
660	He took the shield of the knight;
	Then they mounted and left.
	They rode along all day
	Until close to noon,
664	And remember this was the third day
	That they had not eaten or had anything to drink;
	Just then they saw a knight...

GARLAND LIBRARY OF MEDIEVAL LITERATURE

JAMES J. WILHELM
AND LOWRY NELSON, JR.
General Editors

Series A (Texts and Translations)
Series B (Translations Only)

BRUNETTO LATINI
Il Tesoretto (The Little Treasure)
Edited and translated by
  Julia Bolton Holloway
Series A

THE POETRY OF WILLIAM VII,
COUNT OF POITIERS, IX DUKE
OF AQUITAINE
Edited and translated by Gerald A. Bond;
  music edited by Hendrik van der Werf
Series A

BARTHAR SAGA
Edited and translated by Jon Skaptason
  and Phillip Pulsiano
Series A

GUILLAUME DE MACHAUT
Judgment of the King of Bohemia (Le
Jugement dou Roy de Behaingne)
Edited and translated by R. Barton Palmer
Series A

WALTHARIUS AND RUODLIEB
Edited and translated by Dennis M. Kratz
Series A

THE RISE OF GAWAIN, NEPHEW OF
ARTHUR (DE ORTU WALUUANII
NEPOTIS ARTURI)
Edited and translated by
  Mildred Leake Day
Series A

THE POETRY OF CINO DA PISTOIA
Edited and translated by
  Christopher Kleinhenz
Series A

FIVE MIDDLE ENGLISH
ARTHURIAN ROMANCES
Translated by Valerie Krishna
Series B

THE ONE HUNDRED NEW TALES
(LES CENT NOUVELLES NOUVELLES)
Translated by Judith Bruskin Diner
Series B

L'ART D'AMOURS (THE ART
OF LOVE)
Translated by Lawrence Blonquist
Series B

BÉROUL
The Romance of Tristran
Edited and translated by
  Norris J. Lacy
Series A

GRAELENT AND GUINGAMOR
Two Breton Lays
Edited and translated by
  Russell Weingartner
Series A

GIOVANNI BOCCACCIO
Life of Dante (Trattatello in
Laude di Dante)
Translated by Vincenzo Zin Bollettino
Series B

THE LYRICS OF THIBAUT DE
CHAMPAGNE
Edited and translated by
  Kathleen J. Brahney
Series A

THE POETRY OF SORDELLO
Edited and translated by James J. Wilhelm
Series A

GIOVANNI BOCCACCIO
Il Filocolo
Translated by Donald S. Cheney with
  the collaboration of Thomas G. Bergin
Series B

GUILLAUME DE MACHAUT
The Judgment of the King of Navarre
(Le Jugement dou Roy de Navarre)
Translated and edited by R. Barton Palmer
Series A

THE STORY OF MERIADOC, KING OF
CAMBRIA (HISTORIA MERIADOCI,
REGIS CAMBRIAE)
Edited and translated by
  Mildred Leake Day
Series A

THE PLAYS OF HROTSVIT
OF GANDERSHEIM
Translated by Katharina Wilson
Series B

GUILLAUME DE MACHAUT
The Fountain of Love (La Fonteinne Amoureuse), and Two Other Love Vision Poems
Edited and translated by
R. Barton Palmer
Series A

DER STRICKER
Daniel of the Blossoming Valley
Translated by Michael Resler
Series B

THE MARVELS OF RIGOMER
Translated by Thomas E. Vesce
Series B

CHRÉTIEN DE TROYES
The Story of the Grail (Li Contes del Graal), or *Perceval*
Edited by Rupert T. Pickens and translated by William W. Kibler
Series A

HELDRIS DE CORNUÄLLE
The Story of Silence (Le Roman de Silence)
Translated by Regina Psaki
Series B

ROMANCES OF ALEXANDER
Translated by Dennis M. Kratz
Series B

THE CAMBRIDGE SONGS (CARMINA CANTABRIGIENSA)
Edited and translated by
Jan M. Ziolkowski
Series A

GUILLAUME DE MACHAUT
Le Confort d'Ami (Comfort for a Friend)
Edited and translated by
R. Barton Palmer
Series A

CHRISTINE DE PIZAN
Christine's Vision
Translated by Glenda K. McLeod
Series B

MORIZ VON CRAÛN
Edited and translated by
Stephanie Cain Van D'Elden
Series A

THE ACTS OF ANDREW IN THE COUNTRY OF THE CANNIBALS
Translated by Robert Boenig
Series B

RAZOS AND TROUBADOUR SONGS
Translated by William E. Burgwinkle
Series B

MECHTHILD VON MAGDEBURG
Flowing Light of the Divinity
Translated by Christiane Mesch Galvani; edited, with an introduction, by Susan Clark
Series B

ROBERT DE BORON
The Grail Trilogy
Translated by George Diller
Series B

TILL EULENSPIEGEL
His Adventures
Translated, with introduction and notes, by Paul Oppenheimer
Series B

FRANCESCO PETRARCH
Rime Disperse
Edited and translated by Joseph Barber
Series A

GUILLAUME DE DEGUILEVILLE
The Pilgrimage of Human Life (Le Pèlerinage de la vie humaine)
Translated by Eugene Clasby
Series B

RENAUT DE BÂGÉ
Le Bel Inconnu (Li Biaus Descouneüs; The Fair Unknown)
Edited by Karen Fresco; translated by Colleen P. Donagher; music edited by Margaret P. Hasselman
Series A

THOMAS OF BRITAIN
Tristran
Edited and translated by Stewart Gregory
Series A

KUDRUN
Translated by Marion E. Gibbs and Sidney M. Johnson
Series B

PENNINC AND PIETER VOSTAERT
Roman van Walewein
Edited and translated by David F. Johnson
Series A

MEDIEVAL LITERATURE OF POLAND
An Anthology
Translated by Michael J. Mikoś
Series B

HELYAS OR LOHENGRIN
Late Medieval Transformations of the Swan Knight Legend
Edited and translated by
Salvatore Calomino
Series A

KASSIA
The Legend, the Woman,
and Her Work
Edited and translated by
  Antonía Tripolitis
  Series A

THE SONG OF ALISCANS
Translated by Michael A. Newth
  Series B

THE VOWS OF THE HERON (LES
VOEUX DU HÉRON)
A Middle French Vowing Poem
Edited by John Grigsby and
  Norris J. Lacy; translated by
  Norris J. Lacy
  Series A

MEDIEVAL GALICIAN-PORTUGUESE
POETRY
An Anthology
Edited and translated by Frede Jensen
  Series A

JAUFRE
An Occitan Arthurian Romance
Translated by Ross G. Arthur
  Series B

HILDEGARD OF BINGEN
The Book of the Rewards of Life (Liber
Vitae Meritorum)
Translated by Bruce W. Hozeski
  Series B

BRUNETTO LATINI
The Book of the Treasure
(Li Livres dou Tresor)
Translated by Paul Barrette and
  Spurgeon Baldwin
  Series B

THE PLEIER'S ARTHURIAN
ROMANCES
Garel of the Blooming Valley, Tandareis
and Flordibel, Meleranz
Translated by J. W. Thomas
  Series B

JEAN RENART
The Romance of the Rose or of
Guillaume de Dole (Roman de la Rose
ou de Guillaume Dole)
Translated by Regina Psaki
  Series B

JEAN D'ARRAS
Roman de Melusine
Translated by Sara Sturm-Maddox and
  Donald Maddox
  Series B

ADAM DE LA HALLE
Le Jeu de Robin et Marion
Translated by Shira Schwam-Baird
  Series A

AMADAS AND YDOINE
Translated by Ross G. Arthur
  Series B

THE WRITINGS
OF MEDIEVAL WOMEN
An Anthology
Second Edition
Translated by Marcelle Thiébaux
  Series B

JEAN FROISSART
La Prison Amoureuse
(The Prison of Love)
Edited and translated by
  Laurence de Looze
  Series A

TUSCAN POETRY
OF THE DUECENTO
An Anthology
Edited and translated by
  Frede Jensen
  Series A

THE PERILOUS CEMETERY
(L'ATRE PÉRILLEUX)
Edited and translated by
  Nancy B. Black
  Series A

For Product Safety Concerns and Information please contact our EU
representative GPSR@taylorandfrancis.com
Taylor & Francis Verlag GmbH, Kaufingerstraße 24, 80331 München, Germany